This groundbreaking book is the first comprehensive study of the historical development of Irish language policy in a generation. Drawing on a broad theoretical canvas, Walsh deftly tracks shifts in governance and tensions between the state and civil society groups promoting Irish. Despite significant advances in recent decades, he argues that more robust policy is required to secure the language in the next century. His thorough use of archival sources gives unprecedented insight into the development of Irish language policy in a broader European context. This book is essential reading for anyone interested in minority language revitalisation.

– Bernadette O'Rourke, Professor of Sociolinguistics and Hispanic Studies,
University of Glasgow

This excellent study of Irish language policy is both magisterial in content and arresting in style. It offers a provocative and penetrating inquiry, which will inform public debate and should prompt a government reappraisal of its performance to date. Walsh draws on a wide variety of sources, including government documents, civil society programmes and initiatives, community and individual histories, to reconstruct a fascinating, if daunting, grand narrative of government underperformance. It need not be thus as the insightful cross-referencing to best practice in Wales, the Basque Country and Catalonia suggests fruitful areas where Ireland is lagging behind. Other European contexts could learn a great deal from this interpretation.

– Colin H. Williams, Honorary Professor, Cardiff University and
Senior Research Associate, VHI, the University of Cambridge

GW00659496

One Hundred Years of Irish
Language Policy, 1922–2022

Reimagining Ireland

Volume 112

Edited by Dr Eamon Maher,
Technological University Dublin – Tallaght Campus

PETER LANG

Oxford • Bern • Berlin • Bruxelles • New York • Wien

One Hundred Years of Irish Language Policy, 1922–2022

John Walsh

PETER LANG

Oxford • Bern • Berlin • Bruxelles • New York • Wien

Bibliographic information published by Die Deutsche Nationalbibliothek. Die Deutsche Nationalbibliothek lists this publication in the Deutsche Nationalbibliografie; detailed bibliographic data is available on the Internet at http://dnb.d-nb.de.

A catalogue record for this book is available from the British Library.

Library of Congress Cataloging-in-Publication Data

Names: Walsh, John, 1971- author.
Title: One hundred years of Irish language policy, 1922-2022 / John Walsh.
Description: Oxford ; New York : Peter Lang, [2022] | Series: Reimagining Ireland, 1662-9094 ; vol no. 112 | Includes bibliographical references and index.
Identifiers: LCCN 2022007595 (print) | LCCN 2022007596 (ebook) | ISBN 9781789978926 (paperback) | ISBN 9781789978933 (ebook) | ISBN 9781789978940 (epub)
Subjects: LCSH: Language policy--Ireland. | Irish language--Revival.
Classification: LCC P119.32.I73 W35 2022 (print) | LCC P119.32.I73 (ebook) | DDC 306.44/9415--dc23/eng/20220302
LC record available at https://lccn.loc.gov/2022007595
LC ebook record available at https://lccn.loc.gov/2022007596

Cover image: 'Protest by Irish language groups outside the Department of the Gaeltacht in Galway in 2014 following the resignation of the Irish language commissioner'. Photograph by John Walsh.
Cover design by Peter Lang Ltd.

ISSN 1662-9094
ISBN 978-1-78997-892-6 (print)
ISBN 978-1-78997-893-3 (ePDF)
ISBN 978-1-78997-894-0 (ePub)

© Peter Lang Group AG 2022

Published by Peter Lang Ltd, International Academic Publishers,
Oxford, United Kingdom
oxford@peterlang.com, www.peterlang.com

This publication has been peer reviewed.

Contents

Acknowledgements   vii

Introduction   1

CHAPTER 1
Speakers   29

CHAPTER 2
Gaeltacht   77

CHAPTER 3
Education   141

CHAPTER 4
Legislation   195

CHAPTER 5
Broadcasting   249

Conclusion   305

Bibliography   321

Index   363

Acknowledgements

This book would not have been possible without the support of a large number of people in Galway and further afield. I extend my gratitude to the staff of Archives and Special Collections in the James Hardiman Library at Ollscoil na Gaillimhe - University of Galway (formerly NUI Galway) in particular Marie Boran, Geraldine Curtin, Margo Donohue, Kieran Hoare and Barry Houlihan. Other Library staff Trish Finnan, Hugo Kelly and Rioghna Moggan have assisted in various ways. I am grateful to those Galway colleagues who have supported me to develop the Conradh na Gaeilge archive, Librarian John Cox, Deputy Librarian Monica Crump and especially archivist Niamh Ní Charra, who also helped with sourcing material for this book. Other former and current colleagues Professor Dan Carey, Professor Nollaig Mac Congáil, Séamus Mac Mathúna, Professor Laura McLoughlin, Professor Donncha O'Connell, Tom O'Malley and Dr Jackie Uí Chionna offered support generously.

Further afield, I am deeply indebted to friends and colleagues in other universities who supported me in various ways: Dr Ciara Breathnach (University of Limerick), Dr Rosemary Day (University of Limerick), Professor Rob Dunbar (University of Edinburgh), Professor Michael Hornsby (Adam Mickiewicz University, Poznan), Dr Huw Lewis (Aberystwyth University), Dr Seán Mac Risteaird (Dublin City University), Professor Wilson McLeod (University of Edinburgh), Professor Máirín Nic Eoin (Dublin City University), Professor Bernie O'Rourke (University of Glasgow) and Professor Colin Williams (Cardiff University).

The assistance of the staff of the National Archives of Ireland and of Special Collections in the Boole Library, University College Cork is gratefully acknowledged. I also extend gratitude to Emer Ní Bhrádaigh, Mary Noonan and Cuan Ó Seireadáin who gave me access to quiet workspaces in Clare and Galway in which to complete this book. Gabhaim buíochas chomh maith le Maolsheachlainn Ó Caollaí agus le hÓrla de Búrca (Oifig an Choimisinéara Teanga). I was delighted to return to Peter Lang to publish this volume and I thank the Senior Commissioning Editor for Ireland, Tony Mason and the editor of the Reimagining Ireland series, Eamon Maher for their efficiency and professionalism.

Tá mo mhórbhuíochas tuillte ag na cairde seo a chuir comhairle mo leasa orm go minic, a chabhraigh liom cruacheisteanna a réiteach agus a thug misneach dom in am an ghátair: An Dr Dorothy Ní Uigín agus Dónall Ó Braonáin (Acadamh na hOllscolaíochta Gaeilge) agus an Coimisinéir Teanga, Rónán Ó Domhnaill. My father Peter and my family Clare, Micheál, Jack, Aoife, Jamie and Sharon encouraged me along the way. My husband Declan Coogan has earned my deepest gratitude for his unstinting support and belief in me throughout this project. I dedicate this book to the memory of my late mother Anne, who passed on her respect for Irish to me and re-learned it as an adult.

Galway, January 2022

Introduction

1. Introduction

This book was completed around the centenary of the Anglo-Irish Treaty on the 6th of December 1921 that paved the way for the creation of the Irish Free State. The plenipotentiaries in London signed their names in Irish, and many had been involved in the Gaelic League (Conradh na Gaeilge) since the period of the cultural Revival in the turn of the nineteenth and twentieth centuries. Indeed, many of those who fought for independence, both literally and metaphorically, supported the revival of Irish, and language policy took an ostensibly important place once the new state came into being formally on the 6th of December 1922. The aim of this book is to explore a centenary of policy towards the Irish language since independence in a series of thematic chapters covering speakers, the Gaeltacht (Irish-speaking districts), education, legislation and the broadcast media. Guiding the analysis is the broad framework of language policy, a branch of sociolinguistics that also has links with other social sciences such as political economy, sociology and anthropology. Later in this chapter, I outline some of the key conceptual foundations of language policy as a discipline, but I first present three inter-related anecdotes from the news cycle in late 2021 that shine light between them on many of the key themes in this book.

On the 15th of December 2021, the Official Languages (Amendment) Bill passed its final stage in the Dáil (lower house of parliament) and was sent to the President for his signature (Tuairisc.ie, 2021a). The headline measure in the new legislation was a target of 20 per cent of recruits to public bodies to be competent in Irish by 2030. On the same day, schoolchildren from five gaelscoileanna (primary level immersion schools) in south

Dublin protested outside the Dáil against the failure of the Department of Education to provide a second level Irish-medium school in their area (Nuacht RTÉ, 2021). The following day, the Minister for Justice diminished further the already weak status of Irish in the recruitment policy of the Garda Síochána (police), with the stated aim of attracting immigrants to the force (Tuairisc.ie, 2021f).

Taken together, these three events illustrate some of the ideologies and contradictions in relation to policy on the Irish language, a century after the Irish state was founded. The enactment of the revised Official Languages Bill was a key turning point as it strengthened existing legislation and contained the potential to increase substantially the provision of public services in Irish. It came about due to the doggedness and persistence of activists and the support of a handful of politicians who are committed to promoting Irish as a living, spoken language and to improving public services for Irish speakers. They were aided by a more favourable political climate due to the presence in government of two parties that are relatively supportive of Irish, the centre-right Fianna Fáil and the Green Party. Although there are weaknesses in the new legislation, not least the absence of a date by which all services would have to be provided in Irish in the Gaeltacht, it represents the best political outcome in the current circumstances. However, the fact that it took ten years and three changes of government to achieve illustrates the low priority given to Irish by the other centre-right party, Fine Gael, which held power for much of the decade that the legislation was under review. Furthermore, the passing of almost a century between the foundation of the state and strengthened legislation to provide services in Irish is a telling illustration of the marginalised place of language in the policy arena, despite its exalted constitutional status.

Like its predecessor, the new Act is limited mostly to services provided by public bodies and does not function as a wide-ranging law to promote Irish throughout society. It has nothing to say about educational provision, for instance, and therefore offers no comfort to the gaelscoil students and teachers demanding secondary provision in Irish. Compared to similar minority language contexts in Western Europe, Ireland lags behind considerably in its provision of immersion education, with only c. 8 per cent of students in gaelscoileanna compared to c. 25 per cent in Wales and c.

75 per cent in the Basque Country (see Chapter 3). This low figure also contrasts starkly with the new target of 20 per cent of recruits to public bodies and highlights the absence of joined-up thinking about Irish even after a century of promotional policies. Without developing significantly the position of Irish in education, in particular immersion schooling, there is no chance that the government can meet the targets of its own *20-Year Strategy for the Irish Language* (Government of Ireland, 2010) to increase significantly the numbers of speakers. Due to the weak sociolinguistic base of the Gaeltacht, many new speakers will have to come from the education system, particularly gaelscoileanna. By failing to consolidate the position of Irish in education, the Irish state is undermining one of the central planks of its language policy.

The policy change in relation to the Garda Síochána is relatively in-consequential as an Irish language entry requirement was abolished in 2005. Since then, entrants were required to know two languages, one of which had to be English or Irish. Now, with the ostensible aim of attracting more diverse recruits, only one language is mandatory because, according to the Minister for Justice, the requirement to know two is an obstacle to recruitment and disadvantages those who were not born in Ireland and do not know Irish. Although the change is minimal, the statement speaks volumes about what we can call the 'real' language policy, what is actually going on when the bluster about promoting Irish is stripped away. Firstly, it ignores the fact that many immigrants are already bi- or multilingual and therefore were not disadvantaged by the previous policy. Presenting Irish as an obstacle to their participation when it was not an absolute requirement anyway is disingenuous, and one is tempted to conclude that pressure for change came from Irish-born applicants who did not know enough Irish or any additional language to English. Framing the requirement for two languages as a problem is reflective of a de facto monolingual English-only policy in the public service and society more generally. Secondly, the statement stands in stark contrast with the ambitious recruitment target of the new Act, which includes the Garda Síochána among the public bodies covered. The new policy does nothing to deal with the issue of recruitment of Irish speakers to the force, a clear requirement under the new legisla-tion. The timing and optics of the Department of Justice statement could not have been worse, coming on the same day that the Minister for the Gaeltacht heralded the new Official Languages Act as an historic break-through for the Irish language (Department of Tourism, Culture, Arts, Sport, Gaeltacht and Media, 2021).

A final point relates to media coverage of these stories. Irish language radio, television and online media covered all three items in detail, but they were marginal in English-language media, although one outlet pounced on the apparent contradiction between the new 20 per cent requirement for public bodies and the downgrading of Irish in the Garda Síochána. There was an absence of even a basic understanding of the language policy and the familiar negative commentary claiming a discrepancy between the new Act and a supposedly non-existent Irish-speaking community (e.g. Newstalk, 2021). When it comes to language matters, Irish- and English-language media often inhabit parallel universes.

2. Context and aims

All of the issues touched on in these anecdotes – education, public admin-istration, legislation, media, the Gaeltacht and speakers – are discussed in the chapters that follow. Using the framework of language policy, the book highlights the contradictions between the stated policy aims and their execution, examining how ideological clashes between civil society and the state, or between different arms of the state itself, can impede or retard implementation.

The overall aim is to provide a comprehensive analysis of the policy of the Irish government in relation to the Irish language, on the occasion in 1922 of the centenary of the foundation of the Irish state. In the course of the last century, Irish has shifted from being a marginalised language within the larger British state, lacking a standardised written variety and institu-tional support, to a minoritised language within its own nation-state albeit with considerable legal and administrative backing. Throughout this period, its demography has been transformed: the traditional Gaeltacht districts of the native language in the western half of the country have continued to atrophy but numbers claiming competence in Irish have risen consistently elsewhere and there are active networks of speakers throughout the country. Both trends are largely a result of the language policy measures adopted by successive Irish administrations since independence. At various critical junctures throughout the twentieth century, key institutional supports were provided for Irish in policy domains such as the law, education, media, public administration and the Gaeltacht itself. Constitutionally, Irish became the 'national' and 'first official' language, but without attendant policy measures that could have made greater progress towards turning those legal aims into a sociolinguistic reality. While the measures were significant in themselves, most of them were developed in an era preceding the academic disciplines of applied sociolinguistics and language planning and were less ambitious than policies that would be adopted in later decades in other minority language regions such as the Basque Country, Wales and Catalonia.

Following the rhetoric of poorly defined 'gaelicisation' in the early decades of the state, the policy trajectory has shown slippage towards a vague 'bilingualism' since the 1960s, on the back of broader socioeconomic transformation of Irish society. A discourse of minority rights has emerged since the 1980s, and Irish language policy has since found itself caught between the remnants of the historical rhetoric of the 'national' language on the one hand and on the other by the notion of Irish as a minority language spoken actively only by a small core group. Although the focus of this book is on the Irish state as the main driver of Irish language policy over the past 100 years, I will also examine the impact of Irish language activism in Northern Ireland and consider the role of Irish speakers in the North in the future development of the language. No account of Irish language policy would be complete without an analysis of the situation north of the border, particularly since the late 1960s when the roots of many current initiatives began to crystallise in the context of the Troubles.

Another critical aspect of Irish language policy is its relationship with the broader social and demographic change in Ireland over the past twenty years, which has undermined historical perceptions about ownership of the language. Due to grassroots community initiatives on both sides of the border, the language is no longer strongly associated with historical essentialist ideologies around Irishness. From its inception in the late nine-teenth and early twentieth century, therefore, Irish language policy has shifted from being a central pillar of a young European state's identity con-struct to an optional extra in a hyper-globalised context marked by fluid identities, high levels of immigration and an increasingly neoliberal and weakened state. However, contrary to the predictions of modernisation theory, minority languages such as Irish have not faded away and a small but vigorous community of speakers continues to exist, supported by a larger buffer of what can be called 'supporters' of the language, those with limited passive ability but some level of positive ideological engagement.

A key objective of this book is to contribute to a deeper understanding of a well-known minority language revival effort: policy towards Irish since the foundation of the Irish state. There has been no single in-depth wide-ranging analysis of Irish language policy in twenty-five years since Ó Riagáin's milestone account (1997). In the chapters that follow, I seek to answer the following central questions: how has Irish language policy func-tioned in the historical arc of this study? How have competing ideologies and broader socioeconomic and socio-political contexts shaped its formu-lation and implementation? To what extent can Irish language policy be considered a success or failure? The volume will synthesise existing research on the topic, position it in the context of the theoretical fields of socio-linguistics and language policy and provide a thematic analysis, based on rich primary sources, of various strands of Irish language policy over the past century. The time is ripe, after 100 years of independence, to assess critically the considerable efforts of the Irish state and Irish language civil society to bring about their stated aim of the revival of Irish.

3. Theoretical framework

Many terms are in use to describe the study of the use of given languages or language varieties and attempts to modify such behaviour. Used in a global sense in reference to languages in general, these include language planning, language policy, language management, language governance and language regimes. When discussing minoritised languages such as Irish, terms like language revitalisation, language revival, language normalisation, language recovery and language reawakening are in use, depending on the extent of minoritisation (i.e. 'normalisation' is used by the Catalans but moribund Native American languages prefer 'reawakening'; see Sallabank, 2013). This terminological richness reflects the complexity and breadth of the field, which is in existence only since the second half of the twentieth century. The title of the field is itself a conundrum and depends on the theoretical framework adopted, but one of its leading scholars, Bernard Spolsky, suggests 'language policy' as an umbrella term and that is the title of a landmark handbook about the topic that he edited (Spolsky, 2012). Regardless of the philosophical basis, most of the terms imply some form of deliberate intervention (often but not always by a political authority) in a given language situation, with the aim of influencing use of and/or attitudes towards languages or varieties. In this sense, such intervention has been in existence for time immemorial since emperors and monarchies began promoting certain languages or varieties and marginalising others. Language policy is now a complex and broad interdisciplinary field that encompasses other disciplines such as anthropology, sociology, political science, political economy, geography and economics.

One historical sketch of the field highlights four examples of language policy spanning the seventeenth to the twentieth centuries and representing pre-modern, early modern and modern periods. The first is the establishment of the French Academy (*Académie française*) in 1635 with the aim of purifying French and rendering it capable of dealing with the arts and sciences. The second relates to the early modern European national movements that emerged in the late nineteenth century in countries or regions that did not have political autonomy, i.e., Finland, the Czech lands, Slovakia, Norway and Ireland. These groups made linguistic and cultural demands, and the influence of Romanticism increased the emphasis on the perceived purity and authenticity of their cultural realms. The third, containing both early modern and modern influences, is the example of the Soviet Union in the 1920s and 1930s, where Russian was not prioritised at the expense of everything else and dozens of other languages were supported by the state, particularly in education and standardisation. The final is the modern example of the Prague School, a group of linguists who in the 1920s and 1930s devoted themselves to the 'cultivation' of Czech in the newly independent Czechoslovakia. One of the lasting contributions of the Prague School was to distinguish between 'cultivation' (development of the language itself) and 'policy' (implementation) approaches to language (Jernudd & Nekvapil, 2013: 18–22).

3.1 *The rise of language planning*

Until the emergence of sociolinguistics in the mid-twentieth century, linguists were focused on structuralism and did not generally enter in discussion about behaviours in relation to languages. The field known as language planning has its origins in the post-Second World War period when economists, social scientists and linguists alike believed that 'planning' would provide solutions to social problems. The 1960s and 1970s were the era of 'classic language planning' associated with leading scholars in the new discipline of sociolinguistics such as Einar Haugen, Joshua Fishman, Uriel Weinreich and Charles Ferguson. Attention was paid to the language 'problems' being experienced by newly independent post-colonial states in Africa and Asia as they decided which language or languages to use in public administration or education. The approach was highly interventionist and top-down, with the emphasis on the political authority of central government:

> This classic language planning model is based on the premise that language planning takes place at the level of the nation-state and the plans project onto the development of the *entire* society. Political processes of the state (or government) determine the goals to be achieved. (Ibid.: 26, emphasis in original)

Issues of language and society moved to the forefront of linguistics and language planning became a sub-branch of sociolinguistics, extending its reach into all language situations, not just those in 'developing' countries. There was criticism of the approach, however, and the classic language planning of that era is seen by some as a Western concept that promoted modernisation and development and perpetuated structural inequalities in the process:

> Western-based academic language-planning approaches in the 1950s and 1960s often subsumed a number of ideologies about (1) the nature of language – that is, as a finite, stable, standardized, rule-governed instrument for communication; (2) monolingualism and cultural homogeneity as necessary requirements for social and economic progress, modernization, and national unity (with stable diglossia as a fall-back, compromise position); and (3) language selection as a matter of 'rational choice' in which all options are equally available to everyone, or could be made equally available. These basic assumptions were often consonant with the views of Western-based and Western-trained state planners and policy analysts engaged in national (re)-construction in developing countries during the 1950s and 1960s, and continue to be influential to the present day. (Ricento, 2006: 14–15)

As well as criticism of the functionalism and evolutionism inherent in classic language planning, a 'one language, one nation' approach was dominant and there was little tolerance of diversity within a given political entity (for an analysis of the role of nationalism in language policy, see Wright, 2013). Furthermore, there was the problem that a heavily centralised approach would ignore real world complexities:

> In practice, the linguists' plans (like the plans developed by their economic and social colleagues) seldom worked, for they came up against the counter-pressures of actual demographic situations (the complex sociolinguistic ecology as Haugen 1972 noted that made up the ethnography of communication (Hymes 1974) in a given speech community) and the emotionally powerful factors (nationalism, religion, ethnicity, identity, power, communicative strength) that account for the significant values a language variety had for various members of a society'. (Spolsky, 2013: 4)

The 'planning' approach became further tainted within sociolinguistics in the late 1980s following the collapse of the Soviet bloc, although as Jernudd and Nekvapil point out, this did not prevent liberal democracies throughout the world from continuing to pursue economic planning as a fundamental basis for public policy (ibid.: 27). The increased popularity of critical theory and greater attention to minority rights also influenced changes in the approach. For instance, Europe in the 1970s and 1980s witnessed the flowering of minority language activism from Catalonia to

Wales to Ireland. A key contribution at the end of the decade by Robert Cooper moved the field away from problem solving towards the notion of deliberate intervention in a given language situation. Such '[l]anguage planning refers to deliberate efforts to influence the behaviour of others with respect to the acquisition, structure, or functional allocation of their language codes' (1989: 45). Cooper's 'accountancy scheme' outlined a broader approach involving not only the state but a range of actors including speakers themselves: 'What actors (1) attempt to influence what behaviours (2) of which people (3) for what ends (4) under what conditions (5) by what means (6) through what decision-making process (7) with what effect?' (ibid.: 8). Another of Cooper's contributions was to add 'acquisition planning' (the teaching and learning of languages) to the existing sub-categories of corpus planning (developing the language itself, for instance, grammar and terminology) and status planning (for instance, giving the language legal or constitutional status) (Jernudd & Nekvapil, 2013: 29).

A major influence on the emerging sub-field of minority language promotion came in Fishman's landmark volume *Reversing Language Shift* (1991), a theoretical reflection on ancestral language abandonment in minoritised language communities as well as a guide to action on promoting maintenance. The ideological underpinning of the work was emphasised by its subtitle: 'theoretical and empirical foundations of assistance to threatened languages', placing Fishman firmly within the paradigm of sociolinguists for language revitalisation (O'Rourke et al., 2015: 10–11). The eight stages of his 'Graded Intergenerational Transmission Scale' (GIDS) spanned relatively large languages that were well institutionalised in education and high-level public administration to moribund languages that faced extinction and needed to be re-learned by adults. The fulcrum of GIDS was 'stage 6', intergenerational transmission in the family and community, a fundamental requirement that could not be avoided if 'higher' level aims such as public administration, core education and government were to be achieved.

The Reversing Language Shift (RLS) model gained popularity among minority language activists, including in Ireland, because it provided an apparently linear pathway to revitalisation.[1] However, it has been criticised as being excessively oriented to the revival of native speaking communities based on historical notions of languages as distinct codes and rigid ethno-linguistic identity (García et al., 2017). Romaine (2006) has questioned the emphasis on intergenerational transmission and reconstructing the past rather than bringing the language forward to new spaces and new speakers. Due to its emphasis on intergenerational transmission, RLS can also be seen as fundamentally heteronormative and exclusionary of those not dwelling within traditional nuclear families (Walsh, 2019a). Others have criticised it as functionalist and conservative in orientation, excessively reliant on consensus and oblivious to issues of conflict and power (Williams, G., 1992: 122).

3.2 *From language planning to language policy*

Language policy as a separate approach, as distinct from an umbrella term for the field, has emerged on the back of such criticisms of the top-down, interventionist approaches of language planning. With roots in the critical sociolinguistic approach that emerged in the French and Spanish states in the 1980s, language policy focuses more on understanding official and community ideologies in relation to language than on specific 'planning' interventions, although there is overlap between both terms and the abbreviation LPP (language policy and planning) is common. Shohamy describes language policy as:

> the primary mechanism for organizing, managing and manipulating language behaviors as it consists of decisions made about languages and their uses in society. It is through LP that decisions are made with regard to the preferred languages that should be legitimized, used, learned and taught in terms of where, when and in which contexts. Thus, LP acts as a manipulative tool in the continuous battle between different ideologies. (2006: 45)

---

1   Its traction in Irish language circles was probably boosted by Fishman's harsh criticism of the Irish government in the 1960s (see Chapter 3).

Shohamy draws a distinction between language policy as understood by written documents, laws and regulations governing language use and the 'real' language policy that has to be inferred through other mechanisms and may actually undermine or derail the official policy measures. Therefore, while language policy is often explicit or overt by its codification in national language standards, tests, laws, etc. (the de jure policy), it is also implicit or covert (de facto) and needs to be derived or inferred from other behaviours:

> Implicit language policies can occur also at national level as many nations do not have explicit policies that are formulated in official documents. In the case of the USA, for example, there are no explicit and stated language policies that specify the status and uses of the English language. Yet, it is clear that English is the dominant majority language and this observation can be derived via a number of indicators. It is important to note in this context how the US English movement still perpetuates English by passing state laws that state explicitly that English is the official language. (Ibid.: 50)

In Ireland, a good example of the 'real' language policy can be derived from the use of the Irish and English on road signs. Despite its explicit status as national and first official language, on road signs Irish is in smaller font, italicised and often misspelled (Ó hIfearnáin, 2006). The implicit message from such signs is that English is the more important language and the foreignness of Irish is emphasised by its italicisation. Another example is the frequent contrast between official political rhetoric about the central importance of Irish and its marginalisation in public administration and public life generally (see Chapter 4). Shohamy concludes: 'Overt LPs refers to those language policies that are explicit, formalized, de jure, codified and manifest. Covert LPs, on the other hand, refer to language policies that are implicit, informal, unstated, de facto, grass-roots and latent' (ibid.: 50).

A leading author in the field, Spolsky, has proposed a model of language policy comprising three inter-related components:

(a) Language practices: what people actually do with the language, which varieties do they speak, to whom and for what purpose. This may also be described as the ecology of communication or ethnography of speech. It can be considered an indication of the 'real' language policy.

(b) Language beliefs: the values associated with different varieties of the language(s). This may also be called ideology if the values and beliefs are organised systematically.

(c) Language management: the efforts by authorities or individuals to modify practices and beliefs. Management is similar in meaning to the historical concept of planning as it refers to interventions in given language situations (Spolsky, 2004: 5–15).

However, these may not be successful if the managers do not adequately understand the ecology and ideology:

> In my approach, a constitutional or legal establishment of a national or official language is a clear example of language management, although just as speed limits do not guarantee that all cars abide by them, so a language law does not guarantee observance. (Spolsky, 2013: 5)

Spolsky has also contributed to the concept of language management, defining his use of the concept in the context of developing an overarching theory of how language is used:

> The goal of a theory of language policy is to account for the choices made by individual speakers on the basis of rule-governed patterns recognized by the speech community (or communities) of which they are members. Some of these choices are the result of management, reflecting conscious and explicit efforts by language managers to control the choices. (2009: 1)

Spolsky justifies his use of the term with reference to negative historical connotations of 'planning':

> I use the term 'management' rather than 'planning' because I think it more precisely captures the nature of the phenomenon. Planning was the term used in the 1950s and 1960s in the post-war enthusiasm for correcting social problems; the subsequent failures of social and economic planning have discouraged its continued use. The two areas, health services and education, that still attempt centralized planning in western societies, continue to be problematic. (Ibid.: 4–5)

He argues that a manager must be identified before we can talk about language management, but that managers can take many shapes and forms (for a discussion of this in an Irish context, see Ní Dhúda, 2017). His framework for a theory of language management is based on two assumptions. The first is that language policy is a social phenomenon and dependent on interactions in certain settings with certain participants discussing certain topics (domains). People make language choices appropriate to domain. The second assumption is that it contains the tripartite model outlined above, which each component constituting a force that influences language choices. Spolsky proceeds to analyse ten domains from the family to the supranational level, but cautions that while the domain itself is his starting point, significant influences from outside are at play in each case (Spolsky, 2009: 2–7).

Language management theory was first presented in the late 1970s and 1980s and distinguished between the generation of utterances and the management of utterances. It is divided into 'simple management' where, for instance, a person corrects themselves by substituting a standard for non-standard form in certain domains, and 'organised management' that can operate at various levels in society. The attempt was to broaden the scope of the field beyond focus on the state as the manager, while maintaining a firm connection to linguistics (Jernudd & Nekvapil, 2013: 33). Nekvapil (2006) distinguishes between language planning and language management, comparing the latter to strategies that set general goals but are flexible enough to allow modification. According to this approach, language planning is characterised by rigidity and stasis, and management by contrast is more agile. 'Language management cycles' are feedback processes when speakers note inadequacies, i.e., in terminology creation, and through consultation suggest amendments. Proponents of language management claim that it draws attention to resistance to central imposition of language norms and offers a new perspective on language shift and maintenance:

> The theory has a very broad scope, includes both the *macro* dimension and the *micro* dimension ('agency'), examines language management as a *process*, views it in *communicative* and *socio-cultural* terms (including socio-economic ones), but at the same time is transparently compatible with *linguistics* and good for utilization on

research on *second language* learning and teaching. (Jernudd & Nekvapil, 2013: 36, emphasis in original)

In a recent review of his model, Spolsky stresses the importance of the 'non-linguistic environment', arguing against what he calls 'linguicentrism', the idea that language has no relationship with the world around it. Physical geography, demography, civil strife or warfare, deprivation, technology and climate change can all impede the implementation of language policy. He refocuses attention on the individual, placing the person at the beginning of the analysis and proceeding to other higher-level domains. This, he says, is because of the capacity of individuals to build their linguistic repertoires and cement their practices in spite of external language management:

> Ultimately, the fate of a language policy depends on the ability and willingness of individual members of the speech community to accept it; although perhaps many speakers are unaware of the importance of language and language choice, without acceptance by members of a speech community, any attempt at language management is doomed. (Spolsky, 2021: 14)

Spolsky proceeds to look again at language policy under twelve themes beginning with the individual and the family/home domain, followed by education, neighbourhood/workplace, public institutions, military policy, imperialism/colonialism, economic pressure/neoliberalism, endangerment and language shift, management agencies, treaties and supranational instruments and the nation-state. He concludes that language can be managed but that it is complex because it occurs simultaneously at so many levels. Due to this complexity, it is very difficult to predict which factors (educational, political, historical, sociological, psychological, religious, etc.) most influence how an individual or group maintains a certain language or shifts away from it. While the family is likely to shape the individual's initial repertoire, that could soon be reshaped by other forces from external domains. School is the next key influence, but it too is limited by potential mismatches between language of instruction and teachers' competence in or commitment to it. Family choices of schooling may also have a strong linguistic element: for instance, for identity reasons, parents/guardians may wish their children to acquire a heritage language through immersion schooling, if available in their area, or they might want the family to be educated in the majority language. Movement of families due to socioeconomic or socio-political factors can add new domains and see further modification of their repertoires. This is all before we even begin to consider higher-level domains such as state services, the media, etc.

> Any national management, ideally but seldom recognising diversity and aiming at equality, should recognise all these forces and influences, but implementation still depends on the availability of resources to support any plans. Within these limits, a workable national language policy can be developed and, with ample funding, implemented. (Ibid.: 198–199)

Because language policy is 'a dynamic and indefinite phenomenon' (ibid.: 203), Spolsky concludes that it will always be necessary to review and rethink it based on previous experiences.

3.3 Language governance and social transformation

The final concept to be discussed is language governance, the study of language policy within and between institutions. Governance has conceptual links to public administration, public policy, political economy, political science and business studies and relates to the higher-level domains identified by Spolsky and others. It operates at many levels and analyses a multitude of organisations and their influence on language, although national governments retain a key role. However, governance is wider than government and encompasses a range of institutions from civil society organisations to transnational or supranational bodies such as the European Union. A leading text in the field defines it as follows:

> Government and governance are both ways of governing society yet while government relates to the forms associated with liberal representative democracy, the traditional state, governance involves a much wider set of actors, including elected politicians and public officials, but also various nonelected interest and pressure groups ... as society becomes more complex and differentiated, the traditional method of governing from above – government – becomes more difficult. This leads to governance, understood

as steering rather than directing, which it is claimed supplements or at times even replaces government. Governance is allegedly more bottom-up than top-down and involves a partnership between government and non-governmental elements of civil society. (Loughlin & Williams, 2007: 59–60)

Use of 'allegedly' is important here because a diffuse form of governance may in fact weaken language policy initiatives by transferring them further and further away from the locus of political power through privatisation or outsourcing of functions (the same applies to other aspects of public policy that have been similarly semi-privatised or privatised entirely). However, governance is a very useful tool that allows us take stock of the complexity of interactions between all of the actors involved in a language policy process. Tracking changes in international trends of governance from the welfare state to the post-welfare state and the rise of neoliberalism, coupled with insights from globalisation and cultural counterforces based on regional territorial identities, facilitates a deeper understanding of how national language policies evolve over time. This approach can be used, for example, to explain historical shifts in Irish language policy that were influenced by forces outside Ireland. The role of the European Union in shaping national language policy can also be considered through the lens of supranational governance and in the case of Irish, it has been a crucial (if belated) external support for the language (see Chapter 4).

Finally, a landmark recent volume, *Language Revitalisation and Social Transformation*, draws attention to the need to revisit and rethink historical assumptions about minority language policy in the light of profound social, economic and political transformations in recent decades. Focusing mostly on Western Europe, it argues that both the academic literature and the work of policymakers are not cognisant enough of broader societal changes and their impact on minority languages. Socio-demographic change relates to the new make-up of Western societies in the age of mobility, the ageing nature of the population, the increased participation of women in the workforce, the impact of urbanisation and the explosion of the digital world due to the advance of information and communication technologies (ICT). Economic transformation has occurred due to the shift from industrial production to the services economy. International trade of services relies heavily on ICT, and deeper economic globalisation has reduced the state's capacity to control such processes. Political change has also come about as the nature and role of the nation-state is reshaped. International markets, transnational corporations, regional and minority demands for greater autonomy and the rise of neoliberal ideology increasingly challenge the authority of national governments. Neoliberalism has transformed the nature of the state, marking a profound shift from the public to the private sector, fragmented public services and increasingly complex and cumbersome decision-making processes (Lewis & McLeod, 2021: 6–11).

Noting the historical influence of paradigms such as Fishman's 'Reversing Language Shift' model on the discipline, the authors present four inter-related questions that guide their analysis of the relationship between social transformation and language revitalisation. The first relates to intergenerational transmission and the evolution of the family unit. Profound changes in the structure of the family and in early childhood socialisation have occurred in recent decades. Children are now likely to be cared for by a mixture of family members and professional services, with implications for language policy, and Fishman's notion of the bounded family unit is increasingly untenable. The second question relates to mobility, community and daily language use. The historical emphasis on geographical concentration of minority language communities by Fishman and others requires rethinking in the light of greatly increased personal mobility and decreased social participation in neighbourhood activities. In the age of 'spatially dispersed lifestyles' (ibid.: 18), the notion of territorial community and its implications for language needs to be further problematised.

The third question considers globalisation and the link between language revitalisation and economic development. Although there has been some academic attention to these connections, the relationship is not well understood. Changes in international trade, shifts in labour from Europe and North America to Asia and the growth of financial services have exerted greater influences on urban centres than on rural districts where minority languages tend to have larger concentrations of speakers. However, such economic change may have significant secondary effects on such regions by pulling away qualified young people or undermining regional development. The final question relates to governance and policymaking, the authors arguing that not enough attention has been paid to the impact of regionalisation, internationalisation and post-welfare state governance models on minority language policy. They point to potential improvements in sub-state entities such as Wales, the Basque Country and Catalonia as well as the impact of Europe-wide civil society language groups and the supranational institutions of the European Union. However, they also raise a key question about the nature and impact of relationships between civil society and the state in this regard, and call for attention to how these have influenced the effectiveness of language policy (ibid.: 12–23). These questions are particularly relevant to contemporary Irish language policy and can help us explain key policy shifts in the past, as will be explored later in the book.

3.4   *From new speakers to speakers*

This book also draws on theoretical insights from a European research network entitled 'New speakers in a Multilingual Europe: Opportunities and Challenges' funded by a COST (European Co-operation in Science and Technology) Action between 2013 and 2017. This work is included here because of its implications for language policy spanning transmission, education, status, public administration and informal social and cultural domains. The 'new speaker' concept does not claim to describe a new phenomenon because recorded history is replete with accounts of people crossing linguistic boundaries. However, the idea of the new speaker problematises the presumed link between language, territory and identity and was proposed as a way of identifying patterns in the ways in which speakers acquire and adapt new languages. The Action emerged from existing research in minority language contexts in the Spanish state (e.g. Puigdevall, 2014) and Wales (Robert, 2009) where, as a result of re-vitalisation programmes, people not socialised in the minority language in early childhood were seen to play key roles in its development within society. The Action began with three broad thematic categories: new speakers of indigenous minority languages, new speakers as migrants and new speakers as workers. The following definition was proposed for indigenous minority languages, which is the most relevant category for Irish. A new speaker of such a language was identified as:

> one who generally learns the language in institutional contexts outside the home. S/he often acquires the language to a high degree of competence and uses it actively outside of classroom contexts. New speakers were seen to include individuals with little or no home or community exposure to a minority language but who instead acquire it through immersion or bilingual educational programmes, revitalisation projects or as adult language learners. (O'Rourke et al., 2019: 14)

The Action was particularly useful for studying the transformed context of the transmission and acquisition of indigenous minority languages and provided tools that helped understand how new speakers navigate these processes. One such tool was the notion of *muda* (pl. *mudes*) from the Catalan verb *mudar* meaning to change or transform, which was applied to trajectories of speakers and their stages of acquisition and adoption throughout the lifecycle. It analyses how a knower of a language becomes an active user without necessarily being linked to the ethnonational identity associated with the language or discourses of nationalism or romanticism. Studying speakers' individual journeys towards new speakerhood has allowed researchers track the obstacles faced by (potential) speakers and understand how these are overcome, with obvious implications for language policy. For instance, the research has shown that *mudes* often occur during adult life, thereby emphasising the importance of language programmes aimed at older age cohorts. It also shows that *mudes* must be ratified by others to be successful, underlining the need to support new speakers with the sometimes difficult process of transition into the target community or network. The *muda* concept has analytical purchase beyond minority language settings, as it is irrelevant whether the language is minoritised or not if the speakers themselves are minoritised. This has been seen in the case of migrant workers in Estonia and Norway, whose languages are not under threat in their national contexts but where similar dynamics of legitimacy and authenticity can impede the acceptance of new speakers. Similarly, other strands of the Action studied how *mudes* into a different variety of the same language can also be problematic, as is the case with migrant workers from South American attempting to adopt peninsular Spanish in order to improve their integration and employment prospects. In this case, the legitimacy lies not with a separate named language but with a more prestigious variety of Spanish in the context of the Spanish state (ibid.: 16).

The new speaker research also problematises the notion of 'native speaker' and prompts an investigation of how linguistics as a discipline has reproduced certain language ideologies and hierarchies through abstract notions of nativeness. The remnants of Romanticism linking language, nation and territory cast a long shadow over linguistics and have led to the prioritisation of 'native speech' in domains spanning language policy itself, education, employment, media, etc. Adoption of the new speaker category rejects the simplistic binary of native vs. non-native and moves away from the deficit that is implicit (or sometimes explicit) in well-worn labels of linguistics and related strands such as 'second language learner', 'L2', 'non-fluent learner', 'semi-speaker', etc. (O'Rourke et al., 2015). This is particularly important in the case of Irish where debates about the supposed greater authenticity of Gaeltacht speech have raged for well over a century.

Debates about whether 'new speaker' was an umbrella term, an analytical concept or lens animated the researchers in the Action. There was concern not to typologise speakers and in so doing reproduce dominant ideologies about linguistic hierarchies, and it was argued that social categories were always subject to negotiation and variation depending on speakers themselves. Folk or emic categories exist in certain concepts such as the Basque Country (*euskaldunberri*) and Galicia (*neofalantes*) but not in others such as Ireland where there is no unproblematic or widely accepted term to describe new speakers of Irish ('Gaeilgeoir', while meaning literally 'Irish speaker', is a loaded term with different connotations, some pejorative, in different contexts). While some of the research on minority languages used 'new speaker' as an analytical category, it was also employed as a lens through which to study the processes of acquisition and adoption. In fact, new speaker as analytical category was less useful when examining social outcomes of the process, particularly in relation to the strands of migrants and transnational workers. Cross-strand comparisons showed that experiences of legitimation and de-legitimation could be the same regardless of the mode of acquisition, degree of competence, locus of use and whether the person seeks to use a named language or variety of such language (O'Rourke et al., 2019: 27). The particular challenges facing immigrants as new speakers were explored in a number of contexts including Galicia and Wales (Bermingham & Higham, 2018), the Basque Country and Wales (Augustyniak & Higham, 2019) and Catalonia (Caglitutuncigil, 2018). At the policy level, some sub-state regimes, for instance, Catalonia, have launched campaigns to introduce immigrants to the minoritised language (Plataforma per la Llengua, 2010).

Stating that it was never intended to create taxonomies of speakers, the final report of the COST Action asked whether it was necessary to use 'new speaker' at all when 'speaker' would suffice. The concept, it said, had been useful for understanding language revitalisation but less so when looking at social outcomes in other contexts. It concluded that its main aim had been:

> understanding the political economy of speaker categorisation in specific contexts, and hence shedding light on how language participates in struggles over access to resources. This speaker perspective and specifically a *sociolinguistics of the speaker* can perhaps allow researchers to illuminate who has access to which codes, how and where they are able to deploy them, and with what social and economic consequences, across a wide range of settings in today's multilingual, globalised Europe. (ibid.: 27, emphasis in original)

I am among the authors who adopted the new speaker approach in research about Irish over the past decade (see, for instance, O'Rourke & Walsh 2020 and a fuller list of sources in Chapter 1). This body of work has certainly deepened understanding of the processes that characterise the trajectories of those wishing to adopt Irish in a variety of contexts and led to policy proposals (Walsh et al., 2015). However, there is scope now, as suggested above, to broaden this approach to study how linguistic resources are accessed and deployed by all Irish speakers, regardless of their background.

4. Methodology

This book adopts a qualitative approach to the analysis of historical and contemporary documentary sources linked broadly to the theme of language policy. It is based primarily on an analysis of primary historical documents and archival collections related to state and voluntary language bodies. These were eclectic in nature and spanned reports, discussion papers, press releases, correspondence, word lists, flyers, brochures, diaries, newspaper clippings and various ephemera as diverse as product packaging, receipts and bus tickets. In the National Archives of Ireland, archival records of the Departments of the Taoiseach (Prime Minister), Finance, Posts and Telegraphs and the Gaeltacht were examined in relation to all of the themes. The Conradh na Gaeilge Collection at NUI Galway has yielded valuable insights into campaigns for media and legislation. Historical insights into language shift and ideology in the Gaeltacht were gleaned from records in the National Folklore Collection held by University College Cork. More recent documents published by state agencies, commissions and advisory councils were also examined.

Drawing on the approach of Braun and Clarke (2006), I conducted a thematic analysis of historical documents in order to identify patterns and themes and relate them to each other. In the case of large collections, a more detailed open coding procedure was used. The analytical approach was heuristic and each collection was considered in its historical context and related to the theoretical framework. Braun and Clarke's two levels of theme, semantic (explicit) and latent, were particularly useful because they align closely to some models of language policy (see 3.2 above). The book also draws on interviews, focus groups and participant observation of Irish speakers in community and media settings (see Chapter 5 in particular). Fieldwork was conducted mostly in Irish, and interviews were transcribed and coded in a similar way to the approach to historical documentation. In order to foreground participants' voices and given that many readers of this book will know Irish, original extracts in this text are given in Irish with English translations in footnotes.

Some minor editing of extracts from interviews and focus groups has been done for the sake of clarity but otherwise I have endeavoured to preserve the voices of participants. Therefore, grammatical 'errors' have not been amended and discourse markers from English (e.g. 'you know', 'like', 'so') that are common in informal Irish speech have not been removed. In line with the policy set out in the Official Languages Act, and in order to give them due historical recognition, the original Irish versions of Gaeltacht placenames are used in the text (e.g. An Cheathrú Rua instead of Carraroe, etc.). Irish terms in widespread use among English speakers in Ireland, for example, Dáil (lower chamber of parliament), are not italicised but glossed where necessary for international readers.

5. Structure of the book

Rather than attempting to deal with every aspect of the question over the past century, this book analyses a number of themes related to Irish language policy since 1922. The choice is necessarily subjective but attempts to cover topics that are unquestionably of fundamental importance and others that reflect my personal and professional experience over the past three decades. Although the book focuses mostly on what became the Republic of Ireland, the cross-border governance structure introduced in 1998 is referred to regularly, there are frequent comparisons with the position of Irish north of the border and one of the case studies features an Irish-language media initiative in Belfast. The linguistic and cultural Revival period of the late nineteenth and early twentieth centuries is not considered in detail as the focus is on the 100 years since the establishment of the Irish state in 1922.

The themes discussed in the chapters that follow are speakers of Irish, Gaeltacht policy, the education system, legislation and broadcast media. Each chapter is divided into two sections comprising an overview of the topic, followed by a detailed case study of one aspect of it. This was necessary because of the potentially enormous scope of the five topics over a period of 100 years. In choosing case studies, care was taken not to replicate existing work but rather to investigate aspects of topics that had not been studied in depth previously. The first three thematic chapters cover key topics that are essential to any review of the policy's success or failure over the past century: speakers of the language in the Gaeltacht and elsewhere, state policy on the Gaeltacht and the position of Irish in the education system. Chapter 1 relates to Irish speakers in the Gaeltacht and elsewhere in Ireland, including in Northern Ireland. Taking community as its focus, it gives an overview of census and other quantitative data as well as sociolinguistic, sociological and anthropological studies of speakers in territorially defined communities or networks. The case study covers the Gaeltacht area of west Waterford (Na Déise) from the 1920s to the present day. It begins with an exploration of the insights provided by the diaries of a folklore collector into language use and ideology within his community in the early decades of the century. The case study concludes with an analysis of the community-based language planning process in Na Déise, which is being implemented currently both in the Gaeltacht and in a nearby town.

Chapter 2 is also related to the Gaeltacht but focuses on policy, providing an overview of major government initiatives from the 1920s to the present day, including the geographical extent of the Gaeltacht and its economic development through state agencies such as Gaeltarra Éireann and Údaras na Gaeltachta. It also contains an explanation of the *20-Year Strategy for the Irish Language*, the Gaeltacht Act 2012 and the background to the language planning process. In the case study, the first major policy initiative following the foundation of the state, the Gaeltacht Commission of 1925–1926, is examined in depth. The genesis of the Commission is explained and its membership, methodology and findings analysed. Public and governmental responses to it are considered and its contribution to language policy assessed.

Chapter 3 turns to the education system, an area of central concern to Irish language policy because of the core status accorded to it at primary and post-primary level in the Republic of Ireland. The introduction provides an overview of five aspects of the question: Irish as a standalone school subject in the Republic, the Irish-medium sector, Gaeltacht schools, Irish at university and Irish in the education system in Northern Ireland. The case study focuses on the decade from c. 1965 to c. 1975, when many important changes occurred in language policy with significant implications for the status of Irish in education. The major government retreat of the early 1970s in the realms of education and public administration is analysed in the context of a broader review of language policy in line with changes in economic development policy. Finally, the work of Comhairle na Gaeilge, a high-level advisory group for government is considered, particularly its research and recommendations about education.

The final two thematic chapters relate to legislation and the broadcast media. Chapter 4 offers an overview of the constitutional status of Irish and case law related to efforts by Irish citizens to assert their language rights. Despite the gap between Article 8 and legislative provision for Irish for several decades, its constitutional status facilitated other important policy initiatives. The current legislation governing Irish in the Republic, the Official Languages Act, is discussed, as is the enhanced legal status of Irish as an official working language of the European Union. The chapter considers the limited impact of the European Charter for Regional or Minority Languages on Irish in Northern Ireland and summarises the ongoing campaign for an Irish language act there. The case study draws on archival sources to examine in depth the twenty-five-year campaign for language legislation in the Republic as led by voluntary organisations such as Conradh na Gaeilge and Comhdháil Náisiúnta na Gaeilge. The campaign culminated in the Official Languages Act 2003, which provided limited rights for Irish speakers and imposed duties on public bodies to provide certain services in Irish.

Chapter 5 relates to the position of Irish in the broadcast media, beginning with a review of its status on what was Ireland's single radio station from 1926 to 1972. It outlines the campaigns for a separate Irish language radio station, Raidió na Gaeltachta (1972), and television station, TG4 (1996), and reviews the limited support for Irish language public service media in Northern Ireland. The case study covers two Irish-language community radio stations, Raidió na Life and Raidió Fáilte, in Dublin and Belfast, respectively. Drawing on interviews and focus groups with staff and volunteers, it analyses their history and current operations. The understandings of volunteers of the stations' aims and the inter-relationship between community development and the promotion of Irish are also discussed. Given their location in urban settings far from the Gaeltacht, both Raidió Fáilte and Raidió na Life are sites for activism by mostly new speakers and by concluding the book with this group, we come full circle back to the centrality of the Irish-speaking community in an analysis of this type. The Conclusion chapter draws together the book's conclusions, assesses the relative success or failure of the policy over the past century and makes recommendations for the future.

CHAPTER I

Speakers

1. Introduction

The first part of this chapter provides an overview of contemporary speakers of Irish, ranging from geographically dense communities in the Gaeltacht containing high concentrations of native speakers, to looser networks of people who acquired Irish outside home or neighbourhood settings and can be analysed using the new speaker lens. It also offers an overview of Irish speakers in Northern Ireland where there are no extant Gaeltacht communities, as historically understood, but where Irish continues to be promoted in networks. The second part of the chapter is a case study of historical and contemporary Irish speakers in what is known as Gaeltacht na nDéise in the southeastern county of Waterford (see Map 1).

Irish continues to be transmitted as a family language and spoken in the community to varying extents in the Gaeltacht and in networks elsewhere in the Republic of Ireland where it may also be a family language. There are also Irish-speaking families and networks in Northern Ireland and abroad, including in Britain, the United States and other countries with significant populations of Irish ancestry. Estimating the precise number of speakers of any language is complex but is more challenging in the case of a minoritised language such as Irish where ideological considerations may cloud decisions about language competence and use. Due to its universal nature, the most comprehensive data source is the census of population, which is held every five years in the Republic and every ten in Northern Ireland. However, there are issues with the nature and scope of the questions asked which differ

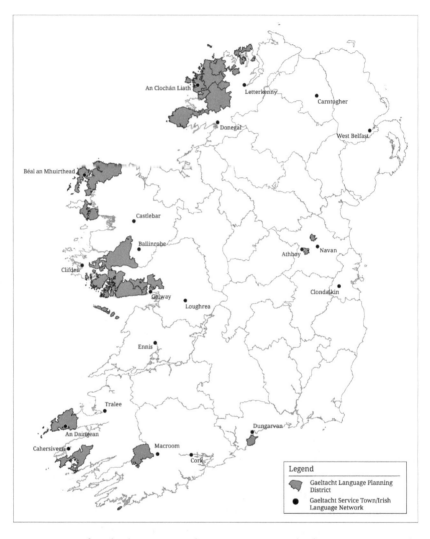

Map 1. Map of Gaeltacht Language Planning Districts, Gaeltacht Service Towns and
Irish Language Networks.

Map kindly created by David Kelly, Moore Institute, NUI Galway.

on both sides of the border and therefore prevent comparisons. Changes in the question in the Republic of Ireland in recent years have also created inconsistencies, in particular a jump of nearly 9 percentage points in the number of 'speakers' between 1991 and 1996. This has been attributed to the removal of the question asking if the respondent could read but not speak Irish, prompting those with moderate or weak speaking ability to record themselves as speakers instead (Ó Riagáin, 2018: 36–37). In the Republic, respondents are asked whether they speak Irish and about their frequency of use, but not about their perceived level of competence. In Northern Ireland, respondents are required to self-assess if they possess certain skills in Irish but are not asked how often they speak the language. The absence of clear guidance about what constitutes a speaker, coupled with both the core status of Irish in education in the Republic and its minoritised status in society, exert influences on individual perceptions of their ability in and relationship to the language. In the North, the strong link between Irish and the nationalist/Catholic community and its historical association with a resistance identity also cast a shadow over the census figures there.

Further sources are smaller survey samples since the 1970s, which combine data about knowledge of and use of Irish as well as attitudes towards it (e.g. Ó Riagáin & Ó Gliasáin, 1994; Mac Gréil & Rhatigan, 2007; Ó Riagáin, 2007; Darmody & Daly, 2015). A landmark historical study of language policy and social reproduction includes a detailed study of Irish and class structures (Ó Riagáin, 1997). A study of the 2002 Census and a government grant to support Irish in the family was the baseline for the *Comprehensive Study of the Use of Irish in the Gaeltacht* (Ó Giollagáin et al., 2007a; see also Chapter 2). There has also been qualitative and ethnographic research into Irish speakers in the Gaeltacht and elsewhere, including Irish-speaking families and networks.

1.1 Census in the Republic of Ireland

The census due to be held in 2021 was postponed to 2022 due to Covid-19. The most recent census for which results are available, that of 2016, is significant because it registered reductions in several key statistics related to general knowledge of Irish and use of it, particularly in the Gaeltacht. The 2016 census found that 1,761,420 people or 39.8 per cent of the population, reported being capable of speaking Irish. This represented a slight reduction of 0.7 per cent on the 2011 figure (1,774,437 people or 41.4 per cent). As in previous censuses, there was a considerable gender difference in terms of reported language ability, with 43.1 per cent of women claiming competence compared to 36.4 per cent of men. There was also a fall in the headline figure of daily Irish speakers outside education to 73,803 (1.7 per cent) from 77,185 (1.8 per cent) in 2011. A further 111,473 people (2.3 per cent) reported speaking Irish weekly (a slight increase on 2011) and 586,535 (12.3 per cent) said they spoke it less often, a decrease on 2011. Significantly, about a quarter of the people who returned themselves as speakers (421,274) said that they never spoke Irish (Central Statistics Office, 2017b: 66). Consistent with previous censuses, professed ability to speak Irish was strongly correlated with attendance at school, with 66 per cent of 17 and 18-year-olds claiming competence. Once again, results were differentiated for gender, with just 60.4 per cent of males in this age cohort stating that they could speak Irish compared to 71.4 per cent of females (ibid.: 67). The gender imbalance is most pronounced in the 35–44-year cohort where there were just 631 male daily speakers for every 1,000 females (ibid.: 2017a). There was also a strong correlation between educational achievement and ability to speak Irish with 49 per cent of Irish speakers possessing a degree or higher qualification compared to just 28.5 per cent in the general population (ibid.).

Of the 73,803 daily Irish speakers outside education, 53,217 (70.1 per cent) lived outside the Gaeltacht (ibid.: 69). Although the largest number of absolute speakers was found in Dublin and its suburbs, this represented a lower percentage than within the national population (14,903 or 1.3 per cent). The town with the highest percentages of daily Irish speakers outside the Gaeltacht was Letterkenny, which is adjacent to the Irish-speaking part of Donegal (771 or 53.4 per cent).

Of the Gaeltacht population of 96,090, 63,664 (66.3 per cent) said that they could speak Irish, down from 66,238 (68.5 per cent) in 2011. There was a sharp decline in the number and percentage of daily speakers outside education to 20,586 (21.4 per cent) from 23,175 (24 per cent) (2017b: 69;

also 2017a). This overall figure masks considerable regional differences across the Gaeltacht with the highest absolute numbers and percentages of daily Irish speakers to be found in the Gaeltacht area of Co. Galway (29 per cent) and the lowest in Galway City (4.3 per cent) (ibid.: 2017a). However, there were declines in numbers of daily speakers in every Gaeltacht with the exception of Galway City and Waterford, where marginal increases were registered (2017b: 69). Of the twenty-six Language Planning Districts in the Gaeltacht, the highest percentage of daily Irish speakers outside education was recorded in the small island of Toraigh in Co. Donegal (85 people or 74.6 per cent) followed by Ceantar na nOileán in Co. Galway (1,474 people or 71.7 per cent). The parts of Galway City officially located in the Gaeltacht were at the bottom of the list (2017a).[1]

1.2   Census in Northern Ireland

The most recent census day in Northern Ireland was held on the 21st of March 2021 and the latest published census data was gathered on the 27th of March 2011. Questions are asked about 'main language' and there are specific questions about Irish and Ulster Scots. 0.2 per cent of the population (4,164 people) recorded Irish as their 'main language' (Northern Ireland Statistics and Research Agency [NISRA], 2012: 17). The local government area with the highest concentration of people claiming Irish as their main language was Belfast where the percentage reached 0.6 per cent (1,650 people), rising to 1.4 per cent (1,269 people) in West Belfast (NISRA, 2014: 66, 70).[2]

Specific questions about Irish relate to self-reported skills in the language but there is no enquiry about level of competence. 10.7 per cent of the population (184,898 people) claimed some ability in Irish (NISRA,

---

1   I thank Emmet Ó Fatharta of the Central Statistics Office for assistance with figures.

2   The published reports provide percentages only in relation to each question. Full statistical information is available at <https://www.ninis2.nisra.gov.uk/public/InteractiveMapTheme.aspx?themeNumber=136&themeName=Census%202011> and has been consulted in preparing this section.

2012: 18), the highest percentage being found in local government areas of Newry and Mourne (19.8 per cent or 18,816 people), Magherafelt (18.5 per cent or 7,924 people) and Dungannon (18.3 per cent or 10,050 people) (NISRA, 2014: 75). In the electoral district of West Belfast, 21 per cent (18,853 people) claimed some ability in Irish with relatively high returns from Mid Ulster and Newry and Armagh (ibid.: 77).

Respondents are also asked if they understand Irish only, speak Irish only, speak and read Irish or speak, read, write and understand the language. Notwithstanding issues about the nature of the questions and the limitation of self-reporting, it is possible to interpret the question covering the four linguistic skills as applying to people with a relatively high level of competence. 3.7 per cent (64,847) of people in Northern Ireland responded positively to that question, with numbers higher in areas with concentrations of nationalists. 8.2 per cent (7,323 people) of the electoral area of West Belfast claimed competence in the four skills, followed by 6.2 per cent in both Mid Ulster (5,885 people) and Newry and Armagh (6,671 people), 5.4 per cent in Foyle (Derry) (5,233 people), 5 per cent in South Belfast (5,351 people) and 5 per cent in West Tyrone (4,329 people) (NIRSA, 2014: 77).

1.3 Other surveys

An all-Ireland Irish language survey conducted by the Economic and Social Research Institute (ESRI) for the all-Ireland language planning body Foras na Gaeilge in 2013 yielded 2,260 adult respondents, 1,125 in the Republic of Ireland and 1,045 in Northern Ireland (Darmody & Daly, 2015: 5). The methodology was aligned with an earlier all-Ireland survey conducted in 2000 (Ó Riagáin, 2008 & 2012). Respondents were asked to characterise their Irish according to six fluency levels in three overarching categories of 'no fluency', 'basic fluency' and 'advanced fluency'. In the Republic of Ireland, 14 per cent ranked themselves as possessing advanced fluency compared to 3 per cent in Northern Ireland. 43 per cent in the Republic reported basic fluency compared to 14 per cent in the North (Darmody & Daly, 2015: 64). The ESRI research found that

6 per cent of respondents in the Republic reported speaking Irish daily, compared to just 1 per cent in Northern Ireland. The total of daily and weekly speakers in the Republic was 13 per cent compared to 2 per cent for the North (ibid.: 66). Interestingly, almost one-third of those in the Republic who chose advanced fluency recalled returning themselves as non-Irish speakers in the Census, with more than half of those with basic fluency in both jurisdictions recalling doing so. The authors of the report argued that this pointed to the need for changes in the census questions:

> This highlights the benefit of including a more detailed question related to the Irish language in the next Census as it is evident from the Irish Language Survey 2013 that many of those who can converse in Irish did not in fact record this ability during the Census. (Ibid.: 68)

The ESRI research found that respondents in rural areas were more likely to use Irish regularly than those in urban centres. There was a strong correlation between younger age, educational attainment and higher class categories and the regular use of Irish. In Northern Ireland, the use of Irish among Catholics was much higher (25 per cent) than Protestants (2 per cent) (ibid.: 66).

In a survey of 1,015 adults conducted in 2007 and 2008, almost 8 per cent of respondents described their Irish as fluent. 42 per cent were classified as 'reasonably competent' (in the top three categories of ability), rising to 47 per cent for the Irish-born sample (Mac Gréil & Rhatigan, 2009: 39). Highest levels of reasonable competence were found among people aged 18–40, brought up in Munster and living in the mid-west and southwest. There was also a positive correlation between reasonable competence and those who had completed secondary or higher education and among those with professional/executive status but no significant gender difference was reported (ibid.: 43–53). 9 per cent of the sample reported using Irish weekly or more often, with a further 11 per cent using it occasionally, a cumulative total of 20 per cent (rising to 23 per cent for the Irish-born sample) (ibid.: 58). Levels of use of Irish were highest when accessing Irish-language media, in the home and with Irish-speaking friends (ibid.: 60). Younger age cohorts (18–40 years) and those brought up in Munster made greater use of Irish and again there was a positive correlation between educational attainment and use of Irish. However, the report pointed to the 'extraordinary depth of the embedded gap between competence and use of Irish' with around half of those with reasonable competence never using the language (ibid.: 69).

1.4   Gaeltacht studies

A large amount of social research has been conducted by sociologists, sociolinguists and geographers in the Gaeltacht since the 1960s. This has documented socioeconomic deprivation as well as an ongoing decline in the use of Irish; for instance, a geographical survey of the Galway Gaeltacht noted that it suffered significant population decline between the 1920s and 1960s and that the skewed age profile and history of underdevelopment had led to social problems (Mac Aodha, 1969). Pioneering sociolinguistic research includes the work of the Committee on Irish Language Attitudes Research (1975), which included the Gaeltacht, and studies of regional planning (Ó Riagáin, 1971) and language shift and maintenance (Ó Riagáin, 1982). A detailed local study of language use patterns in the west Kerry Gaeltacht was conducted in the late 1980s (Ó Riagáin, 1992). A geographical study that proclaimed the death of Irish attracted much attention in the Gaeltacht and elsewhere (Hindley, 1990 & 1991).

Various strands of research in recent decades have emphasised the pressure on Irish as a vernacular in the Gaeltacht, particularly among young people. A study of pre-school children revealed that native Irish speakers switch to English when children with limited Irish are present (Hickey, 2001). A survey of young people in the Gaeltacht, conducted as part of the *Comprehensive Linguistic Study of the Use of Irish in the Gaeltacht* (CLS; see Chapter 2), examined the use of Irish among young people themselves and with other age cohorts and tracked changes in language use as they got older. It noted a disparity between overwhelmingly positive attitudes towards Irish and patterns of use. In the core category A areas, 53 per cent of young people said they were raised with Irish only or for the most part, while 91 per cent reported being able to speak Irish well or very well. However, only 60 per cent of respondents in these areas used Irish for the most part within these domains. 24 per cent of those in category A areas spoke Irish for the most part with their peers (9 per cent for all Gaeltacht areas), with the level of use falling as they advance through the education system (Ó Giollagáin et al., 2017a: 25–27; see also Ó Giollagáin et al., 2017b: part 4).

Gaeltacht teenagers have been shown to possess superior competence in English than in Irish (Pétervary et al., 2014) and it has proven challenging for schools to stimulate social use of Irish outside the classroom (Ní Shéaghdha, 2010). English is frequently the language of socialisation of children and teenagers even in cases where they have high levels of competence in Irish. One study showed that almost 49 per cent of pupils spoke English only or mostly to their friends at school, rising to 70 per cent outside school (Ní Thuairisg & Ó Duibhir, 2019: 31–34). This suggests that in institutional settings where Irish is dominant (i.e. schools), teenagers speak more Irish to each other.

Other research has focused on how Gaeltacht families interpreted the guidelines of the former support scheme for speaking of Irish in the home, Scéim Labhairt na Gaeilge (SLG), that operated between 1933 and 2011 (Ó hIfearnáin, 2007; see also Chapter 2). The relationship between the standard language and use of Irish as a home language in the Gaeltacht has also been explored, as have family responses to language shift in the Gaeltacht (Ó hIfearnáin, 2008 & 2013). Relatedly, recent ethnographic research has investigated use of Irish among children in families in the Corca Dhuibhne Gaeltacht (Smith-Christmas & Ruiséal, 2019; Smith-Christmas, 2020).

A report for the parents' support network Tuismitheoirí na Gaeltachta ('Gaeltacht Parents') found that only a small percentage of Gaeltacht families are raising children with Irish. Based on the census of 2016, 2,889 families with children between 0 and 18 years reported speaking Irish daily both within and outside the education system (23 per cent of a total of 12,586 Gaeltacht families). Almost half of the families (1,414) are based in Galway, 857 in Donegal and 621 spread across the remainder of Gaeltacht counties (Ní Chuaig et al., 2021: 2). Most pre-school education in the Gaeltacht is provided by Comhar Naíonraí na Gaeltachta ('Gaeltacht Pre-Schools Partnership') and organisations such as Tuismitheoirí na Gaeltachta and Oidhreacht Chorca Dhuibhne ('West Kerry Heritage') provide supports for families, but there is considerable variation among different Gaeltacht Language Planning Districts. The low level of family use of the language emphasises the importance of the Gaeltacht education system in supporting acquisition of Irish (ibid.: 3–4). The authors of the report describe the findings as bleak for the sustainability of Irish in the Gaeltacht and state that the low number of families using Irish is a cause of concern given the centrality of intergenerational transmission to the *20-Year Strategy for the Irish Language* (ibid.: 55). The report recommended providing every support to these families so that they do not become despondent and give up their efforts to transmit Irish to their children. It proposed that all relevant agencies come together to agree a plan to provide long-term support. Recognising seven different combinations of family use of Irish and English, it recommended targeting specific support mechanisms at each category (ibid.: 56–58).

Considerable research on use of and attitudes to Irish in the community has been conducted as part of the Gaeltacht language planning process (see Chapter 2), as local committees gathered data to inform their language plans. The quality of the data varies, reflecting the limited support offered by the state to such groups, but some Language Planning Districts have assembled comprehensive quantitative and qualitative data (e.g. Gaeilge Iorrais, 2018). The Waterford Gaeltacht (Gaeltacht na nDéise) is discussed in the case study of this chapter (for an analysis of language plans as they relate to family use of Irish, see Ní Chuaig et al., 2021).

1.5 Other networks of Irish speakers

There have been various attempts since the foundation of the state to create other Irish-speaking communities outside the Gaeltacht. While principles of territoriality and intergenerational transmission have been central in most of these initiatives, some have eschewed the Gaeltacht label because of its historical connotations. What the vast majority of the projects have in common, however, is that they failed to create any sizeable, sustainable communities of Irish speakers. With the exception of the Ráth Chairn Gaeltacht in the 1930s (see Chapter 2), no other new

Irish-speaking geographical community of appreciable size or linguistic success has been established in the Republic. A list of historical efforts in Ó Murchú (2007) covers both urban and rural initiatives. Heavily influenced by Fishman's RLS model, a more recent journalistic account by Dunbar (2021) focuses on territorially defined communities and does not engage with the extensive body of research on new speakers of Irish (see 1.6 below).

An initiative to build housing for Irish speakers in one of the new Dublin suburbs in the 1920s was not successful and all that remains today is a series of roads called after Gaeltacht areas (McManus, 2021: 273–280). In the 1960s, a group called 'Iosrael in Iar-Chonnachta' (Israel in west Connacht) did not attempt to establish a new community per se, but rather to attract Irish speakers from elsewhere to resettle in the Gaeltacht in order to strengthen it (Fennell, 1969). In 2007, a group calling itself 'Baile Gaelach' (Irish-speaking home or village) announced its intention to buy land for Irish speakers in Leinster, avoiding the Gaeltacht label because it felt that the concept was too narrow, but it too came to nothing (Walsh, 2012: 404). The small left-wing activist group Misneach ('courage'), established in 2013, has said that it wishes to set up 'Gaelphobail' (Irish-speaking communities) either within or outside the Gaeltacht (Mac Aoidh, 2016). One critic and activist has suggested establishing a tightly knit community of ideologically committed speakers that would grow to 50,000–100,000 people over time. Such a community would shift the discourse away from an attitude of antiquarianism (*meon na hársaíochta*) to one of reclamation (*meon na hathghabhála*) in relation to Irish (Mac Síomóin, 2006). Arguing that the sociolinguistic distinction between the Gaeltacht and the rest of Ireland has reduced, another scholar has suggested the term 'Nua-Ghaeltacht' (New Gaeltacht) to refer to a dynamic but dispersed national community of Irish speakers (Ó Riagáin, 2011).

The most successful historical example of a new, intentional Irish-speaking community is the Shaw's Road 'Gaeltacht' (*Gaeltacht Bhóthar Seoighe*) in west Belfast, established in 1969 at the start of the Troubles. A group of Irish speakers motivated by the importance of creating a territorial community came together and built a handful of houses on available land in the west of the city. They also established their own Irish-medium school, the first of its kind in Northern Ireland. The school was not recognised by the British authorities for over a decade and relied for its survival on voluntary contributions. The initiative was marked by a resistance identity and a can-do mentality characteristic of Irish language initiatives in the hostile political context of the time (see Chapter 5). Mac Póilin, who himself moved into the Shaw's Road in 1976 and raised his family there, deftly explained the unique circumstances that supported the development and maintenance of Irish in Belfast:

> The socio-linguistic and political circumstances in which Irish has survived in Belfast are distinctive; a small organic Irish-speaking community within an urban network of language learners within a large disaffected Catholic/nationalist minority with a high birth-rate in a Protestant/unionist city in an unstable Protestant/unionist state within a Catholic/nationalist island. (2003b: 129)

By 2008, there were twenty-two houses in the community and the third generation of children was being raised in them through Irish, but suburbanisation meant that there was no more room for expansion. Despite its small extent, the Shaw's Road Gaeltacht punched above its weight in terms of psychological influence on Irish speakers across Northern Ireland and further afield (Mac Póilin, 2007: 41). Recently, the west Belfast area, including the Shaw's Road, has been recognised as an Irish Language Network as part of the Irish government's language planning process. A rural community in Co. Derry, Carn Tóchair, has similarly been recognised and bases its philosophy on linking the Irish language to community development and sustainability (Armstrong, 2012). Both networks are funded by Foras na Gaeilge.

1.6 'New speakers' of Irish

Over the past decade, a large volume of research has been conducted on 'new speakers' of Irish, people of varying degrees of fluency and commitment who use Irish regularly although they were not socialised in it in early childhood in the Gaeltacht. I co-led, with Bernadette O'Rourke, a large-scale qualitative research project in Ireland, comprising 100 semi-structured narrative biographical interviews with people fitting the new speaker profile from various backgrounds, locations and genders and ranging in age from the late teens to the 70s. The majority of participants had no Irish language background and acquired the language in the mainstream English-medium education system in the Republic of Ireland, with smaller numbers attending Irish-medium schools. A number of people raised with English in the Gaeltacht were interviewed, as were new speakers from both backgrounds in Northern Ireland. The sample also contained adult learners in the United States who learned Irish from classes or self-tuition. The majority of participants had spent periods in the Gaeltacht and believed that its continued protection was important, although not all wanted to model their speech on Gaeltacht varieties.

In terms of competence, five subgroups were identified: (a) 'expert speakers' (Piller, 2002), so defined because they attained a high level of competence although this did not always involve acquisition of a Gaeltacht variety; (b) those who modelled their speech on Gaeltacht dialects and sometimes 'passed' as native speakers; (c) those who spoke more hybridised forms of Irish involving greater use of post-traditional features; (d) people raised with Irish or bilingually outside the Gaeltacht who do not consider themselves native speakers and (e) potential new speakers, people who have begun a trajectory towards greater social use of Irish but are at lower levels of competence (Walsh et al., 2015; O'Rourke & Walsh, 2020).

Several interlinked themes related to Irish have been analysed within this body of research. These include the process of becoming a new speaker of Irish, which is explored in ten case studies (O'Rourke & Walsh, 2020: 73–117) and in a comparative study of linguistic *mudes* in three minority language contexts including Irish (see Introduction; Puigdevall et al., 2018). An ethnographic study of Irish in west Belfast includes a further ten case studies about the process of becoming an Irish speaker in that specific sociopolitical context (Zenker, 2013: 55–90), while Mac Giolla Chríost (2012) and Mac Ionnrachtaigh (2013) study the acquisition of Irish by Republic prisoners in the North.

Another strand relates to different types of identity construction and new speakers (O'Rourke & Walsh, 2020: 118–148) and the identity choices made by new speakers of Irish identifying as gay (Walsh, 2019a). Questions

of identity also arise in a study of new speakers of Irish in the United States
(Walsh & Ní Dhúda, 2015). The emotional experiences of new speakers as
they adopt and use Irish are explored in Walsh (2019c). A further salient
theme is the positionality of new speakers and their relationship with the
Gaeltacht (O'Rourke & Walsh, 2015). This is related to discourse about
ownership of Irish, which has been studied among (potential) new speakers
in university (O'Rourke, 2011).

Questions related to new speakers in education are analysed in
O'Rourke et al. (2017). The social use of Irish among immersion students
is discussed in Ó Duibhir (2018: 139–152) and although employing a second
language acquisition perspective, the analysis by Flynn (2020) of adult
learners of Irish is relevant to the new speaker theme. Attitudes of trainee
teachers of Irish to linguistic variation are discussed by Ó Murchadha
and Flynn (2018), while Ó Murchadha (2019) explores perceptions of linguistic variation, including the varieties of Irish used outside the Gaeltacht.
Petit (2016 & 2020) assesses the experiences of Irish learners in Gaeltacht
summer immersion colleges. O'Rourke (2015) and O'Rourke & Walsh
(2020: 149–168) analyse the phenomenon of *ciorcail chomhrá* (informal
conversation circles) for emerging new speakers while the type of Irish used
by new speakers on radio is considered in Moal et al. (2018). The use of
Irish in popular culture genres such as comedy and hip-hop involves people
who fit new speaker profiles and is discussed by Kelly-Holmes (2011) and
Moriarty (2015). Seoighe (2018) explores the social and cultural spaces
created by new speakers (see also the discussion of Irish language community radio in Chapter 5).

2. Case study: Gaeltacht na nDéise

This case study focuses on the coastal Gaeltacht area of Na Déise in west
Co. Waterford in the southeast of Ireland. Na Déise ('Decies' in English)
is a tribal name referring to a much larger historic barony covering
Waterford and part of Tipperary and the present Irish-speaking district
is the remnant of a larger Gaeltacht area as defined by the Gaeltacht

Commission of 1926 (see Chapter 2). Even in the 1920s, however, Na Déise was cut off from other Gaeltacht areas of Munster and was the only Irish-speaking area in the east of the country. Today, this Gaeltacht area (henceforth referred to in Irish as 'Gaeltacht na nDéise') comprises only 6,110 hectares or 37.8 square kilometres and consists of the districts of An Rinn and An Seanphobal.[3] Although slightly increased in size following a review of the boundaries in 1974, it consists of just one full electoral division (ED) and parts of two others and contains a population of less than 2,000 people. This makes it one of the country's smallest Gaeltacht areas in terms of population and size. Following a fall in the percentage of daily Irish speakers up to the early 2000s, its core base of daily Irish speakers has stabilised at less than 30 per cent of the population and the local iteration of the language planning process aims to ameliorate the linguistic balance between Irish and English. While predominantly rural until recently, proximity to the town of Dungarvan and increased demand for property in coastal areas has changed its character and housing developments have attracted controversy due to their potentially deleterious influence on the Irish language. Historically the economy was reliant on fishing, agriculture and forestry and more recently, a television production company making media content for TG4 has created further language-based employment. The area has a rich cultural tradition based on the language and many of its traditional singers and writers have achieved critical acclaim. The presence of an Irish language boarding school for over a century has boosted the position of the language locally (Walsh, 2012: 227).

Gaeltacht na nDéise is a microcosm of the Gaeltacht where there is considerable pressure on Irish but is distinctive due to its unique geographical location both remote from other Irish-speaking districts and adjacent to urban centres such as Dungarvan, Cork and Waterford. The position of Irish as not particularly strong by comparison with other Gaeltacht areas brings it closer in profile to the remainder of Ireland where loose networks use Irish to varying degrees. As would be expected in a small Gaeltacht area, the local population is mixed linguistically and includes families that have

---

3   The Irish versions of Gaeltacht placenames are used throughout this book. For further information, see the national database of placenames <www.logainm.ie>.

spoken Irish for generations, people closer to the 'new speaker' profile who moved into the area, locals with limited or no competence in Irish and recent incomers who speak only English. Despite its small extent, a considerable baseline of research about Gaeltacht na nDéise has been developed in recent years, including detailed sociolinguistic and socioeconomic surveys of the area. For these reasons, Gaeltacht na nDéise has been chosen for this case study. In the first part of this chapter, we summarised recent data about speakers of Irish nationally and in the Gaeltacht. This case study focuses on language policy interventions – similar to Spolsky's 'language management' concept – aimed at increasing the use of Irish among speakers and potential speakers in one Gaeltacht district where Irish has a moderately strong presence already. It begins with an examination of sources about language, identity and ideology in west Waterford in the early twentieth century before proceeding to analyse the current language planning process being conducted in the region.

2.1 Irish speakers in Gaeltacht na nDéise in the early twentieth century

Almost 100 years ago, Gaeltacht na nDéise comprised sixty-one electoral divisions and covered more than half of Co. Waterford, parts of south Tipperary and east Cork (Gaeltacht Commission, 1926: 8). Many of these areas were defined as 'Breac-Ghaeltacht' (literally 'speckled' or partial Gaeltacht) by the Gaeltacht Commission of 1925–1926 (see Chapter 2), a mixed linguistic zone seen as a buffer to protect the core 'Fíor-Ghaeltacht' ('true' or fully Irish-speaking) areas. In the evidence gathered by the Commission, concerns were expressed about the position of Irish, with particular attention being paid to the plight of those involved in the fishing and maritime industries (Walsh, 2002: 36). A study of a wide range of sources – linguistic, sociolinguistic, biographical and folkloric – from the early decades of the twentieth century reveals rich and complex insights into language policy – in the sense of practices, beliefs and management – in Gaeltacht na nDéise (for a full account, see Walsh, 2016). The following sections focuses on one such source, the diaries of local folklore collector Nioclás Breatnach (1912–2002), but first we examine the concept of 'Breac-Ghaeltacht' itself.

The Breac-Ghaeltacht as a sociocultural and sociolinguistic concept remains relatively unexplored and we have only a poor understanding of the language practices of its inhabitants and their attitudes to Irish and English. Although the category was never formally recognised in legislation and was shelved in 1956 when the boundaries were redrawn, it caught hold of the public imagination as a way of distinguishing between different profiles of Gaeltacht. In essence, the label entered Gaeltacht folklore and retains currency among generations of people old enough to remember the distinction between 'Fíor-Ghaeltacht' and 'Breac-Ghaeltacht'. Based on a renowned autobiographical account of a bilingual Irish-German family in Dublin (Hamilton, 2003), Ó Laoire describes Irish speakers as 'breacdhaoine' ('speckled people') because they have no option but to deal with English (2004: 61). The people of the Breac-Ghaeltacht of the early twentieth century can be seen as the 'speckled people' par excellence, grappling with two languages and cultures in the midst of rapid language shift from Irish to English. While information about the Breac-Ghaeltacht is available in the Commission's documentation, other sources from folklore studies, dialectology and autobiography shed further light on the complexities of the concept. This type of data helps us to understand language shift around the edges of the core Gaeltacht areas in the decades following the foundation of the state, insights that are highly pertinent today given the hybridised nature of the remaining Irish-speaking districts and indeed of all networks of speakers of Irish.

Use of sources such as folkloric or dialectal studies conducted in the first half of the twentieth century also requires attention to the ideological underpinnings of such work. The rigid parameters of both disciplines at the time prioritised small numbers of informants deemed to be exemplars of local lore or language, thereby marginalising other people whose cultural or linguistic knowledge was judged incomplete or corrupted (Ó Cadhla, 2011: 139–153). The simplistic binary distinction between 'Fíor-Ghaeltacht' and 'Breac-Ghaeltacht' does not deal satisfactorily with the social position of Irish in its receding core communities during this period or since. As will be argued in this section, the varied evidence available shows that the

Breac-Ghaeltacht contained many Irish speakers who could not be easily categorised as 'native speakers of English' or 'native speakers of Irish' and that further recognition is needed for the interstitial spaces in which hybridised forms of language practice prevailed. The dominance of simplistic and rigid linguistic or cultural categories calls for additional analytical tools in order to understand what has been called 'an fearann breac' (the speckled ground) of Irish language literature that is forged in the spaces between two languages and cultures (Nic Eoin, 2005). Although many Breac-Ghaeltacht speakers displayed what are seen as classic signs of linguistic obsolescence, and notwithstanding the fact that the fate of the Breac-Ghaeltacht was the retreat of Irish, the language shift was not a simple, linear process. The situation can also be framed in terms of identity negotiation in areas without strong ethnocultural boundaries, long affected by cultural and linguistic hybridity. As well as an Irish national identity cemented by the nation-building of the Irish Free State, the Breac-Ghaeltacht contained people who adhered to an Irish-speaking or a local identity or identified primarily as English speakers, or indeed shifted between various identity options according to their sociolinguistic environment. This microstudy is an attempt to deal with the lack of attention to the bilingualism of the Breac-Ghaeltacht in official sources and – by sifting through evidence about language practice and ideology – to illustrate the sociolinguistic complexity of those communities.

The Breac-Ghaeltacht is worthy of attention because it comprised areas where language shift was well advanced by the foundation of the state, illustrated by the fact that only relatively small parts of Co. Waterford were designated as 'Fíor-Ghaeltacht' by the Commission. The sources are both linguistic – providing evidence of the language shift from Irish to English – and sociolinguistic – detailing the changing social conditions in which Irish was spoken in these areas.

2.2 Dialectology

Irish language dialectology experienced a golden age at this time, with large-scale studies of all varieties of Irish by international linguists and a

series of microsurveys of individual dialects, particularly after the foundation of the Dublin Institute of Advanced Studies in 1940, one of whose
specialisms was Celtic linguistics. The Prussian linguist Wilhelm Doegen
made wax cylinder recordings of native speakers of Irish throughout
the country in the 1920s. He recorded seven speakers in Na Déise, six in
Waterford and one in Tipperary (Royal Irish Academy, 2009; see also Mac
Congáil and Ó Duibhín, 2009 and Ní Bhaoill, 2009). A general source
from the mid-twentieth century is the *Linguistic Atlas of and Survey of
Irish Dialects* (henceforth LASID) by the Swiss linguist Heinrich Wagner
(1958, republished 1981), six points of which relate to Na Déise. The variety
and quality of information at the eighty-eight points chosen by Wagner
gives an indication of the uneven language shift at the time. While an
ideology of seeking out the most authentic native speakers underpinned
the work, many of Wagner's informants showed evidence of the influence
of English on their speech. Indeed, his definition of a 'native speaker' contained a degree of flexibility to reflect the fact that in some places, the
dialect no longer had any currency as the vernacular:

> My definition of a native speaker was as follows: a person brought up to speak the
> Irish dialect which still is, *or was once spoken in a given place*. I claim that such a person
> is representative of this local dialect. (1981, ix, emphasis added)

This caveat allows that in some places, the informant was among the final
speakers of a given dialect and that it had ceased to have any communicative function locally. In many places where LASID informants were
located, Wagner had no option but to choose people who fell short of the
classic requirements of such studies, i.e. as little knowledge as possible of
the dominant language:

> I was most anxious to collect my material as soon as possible in those places where
> there were only a very few native speakers left. I worked only with people who whose
> first language had been Irish only, *or both Irish and English* … [I] confined myself to
> the study of the speech of people who, *at least in their youth*, spoke the Irish dialect
> of their locality. In most places I was dealing with people who had not spoken Irish
> for, perhaps, upwards of sixty years, *English having become the vernacular of the place
> at an early stage in their lives*. Thus, it was seldom possible to get all the words and
> grammatical forms needed for my questionnaire. Most of the subjects were aged

between seventy and ninety-five years, and although they did their best in answering my questions, *they were inevitably at a loss from time to time, as their Irish had become rusty.* A number of those interviewed had been bedridden for years, including some who were inmates of hospitals and institutions ... *If we have corrupt material en masse,* i.e. sentences which are mere translations of our English questionnaire sentences, it is not due to inefficient methods of interrogation, but to the fact that *most of our informants have not spoken Irish for many years.* If Irish were to become their vernacular once more, it would be different in many ways from the language spoken by the preceding generation who knew very little English. We are concerned with linguistic reality. Our material will, therefore, also show the influence which English has exercised on Irish over the past hundred years (Ibid.: x, emphasis added)

Wagner had no choice but to recognise the 'linguistic reality' if he wanted to gather evidence of extant native speech in Irish, but his commentary nonetheless reflects the ideological basis of the 'salvage' linguistics (O'Rourke and Walsh, 2020: 30) associated with this approach and period:

> We are not dealing with a language spoken over a wide area, but rather with the ruins of a language. We compare our work with the archaeologist's task of reconstructing an old building from a few heaps of stones, lying here and there in the place where the original building stood. (Ibid.: x)

Studies of individual dialects such as in Gaeltacht na nDéise often contain useful additional information about language profiles of the informants or specificities of the areas where they lived. An iconic early twentieth century compendium of local speech contains a description of the state of Irish in the west Waterford area (Sheehan, 1906: 239–279). Basic sociolinguistic information is provided in Breatnach (1945). A later study of the morphology of the irregular verb in Na Déise is of interest because of the places where informants were living, providing information about the locations of individual Irish speakers even if the language had ceased being a vernacular across most of the area (Uí Fhoghlú, 2004). The same can be said about a late twentieth century word list, which contains a detailed list of informants and their places of residence (Ó hAirt, 1988: iv–vi). This was based on vocabulary gathered by a local priest, Fr Piaras de Hindeberg, in the 1970s. A further 540 hours of audio recordings by Fr de Hindeberg remain to be analysed and could yield valuable further linguistic and sociolinguistic information (Ó Drisleáin, 2012).

2.3 Official and biographical sources

There is plenty of evidence in the minutes of meetings conducted by the Gaeltacht Commission around the country and the evidence of people from across the Fíor-Ghaeltacht and Breac-Ghaeltacht regions. A meeting was held in Dungarvan on the 9th of October 1925 and the account contains evidence about language practice and language ideology across the Breac-Ghaeltacht area. Additional information about the Munster Gaeltacht areas is provided in submissions made by people in Cork, Tipperary and Waterford (Gaeltacht Commission, 1926: 70–72). Similarly, various autobiographical and biographical accounts offer further glimpses into the state of Irish in Na Déise in the twentieth century (see a full list of sources in Walsh, 2016).

2.4 Folkloric sources

Sources related to the collection of folklore can also provide linguistic and sociolinguistic insights into individual storytellers or the areas where they lived. Some of the material gathered by the Irish Folklore Commission has been analysed and presented in key volumes (see the analysis of material from Cork in Walsh, 2011). Caution is needed with the linguistic veracity of the material, however, as ideological considerations may have prompted collectors or editors to 'correct' material that showed evidence of language shift. It has been argued that much of the collection was considered canonical folklore, a reflection of both Victorian values of antiquarianism and the purist culture of revivalism (Ó Cadhla, 2011: 242). Although folklore collectors were advised to transcribe material accurately and not to alter the original text (Briody, 2007: 418), in the absence of audio recordings this cannot always be verified. Wax cylinders were frequently re-used due to financial considerations, destroying the original recordings and therefore the ability to compare them with transcripts (ibid.: 245). Even if transcription was conducted diligently and no attempt made to amend the original material, no system can fully capture every aspect of the linguistic competence of an individual storyteller. Furthermore, no editor is uninfluenced by some ideological frame that would influence the presentation of material in written form. Often in the areas in question, folklore was gathered from people recognised as the last fluent speakers in their localities, some of whose Irish was rusty due to lack of use. A similar situation prevailed in the Isle of Man when the Irish Folklore Commission – following the intervention of Taoiseach Éamon de Valera who visited the island privately while on holidays – began gathering material in Manx Gaelic in 1948 (Manx National Heritage, 2003: 7).

In the case of Na Déise, several folkloric sources are relevant to a discussion of the position of Irish in the area. The 1930s Schools Collection (Bailiúchán na Scol)[4] contains information about the language itself (Ó Cadhla, 2001) and the tape recordings made by de Hindeberg are particularly valuable because they contain less 'canonical' folklore and more evidence of language use and form, as well as attitudes towards it, in a later period. They are also of interest because much of the material was collected from a woman, marking it as exceptional in folkloric research from that period (Ó Cadhla, 2011: 176–198). The fieldwork of Pádraig Ó Miléadha in the 1930s in Sliabh gCua in south Tipperary also provides an insight into the state of Irish in that district. Although Irish was said to be in rapid retreat in the area, it was still possible to find twenty informants (Ó Miléadha, 1936). Of particular relevance to this chapter are the diaries kept by folklore collectors when conducting fieldwork because they contain references to the position of Irish and ideologies towards it. For instance, in a visit in 1945, the collector Seosamh Ó Dálaigh claimed that language shift was underway even in the family of the renowned local storyteller Mícheál Turraoin (Maidhc Dháith) (Verling, 2007: 76).[5] The

---

4   For further information about this collection, see <https://www.duchas.ie/en/info/cbe>.

5   It appears that any language shift was reversed in the next generation of the family. An account of the history of the Seanphobal Gaeltacht includes a reference to an

diaries of local folklore collector Nioclás Breatnach are a rich source of sociolinguistic information about the complexities of language practices, beliefs and managements in Na Déise in the early decades of the twentieth century and it is to these that we turn now.

2.5 Nioclás Breatnach

Following the establishment of the Irish Folklore Commission in 1935, collectors were asked to keep field diaries documenting their work. While the focus of these diaries was not primarily linguistic, many of them contain fascinating insights into language policy, in Spolsky's sense, on the ground in various Gaeltacht areas. One such collector was Nioclás Breatnach, who was born near Dungarvan in 1912, and began working for the Commission when he was only 23 years old. His youthful enthusiasm brings vitality to the accounts, which provide a perceptive and detailed insight into local life, including the position of Irish, in his own area. Breatnach travelled all over the Irish-speaking districts of west Waterford, east Cork and south Tipperary and kept a diary for almost two years from November 1935 to June 1937. The geographical distribution of his informants did not always coincide with the official borders of the Gaeltacht and he occasionally collected material from further afield. It is salient that he found a large number of informants in the Breac-Ghaeltacht areas where Irish was supposedly in a weak position, particularly around the town of Dungarvan. Sixty years later, shortly before his death in 2002, he published an autobiography that contains further information about Irish in Waterford in the 1930s (Breatnach, 1998).

Given the ideological requirements of his employer – to seek the best of folklore from the most fluent speakers, usually men – it is to be expected that Breatnach's diaries are replete with praise for the high linguistic standards of many of his informants. His limited agency was likely further restricted by his youth and lack of experience, but the diaries nonetheless

---

Irish-language play written by Maidhc Dháith's grandson, Déaglán Turraoin (de Paor, 2000: 649; see also Turraoin, 2019).

deal sensitively and perceptively with language shift in Gaeltacht na nDéise at the time. He noted speakers who fell short of the Commission's high standards and their less than optimal linguistic production according to the dominant norms but his tone was never condemnatory (Breatnach, 1998: 175–191). The diaries also reveal Breatnach's role as a mediator between his community and the Commission, where local ideology and practice often contradicted the aims of the state Revival project. He can be seen as an organic intellectual (Hoare & Nowell Smith, 1991: 6–23) with a deep understanding of local sensitivities, frequently referring to linguistic and cultural change as well as documenting folklore. Breatnach's work ethic was impressive, writing almost 450 pages of notes in the first half of 1936 alone. He also possessed an in-depth knowledge of the local dialect, noting minutiae of variation in lexicon and phonology from one district to the next and reflecting it in his idiosyncratic orthography.

A detailed analysis of the diaries found ninety direct or indirect references to Irish in the text based on ten themes including use of English itself, high standard of Irish, no mention of Irish where it would be expected, lack of experience of the oral tradition, age and ill-health of informants and language use and attitudes among the young. The references to language practices of individuals or in communities are direct but the discussion of ideology is often more nuanced and subtle. Occasionally, Breatnach's own belief is clear or there are overt references to the language ideologies of others but in many cases, it has been necessary to draw inferences from the data. The background ideology of the Commission itself, as noted previously, is another key influence on the data at every stage of its production and processing.[6]

References to the use of English, particularly in the Breac-Ghaeltacht, are the most common in the diaries. For instance, Breatnach frequently visited an informant in Cill Rosanta, a Breac-Ghaeltacht area to the east of Dungarvan, and commented that he switched regularly between Irish and English, using terms such as 'staters' and 'Black and Tans' in an account

6   Spelling in Irish reveals many phonetic features of the dialect of Na Déise and is left unstandardised. It has not been possible to give this local flavour in the translations but punctuation has been regularised for the sake of clarity. For a fuller account of this collection in Irish, see Walsh, 2016.

of the Civil War (CBÉ, 205: 204–206). This most likely reflects the influence of English-language media in disseminating terminology about
contemporary events. Another informant, Min Power from Dungarvan,
is noteworthy because she spoke English and had only passive ability in
Irish, evidence that Breatnach occasionally ignored the instruction to seek
only the most fluent Irish speakers. This account is worth quoting in full
because of the salience of the encounter:

> Beurla do bhí aici bíodh agus [...] t[h]uigfeadh sí an Ghaoluinn acht bhí neamh
> thaithighe uirthi agus dubhairt sí gur bhfeárr a gheobhadh sí é dhéanamh as B[e]
> urla agus thugas cead a cinn di. Bhí mo chara ana-s[h]ásta leis sin mar bhí sé ar
> bheagán Gaoluinne agus bhain sé deatach as an seanchas agus ní mó ná minic a
> thagadh draid an gháire air. As lár an chibeal cé rángóch bualadh isteach nach mac
> a h-ing[h]-íne: geafar óg ba eadh é agus bhain sé tamall maith dhe an t-iongantas
> a chur de nuair a chonnaic sé mise i mbun pinn. (22.10.36) (CBÉ, 294: 188–189)[7]

English was the dominant language in Dungarvan, and on this occasion, Breatnach visited Power with a friend who spoke only limited
Irish. Power explained that she could understand Irish but lacked experience in speaking it, a frequent occurrence in the mixed zone of
the Breac-Ghaeltacht (see discussion of a similar dynamic in Cork in
Walsh, 2011: 133). Preferring to tell her story in English, this was a relief
for Breatnach's friend who enjoyed the performance immensely. When
Power's grandson returned to the house, he was amazed to see Breatnach
transcribing the story, presumably because no-one else in a position of
authority had considered his grandmother a legitimate source of folklore.
There are also references to other informants with less than perfect command of Irish and to a slippage between the generations:

> Siar go dtí an Teampall Geal [Breac-Ghaeltacht in west Waterford] a bhuaileas indiu
> siar go dtí an cnocán áit a bhfuil Mícheál Breathnach 'na chomhnaidhe ... Maidir

---

7   She spoke English even though [...] she could understand Irish but had little ex-
    perience of it and she said she could do it better in English and I allowed her do
    that. My friend was very happy with that because he didn't speak much Irish and he
    really enjoyed the storytelling and often laughed at it. In the middle of the commo-
    tion who would happen to call in but her daughter's son: he was a young gaffer and
    it took him some time to get over his wonder when he saw me writing.

leis an gceann óg thá croiceann na sláinte uirri acht maidir le Gaedhilg thá snaidhm
bhéil uirri. Níl an t-atha[i]r fhéin ró-líomhtha chúiche. (19.03.37) (CBÉ, 382: 93–96)[8]

In this case, a young girl in another Breac-Ghaeltacht home is said to be
unable to speak Irish at all while her father is deemed less than fluent,
further evidence of language shift in an individual family. The diaries
also contain evidence of the extent of English-language culture in the
area, a fact apparently accepted as normal by Breatnach. For instance, his
account of the influence of the cinema in Dungarvan emphasises how
it has put pressure on a local drama company and does not mention its
impact on Irish (04.01.36; CBÉ, 205: 114). Both cultures existed side by
side in the Breac-Ghaeltacht, with folklore collectors themselves often
straddling the worlds of Irish and English. As well as the obvious mod-
ernising advances represented by the recording equipment, the collectors
themselves partook in English-language culture also. For instance, the
diaries of Séamus Ennis from other parts of the Gaeltacht contain references to his visits to the cinema in nearby towns on his days off (uí Ógáin,
2009: 86 & 326).

As is to be expected, the diaries also contain much admiration for the
linguistic prowess of many of the informants who were indeed aligned with
the expectations of the Commission. For instance, Breatnach had warm
praise for one of his contemporaries, 23 year-old Tadhg Cúnún from a renowned family of storytellers in An Seanphobal, whom he deemed unparal-
leled in his knowledge: 'ní' chasag a leithéid de bhuachaill fós orm a' raibh an
oiread aige agus athá age Tadhg. Go mba fada buan é chún iad a dh'innsint'
(20.03.36; CBÉ, 205: 283–284).[9] A second account praises the fluency of
two eloquent storytellers, one of them from the Breac-Ghaeltacht area of
south Tipperary: 'ní mhairfeadh aoinne ar aon úrlár leis an mbeirt acu leis
an raise cainnte – ba mhaith i gcóir a chéile iad – ní baol ná coinneoifí an

---

8   I went west to An Teampall Geal [Breac-Ghaeltacht in west Waterford] today to
    the hill where Michéal Breathnach lives ... Regarding the young girl, she looks very
    healthy but as regards to Irish her mouth is tied with a knot. The father himself is
    not too fluent in it.

9   I have not met a boy before now who knew as many [stories] as Tadhg. May he live
    long to tell them.

teangain i mbun a' tsiubhail acu araon – chuirfidís slabhra cainnte orm' (25.03.36; CBÉ, 205: 322–323).[10] A third extols the Irish language ability and commitment of a family in the extreme west of the county: 'Gaoluinn ar fad a labhartar sa tig agus thá a rian ar an murar óg. Táid Gaolach go smior' (23.03.36; CBÉ, 205: 286).[11]

Another theme identified in the analysis was an absence of reference to Irish where it might be expected. I included this innately subjective category because of the salience of the many examples in the diaries where Irish was not mentioned although it seemed to me to be relevant to the context. For example, an account of another storyteller from Dungarvan, Bríd (Biddy) Ní Dhúnaill, refers to a group of children listening but does not say if the story was told in Irish or English (25.04.26; CBÉ, 205: 342–344). Children in the mostly English-speaking town could not be expected to be fluent in Irish, although they may have had passive knowledge due to exposure to older Irish-speaking relatives. Similarly, an account from a Breac-Ghaeltacht area mentions the fact that the house had received a Gaeltacht housing grant from the government (see Chapter 2) but makes no reference to the Irish language ability of the family (05.03.37; CBÉ, 382: 84–85).

Another frequent theme relates to lack of experience of the oral tradition among storytellers, in keeping with the common complaint in cases of linguistic endangerment that previous generations had higher competence in the language. This was often due to language shift and cultural change, meaning that those who had learned stories in their youth and could impart them no longer had an audience and were out of practice. For instance, in this account of an informant in An Rinn, Breatnach writes:

> Dúirt Mícheál liom dá mbeinn a' góilt thimpall fiche bliain ó choin ner a bhí na seananndúirí cearta suas ná beinn i bhfad á líona – dos na firéain a bhí sé a' tagairt. 'Fiú mo sheanamháthair féin' arsa sé 'bhí sí as meán chúca bhíoch scéal aici ga haon oíche agus ní hé an scéal céanna a bheadh aici aon dá oíche'. Agus buil a cuid scéalta ag aoinne eile thimpall arsa mise 'nó a' mbíoch aoinne eile ag éisteacht léi'. 'Ní bhíoch'

---

10 No one would last on the same floor as the two of them because of the rush of speech – they were good for each other – there is no risk that they won't both keep the language alive – they would engage me with talk.

11 Irish only is spoken in the house and the effects can be seen on the children. They are Irish speaking to the core.

arsa Mícheál 'ach ar linn sinne bhe' nár ngarsúin bhíoch sí ag seanchas dúinn cois na
tine agus do phioc mé suas roinnt uaithe'. (22.01.36) (CBÉ, 205: 164–165)[12]

In this case, the informant believes that Breatnach has come twenty years
too late and that competent storytellers no longer exist. He recalls that
the practice was in retreat even in the previous generation, referring to
how his grandmother had no audience other than her own family and
that his knowledge of the tradition was limited to his fading memories of
her stores in his childhood. Another account from the Breac-Ghaeltacht
paints a stark picture of the cultural change that had occurred by the 1930s:

> Deallruigeann leis ón tslighe a bhíodh sé ag innsint na sceul go bhfuil neamh-thaithí
> air agus nuair a d'iarrfa mé dhe ar innis sé na scéalta san cheana ba é an freagra a
> fuaireas 'cé dó a niúsainn iad, anú níl aoinne suas anois a dh'éisteoch liom nach tú
> féin [agus] cúpla sean-[duine] agus diombainte roinnt eile a' mbeadh caitheamh i
> ndiaidh an fhoghluma acu'. Is dócha go mbfhíor dho – chuir an neamh shuim san
> Seán cúl lámhach le haithris na sceul. (10.10.36) (CBÉ, 294: 160–162)[13]

Despite several decades of Irish language activism and the ostensibly pro-
Irish policies of the new state, the storytelling tradition in this particular
Breac-Ghaeltacht was in rapid decline by the time that Breatnach began
his work. Despite (or perhaps because of) the far from ideal situation
facing him, he gathered a range of material and unwittingly bequeathed
us a fuller picture of the sociolinguistic context.

12   Mícheál said to me if I was going around twenty years ago when the real old stock
      was about, I wouldn't be long filling [cylinders] – he was referring to the rare people
      [who knew stories]. 'Even my own grandmother', he said, 'she was incredible at
      them, she would have a story every night and would never tell the same story two
      nights in a row'. 'And does anyone else around have her stories' said I, 'or did anyone
      else listen to her'? 'No', said Mícheál, but when we were children she used to tell us
      stories by fire and I picked some up from her.
13   It seems from the way that he was telling the stories that he lacked experience of it
      and when I asked him if he told those stories before, I received the answer: 'Who
      would I tell them to? Of course there's nobody around now who would listen to me
      except yourself and a few old people and apart from a few others who would want
      to learn.' I suppose he was right – that lack of interest stopped Seán telling stories.

This analysis of the Breatnach diaries is a microstudy of how language policy operates in one area according to Spolsky's model. It draws on a folkloric source to uncover how Irish was used (language practices), how people felt about it (language beliefs) and how the state attempted to influence practices and beliefs (language management), in this case through the work of the Irish Folklore Commission. The complexities of the situation were captured in a detailed and sensitive manner by a local collector operating as an intermediary between his community and the Commission. This study reveals a variety of language practices ranging from exemplary speakers aligned with the Commission's ideological frame, to those successfully transmitting Irish in the family, to hybrid speakers moving between Irish and English, to those with passive knowledge of Irish only and to monolingual English speakers. This is not surprising given the fact that most of the area in question was classified as Breac-Ghaeltacht, but it also serves as a reminder about the porosity of the Gaeltacht itself despite the apparently neat binary divisions between 'Gaeltacht' and 'Galltacht'[14] and English and Irish. The idea of Breac-Ghaeltacht problematises and destabilises these rigid categories.

In terms of beliefs, the diaries themselves, and the project from which they emerged, required Breatnach and his fellow collectors to work according to ideological parameters that promoted the maintenance of the Gaeltacht as an Irish-speaking entity. That is the covert ideology underpinning the entire enterprise, although it is not articulated overtly in the diaries themselves. The many, often successful attempts by Breatnach to find exemplary speakers is evidence of this, as is the praise given to those with high levels of ability in linguistic and folkloric terms. However, Breatnach knew that he was working in a mixed linguistic zone where attitudes to Irish were complex and he gathered a great deal of material from informants who would be considered deficient in another, more Irish-speaking context. Therefore, while we cannot state with certainty that he challenged the Commission's ideology overtly, clearly he accepted the sociolinguistic reality and worked with the material available.

14   A historical term referring to English settlers in Ireland but later used to describe English-speaking areas outside the Gaeltacht (O'Rourke & Walsh, 2020: 45).

There is little overt evidence of the public's ideologies towards Irish in the diaries but it is important to remember the macro-context of support for political nationalism and general acceptance of the official pro-Irish policy. Other local factors would include the over-representation of Na Déise on the Gaeltacht Commission a decade before and the national renown of the local all-Irish boarding school, Coláiste na Rinne (see Chapter 2). The diaries also contain some overt evidence of hostility towards Irish or lack of enthusiasm about the revival effort and there are references to lack of interest in traditional culture among the young, women and those who had emigrated, although these are not always linked specifically to the language itself. A language policy that in this case prioritised men with high competence in language and lore silenced the voices of others who did not reach these standards. In terms of language beliefs, therefore, this study highlights tensions between, on the one hand, the official hegemonic ideology promoted by the state through the work of the Commission and on the other, public ideologies that ranged from engaged to apathetic to hostile.

The microstudy of Na Déise in the 1930s opens up the possibility of similar research in other parts of the historical Gaeltacht, using folkloric and other sources, in order better to understand the complexity of language practices and ideologies on the ground. The idea of Breac-Ghaeltacht, the buffer zone surrounding the core areas, obliges us to challenge simplistic binary divisions between 'Irish speakers' and 'English speakers' and between 'Gaeltacht' and 'Galltacht'. This has implications for our understanding of the contemporary Gaeltacht that, following further decades of language shift, is similar to the Breac-Ghaeltacht of the past. Although the Gaeltacht Commission went some way towards recognising internal variation in its distinction between Fíor- and Breac-Ghaeltacht, binary discourses have dominated research and public debate about the Gaeltacht for decades. In an apparent echo of the 1926 report, the *Comprehensive Linguistic Study* (CLS) by Ó Giollagáin et al. (2007a) recommended stratifying the Gaeltacht into A, B and C districts according to language vitality, but its conclusions focused on the need to strengthen the core A districts (see Chapter 2).

The next section reviews the development of language policy as it applies to Gaeltacht na nDéise over the past two decades, since the emergence of the language planning process in the early 2000s. We begin with data about linguistic vitality in recent years before considering recent developments in language management aimed at speakers of Irish and those who could become speakers of the language.

3. Contemporary Irish speakers in Gaeltacht na nDéise

The extent of the Gaeltacht was reduced significantly following a review of the boundaries in 1956, which led to the establishment of the Department of the Gaeltacht. The reduction in the southeast was particularly dramatic, falling from sixty-one electoral divisions to just one with part of one other in An Rinn and An Seanphobal. There is a perception locally that Irish underwent a revival in the late 1960s and 1970s when Irish-speaking families came into the area and contributed to a language shift back to Irish among many local people (Uí Fhoghlú, 2000: 635). The percentage of families receiving the full Scéim Labhairt na Gaeilge (SLG) grant increased during this period and in 1974, the Gaeltacht was extended by adding an additional thirty townlands to the south encompassing much of An Seanphobal (Walsh, 2012: 207–208).

3.1 Census returns

Due to changes in the Census questions about Irish in 2006, long-term comparisons are fraught with difficulties but in line with other Gaeltacht areas, the position of Irish in Na Déise has weakened over the past four decades although there has been stabilisation in recent years. Considerable population increases since the late 1990s, encouraged by weak controls on housing developments, have put Irish under additional pressure. Imbalances between the two parishes – with Irish in a stronger position in An Rinn than An Seanphobal – are concealed by the aggregate results for the Gaeltacht as a whole. The headline figures of people claiming competence in Irish remained between approximately 80 and

85 per cent between 1981 and 1996 but fell back to 72.5 per cent (1,006 people) in 2002, in line with a significant increase in the population. A sharp drop from 53.5 per cent (692 people) to 39.8 per cent (552 people) in the percentage of daily Irish speakers was recorded in the same period (Central Statistics Office, 2004). This decline galvanised local Irish speakers into action and prompted interest in the nascent language planning process emerging following the report of the Gaeltacht Commission of 2000–2002 (see Chapter 2 and below). Based on the 2002 census, the CLS found that the Waterford Gaeltacht should be placed in the C category, as the percentage of daily speakers fell below 44 per cent in each of the three EDs. An Rinn was only marginally below that threshold (43 per cent) and similar to the profile for Category B, whereas the other two EDs (covering An Seanphobal) were consistent with Category C status. However, because of the small extent of Gaeltacht na nDéise in total, it was recommended that the entire area be reclassified as Category B (Ó Giollagáin et al., 2007a: 17). Although the A, B and C categories were never adopted by policymakers, the fact that Na Déise escaped C status may have given local language planning efforts an additional psychological boost.

Despite the pressures on Irish locally, the headline figure of reported competence has remained stable over the past two decades and, in fact, Na Déise was the only Gaeltacht in the country to register a slight increase to 73.9 per cent (1,286 people) in 2016. 26.8 per cent of the local population (467 people) were recorded as speaking Irish daily either outside the education system or both within and outside the education system (Ó Faoláin et al., 2018: 21). Commenting on the census returns, the authors of the Déise Language Plan (see below) concluded that there was still a loyal Irish language community in the area but pointed to signs of language shift, such as higher percentages of Irish speakers among cohorts attending full-time education. However, it noted improvements in recent years in the use of Irish in every age cohort, particularly the young (ibid.: 30–31).

3.2 Survey of socioeconomic and cultural needs

Comhlacht Forbartha na nDéise (CFND, Déise Development Body) was established in 2005 with state support and co-ordinates the area's social, cultural and economic development. Intersecting with both voluntary and community groups and state agencies, it is part of the increasingly complex local governance of Irish by a myriad of organisations and led the development of the area's first statutory Irish Language Plan (see below). One of CFND's first actions was to conduct a study of the socioeconomic and cultural needs of the Gaeltacht, which provided further information about knowledge and use of Irish locally. Following an exhaustive methodology involving visits to all households in the area, the report was based on 477 responses representing an astonishing 97 per cent of the total (O'Connor et al., 2007: 14–15). The demographic background of the participants was significant in terms of language policy, with just slightly over 50 per cent of respondents originally from the area and therefore more likely to know Irish and 41.5 per cent from elsewhere in Ireland (ibid.: 15). In light of this baseline figure, the fact that slightly under a third (29.7 per cent) of households reported using Irish as their principal language is not surprising. This finding was also broadly in line with census returns for the core category of 'daily Irish speakers'. Two-thirds of households (68.6 per cent) reported using English as their main language and Irish was the mostly commonly used 'second language' for almost the same amount (64.8 per cent), although what is meant by this was not defined. 86.3 per cent reported an ability to speak Irish, about ten points higher than census returns, while 13.7 per cent reported that they could not speak Irish, a figure close to the 7.7 per cent who are not from an Irish background. Of those who spoke Irish, the vast majority (85.2 per cent) reported speaking it at home with over half (53.5 per cent) speaking it at home daily. Over seven out of ten Irish speakers spoke Irish with their relatives (71.1 per cent), friends (73.9 per cent) and neighbours (71 per cent). A majority of Irish speakers said that they did not speak Irish at work (41.3 per cent) but about one-third (33.6 per cent) reported that they did so. An overwhelming majority of people (98 per cent) favoured the retention of Gaeltacht status for the area (ibid.: 17).

Other data with relevance for language maintenance and/or acquisition included educational attainment, with 68 per cent possessing a Leaving Certificate qualification compared to 80 per cent nationally, leaving 32 per cent who could be classified as early school leavers (ibid.: 21). In terms of employment, 46 per cent of respondents reported that they worked locally in the Gaeltacht while 70 per cent expressed the desire to do so (ibid.: 27). There was a healthy occupational spread and the region was not overly reliant on any one occupation. However, reflecting the economic boom at the time, one person in eight was employed in the building industry, a significant figure when considered against the backdrop of housing controversies (ibid.: 29; see 3.5).

On the strength of what it saw as positive figures in relation to the use of Irish, the report recommended greater provision of Irish classes, with particular attention paid to the 42 per cent of the population not from the local area. In response to the almost unanimous demand that the Gaeltacht status be maintained, it concluded that 'there is an overwhelming mandate for policy makers to preserve the distinct identity of the area' (ibid.: 33). It also recommended urgent action in relation to early school leavers, many of whom could be experiencing problems with literacy, and recommended urgent measures in relation to housing to ensure that Irish speakers could continue to live in the area (ibid.: 35).

3.3   Use of Irish in the family

Based on census returns from 2016, a study of Gaeltacht families raising children with Irish reported that 151 children in Gaeltacht na nDéise spoke Irish daily outside education. There were eighty-one families (31 per cent of a total of 260) with children under 18 years in the area who spoke Irish daily outside education (Ní Chuaig et al., 2021: 115). This is in keeping with other characterisations of the strength of Irish in this Gaeltacht area.

3.4 Language planning

Separate inter-related language planning initiatives are underway in Gaeltacht na nDéise and its environs. The Gaeltacht area has its own plan based on an extensive local survey and Dungarvan, recognised as a Gaeltacht Service Town, is beginning its own language planning process. Under the Gaeltacht Act 2012 (see Chapter 2), both processes are supposed to complement each other.

3.4.1 Na Déise Irish language survey

In 2015 with the support of Údarás na Gaeltachta, work began on the Déise Irish Language Plan (Plean Teanga na nDéise), in line with the government's language planning process. The work was led by CFND and the methodology comprised an analysis of census data, new surveys of all households and schoolchildren and focus groups. The team stated that its vision was to ensure that the community could live every part of its life through Irish, that Irish would be the dominant language and that it would be transmitted intergenerationally. More specific aims were that Gaeltacht na nDéise would not experience a decline in any Irish language indicator in the next census and that there would be a 1 per cent increase per year over the seven-year term in the number of daily speakers outside education, or at least an increase to 500 speakers by the end of the term (Ó Faoláin et al., 2018: 2). The survey sought information about use of and attitudes to Irish and the Gaeltacht and to community and state services available in the area. Respondents were also offered the opportunity to make suggestions. 497 of 600 surveys were collected, representing a very healthy response rate of 83 per cent (ibid.: 23). Eight areas of social, cultural and economic life were covered: (1) competence in and use of Irish; (2) families and youth; (3) education; (4) culture and arts; (5) community and sport; (6) business and employment; (7) tourism and heritage and (8) the state.

In terms of use of Irish as a household language, 5.7 per cent of respondents said that Irish was the only language spoken at home with a further 8 per cent saying it was used for the most part. A further 20.1 per cent reported that both Irish and English were used equally. Although the change in question does not facilitate a valid comparison, the total of 13.7 per cent using Irish only or for the most part represents a significant decline from 2007 when almost 30 per cent reported using Irish as the principal language of the household. However, combining all categories where Irish has at least an equal presence with English gives a total of 33.8 per cent, a figure not dissimilar to 2007. A large majority of the population reported using English exclusively (28.5 per cent) or for the most part (37.7 per cent), a total of 66.2 per cent, close to the 2007 total of 68.8 per cent (ibid.: 32). Overall, the baseline information is similar to that identified in the census category of daily speakers and in the 2007 research: approximately one-third of the population of Gaeltacht na nDéise uses Irish regularly, often in combination with English, with the remaining two-thirds using English for the most part or exclusively.

In terms of demographic origin, slightly over half (51.2 per cent) of the population reported that they were from the Gaeltacht, in line with the previous survey (ibid.: 33). Unsurprisingly, those who grew up locally reported the highest level of competence in Irish, with 77 per cent of people from the Gaeltacht claiming that their Irish was 'fairly good', 'good' or 'fluent'. This fell to 56 per cent when all of the local population was included. The highest levels of competence were found within younger cohorts, reflecting the efforts of local schools (ibid.: 34–35). Similar to the earlier survey, there was almost unanimous agreement (96.5 per cent) that the area should maintain its Gaeltacht status, even among those who were not born in the area (ibid.: 36–38).

Large majorities across all age cohorts and places of origin were in favour of the statement that 'it is good to raise children speaking Irish'. While support was strongest from those with higher levels of competence, a clear majority of those whose Irish was weak also supported this statement (ibid.: 40). A majority of young people in the area reported that their Irish was either 'good' or 'fluent' despite the fact that most were raised in homes where English was dominant. Use of Irish by young people was strongly associated with the school while hobbies where Irish was most likely to be used included Gaelic games and music or singing (ibid.: 41–44). According to focus group research, there was a perception that the use of Irish in the family and among young people had increased in recent years but that a new youth club functioning in Irish was needed. The work of the local Gaelic Athletic Association (GAA) was praised but additional social and cultural activities for young people were also recommended (ibid.: 44).

The survey provided information about the take-up of local educational services at pre-school, primary and secondary level. This data is useful because all local education levels use Irish as the medium of instruction and are therefore an important boost to language acquisition in institutional settings. The Language Plan described such services as 'language sanctuaries' (*tearmainn teanga*) because they provided Irish-only spaces (ibid.: 45). Around three-quarters of local children attended the local pre-school (75.5 per cent) and primary school (73.1 per cent), but numbers fell off at secondary school (51.3 per cent), with almost half of teenagers attending schools outside the Gaeltacht. As is the case with national census data on Irish, there was a strong correlation between educational attainment and Irish language competence. For instance, 50 per cent of those who received a primary education only assessed their Irish as 'weak', while 42.7 per cent of those possessing a postgraduate degree described their Irish as 'fluent' (ibid.: 44–47). Focus group research about education again confirmed strong local demand for Irish language classes and a homework or after-school club. It was argued that the link between local primary and secondary education should be strengthened (ibid.: 49–50).

The focus groups also enquired about arts and cultural initiatives and local sporting associations and further expansion of activities in all areas was suggested in order to provide more opportunities for young people to use Irish (ibid.: 50–53). In terms of business and employment, 37 per cent said that they were working in the Gaeltacht, with a further 29 per cent in Dungarvan. English was by far the dominant work language (79 per cent) with bilingual or Irish-only employment amounting to 22 per cent (ibid.: 55). The survey also confirmed that there was a strong local sense of identity based on the Irish language and associated culture, a factor that has contributed to local language maintenance (Breathnach, 2019). A similar dynamic may be at play in other small but relatively vibrant Gaeltacht communities such as Múscraí (west Cork) and Ráth Chairn (Meath) where there is a strong local cultural tradition.

3.4.2 Measures of the Plan

The Plan proposed fifty-eight measures encompassing all of the areas covered by the survey. In the category of Families and Youth, these included a support network, a dedicated officer, family support services, social events for families, a childcare centre, youth 'language sanctuaries', youth clubs and camps and additional supports for young people to acquire Irish outside education (ibid.: 59–81). Under Education, the Plan proposed the establishment of a Gaeltacht education network, a school language policy, greater linkage between various levels of Irish-medium education, extra-curricular activities in Irish, language enrichment materials, a programme to support learners to gain fluency, an adult education centre, deeper links with third-level institutions and a permanent third-level centre in the Gaeltacht (ibid.: 82–101). Cultural measures included a residential artist, additional cultural events and a local cultural festival, links with other Celtic countries, a project to develop online resources about traditional *sean-nós* singing and the creation of additional cultural and artistic resources (ibid.: 102–112). Under Community and Sport, the main recommendation was the establishment of a network to investigate the problem of local housing and to pursue the development of a social housing scheme (ibid.: 114). Other recommendations included developing cultural and social centres and a welcome pack for people new to the area (ibid.: 113–128). Under Business and Employment, measures included a pro-Irish language policy in local companies, business training opportunities and a local business network, awards for the use of Irish in business, awareness about careers in Irish and additional information about local employment opportunities (ibid.: 129–139). Proposed measures under Tourism and Heritage included a local publicity campaign, events and additional signage for visitors, the promotion of the sea as a resource and the protection of local heritage sites (ibid.: 140–151). The section on the State pointed to the contradiction between the language planning process on the one hand, where communities were expected to produce plans to strengthen Irish in the Gaeltacht, and the dominance of public services in English (ibid.: 152). It recommended the recruitment of bilingual staff to state bodies and the development of a local housing strategy to provide affordable and social housing based on language conditions in order to strengthen the Gaeltacht as an Irish-speaking community (ibid.: 153–154; see 3.5 below). The Plan also proposed that the borders of the Gaeltacht be expanded slightly to include all townlands in the two part-EDs added to the Gaeltacht in 1974 (ibid.: 154–155).

Adding together administrative and implementation costs, the Plan was costed at €2.3 million over a seven-year period (ibid.: 156). A three-part governance system was suggested comprising a language planning team, working groups and the board of CFND. Progress would be monitored based on annual work plans and ongoing research conducted to assess the progress of measures (ibid.: 161–163).

3.4.3 Dungarvan Irish Language Plan

Dungarvan has long played an important role in the life of the Waterford Gaeltacht, as it is the major urban centre in the west of the county. As we saw earlier, although a predominantly English-speaking town in the early decades of the twentieth century, many Irish speakers lived in its environs and there was at least passive knowledge of Irish among some of the population. Nioclás Breatnach himself was born near the town and it was in Dungarvan that the Gaeltacht Commission held its public meeting in 1925. It heard evidence from Domhnall Ó Fearachair, an Irish-speaking merchant from the town who was involved in the language movement locally. Ó Fearachair declared that being bilingual had been no disadvantage to his business (Coimisiún na Gaeltachta, 1925: 368–369).

In line with the retreat of Irish in the Gaeltacht, English has become more dominant in Dungarvan in recent decades and its linguistic profile is little different to the national average (2 per cent vs. 1.7 per cent of daily speakers) (Department of Tourism, Arts, Heritage, Gaeltacht, Sport and Media, n.d.). However, its proximity to Gaeltacht na nDéise led it to be proposed as a Gaeltacht Service Town and in 2020, Dungarvan embarked on its own language planning process, establishing the co-ordinating group Dún Garbhán le Gaeilge ('Dungarvan with Irish'). Following local consultation, a draft of thirty-nine measures was published in 2021 covering governance of the Plan, awareness raising, the presence of Irish in the town, families and youth, business and education. Governance measures included establishing Dún Garbhán le Gaeilge as a co-operative, appointing a Language Planning Officer and setting up structures to foster communication with others involved in language planning in Waterford and in other Gaeltacht Service Towns. Awareness raising measures included creating a database of Irish language services and a campaign launch. Recommendations to strengthen the presence of Irish in the town covered setting up an Irish language centre, improving Irish language signage and establishing Irish language conversation groups and social events. Suggestions to boost Irish among families and youth included support for the 'Teanga Tí' (home language) scheme operated by voluntary body Glór na nGael, an Irish language play group, language support for families, a youth network and scholarships to attend Coláiste na Rinne. A free translation service was to be provided for businesses, tailored language classes offered to that sector and an Irish language business award re-established. Among the measures related to education were additional Irish classes for the public, an exchange programme with Gaeltacht schools, an Irish language programme for transition year students and an Irish teachers' forum (Dún Garbhán le Gaeilge, 2021).

3.5 Housing

The thorny question of housing has provoked considerable controversy in Gaeltacht na nDéise since the late 1990s, with large increases in population and the subsequent decline of Irish being linked to weak controls on housing developments. The issue gained traction during the 'Celtic Tiger' economic boom of the late 1990s and 2000s, when the value of land and housing increased exponentially alongside strong demand. Gaeltacht areas closest to urban centres, particularly in Waterford and Galway, were most adversely affected and the linguistic impact of housing became a live political issue in both counties. This aspect of physical development cuts to the heart of the language planning process as it throws into stark relief the challenges in protecting an endangered language in contexts where neoliberal approaches hold sway and where there is little appetite for interventionism to control the market. Additional complications are

Ireland's entrenched accommodation crisis, with unprecedented demand for housing, spiralling prices and rents, and increasingly stringent measures to mitigate the effects of climate change.

As noted above, there was a sharp decline in levels of competence in and use of Irish in Gaeltacht na nDéise between 1996 and 2002, in line with a population increase in the area on the back of the economic boom. The 1999 County Waterford Development Plan referred to the Gaeltacht in vague cultural terms only and made no firm commitments to the protection of Irish there (Waterford County Council, 1999: 17). It was published before the enactment of the Planning and Development Act 2000, which obliged local authorities to state how they would be protect the Irish language in the Gaeltacht if there was such a district in the area of their development plan. In 2001, the environmental consultancy CAAS was commissioned by the Council to write a local plan for the Gaeltacht and recommended restricting development to existing villages in order to preserve the area's rural character (CAAS, 2001: 38). Reflecting the new Planning and Development Act, it also recommended the imposition of a Linguistic Impact Statement if it was felt that a given development would have a negative effect on Irish. Despite appearing to be supportive of Irish, a proposal by CAAS to allow densities of up to eight houses per acre (although only three would be permitted on most of the zoned land), sparked controversy. A local group, Gaeltacht i mBaol ('Gaeltacht in Danger') was formed to oppose the plan, claiming that it would encourage housing estates, turn the area into a suburb of Dungarvan and weaken Irish further. However, the matter was divisive locally and the chairman of the local community council, himself the owner of land with development potential, refused to put his view on the record (*The Irish Times*, 2001).

A central policy plank of the CLS was to recommend the protection of existing densities of Irish speakers in the Gaeltacht through controls on housing development and social and demographic changes. A large part of the extended Irish version of the CLS (Chapters 7–12) was dedicated to the planning issue in the Gaeltacht and recommended that such changes be managed and reduced in order to protect the vitality of Irish in the community (Ó Giollagáin et al., 2007b: 266–267). It concluded that the Planning and Development Act was being implemented unevenly by various local authorities in Gaeltacht counties and that a co-ordinated national approach and Gaeltacht planning policy was required (ibid.: 275–277). In its study of Gaeltacht na nDéise, the CLS found that of 442 planning applications made between 2000 and 2005, 63 per cent of them were for individual houses, but that only 31 per cent could be said with certainty to have been made by people connected to the local area (ibid.: 184, 228). It found a large number of applications (40) for developments of more than two houses (296 in total), 58 per cent of which (168 houses) were permitted by Waterford County Council (ibid.: 231, 237). With most of this new housing situated in the ED of An Rinn, what was previously a rural area became heavily urbanised, confirming the fears of Gaeltacht i mBaol a few years previously (see also Ó Ceithearnaigh, 2006).

The publication of the 2002 census returns, showing a sharp decline in Irish locally, prompted deep concern among many Irish speakers in the Gaeltacht and became a divisive issue in the community. On the one hand, the fact that one in eight local workers was reliant on the building industry for employment prevented many locals from opposing housing developments, even though many such people were themselves Irish speakers. On the other hand, local people who had campaigned for decades for the protection of Irish were dismayed to witness what appeared to be untrammelled development that often failed to meet local housing needs, as potential buyers from the Gaeltacht were priced out of the market. Waterford County Council was blamed for what was seen as its tepid policy on housing in the Gaeltacht, as expressed in the 1999 County Development Plan. One such person, whose Irish-speaking parents had moved into the area in the late 1960s, offered this negative assessment of the Council's policy:

> Ón taithí athá agam féin ar Chomhairle Chontae Phort Láirge, níl sé iontach oiriúnach Comhairlí Contae a bheith freagrach as ceantacha Gaeltachta. Níl mé á lochtú á rá go bhfuil gach aon rud a dheineann siad go holc ach dáiríre is *disaster* iomlán a bhí i gceist le pleanáil anso. Bhí ana-bhaint agam féin le Gaelacht i mBaol, eagaíocht a bhí againn [anso]. Chuireamar i gcoinne iarratas pleanála amháin mar chás samplach agus idir comhairleoirí contae agus oifig na pleanála, bhí sé fé mar a bheifeá amannta le caint le falla. Ní chíonn siad, ní thuigeann siad i mo thuairim féin tábhacht na Gaeltachta, ní thuigeann siad gur suíomh fé leith athá ann agus thá

na comhairleoirí contae, thá siad oscailte do bhrú ó dhaoine. (Mhic Ghiolla Chuda, 2004, cited in Walsh, 2012: 225)[15]

A new draft County Development Plan published in 2005 showed a greater awareness of the sensitivity of housing in the Gaeltacht and, following the CAAS recommendations four years previously, suggested that restrictions could be imposed on certain housing developments:

> Such measures *may* include an obligatory Linguistic Impact Statement (LIS) outlining how the proposed development will support and sustain the Gealtacht [sic] community and any reconsideration of the zoning policy for the area. (Waterford County Council, 2004: 24, emphasis added)

While the draft Plan was a clear improvement on its predecessor, the conditional wording of the section above did not go far enough for those concerned about the impact of housing on Irish. A public meeting was organised by the community council in An Rinn in February 2005 to discuss an agreed response to the draft and a language sub-committee was formed to lobby the Council for greater protection for Irish. A headline story in an Irish language newspaper painted the challenge in stark terms: 'Éirigh as do shuan!' (Wake up!) (Ó Néill, 2005). A submission to the Council demanded that the new Plan contain an obligatory Linguistic Impact Statement in relation to all future developments in the area. Ironically, it quoted from the CAAS report that had been opposed previously on the basis that it would encourage excessive housing densities. The inflamed rhetoric reflected strongly held opinions on the matter: 'Tá baol ann go mbeimis ag féachaint ar scrios iomlán eacnamaíochta, sóisialta, oideachasúil agus cultúrtha an cheantair, má chailltear stádas Gaeltachta'

---

15 From my experience of Waterford County Council, it's not very suitable for County Councils to be responsible for the Gaeltacht. I'm not blaming them by saying that everything they do is bad but really planning here has been a disaster. I was very involved with Gaeltacht i mBaol, an organisation which we had [here]. We opposed one planning application as a test case and, with county councillors and the planning office, it was sometimes like talking to the wall. They don't see, they don't understand, in my view, the importance of the Gaeltacht, they don't understand that it's a specific case and the county councillors are open to pressure from people.

(Comhairle Pobail na Rinne, 2005: 6).[16] Planning was an issue locally in the subsequent elections to the board of Údarás na Gaeltachta in 2005, but a candidate who did not support a Linguistic Impact Statement on housing was elected while another person who stood specifically on the issue of planning did not take a seat (Walsh, 2012: 223–224).

Following the housing boom of the 2000s and the local opposition it generated, subsequent County Development Plans have become more closely aligned to the provisions of the Planning and Development Act. For instance, the 2011–2017 Plan stipulated that an Irish language requirement be applied to a minimum of 60 per cent of housing developments (Waterford County Council, 2011), rising to 80 per cent in the draft Plan for 2022–2028 (Breathnach, 2021; Waterford City & County Council, 2021).

Previous surveys conducted in Na Déise have illustrated local concern about the excessive cost of housing and complaints that local people cannot afford to buy homes locally (O'Connor et al., 2007: 31; Ó Faoláin et al., 2018: 53). The development of the statutory local Irish Language Plan brought greater awareness of language policy in general, including in relation to housing. The Plan referred specifically to housing, which it said had been identified as a challenge in previous non-statutory plans and policy initiatives and was forcing Irish speakers to leave the area (ibid.: 114). It recommended the implementation of a Gaeltacht Residency Qualification in the planning process that would encourage a more favourable approach to local people and Irish speakers applying for planning permission for single houses. The Plan also urged the implementation of restrictions on all housing developments of two or more houses (ibid.: 154).

The new draft County Development Plan for 2022–2028 stipulated that a 'Language Enurement Clause (LEC)' be applied to any development of two or more houses in order to ensure that occupants 'be capable of using the Irish language on a daily basis' (Waterford City & County Council, 2021: 164). The LEC is to remain in place for fifteen years and the remaining 20 per cent of units would be made available to those 'who have a local or other need to reside in the Gaeltacht' (ibid.: 165). Applications for single

16   There is a risk that we would be looking at the complete economic, social, educational and cultural destruction of the area if Gaeltacht status is lost.

houses would need to show that the persons had a 'demonstrable economic, social or local need to live in the area', or residents would have to agree to occupy the houses and adhere to an LEC for fifteen years (ibid.: 165). The level of fluency of Irish required would be equivalent to B2 (upper inter-mediate) of the accredited system for adult language learning, Teastas Eorpach na Gaeilge (TEG, European Certificate in Irish). This was a con-siderable advance on the vagueness of the 1999–2005 Plan, but it should be noted that the sociolinguistic balance of the community was altered in the interim period due in part to the policy of minimal intervention by the local authority. However, in 2021, the Council rejected planning permis-sion for a development by Shinebright Ltd of forty-six houses in Maoil an Choirnigh in An Rinn (Tuairisc.ie, 2021h). The main reason given was the negative impact on Irish of the project and the failure of the developer to provide an adequate Linguistic Impact Statement. At the time of writing, Shinebright had appealed the decision to the planning appeals board, An Bord Pleanála (McMorrow, 2021).

3.6 Discussion

The housing crisis continues to be one of Ireland's most severe challenges, and successive governments have so far failed to tackle it successfully. After a quarter-century of boom and bust, its influence has spread beyond the working class and it is now a key issue of concern to young middle-class voters (Ó Broin, 2019). These are increasingly abandoning the two main historical political parties in favour of opposition promises to solve the housing issue. Planning regulations and environmental governance often clash with the desires of people to live close to their families in rural areas. The statutory requirement to protect Irish in the Gaeltacht intro-duces an additional complication in areas that have long been mixed lin-guistically. After a long period of inaction that led to irreversible change in the demography of the Gaeltacht, Waterford County Council has belatedly adopted a robust housing policy that attempts to balance the requirements of environmental and linguistic protection with providing housing. However, local authorities have only limited ability to intervene in the market under the existing policy framework and unless the state undertakes to provide more stock directly – seeing housing as a social good rather than a private gain – spiralling prices will continue to push existing supply beyond the reach of most people in the Gaeltacht. There have been high-profile cases involving planning in other Gaeltacht areas in recent years, underlining the extent of this challenge and the tensions it generates. For instance, the language Commissioner found that Kerry County Council contravened the 2000 Act by failing to implement a language condition attached to a housing development in the Gaeltacht village of Baile an Fheirtéaraigh, describing it as 'a very serious breach' (An Coimisinéir Teanga, 2020: 20). In 2021, the High Court upheld on linguistic grounds an appeal by a local co-operative in Co. Meath against permission that was granted to a proposed development of housing and a hotel in the heart of the Ráth Chairn Gaeltacht (Tuairisc.ie, 2021e).

4. Conclusion

This chapter analysed speakers of Irish in the Gaeltacht area of west Waterford from the early twentieth century to the present day. The case study focused on Gaeltacht na nDéise, one of only two Irish-speaking areas in the east of Ireland which has maintained Irish beyond all the odds into the twenty-first century. Although its extent has shrunk considerably, predictions of its demise made to the Gaeltacht Commission a century ago proved to be premature. Although his focus was on collecting folklore, local man Nioclás Breatnach unwittingly bequeathed us rich insights in his diaries into language practice and beliefs within his own community, which was undergoing language shift in the 1930s. His employer, the Irish Folklore Commission, was an arm of the language management practised by the state in the early decades of the Revival project in that it aimed to collect, preserve and valorise extant lore from exemplary speakers. While the best folklore from the most fluent speakers was favoured, Breatnach occasionally took liberty with the rules and collected less than optimal material from people whose Irish was less traditional or even who had only passive ability in the language. Greater attention to the concept of Breac-Ghaeltacht reminds us of the blurred spaces between Irish and English and allows us to create a fuller picture of embodied language practices on the ground. The work of the Commission in general and of Breatnach in particular no doubt exerted a positive influence on many future generations of Irish speakers who looked to the collection with respect as a valuable cultural repository. Desire to ensure the continuity of the tradition has also underpinned the extensive body of cultural output from this small corner of Waterford, contributed to a strong local linguistic identity and may also have encouraged intergenerational transmission of Irish by some families (Breathnach, 2019).

Whereas Breatnach and others like him were involved only indirectly in the promotion of Irish as a community language, today's language management has been formalised and put on a statutory footing as part of the state's 'language planning process'. Activists in Gaeltacht na nDéise have been enthusiastic participants in language planning since the early days of its roll-out in the 2000s, with two previous non-statutory plans devised. Following comprehensive local research, the area is in the process of implementing a detailed Plan for the Gaeltacht and preparing a similar initiative for Dungarvan.

It goes without saying that implementation is the most challenging part of any language policy, and the past century of Irish history is replete with examples of failed language initiatives. The language planning process has been undermined by a number of factors: it was virtually stillborn, emerging from the rubble of the financial crash of the late 2000s, it was poorly conceived and set up on foot of rushed legislation, it remains underfunded and progress is slow almost a decade after its establishment. A key flaw is the transfer by the state of a key responsibility further and further away from its core operations to voluntary committees, often well-meaning, but lacking expertise in the field. While many Language Planning Officers are qualified and committed, the daunting nature of the task risks becoming overwhelming (Walsh, 2021b). Another uncertainty relates to the provisions of the plans themselves: if a language planning committee in a given district establishes through research that there is strong local demand for an Irish language centre costing €1 million, there is no mechanism to ensure that such an objective is achieved. A similar conclusion can be reached about provisions on housing contained in the Déise Plan and others: to what extent does the committee or Language Planning Officer have any real agency to bring about the change in the situation given the current governance arrangements?

The language planning process is extremely complex and requires a unique skill set including lobbying for increased resources, cajoling reluctant stakeholders, persuading fluent speakers to participate, balancing the often conflicting needs of fluent speakers and learners, conducting ongoing monitoring of the plans and fighting with the state over intractable systemic issues such as infrastructural planning and health. Because of the novelty of the process, there is as yet no established career path for Language Planning Officers and no guarantee of long-term employment or progression. Furthermore, to date no detailed research has been undertaken on the success of the initiative and devising a transparent and fair monitoring process will be challenging given the uneven balance between the plans, some of which are more robust and research-based than others.

Notwithstanding these serious shortcomings, the language planning process is here to stay and will remain the state's main community language initiative for the foreseeable future. At the very least, it has encouraged a cross-section of districts with very different linguistic profiles to take stock of the state of Irish in their midst, identify priorities for the future and rally local support for the language. A more active role by the state, both in terms of finance and governance, could smooth the way for the process, but concrete progress would also be required across all of the domains discussed in this book. In Chapter 2, we move from a focus on speakers and community-based language planning to historical language policy in relation to the Gaeltacht.

Gaeltacht

1. Introduction

The Gaeltacht has loomed large in Irish language policy since before the foundation of the state, as it occupied a central position in the Revival movement of the late nineteenth and early twentieth centuries. Historically used to refer to Irish-speaking people, it developed a new meaning of territory during the Revival period and, in line with dominant ethnolinguistic ideologies of the time, came to be seen as the source from which the restoration of Irish as the vernacular would be achieved. The networks of branches of the Gaelic League (Conradh na Gaeilge), established in 1893, brought Irish people in contact with their ancestral language, many for the first time, and the promotion of the language became part of the broad canvass of artistic, sporting, musical and cultural strands of the Revival. Following an analysis of speakers of Irish in the Gaeltacht in the previous chapter, Chapter 2 turns to policy initiatives aimed at strengthening the Irish-speaking districts. It focuses on the first major state intervention on behalf of the Gaeltacht, the Gaeltacht Commission of 1925–1926.

2. Context

As the remnants of what had once been a predominantly Irish-speaking Ireland, the Gaeltacht areas of the western and southern coasts loomed large in the Revival movement of the late nineteenth and early twentieth centuries. Although deeply impoverished due to the political economy of British rule and bleeding its population through out-migration, the Gaeltacht was recast by cultural and political nationalism as a cultural touchstone for the nation from which the revival of Irish would radiate (O'Leary, 2004). Newspapers of the Revival period, themselves established by mostly middle-class learners of Irish from the cities, are replete with accounts of the 'trip west' (*an turas siar*) to the Gaeltacht to learn Irish, an early form of cultural tourism (Ó Torna, 2005: 75–95). It was during this period that the understanding of the word 'Gaeltacht' as a defined geographical region began to take shape, replacing its earlier sense of Irish-speaking people (ibid.: 44). As the notion of the Gaeltacht as space began to solidify in public consciousness, the question of language maintenance and shift within its borders came into sharp focus. This was further intensified by the mapping of the Gaeltacht which was undertaken by the Irish Free State from the 1920s.

Many of those involved in the campaign for Irish independence were involved in Conradh na Gaeilge (Ó Flaitheartaigh & Weeks, 2021: 82) and although not all were fluent Irish speakers, there was strong political support for the idea that the Gaeltacht deserved special protection. The first Dáil, sitting before the foundation of the state, appointed sitting TD (member) and Ceann Comhairle (speaker) Seán Ó Ceallaigh ('Sceilg') as Minister for Irish. Ó Ceallaigh was also president of Conradh na Gaeilge (Ó Gadhra, 1989a: 167–171, 174).[1] The first and second Executive Councils (cabinets) of the Irish Free State contained seven ministers, three of whom were strongly associated with the League and fluent Irish speakers: Eoin MacNeill (a co-founder along with Douglas Hyde), Ernest Blythe and

---

1   For a biography of Ó Ceallaigh, see Breathnach and Ní Mhurchú, 2021c.

Richard Mulcahy.[2] The President, WT Cosgrave, had been a member of the League and was sympathetic to its aims, but knew little Irish and had to rely on crude phonetic renderings in English orthography for his limited use of Irish in speeches on radio (Department of the President, 1926a). In his study of the period 1893–1993, Ó Riagáin outlines four elements to the new state's language policy: (a) the maintenance or preservation of Irish in the Gaeltacht, (b) the revival of Irish in the remainder of the country, sometimes referred to as 'gaelicisation', (c) the use of Irish in public administration and (d) the standardisation of Irish to facilitate its use in domains such as public administration, education, broadcasting, etc. (1997: 15). Following the introduction of key measures such as the constitutional status and the use of Irish in the civil service and education, the government's first major policy initiative on the Gaeltacht was to establish a Commission in 1925 to investigate the extent of the Irish-speaking areas and to make recommendations for strengthening the use of Irish in them. The Commission published its report in 1926 and is studied in detail in the case study later in this chapter.

2.1 Geography of the Gaeltacht, 1926–1956

The Gaeltacht Commission recommended the inclusion of 585 electoral divisions (EDs) in the Gaeltacht in 1926. From 1928 to 1956, conflicting geographical definitions of the territory remained on the statute books and there was considerable variation between government schemes in the way that a given area was considered to be in the Gaeltacht. Most of the definitions were related to specific services or supports and did not aim to provide a definitive sociolinguistic explanation of the Gaeltacht, but the geographical uncertainty caused administrative confusion at least. For instance, the 585 EDs recommended by the Commission were formalised in the Local Offices and Executives Order (Gaeltacht) 1928, an enactment

---

2   These were known also by their Irish names Eoin Mac Néill, Dubhghlas de hÍde, Earnán de Blaghd and Risteárd Ó Maolchatha. In this text, the English version is used except in references containing the Irish version.

that aimed to set salaries for public servants working in the Gaeltacht. In 1929, 660 EDs were included in the Housing (Gaeltacht) Act, legislation that provided grants and loans for improvement of housing stock and outhouses for animals. This amounted to the most generous ever legal definition of the Gaeltacht that even included EDs in Counties Cavan, Leitrim, Limerick, Louth and Sligo, areas where Irish had long ceased to be used. There were further contradictions between legislation and schemes related to school meals, vocational education, local officials and an incentive to promote Irish in families (see below). Despite the establishment of Gaeltacht 'colonies', predominantly in Co. Meath, between 1935 and 1940, such areas did not gain official Gaeltacht status until 1967 (for a more detailed discussion, see Walsh, 2019b: 190–191 and Ó Gadhra, 1989b: 30–36).

2.2 Gaeltacht Services

Rural industries originally under the control of the Congested Districts Board (CDB) were transferred to the Land Commission in 1923 and in 1924 to the Department of Fisheries. As the CDB was largely coterminous with the Gaeltacht (Breathnach, 2005: 168, 183–184), many such industries were at least nominally located in Irish-speaking districts. In the White Paper of 1928 outlining the government's response to the Gaeltacht Commission's proposals, responsibility for Gaeltacht policy was transferred formally to the Department of Fisheries, which established a Gaeltacht Services Division. In 1934, Fisheries became part of the Department of Agriculture and Gaeltacht Services moved to the Department of Lands (Department of Lands, 1938: 3). Rural industries supported included lace-making, knitting, weaving, packing of carrageen and producing of kelp. Gaeltacht Services had responsibility for another initiative that emerged from the work of the Commission, grants for Gaeltacht housing. The division also had responsibility for administering financial support under the Housing (Gaeltacht) Act in 1929. The original act had stated that priority would be given to Gaeltacht dwellers proficient in Irish but this provision was tightened in 1934 in revised legislation that made normal use of Irish by the household a condition of funding (ibid.: 12). Gaeltacht Services also arranged for domestic economy instructors to support Gaeltacht women and in 1935, it revived an earlier interdepartmental committee to co-ordinate state actions in relation to the Gaeltacht economy (ibid.: 13). Gaeltacht Services continued until the establishment of new Gaeltacht institutions in the 1950s but its work was limited to relief measures and small-scale industrial activity and there was no strategic attempt to bring about meaningful structural change in the Gaeltacht economy during this period. One historian has described Gaeltacht economic policy in the period 1922–1960s as one of 'retardation' and 'stagnation', which failed to stabilise the population but was minimally disruptive to Irish (Ó Tuathaigh, 1990: 11).

2.3 Scheme to support Irish in families

An important initiative with a direct language policy impact was a scheme introduced in 1933 to support the transmission of Irish within the family, Scéim Labhairt na Gaeilge (SLG, 'Scheme for speaking Irish'). Under SLG, families were paid an annual grant of £2 if the children were fluent Irish speakers, according to an oral examination carried out at school by Department of Education inspectors. The grant slowly increased in value and was raised to £200 per family in 1993, with a reduced grant of £100 paid to those who had not made satisfactory progress. This was to be an incentive for parents or caregivers to speak more Irish to the children. In its final years, SLG was worth €260 per family (reduced rate of €130) and the *Comprehensive Linguistic Study of the Use of Irish in the Gaeltacht* (CLS) recommended that it be increased to €5,000 per year (Ó Giollagáin et al., 2007a: 45). It was abolished as an economy measure in 2011 and replaced with a support package aimed at Irish-speaking children regardless of location. Although SLG had its critics both within the Gaeltacht and among researchers, it was a rare example of a policy intervention aimed directly at supporting the use of Irish as a family language in the Gaeltacht. Its successor support package is poorly resourced and less well known and unlikely to have a significant impact of a family's use of Irish (O'Rourke & Walsh, 2020: 47–48).

2.4 Changes in governance in the 1950s

A major shift in the governance of the Gaeltacht and its industry was announced in the 1950s. In 1956, the government established the Department of the Gaeltacht, thirty years after the Commission had re-commended a high-level body that would co-ordinate Gaeltacht affairs. The extent of the Gaeltacht was reduced radically following a review of the boundaries, which was undertaken to delineate a clear territory where the Department's writ would run and tidy up the geographical inconsist-encies (Ó Riagáin, 1997: 271). The much-reduced territory was defined in the Gaeltacht Area Orders, 1956; only 84 full electoral divisions and part of another 58 remained in the Gaeltacht (Walsh, 2019b: 190–192). The new Department would be responsible for promoting the cultural, social and economic welfare of the Gaeltacht, for assisting with the maintenance and extension of Irish as vernacular and consulting with other govern-ment departments about services they provide to the Gaeltacht or to the 'national aim of restoring the Irish language' (Article 3.2, Ministers and Secretaries (Amendment) Act, 1956). Description of the Revival policy as a 'national aim' begs the question why the aim was not important enough in the 1920s to agree to the Commission's proposal. The definition of Gaeltacht provided in the founding legislation is also worthy of comment because of its inherent flexibility:

> specified areas, being substantially Irish-speaking areas and areas contiguous thereto which, in the opinion of the Government, ought to be included in the Gaeltacht with a view to preserving and extending the use of Irish as a vernacular language. (Article 2.2, Ministers and Secretaries (Amendment) Act, 1956)

Admitting that areas outside the Gaeltacht had been included in the hope that they would become Irish speaking was related less to lin-guistic factors than to political considerations that weighed heavily on decisions about the boundaries. Large areas which had long ceased to be

Irish-speaking were included in the Gaeltacht, particularly in Co. Mayo where the Minister for the Gaeltacht was based (Ó Giollagáin, 2006). There were minor changes to the Gaeltacht between 1967 and 1982 but otherwise the borders have remained unchanged since 1956 (Walsh, 2019b: 192–193). Another change in governance related to shifting industrial policy as Ireland began to emerge from protectionism. Following the establishment in 1949 of the Industrial Development Authority (IDA) to attract foreign direct investment (FDI) to Ireland, the government in 1957 established Gaeltarra Éireann ('Gaelic Products of Ireland') as an industrial body for the Gaeltacht. The initial aim of Gaeltarra was to take over the administration of existing Gaeltacht industries from Gaeltacht Services but from 1965, it was given powers to attract FDI like the IDA. From then on, it became more of a facilitator of private development in the Gaeltacht than a co-ordinator of small home industries. Through a strategy of promoting growth poles of development, Gaeltarra set up industrial estates in Gaeltacht regions that had reasonably good infrastructural connections with other parts of Ireland, primarily in Co. Cork, northwest Donegal and south Connemara. The secondary aim of Gaeltarra related to language, the act referring to the duty of the board to assist with the maintenance and extension of Irish as the vernacular in the Gaeltacht (Article 4.2, Gaeltacht Industries Act, 1957). Significantly, from 1957 to 1969, the head office of Gaeltarra was not in the Gaeltacht but in Dublin, fuelling a sense of remoteness from the people it was supposed to serve.

Severe emigration in the 1950s left its mark on the Gaeltacht as Irish speakers left in droves in search of work in the cities of Britain and the United States, a phenomenon highlighted by the extensive literature in Irish about emigration in the twentieth century (Nic Eoin & Nic Dhonnchadha, 2008). Following the liberalisation programmes of Seán Lemass and T. K. Whitaker in the late 1950s and 1960s, the Gaeltacht witnessed its own industrialisation and socioeconomic change and the position of English was consolidated further (Ó Tuathaigh, 1990: 11). A Gaeltacht Civil Rights Movement (Gluaiseacht Cearta Sibhialta na Gaeltachta) was established in 1969 and included among its key demands a democratic authority for the Gaeltacht and a Gaeltacht radio service. This led to an Irish-language station Raidió na Gaeltachta in 1972 (see Chapter 5) and may have influenced the decision of Gaeltarra Éireann to move its headquarters to Co. Galway. In 1971, a joint working group of Gaeltarra and the Shannon Free Airport Development Company (SFADCO), a regional development body in the area around Shannon Airport in Co. Clare, produced a report called *Gníomh don Ghaeltacht: An Action Plan for the Gaeltacht*. While modernisationist in its approach in line with the liberalisation of economic policy, the report also recognised that Gaeltacht development had to include sociolinguistic factors (Gaeltarra Éireann & SFADCO, 1971). All of these factors fed into the debate about the nature of the governance of the Gaeltacht that would culminate in the establishment of Údarás na Gaeltachta ('Gaeltacht Authority'), a quasi-democratic industrial development body in 1979.

2.5 *Údarás na Gaeltachta*

The story of Údarás na Gaeltachta encompasses debates about the nature of socioeconomic development and how it may or may not be amenable to the promotion of a minoritised language such as Irish. Over the four decades of its existence, Údarás has been transformed from a regional industrial development agency with a secondary linguistic remit to a hybrid development and language body with direct responsibility for local language planning in the Gaeltacht. It never became the democratic authority demanded by the Gaeltacht Civil Rights Movement or even the modified version proposed by Comhairle na Gaeilge in 1972 (see Chapter 3), but through the direct election of board members by Gaeltacht residents, it developed a quasi-democratic function. This gave it a stronger sense of connection to the community even if elected members tended to reflect local party political rivalries and had very limited powers.

The Údarás na Gaeltachta Act, 1980 gave the impression that the promotion of Irish was paramount to the new organisation's operations by placing linguistic considerations first in its list of functions. Article 8.1 stated that Údarás would promote the maintenance and extension of Irish as the principal language of the Gaeltacht and Article 8.2 stated that it would take over the industries and 'productive schemes of employment' that had previously been administered by Gaeltarra Éireann. However, the experience of subsequent decades would underline how Údarás was limited to supporting certain economic activities (industries and 'productive schemes of employment', i.e. not services) and had a peripheral role in relation to Irish. In essence, with the exception of direct elections of the board, the differences between Gaeltarra and Údarás were largely cosmetic (Walsh, 2012: 303). Research about the potentially damaging effects of industrialisation on weak linguistic communities (e.g. Ó Cinnéide et al., 1985) and a damning study by an English geographer that announced the death of the Irish language (Hindley, 1990), led to further questions about the direction of Gaeltacht development. From the 1990s onwards, during the period of Professor Gearóid Ó Tuathaigh of the National University of Ireland, Galway (now University of Galway) as chairperson, debates intensified about the extent to which Údarás should support the social economy and the Irish language itself.

There are also studies of aspects of economic development in the Gaeltacht, including the impact of industrial development on the vitality of Irish (Ó Cinnéide et al., 1985; Ó Tuathaigh, 1990) and the history of Gaeltacht entrepreneurship (Ní Bhrádaigh, 2008a & 2008b). The intersection between language policy and socioeconomic development in several Gaeltacht areas and changes in the policies of Údarás na Gaeltachta has also been analysed (Walsh, 2012).

2.6 The planning process in the Gaeltacht

We saw in Chapter 1 that the issue of housing has become a matter of concern in the Gaeltacht, because of the potentially damaging impact of housing estates on the delicate linguistic balance. The issue came more into focus in the 1990s due to the Celtic Tiger housing boom, and was intended to be controlled by a provision in the new Planning and Development Act 2000. Section 10 (2) (m) was introduced in an attempt to modify the impact of housing developments on the strength of Irish in the Gaeltacht by obliging local authorities to take this into account in their development plans. Every subsequent plan was required to include an objective related to:

> the protection of the linguistic and cultural heritage of the Gaeltacht including the promotion of Irish as the community language, where there is a Gaeltacht area in the area of the development plan.

The new provision has led to quotas of housing being reserved for Irish speakers in certain Gaeltacht counties, along with examinations for purchasers. Developers have been asked to produce 'language impact statements' explaining how the proposed development will affect the Irish language in the area in question. However, as we saw in Chapter 1, there is no coherent policy in place with the result that implementation of the provision varies considerably from one Gaeltacht county to another. A campaign for a Gaeltacht housing policy has been launched in recent years (Conradh na Gaeilge, 2021b).

2.7 Gaeltacht Commission 2000–2002

Another Gaeltacht Commission that operated from 2000 to 2002 provided further data about the weak position of Irish in the Gaeltacht. It found that only 18 of the 154 electoral divisions contained populations with more than 75 per cent daily speakers of Irish (Coimisiún na Gaeltachta, 2002: 10). The Commission recommended a change in the focus of Údarás na Gaeltachta away from employment creation and towards 'the development and implementation of sustainable language-centred initiatives. In this way it will champion the educational, linguistic, cultural, social and economic development of the Gaeltacht' (ibid.: 16). It proposed a radical restructuring of Údarás with equal amounts of its budget to be spent on (1) Irish language, education and culture, (2) economy and infrastructure and (3) community, social and health affairs and called for the introduction of a more holistic development model with a strong language policy foundation (ibid.: 17). An ancillary study to the Commission's report found that the budget of the language and culture division of Údarás was miniscule, amounting to only 1 per cent of its total funding (Ó Cinnéide et al., 2002). Following such criticism, Minister Éamon Ó Cuív in 2003 ordered Údarás to begin spending 20 per cent of its capital budget on language-related projects. However, despite limited forays into support for co-operatives and cultural tourism, the executive deemed that any further extension of its role into non-economic spheres was impossible due to the constraints of the legislation (Walsh, 2012: 309–315).

2.8 Comprehensive Linguistic Study

In 2004, on foot of a recommendation by the Gaeltacht Commission, the government commissioned a major sociolinguistic study of the Gaeltacht to inform policy in the years ahead. The *Comprehensive Linguistic Study of the Use of Irish in the Gaeltacht* (CLS) was directed by the National University of Ireland, Galway and based on an analysis of 2002 census data, data from SLG and qualitative research throughout the Gaeltacht, including the study of youth attitudes and self-reported use of Irish mentioned in Chapter 1 (Ó Giollagáin et al., 2007a & 2007b). A revised version of the data was published at a later stage (Ó Giollagáin & Charlton, 2015). In an echo of the Gaeltacht Commission of 1926, CLS recommended the division of the Gaeltacht into three separate geographical districts, based on the use of Irish, in order to prioritise language planning measures according to profiles of communities:

1. Category A districts, containing 67 per cent or more daily Irish speakers. There were twenty-four such EDs, located mostly in Connemara, northwest Donegal and west Kerry. Irish was stable in all age cohorts except among the young;
2. Category B districts, containing 44–66 per cent daily Irish speakers. There were twenty such EDs, located in Waterford, Cork, central Donegal, Mayo/Galway border and Meath. These districts showed evidence of language shift but Irish maintained a presence in networks;

3. Category C districts, containing less than 44 per cent daily Irish speakers. This comprised 111 EDs, the majority of the Gaeltacht, and in many EDs there was little appreciable difference with areas outside the Gaeltacht (Ó Giollagáin et al., 2007a: 13–17).

CLS recommended amending existing legislation to give legal force to the new geographical arrangement and said that areas failing to adhere to certain language planning criteria (for instance, primary and secondary education delivered in Irish) should lose Gaeltacht status (ibid.: 31–32). The stark conclusion – and one that gained the most media attention – was that Irish would only remain the dominant language of the Category A districts for another 15–20 years (i.e. by 2027) 'without a major change in language use patterns' (Ó Giollagáin et al., 2007: 27).

2.9 20-Year Strategy and Gaeltacht Act

The government claimed that it accepted the general thrust of the CLS proposals to base the status of the Gaeltacht on linguistic criteria and announced that language planning would henceforth be put on a statutory footing in a new Gaeltacht act (Government of Ireland, 2010: 20). The lead author of CLS has repeatedly criticised the government for failing to implement the recommendations in full (e.g. Ó Giollagáin, 2014) but the 'language planning process' has in fact been shaped in a large part by the 2007 report. The Gaeltacht Act 2012 did not codify the A, B, C categories proposed in the CLS, but created three spatial arrangements on which language planning would be conducted: (1) Gaeltacht Language Planning Districts (LPD), (2) Gaeltacht Service Towns (GST) and (3) Irish Language Networks. Under article 7 (2) of the Act, the Minister was empowered to designate a Gaeltacht area as a Language Planning District and twenty-six such areas were announced between 2014 and 2017. These included strongly Irish-speaking areas in Donegal, Galway and Kerry as well as overwhelmingly English-speaking suburbs of Galway city that remained in the Gaeltacht since the 1956 revisions. The act created a process for every LPD to prepare its own language plan, giving Údarás na

Gaeltachta a direct language planning function for the first time since its establishment. In every LPD, local 'lead' organisations are eligible to apply to Údarás na Gaeltachta to prepare a language plan and if accepted, such bodies must submit the plan to the Department of the Gaeltacht for approval within two years. Once accepted, plans last for seven years and are implemented by the lead organisation. If no organisation applies to prepare a plan in a given LPD, the Minister may invoke articles 5 and 13 (b) to remove that area's Gaeltacht status. No Gaeltacht area has lost its status since 1956 and at the end of 2021, twenty-five of the twenty-six LPDs were implementing language plans with the final area's plan still under consideration.

The second category of language planning district, Gaeltacht Service Town (GST), was proposed in the CLS, given the influence of urban centres on language use patterns (Ó Giollagáin e al., 2007: 31). In article 9 of the Act, GST is defined as a town of at least 1,000 people within or outside the Gaeltacht that provides public services or social or commercial facilities of benefit to the Gaeltacht. The Department has stated that the aim of the Act in this regard is to investigate how the potentially positive impact of GSTs on the use of Irish as a community language in the Gaeltacht could be encouraged and strengthened (Department of Tourism, Arts, Heritage, Gaeltacht, Sport and Media, 2020). The same approach to language planning applies in GSTs as LPDs: a local organisation may apply either to Údarás na Gaeltachta or Foras na Gaeilge (depending on the GST's location inside or outside the Gaeltacht) to prepare a local language plan and if approved, must implement the plan over a seven-year period. A list of eighteen urban centres was published comprising towns mostly outside the Gaeltacht including major urban centres such as Galway and Cork. The progress of the language planning process in GSTs has been much slower than in the Gaeltacht, reflecting the latter's greater political importance to the government. At the end of 2021, only three GSTs had language plans in place, Letterkenny (Co. Donegal) and Galway outside the Gaeltacht and An Daingean in the west Kerry Gaeltacht. I was lead researcher on the Galway City Language Plan that was agreed under this process in 2021 (Walsh et al., 2021). The third category, that of Irish Language Network, relates to areas outside the Gaeltacht and was discussed in Chapter 1.

While the development of language plans has allowed communities to identify priorities for the development of Irish in their districts, the process has been criticised for transferring most of the responsibility for language planning to under-resourced voluntary groups. Given the governance structures in place, there are also concerns about the ability of language planning officers, no matter how well intentioned or committed to their work, to bring about real change in their communities.

3. Case study: Gaeltacht Commission 1925–1926

The case study in this chapter focuses on the origins, members, findings, evidence and results of the Gaeltacht Commission of the 1920s. Set up in 1925, less than three years after the first independent government came to office, it delivered its report in 1926 and the government responded in the form of a White Paper in 1928. The Commission's work and the fallout from its report reveal ideological tensions between enthusiastic language activists, disengaged Gaeltacht speakers, occasionally hostile civil servants and ministers with various levels of commitment to the Revival.

3.1 Origins

The origins of the Gaeltacht Commission of 1925–1926 go back to a motion from the representative body of the country's local authorities to President Cosgrave on the 12th of January 1924 calling on the Dáil to 'devise means of coping with the all-important problem of the Gaeltacht and with the Gaelic Culture generally' (County Councils' General Council, 1924). The authorities requested a meeting with Cosgrave but, reflecting the locus of language policy in the formative years, they were met instead by Minister for Education, Eoin MacNeill.[3] Following the

---

3   Eoin MacNeill was minister for Education from 1922 to 1925 and resigned before the Commission report was published (Lee, 1989: 149). He was replaced by John

meeting, a memorandum was circulated to government recommending measures to increase the use of Irish by representatives of the state in the Gaeltacht including Gardaí, customs and excise officers, the army and the Land Commission. The memorandum recognised the particular authority of Land Commission staff in Gaeltacht areas and their influence on language ideology and practice:

> Officials on the same plane of importance as law officers and clerks of courts, they wield a great deal of power and are greatly respected or feared. They are the men with the power; and the language such men speak in the exercise of their authority is the one that gets the allegiance of the public. Hitherto it has been English. (Department of the President, 1924)

A memo by MacNeill, 'The Gaelicizing of Ireland', circulated to his colleagues on the 29th of April 1924, gives an insight into the thinking of someone who had crossed the line from language activism in Conradh na Gaeilge into the most language-sensitive post in the first post-1922 cabinet. MacNeill explained that the policy had been to make Irish compulsory for one hour per day in all primary schools, to introduce Irish as a means of instruction in infant classes and for History and Geography lessons for all students, and to teach entirely in Irish in the Gaeltacht. However, he estimated that only about one-third of teachers were fully competent to carry out the policy and said that until Irish was established as the medium of instruction in the training colleges, no real progress could be made in the schools. Optimistically, he predicted that once the training colleges operated in Irish, schools would change from the present stage of monolingual English, to a bilingual stage, to the goal where Irish would be the exclusive means of instruction and the normal language of teachers and pupils. MacNeill saw the schools as 'Gaelic centres' from which the language could be spread throughout the country. This depended, however, on the preservation of the Gaeltacht as an Irish-speaking district. He urged:

Marcus O'Sullivan who was not as closely associated with the Revival movement (ibid.: 132).

that the Irish-speaking districts of Ireland be preserved as reservoirs of Gaelic from which the language may generally flow out organically to the surrounding districts. If Irish dies in the Irish-speaking districts the Irish of the schools will become an artificial language with no background of reality behind it and as such have no real roots and no lasting effect on the development of our people. (Mac Néill, 1924)

MacNeill acknowledged that there were challenges but nonetheless felt that gaelicisation could be brought about, claiming that the Free State could 'do a great deal ... by making Irish the normal official language in both the Gaoltacht[4] and the English-speaking districts'. Aligned with the dominant ideology of the time, he stated that priority should be given to the Gaeltacht in this task. In a warning that could be applied equally to every subsequent decade of language policy, MacNeill cautioned that Education alone could not achieve these aims and that cross-government support was required in ensuring life-long use of Irish.

The presence of Irish speakers in key roles in government and parliament encouraged the eventual establishment of a Commission on the Gaeltacht. Another former Gaelic League activist, Minister for Finance Ernest Blythe, discussed the matter with former Minister for Defence, Richard Mulcahy and Ceann Comhairle (speaker) of the Dáil, Michael Hayes, in the autumn of 1924. Mulcahy, sacked from his ministerial role that spring following a crisis in the army (Lee, 1989: 96–97), was a leading supporter of the Revival policy and Hayes was also an Irish speaker who would go on to become an academic and eventually a professor of Irish at University College Dublin. Blythe circulated a memorandum to government on the 17th of December, describing the importance of preserving the Gaeltacht as 'unquestionable', warning that a plan to support it would be difficult and that a Commission was required to investigate the matter fully. It appears from the records that Blythe also proposed terms of reference and these were approved by cabinet on the 2nd of January 1925 and appointments made, with Mulcahy becoming chairman (Executive Council, 1925a & 1925b).

4   There was inconsistency in the spelling in the period under study (Gaeltacht, Gaedhealtacht, Gaoltacht). Spelling was standardised in the 1940s (Nic Pháidín, 2008).

3.2 Membership

The membership of the Commission reflected the dominant ideological currents of the time: twelve men representing the middle-class Catholics who had taken control of the newly established Irish Free State, people who had supported the Treaty and were engaged in the business of building and stabilising the machinery of state. They included politicians, civil servants and language activists, many of whom had been deeply involved in the Revival movement since the late nineteenth century. Mulcahy as chair had impeccable credentials as a learner who had acquired Irish to a high level through self-study and periods spent in Gaeltacht areas of Co. Cork (Ó Caoimh, 2019: 12). His son Risteárd recalled how Irish was spoken at home and emphasised his father's commitment to the language, claiming that he rather than Blythe had initially floated the idea of a Commission (Mulcahy, 2009: 185). Other members of the Commission were linked in various ways to the ideals of Irish-Ireland, with some playing key roles in the Revival movement and others having more tenuous connections.

One of those whose links with the Commission's work is not obvious was Patrick Baxter (1891–1959), a TD for the Cavan constituency for the Farmers' Party, a small parliamentary grouping that would eventually merge with other parties to form one of Ireland's largest political parties, Fine Gael, in 1933. Baxter later became a Senator for another farmers' party Clann na Talmhan but when proposed for the post of Leas-Chathaoirleach (deputy speaker) of the Seanad, his lack of competence in Irish was criticised by some colleagues (Seanad Éireann, 1938). An appreciation read on the occasion of his death said that he had been associated with 'all Gaelic activities' in his area following the 1916 Rising, but no further details were given (Seanad Eireann, 1959). It seems that Baxter's ability in Irish was minimal but the presence of Gaeltacht pockets in west Cavan may have influenced his appointment to the Commission (Ní Bhrádaigh et al., 2008).

Others had more obvious connections with the Revival and the Commission's work. Dr Tomás Breathnach (Thomas Walsh) (1877–1960) was Professor of Pathology at University College Galway and prepared a groundbreaking glossary of medical terms in Irish for use in teaching and research (Breathnach, T., c. 1937). He was a member of Galway Sinn Féin and of the Executive Committee of Conradh na Gaeilge (Cunningham,

2012). His brother Micheál, also a graduate of UCG, was also involved in Irish language activism in the city (Breathnach, M., 1966).[5]

Pádraig Ó Cadhla (1875–1948), a teacher based in Co. Clare, was born in the Sliabh gCua Gaeltacht area on the Tipperary/Waterford border and was a well-known Irish language activist in that area. He worked as an organiser (*timire*) for Conradh na Gaeilge and was involved in setting up Irish-language education in An Rinn, Co. Waterford, including the renowned college Coláiste na Rinne (Breathnach & Ní Mhurchú, 2021d). He was also a skilled translator (Ó Macháin, 2019).

Fr Seaghan Mac Cuinnigeáin (1877–1958) was from the Gaeltacht village of An Charraig in Co. Donegal and inspector of the diocese of Raphoe. He wrote a dissenting report of his own that was added to the main Commission document as an appendix (see below). A newspaper report later referred to a translation of the catechism by a Fr John Cunningham, whose 'fine scholarship and wide knowledge both of the literary and spoken language are known and appreciated not merely throughout Donegal, but far beyond its broad confines' (Mac Airt, 1929). Fr Mac Cuinnigeáin was appointed parish priest of Glenties in 1944 and canon in 1950 (*The Derry Journal*, 1953 and *The Cork Examiner*, 1958).[6]

Seámus Ó hEocha (1880–1959; known colloquially as 'An Fear Mór' (the big man, due to his height), was a towering figure in the Irish Revival in the first half of the twentieth century. Originally from Limerick, he was associated with the Waterford Gaeltacht through his work there, particularly in relation to Coláiste na Rinne. He was also involved in Conradh na Gaeilge and worked as a travelling teacher for a time. Ó hEocha later became a senator and one of his sons, Colm, became president of University College Galway (Breathnach & Ní Mhurchú, 2021g).

Risteárd Ó Foghludha (1871–1957, who used the *nom de plume* 'Fiachra Éilgeach') was a leading member of Conradh na Gaeilge. He established the influential Craobh an Chéitinnigh branch, worked as a journalist with the *Freeman's Journal* and translated plays from English and French to Irish. Born in east Cork where Irish was still spoken at the turn of the century, he was friendly with other language activists such as Tórna (Tadhg

---

5   I thank Dr Jackie Uí Chionna for her assistance with information.
6   Thanks to Prof. Nollaig Mac Congáil for his assistance with these references.

Ó Donnchadha)[7] and Fr Pádraig Ó Duinnín. He went on to work for the government's Irish language publishing agency An Gúm from 1936 and edited the Irish text of the 1937 Constitution (Ó Cearúil, 2002; Breathnach & Ní Mhurchú, 2021f).

Joseph Hanly (1880–1960) was General Inspector of Rural Science in the Department of Education. Originally from east Galway where Irish was still spoken to some extent in the early twentieth century, it is unclear how much Irish he knew himself. He was a proponent of a Catholic, Irish-speaking state based on co-operatism, argued that agriculture formed the basis of the Irish economy and claimed that there was ample evidence for this in Irish language literature (Hanly, 1932). He also published *The National Ideal: A Practical Exposition of True Nationality Appertaining to Ireland* (Hanly, 1931). This was described as 'fanaticism' and Hanly was linked to the 'semi-fascist' Ailtirí na hAiséirighe movement that emerged in the 1930s (Murphy, 1976; see also *Irish Farmers' Journal*, 1960).

Pádraig Ó hÓgáin (1885–1969) was a TD representing the Labour Party in Co. Clare. From Kilmaley, still an Irish-speaking area in the west of the county, his parents were Irish speakers but he was raised in English as was so often the case in the context of language shift in Ireland. Ó hÓgáin learned Irish from his next-door neighbour and then became involved in Conradh na Gaeilge (Breathnach & Ní Mhurchú, 2021h).

Lawrence Moriarty (1873–1958) was Secretary of Fisheries, a small government department but of relevance to Gaeltacht communities due to their largely maritime nature. Born in Laois (Queen's County), he was returned as not speaking Irish in the census of 1911 ('Laurence C. Moriarty', 1911)[8] but his father was from Cathair Dónall in the south Kerry Gaeltacht.[9] The founder of Sinn Féin, Arthur Griffith, saw fishing as an unexploited natural resource and the establishment of a dedicated department after independence raised hopes that it could make a difference to coastal communities

---

7   Ó Donnchadha gave evidence to the Commission in Dublin on the 4th of June 1925 (Gaeltacht Commission, 1926: 70).

8   There is variation in spelling between 'Lawrence' and 'Laurence'. I am very grateful to Dr Ciara Breathnach for her generous assistance with sources. See also 'Laurence Moriarty', 1958.

9   I am grateful to Michael Lynch, archivist, Kerry Library, for this information.

(Ó Flathartaigh, 2008: 78; Corcoran, 2013: 171). The Minister for Fisheries, Fionán Lynch (Ó Loingsigh) was an Irish speaker, also from south Kerry, and a member of the Craobh an Chéitinnigh branch of Conradh na Gaeilge (Breathnach & Ní Mhurchú, 2021i). Moriarty wrote an appendix of his own to the Commission's report urging the establishment of a properly funded permanent commission. His department would later be asked to collate the government's response to the Commission's findings and henceforth to co-ordinate Gaeltacht development schemes (Gaeltacht Commission, 1926: 68).

Pádraig Ó Siochfhradha (1883–1964, also known as 'An Seabhac' (the hawk), apparently due to his efficiency as a travelling teacher) was from An Daingean in Co. Kerry and was one of the most renowned activists of the Revival period, working as an author, scholar, teacher, translator and businessman. He worked as a travelling organiser for Conradh na Gaeilge throughout Munster until 1922 and was a member of its Executive Committee. Later he was employed in the Department of Education, where he had responsibility for the preparatory colleges that aimed to ensure fluency in Irish among teachers. Taoiseach Éamon de Valera appointed him as a Senator in the 1940s (Breathnach & Ní Mhurchú, 2021k; see also Ní Mhunghaile, 2015).

Michael Tierney (1894–1975) from Dublin was Professor of Greek at University College Dublin at the time of the Commission. Originally from Castleblakeney in east Galway, still partly Irish-speaking at the turn of the century (Gaeltacht Commission, 1926: 87), he served first as a TD and later as a Senator for Cumann na nGaedheal/Fine Gael. Tierney was elected president of UCD in 1947 and led the development of the university in the mid-century period (McCartney, 2009). He was connected to the Revival movement through his marriage to a daughter of Eoin MacNeill and later wrote a biography of his father-in-law that was published posthumously (Martin & Tierney, 1980). The editor of the biography claimed that Tierney spoke Irish fluently (Martin, 1980: xi) and his successor as president of UCD wrote that he had a 'near-native' command of the language (Hogan, 1976: 177), but other sources suggest that his competence was more limited. For instance, an account of his dispute with classical scholar Seoirse Mac Tomáis (George Thomson) about the use of Irish as medium of instruction in universities illustrates that Tierney told Mac Tomáis that he could not debate fully in Irish with him and would be more effective in English (Mac Conghail, 2009: 128). Tierney was committed to preserving Irish folklore and appointed to the first Irish Folklore Commission in 1935, receiving correspondence in Irish about the role (Briody, 2010: 172). He also reviewed a translation from Greek to Irish for the Irish language publishing body An Gúm (Coilféir, 2020: 54). We can conclude that Tierney was capable of reading and writing Irish and could speak the language relatively well, possibly better than some other Commission members. Where he differed from the bulk of his colleagues, however, was in his ideological disposition to the Revival. Briody argues that despite Tierney's obvious commitment to Irish folklore, his resolute opposition to even a modest amount of teaching through the medium of Irish in UCD damaged both the Revival and the university's reputation among Irish speakers (2007: 481–482).[10] An analysis by Tierney of the language Revival published shortly after the Commission completed its work was criticised as overly pessimistic by Mulcahy (Tierney, 1927: 11).

The Secretary of the Commission was Tadhg Ó Scanaill (1883–1967), a translator in the Dáil. From the Baile Bhuirne Gaeltacht of West Cork, he was involved in setting up An Fáinne ('the ring'), an organisation to promote an emblem worn by Irish speakers with the aim of fostering greater social use of the language. After the Commission, Ó Scanaill spent the remainder of his life working as a civil servant with responsibility for Irish language matters (Breathnach and Ní Mhurchú, 2021j).

The geographical spread of the Commission is worthy of comment, as the extent to which various Gaeltacht areas were represented drew some controversy. There was a strong Munster flavour to the list of commissioners: Mulcahy was from Waterford and learned Irish in Cork, Ó Cadhla was from Na Déise and Ó hEocha strongly associated with there, Ó Foghludha was from Cork, Ó Siochfhradha from Kerry and Ó hÓgáin from Clare, and Ó Scanaill as Secretary was also from Cork. In contrast, only three commissioners represented the entire Connacht and Ulster region,

10   I am very grateful to Séamus Mac Mathúna and Dónall Ó Braonáin for assistance with references in this section.

despite the fact that it contained the largest Gaeltacht areas. Following the appointment of Professor Tomás Breathnach of University College Galway, the university's Registrar Monsignor John Hynes wrote to the government to express concern at lack of representation for Connacht and Ulster (University College Galway, 1925). There was also a concerted attempt by MacNeill to recruit the renowned Irish linguistics scholar Prof. T. F. O'Rahilly, another Kerryman, but he declined the invitation (Mac Néill, 1925).

3.3 Evidence

The Commission's secretariat was located in the former Sinn Féin bank at 6 Harcourt Street in Dublin, a building that would subsequently be occupied by Conradh na Gaeilge from 1966 (New Departures Media, 2021). It held fourteen public meetings in Harcourt Street from April to July 1925 and heard evidence from thirty-seven witnesses. A further ten meetings were held in the Gaeltacht from August to October and evidence gathered from sixty-three witnesses. Groups of commissioners visited Counties Donegal, Mayo, Galway, Clare, Kerry, Cork and Waterford. Two commissioners went to Omeath in Co. Louth, where there were still some native speakers, but unfortunately, no record of their visit remains (Gaeltacht Commission, 1926: 4–5). The surrounding area, Oriel (Oirialla), had been a stronghold of Irish in east Ulster and possessed a rich cultural tradition that persists to the present day (Ní Uallacháin, 2003) but Irish had retreated as a spoken language there by the early twentieth century. Omeath was not included in the Gaeltacht by the Commission but an electoral division in that area was added to a schedule of the Housing (Gaeltacht) Act, 1929 (Ní Bhrádaigh et al., 2007).

Witnesses consisted mostly of middle-class men who worked for the new state or occupied other positions of authority. These included customs officials and inspectors, army officers, tuberculosis officers, senior civil servants (e.g. the chairpersons of Clare County Council and the Land Commission), educators (teachers, teachers' unions, university lecturers, professors), doctors and priests (many of whom were in educational roles).

Business people such as merchants, factory and co-operative managers and representatives of chambers of commerce were also present. Those loyal to the Revival were invited to give evidence, including members of the business committee of Conradh na Gaeilge and renowned folklore collectors such as Seán Bán Mac Meanman[11] (Baile na Finne), Pádraig Mac Seáin[12] (Teileann) and Fionán Mac Coluim[13] (from Antrim but who worked in Munster). The Secretary of the Department of Justice, Éinrí Ó Frighil was questioned at one of the Dublin meetings.[14] Some Gaeltacht fishermen and farmers were consulted but the Commission chose to speak to representative bodies for the most part. Twenty-eight written submissions were received from the public, including a judge, a senator, teachers, priests and language activists (ibid.: 72). All of the commissioners were men and of a total of 100 witnesses, only one woman gave evidence at the public meetings, Máire Ní Mhainín, a primary school teacher from Baile an Fheirtéaraigh, Co. Kerry (Gaeltacht Commission, 1926: 71). Other women may have attended the meetings as members of the public and it is most likely that women working in the civil service were given the responsibility of keeping notes and typing the report, but the written record relating to the Commission is almost exclusively male.

The extent of the challenge facing the new state in relation to Irish was thrown into stark relief by a passing comment on the taking of evidence in the introduction:

> Difficulty was experienced in having oral evidence in Irish taken verbatim, and it was only found practicable to have an English rendering of such recorded in shorthand; accordingly, in respect of oral evidence given in Irish, the English renderings, only, are presented. (Ibid.: 5)

Given the low levels of literacy in Irish at the time and the fact that only four years had passed since the state made Irish a core school subject, it was unsurprising that there would be practical difficulties with this aspect

---

11 See Breathnach and Ní Mhurchú, 2021b.
12 See Breathnach and Ní Mhurchú, 2021c.
13 See Breathnach and Ní Mhurchú, 2021a.
14 Ó Frighil also penned *Handbook of Irish Terms for the Use of Public Bodies* (1921).

of the work. Where evidence given in Irish is translated, this is indicated
in the report. Several of the written submissions were in Irish but with
the exception of the translation of Cosgrave's letter to Mulcahy wishing
the Commission well in its work (ibid.: 2), there is very little Irish in the
Commission's report. Spelling of Irish text in the report is inconsistent
and contains many errors, reflecting the absence of widespread literacy
or standardisation at the time. Extracts below have been left unamended
unless correction was necessary for the sake of clarity. The minutes of
evidence comprise notes taken at the public meetings and written submissions received. They provide information about the extent of the
Gaeltacht, its economy, education, administration and the Irish language
itself.

3.3.1 Extent

The evidence contains many references to the extent of the Gaeltacht at
the time. This data is by its nature impressionistic and subjective but provides a valuable insight into the views of witnesses on the vitality of Irish
in various districts. A teacher from west Clare, much of which would be
designated Breac-Ghaeltacht, described the decline of Irish in that area:

> It is seldom spoken except by the old people, and is decaying rapidly ... The English
> spoken is incorrect, being mainly acquired through what was taught to the children
> and attempted translation of their own Irish constructions ... While the old people
> are well able to converse in Irish, they generally speak broken English ... All the old
> fishermen speak Irish freely and have the old stories, place names, historical references
> and all that, but they use broken English too in all the sea-coast districts.

> Micheál Ruadh Ó Catháin, teacher, An Corrbhaile, Kilkee, Co Clare, 3rd of June
> 1925.[15]

West Clare was also mentioned in a statement from the Christian Brothers
in Dublin, which began by commenting on the extent of Irish in west Kerry:

---

15   All extracts in this section are from an appendix to the main report containing
      minutes of evidence, compiled by the James Hardiman Library, NUI Galway
      (Gaeltacht Commission, 1925). The format of the minutes varies from one library
      to another.

Ó Dhaingean Uí Chúise siar tá fíor Ghaeltacht fós. Ó dheas go Cathair Shaidhbhín ta Breac-Ghaeltacht – tá an Béarla brúighte isteach. Gaoluinn a labhraid ó aois a dathad amach sa cheanntar so. Is fearr atá an Béurla ná an Ghaoluinn ag an aos óg. Ó Lios Póil siar ta an scéul céadna le h-innsint. Breac-Ghaeltacht atá ó Thrá Lí siar go Lios Póil, as san siar tá an Ghaoluinn na steille bheathaidh, ach amháin in Daingean Uí Chúise féin. An Béarla atá in uachtar sa bhaile seo, cé go dtuigid go léir an Ghaoluinn, níl an t-aos óg ábalta ar í a labhairt. Fan a chósta ó Ceann Léime suas amach go Sligeach sí an Ghaoluinn gnáth theanga na ndaoine. Tá áiteanna gur treise í ná a chéile. In iarthar na Gaillimhe tá bailte agus gan aon tuisgint ag na daoine ar an mBéarla. Ins na ceanntair timpall ar na bailtí seo leanas tá an Ghaoluinn ar a bonnaibh fós: Lios Dún Bheárna, Baile Beacháin, Inis Díomáin, Cill Fionnóra, an Currach Fionn. Breac-Ghaeltacht do b'fhearr thabhairt ar na ceanntair seo thuas is dócha. Ach tá Breac-Ghaeltacht dá dhéanamh de'n nGaeltacht go tapaidh agus is le bás na sean-ghlún agus na mean-ghlún sa Bhreac-Ghaeltacht tá an Béarla ag dul i neart agus i neart go dtí sa deire ná beidh ann ach Galltacht.[16]

Statement from the Christian Brothers, Dublin, 9th of June 1925.

A primary school teacher from Acaill in Co. Mayo gave an account of the mixed linguistic nature of the island, noting that Irish was spoken in the most remote areas:

Curraun, Derreens, Saula – Irish-speaking, because of the remoteness from public highway traversed by foreigners who sneered at Irish.

16 From Dingle west it is still Fíor-Ghaeltacht. To Cahersiveen in the south is Breac-Ghaeltacht – English has pushed in. They speak Irish from age 40 up in this area. Young people speak English better than Irish. West from Lispole is the same story. There is a Breac-Ghaeltacht from Tralee west to Lispole, from there westwards Irish is alive and well, except in Dingle itself. English is dominant in this town, although they all understand Irish, the young people are unable to speak it. Along the coast from Loop Head up to Sligo, Irish is the language of the people. There are places where it is stronger than others. In west Galway there are villages where people do not understand English. In the areas around these towns, Irish still has a presence: Lisdoonvarna, Ballyvaughan, Ennistymon, Kilfenora, Corrafin. We believe it would be better to call this area Breac-Ghaeltacht. But the Gaeltacht is being turned into Breac-Ghaeltacht quickly and with the death of old and middle-aged generations in the Breac-Ghaeltacht, English is getting stronger and stronger until in the end there will be only Galltacht.

Achillbeg, Dooega, Bullsmouth – partly Irish-speaking though quite as remote from the public highway, but foreign influence operated from British coastguard stations situated in each of these districts.

Bunnacurry, Binnacurry, Touragee – partly Irish-speaking, skirting public highway.

The Valley – English. Proximity to Nangle and his English-speaking entourage, and being the seat of Lord Cavan and succeeding landlords.

Crumpaun, Dooagh, Dukinella – English-speaking. (1) Coastguards at Keel; (2) migration to Scotland much easier than the people of Upper Achill; (3) landlords; (4) tourists wanted only English-speaking guides.

Francis Moran, primary teacher, Sáile, Acaill, Co. Mayo, 21st of September 1925.

3.3.2 Economy

Another salient theme identified in the evidence is the poverty affecting the Gaeltacht in the 1920s. The dire state of the Gaeltacht economy and subsequent congestion and emigration were considered its most serious challenges, as recognised by the Commission itself in its introduction:

> Without effectively dealing with the very congested Irish Speaking populations, all hope of relieving the congestion in those areas will have vanished, and no future can be open to the traditional Irish Speakers affected but one of continued poverty and degradation in his native surroundings, involving dependence on American money, old age pensions, migratory labour in Britain or elsewhere, and Government relief; or emigration, with the consequent loss to the living language position. (Gaeltacht Commission, 1926: 45)

A submission from the Christian Brothers emphasised the pull factor of emigration because of the absence of economic choices at home:

> Meirice Mecca na Gaeltachta. Níl sa bhaile ach an dealús agus an t-ocras. Caithfidh siad dul lasmuigh chun an greim a chur ina mbéal. Ní haon mhaith dóibh a gcuid Gaolainne. Thar lear atá an uaisleacht agus an saibhreas – thall atá an t-ór le bailiú ar na sráideanna.[17]

> Statement from the Christian Brothers, Dublin, 9th of June 1925.

---

17   America is the Mecca of the Gaeltacht. There is only misery and hunger at home. They have to leave to put food in their mouths. Irish is no good to them. Nobility and wealth is abroad – there is gold to be gathered on the streets over there.

A co-operative manager spoke of the disadvantage faced by Irish speakers when seeking work:

> Cé a thógfadh ar aithreacha agus ar mháithreacha Béarla a labhairt lena bpáistí anois má b'fhéidir agus a gcúl a thabhairt don nGaolainn. Chonaic a bhformhór acu cad a bhain dóibh féin de dheasca na Gaolainne. Gach post i mbun aon dealramh a bhíodh ag imeacht, ba leis an mBéarlóir blasta a thitfeadh sé ... Táthar ag toghadh Béalóirí, fé láthair, os cionn Gaeilgeoirí atá comhoiriúnach le haghaidh postanna poiblí agus lánchead an rialtais leis an obair sin.[18]

> Liam Ó Míodhacháin, co-operative manager, An Rinn, Co. Waterford, 9th of October 1925.

However, a priest in west Clare believed that such was the advance of English in the Gaeltacht, developing its economy would have no positive impact on Irish:

> I do not believe that an improvement in the economic and social condition of these people will of itself make them a bit prouder of their language or stimulate them to speak it more freely. The trend, I think, would be all the other way ... It is hopeless, I think, to try and dam round any exclusively Irish-speaking district so as to effectually beat back the oncoming tide of English. I think circumstances geographical and commercial make that impossible. The corrosion of the Gaeltacht is bound to go on, every inch of it is bound in course of time to become bilingual.

> Canon Denis O'Dea, parish priest, Cora Chaitlín, Co. Clare, 26th of September 1925.

3.3.3 Education

Just a few short years after Irish had been made a core subject in the schools, teachers were carrying the bulk of the burden of the language policy (see Chapter 3). One teacher from Kerry reported that parents

---

18 Who would blame fathers and mothers for speaking English with their children now if they can and give up Irish? Most of them saw what happened to themselves because of Irish. Every decent post that was available, it would go to the fluent English-speaker ... English speakers are being chosen at the moment over Irish speakers who are equally suitable for public posts and the government is giving its full permission for that.

were complaining about the new policy of part-immersion, where the junior classes were taught entirely in Irish:

> Daoine go leor ag gearán ar neamh-oireamhnaighe an Chláir Oibre ins na sgoileanna. Gaedhilg ar fad i gcomhair na naoidhneán an locht is mó gheibhtear air ... Na daoine is mó bhíonn an lochtú an Chláir na daoine go bhfuil a súile ar an nDomhan Thiar aca.[19]
>
> Micheál Ó Conchubhair, teacher, Lios Póil, Co. Kerry, 1st of October 1925.

A priest from the Aran Islands in Co. Galway complained that the curriculum was not suitable for native speakers and complained that there was not enough emphasis on national identity:

> Chidhtear dam-sa nach gcuidigheann an cúrsa oideachais atá 'sna Bunsgoileannaibh leis an gcainnteóir dúthchasach chum muinghin as féin do chothughadh ... Níl spiorad na náisiúntachta 'san gcúrsa oideachais atá 'sna bun-sgoileannaibh. Ní leór leabhra Gaedhilge muna gcothuightear spioraid fhíor-Ghaedhealach.[20]
>
> Fr. M. Ó Domhnaill, Cill Rónáin, Árainn, Co. Galway, 20th of May 1925.

In an articulation of the dominant ethnolinguistic ideology of the time, the Commission romanticised the native speaker of Irish and emphasised the importance of the unbroken link with the historical language. It recommended that instruction about the richness of Irish language culture be incorporated into vocational education in the Gaeltacht:

> The Commission realises that in the memories, stories, folklore, songs and traditions of the Gaeltacht there is preserved an uninterrupted Gaelic culture which constitutes the very soul of the Irish language. The Native Irish Speaker has a command of the beauties of language which is inculcated amongst English speakers only by the laboured teaching of the classics. There is no parallel in English for this refined popular

---

19 Many people are complaining about the inappropriateness of the Work Programme in the schools. Irish only for the junior classes is the greatest cause of complaint ... The people who criticise the Programme the most are those who wish to go to America.

20 I believe that the educational course in the primary schools does not help the native speaker to have confidence in himself ... The educational course of the primary schools does not contain a spirit of nationality. Books in Irish are not enough if a fully Irish spirit is not encouraged.

culture, which is the highly wrought product of generations of Gaelic civilisation. This popular culture is in grave danger of being lost, and the Commission feels that the revival of the language, without the preservation of this culture, would rob Ireland of one of its richest and most dignified inheritances. A proper utilisation of this material, especially in connection with vocational training would, the Commission believes, serve to raise the whole mental and economic standard of the Gaeltacht to a level that could not otherwise be achieved. (Gaeltacht Commission, 1926: 24)

3.3.4 Administration

The report is replete with complaints about public administration and the inability of officials to deal in Irish with the people of the Gaeltacht, where some people had little or no competence in English (see Chapter 4). This example from Donegal points to the practical difficulties encountered by monolingual English-speaking officials in strongly Irish-speaking districts:

The Pension Officer, otherwise unobjectionable, neither understands nor speaks Irish. His clients are perpetually complaining that he misinterprets their 'broken' English with damaging results. Frequently the statistics he gathers from such people are ludicrous in the extreme ... Within my own experience there came five of these pensions officers within seven months, and not one of them knew Irish.

Canon E. Maguire, parish priest, An Charraig, Co. Donegal, 17th of August 1925.

The following teacher from Acaill provided a list of local public officials on the island, giving a mixed picture of their ability to speak Irish:

1. An sagart paráisde – togha Gaedhilgeóra. Is annamh a chloistear focal Gaedhilge uaidh ó'n Altóir amhthach.

2. Na seiplíneacha – Gaedhilg ag duine aca agus is Gaedheal é. Níl Gaedhilg ag an mbeirt eile.

3. An Dochtúir – gan Gaedhilg.

4. An Banaltra – gan Gaedhilg.

5. An Giustis – Tá Gaedhilge aige agus oibrigheann [labhraíonn] sé í amannta.

6. Cléireach na Cúirte – Tá Gaedhilge aige.

7. Na Gárdaí Síothchána – Tá Gaedhilg ag an Searsint.

8. Oifigeach Cáin agus Custaim – Níl aon Gaedhilg aige. Sasannach iseadh é.

9. Oifig an Posta – Tá Gaedhilg ag an Post Máistir agus ag na fearaibh posta.

10. Oifigeach na mBocht – Tá Gaedhilge aige. Dá mbeadh sé de mhisneach aca seo uilig an teanga do labhairt leis na daoinibh dhéanfadh sé maitheas do'n teanga. Bheidís na eisiomplar do na comharsannaibh.[21]

Aodh de Paor, teacher, Acaill, Co. Mayo, 21st of September 1925.

3.3.5 Ideology

The report revealed the complex ideological currents about Irish that were circulating in the Gaeltacht and in society generally at the time. On the one hand, there was the ideology of the Commission itself, many of whose members were formed in the context of Irish-Ireland in the final decades of the nineteenth century and had learned Irish through Conradh na Gaeilge and by visiting the Gaeltacht. The following statement from a Co. Waterford priest is a good example:

It should be shown that as long as we are confined to English as our sole vernacular, we can have no hope of ever building up a healthy, virile Irish nation. England will remain our intellectual and cultural centre, and we shall be simply the backwash of English civilisation. Our tastes, ideas and outlook on life will inevitably be fashioned in England. Without some spiritual bond and visible symbol of national solidarity, such as a common Irish language would afford, it is difficult to conceive, with our

---

21 The parish priest – an excellent Irish speaker. However, he rarely speaks Irish from the altar.
The chaplains – one of them speaks Irish and he is committed to Irish. The other two do not speak Irish.
The Doctor – no Irish.
The Nurse – no Irish.
The Judge – he speaks Irish and sometimes uses it.
The Court Clerk – he speaks Irish.
The Gardaí – the sergeant speaks Irish.
Tax and Customs Oficer – he speaks no Irish. He is English.
The Post Office – the Postmaster and postmen speak Irish.
Poor Officer – he speaks Irish. If they all had the confidence to speak Irish with the people it would be a benefit for the language. They would be examples to the neighbours.

proximity and inevitable close intercourse with England, how we can develop a consciousness of real independent nationality. We can never rise to a true realisation of common ideals and mutual interests ... We need not pretend that the mere re-introduction of Irish would of itself settle all these difficulties. But it would put it in our power to deal with them ourselves. It would give us a sense of power and responsibility which would certainly make us more active and practically interested in them and give us just ground for hope that our exertions may not be altogether in vain.

Fr. Kelleher, St John's College, Waterford, 9th of September 1925.

On the other hand, there was evidence that many Gaeltacht people had disdain for Irish and wanted to give it up or ensure that their children did not speak it:

I think they feel ashamed of it. I heard girls from the fíor-Gaeltacht trying to pretend that they knew very little Irish, but the English was so bad that anyone would know that they spoke some other language ... the breac-Gaeltacht is the most unpatriotic part of the country as far as the language is concerned. The old people have the Irish and they don't want their children to learn it ... I am afraid it is the traditional system that has come down since the time the Irish language was persecuted. It is a sort of unconscious memory with them.

Fr. Tadhg Ó Cúrnáin, An Dromaid, Co. Kerry, 7th of July 1925.

Dr Bartley O'Beirne, the tuberculous officer in Galway, said: 'They look on it more or less as the badge of slaves' (evidence of 3rd of June, 1925). A folklore collector from Co. Donegal spoke of how his own community had no respect for Irish and associated it with poverty:

Níl uathu ach a gclann a fháil faoi lámh Easpaig agus oiread eolais a fháil ar léitheoireacht agus ar scríbhneoireacht agus go mbeidh siad in inmhe litir a léamh agus a scríobh. Tchítear don mhórchuid acu sa Ghaeltacht nach bhfuil ann ach am amú a bheith ag teagasc Gaeilge dá gclann mar nach ngnóthaíonn siad dadaí uirthi agus gur comhartha bochtaineachta agus ainbheasa í.[22]

---

22   They just want to get their children confirmed and obtain enough knowledge of reading and writing so that they would be able to read and write a letter. Many of them in the Gaeltacht believe that teaching Irish to their children is just a waste of time because they earn nothing from it and because it is a sign of poverty and ignorance.

Pádraig Mac Seáin, Teileann, Co. Donegal, 2nd of July 1925.

3.4 Findings and Recommendations

Of eighty-two recommendations, twenty-seven related to education, twenty-five to economic conditions, twenty-four to administration, four to general matters and two to the extent of the Gaeltacht.

3.4.1 Extent

The first matter dealt with by the Commission, as requested by the government, was the extent of the Gaeltacht and the strength of Irish in specific areas. It found that Irish was still spoken in twelve of the twenty-six counties, but that it had ceased to be a community language in most of them. As well as large Irish-speaking areas in Counties Donegal, Mayo, Galway, Kerry, Cork and Waterford, it identified smaller Gaeltacht pockets in south Kilkenny, south Tipperary, southwest Cork, east Cork, west Clare and small parts of Sligo, Cavan and Limerick. The Commission stated that it was necessary to distinguish between parts of the Gaeltacht where Irish 'may or should be restored at once in matters of education, administration and for general purposes, to the position that, for example, the French language occupies in fact in France, and the English language in Ireland' and areas where it should be restored to such a position by a more gradual process (Gaeltacht Commission, 1926: 6). It sub-divided the territory into Fíor-Ghaeltacht, where 80 per cent or more of the population was Irish speaking, and Breac-Ghaeltacht, where between 25 and 79 per cent was Irish speaking (see Chapter 1). The 80 per cent threshold was justified on the basis that it represented a fairly small area where efforts could be concentrated and where changes could be effected reasonably quickly 'without inflicting appreciable inconvenience on any section of the people' (ibid.: 7). There was no clear rationale for the 25 per cent limit other than a claim that a lower percentage would require detailed local investigation (ibid.).

There were occasional inconsistencies between the tables based on the special enumeration and the coloured maps, with areas containing less than 80 per cent sometimes returned as Fíor-Ghaeltacht. The Commission noted that it sometimes deviated from the 80 per cent rule in the case of towns adding, somewhat optimistically: 'Towns and villages are weak spots for the Irish language, but their presence must not be allowed to hinder the application of measures deemed to be necessary for the preservation and development of the Gaeltacht' (ibid.: 7). Based on previous census data, the special enumeration and the data gathered during its work, it identified areas of Donegal, Mayo, Galway, Clare, Kerry, Cork and Waterford as either Fíor-Ghaeltacht or Breac-Ghaeltacht, with small extensions into Sligo and Tipperary. It found that there were 146,821 Irish speakers in the Fíor-Ghaeltacht, representing just over 89 per cent of the population there, and 110,585 speakers in the Breac-Ghaeltacht, or 37.5 per cent. Notwithstanding an increase in the percentage of Irish speakers in the Fíor-Ghaeltacht be-tween 1911 and 1925, it warned that the Irish-speaking population was in a rapid state of decline, recording a fall of 31.5 per cent during that time in the seven counties surveyed, or 22.5 per cent each decade (ibid.: 10). The Commission concluded that there was now no area where English was not spoken to some extent and that many of the younger speakers returned in the 1925 enumeration were a product of the new language-in-education policy rather than community or family transmission:

> In prestige, the position of the language in the Gaeltacht is low. The influence of a hostile Government was thrown against it in the past; it was denied as a vehicle of education; it was ignored and repressed in administration. Generally, public repre-sentatives, businessmen, Church authorities, ignored it. The educated were ignorant of it; and they protected their position by affecting to despise it, or often despising it with conviction. Those who spoke it traditionally saw no avenue of advancement open to them or their children without English. Thus, it came to be accepted that the language was destined to pass. (Ibid.: 10)

The accuracy of the Commission's enumeration of the western counties has been questioned (see below). However, the evidence contains useful impressionistic information of the extent of the Gaeltacht from those mostly sympathetic to Irish.

3.4.2 Education

The twenty-seven recommendations on education covered primary
and secondary schools, teacher training and deployment, provision of
schoolbooks and meals and the development of technical and university education. The first set covered the language competence of primary school teachers, many of whom were thought to be unable to teach
through Irish in the Gaeltacht. The Commission urged that fluency in
Irish be considered an essential qualification for such a role and recom
mended that unqualified teachers be removed from their posts if they
could not gain fluency within three to five years, depending on the district. It suggested the provision of special local courses, outside school
hours, aimed at such teachers. This proved the most controversial of its
proposals when commented on by government (see below). The numbers of qualified teachers exiting training colleges should be increased
and faster pathways into training and towards qualification provided
for Gaeltacht pupils aged 16 and over with fluency in Irish. For instance,
the Commission suggested that pupils in the new preparatory colleges
who already possessed an Intermediate Certificate have their period of
training shortened from four to two years in order to boost supply.

It also recommended salary bonuses of between 5 and 10 per cent for
teachers deemed 'efficient' or 'highly efficient' in Gaeltacht schools teaching
entirely through Irish and that separate educational inspectorates be established for the Gaeltacht. Schoolbooks should be provided in Irish and
sold at cost price to Gaeltacht families. The state must ensure an adequate
provision of schools and equipment. In areas of dire poverty, the exchequer
should provide the entire initial cost where local rates or parish contributions could not be expected to do so. The Commission also recommended
the provision of a free school meal each day. It suggested the establishment
of free day secondary schools in the Fíor-Ghaeltacht and stronger areas
of the Breac-Ghaeltacht and the provision of scholarships to students of
such schools to allow them to attend universities or further education. It
recommended also that existing secondary schools be required to switch
to teaching through Irish if they were not already doing so ('A-schools';
see Chapter 3).

A scheme for rural continuation education (agriculture, manual instruction, poultry keeping, dairying, domestic economy, etc.) should be set up as well as training colleges in such subjects, operating in Irish. It was also recommended that a parallel commission on technical education be asked to investigate possibilities related to the Gaeltacht and that a quarter of places in all training courses for technical instructors be reserved for fluent Irish speakers. The Commission recommended the development of Irish-medium education at university level, in particular University College Galway (ibid.: 11–27; see also Chapter 3).

3.4.3 Economy

The most far-reaching of the recommendations to economic policy related to the redistribution of land and the migration of Irish speakers from the Gaeltacht to better holdings elsewhere. The Commission summarised its main proposal as follows:

> That all grass lands of the Western counties be broken up; that in the resettlement of these lands, especially in the Gaeltacht, none but Irish Speaking families be resettled; that English Speaking families with claims to lands have their claims satisfied outside the Gaeltacht. (ibid.: 63)

With regard to migration, the Commission focused its attention on the severely congested areas of west Donegal, west Mayo and Connemara and recommended the migration of Irish speakers 'in suitable and large homogenous groups, to available lands elsewhere' (ibid.: 45) and their resettlement in economic holdings. It also recommended research on the remainder of the Gaeltacht population to establish the extent to which resettlement might be required or another local solution found through fishing or industry, for example.

Another major proposal related to the dire state of Gaeltacht housing stock, the Commission recommending that loans and grants be provided for improvements. Grants to improve livestock should similarly be made available and veterinary dispensaries established. Other suggestions included grants for land reclamation and drainage, improved seed distribution, the establishment of a state tree nursery and an afforestation scheme.

The Commission also made a number of proposals about fishing, reflecting its importance for the Gaeltacht economy, including the establishment of fishery technical schools with modern boats provided by the state and the provision of up-to-date fishing methods. State loans for large boats and fishing equipment should also be provided. The Commission recommended establishing a state brand for mackerel, investing in kelp production and improving small piers. It suggested better organisation of the homespun industry with additional grants and marketing and the establishment of an employment bureau aimed at securing work for the Gaeltacht population (ibid.: 36–55).

3.4.4 Administration

Of the proposals related to Irish in administration, the recommendation that non-Irish-speaking officials be replaced by Irish speakers was the most contentious (see below). Such officials should include Gardaí, post office workers, Land Commission representatives, pension officers and staff of the Department of Agriculture. Sub-postmasters and their officials would be required to know Irish, or to acquire knowledge of it, and Irish-speaking Gardaí should be transferred to the Gaeltacht as soon as possible. All Gardaí based in or transferred to the Gaeltacht should also benefit from salary bonuses of between 5 and 10 per cent, depending on rank, and three-quarters of all vacancies in the force should be reserved for Irish speakers. Other recommendations were that Irish-speaking officials in the Gaeltacht be required as a matter of discipline to use Irish in the course of their work and that communication between such officials and their headquarters be in Irish. The Commission recommended paying a bonus of 10 per cent to all officials in the Gaeltacht who were capable of doing business in Irish, and to those transferred to such areas because of their competence in Irish. Recommendations related to the legal system included that district courts in the Gaeltacht use Irish as their working language and that all court documentation be issued in Irish. No witness should be obliged to give evidence in English in district, circuit or higher courts and district justices or other officials should not be appointed to Gaeltacht courts without full competence in Irish.

The Commission also recommended that a quarter of clerical vacancies in the civil service be reserved for native speakers and that all civil service examinations be set in both Irish and English, with a quota of vacancies reserved for those answering the paper in Irish. It also proposed a requirement for all civil servants under 26 years of age (i.e. those born since 1900) to have competence in Irish in order to be eligible for promotion. One brigade of the army should use Irish as a working language and be reserved for Irish speakers, Irish should be a requirement for promotion for all officers under twenty-six years, and a third of future vacancies should be reserved for applicants answering the examination paper in Irish. The Commission also recommended that all permanent posts in local government in the Gaeltacht require competence in Irish and that all clerical appointments in the Gaeltacht counties would have the same requirement with all written notices issued in Irish only (ibid.: 27–36).

3.4.5 Other recommendations

Of the remaining general proposals, three were vague exhortations about the need to influence sectors of society beyond the state's immediate sphere of influence: the Catholic Church, the legal, medical and engineering professions and the private sector including the banks and the newspapers (ibid.: 56). The newly founded radio service was not mentioned despite its significance for language policy, an influence that was underestimated in the early years of wireless broadcasting (see Chapter 5). The fourth recommendation was more significant as it related to how the myriad proposals, many of them contentious and far-reaching, would be implemented, the institutional arrangements for what would today be called language policy or governance (Williams, 2007; see Introduction). The Commission noted that many witnesses had urged that either a special Ministry to deal with the Gaeltacht or a dedicated agency similar to the Congested Districts Board be set up but it did not endorse either option, claiming that such a special administrative authority would create 'difficulties', without spelling out what these may be. It did, however, recommend the establishment of a special commission, answerable to the Department of the President, to communicate with various government departments and oversee the implementation of the recommendations. It would have a full-time commissioner and staff and produce an annual report but its functions were to be advisory only. This, the Commission said, would go some way towards filling the gap left by the disbandment of the Congested Districts Board a few years previously (ibid.: 56–57; Breathnach, 2005: 173).

A dissenting statement by Fr Seaghan Mac Cuinnigeáin from Co. Donegal is attached to the main report. While supporting most of the recommendations, he did not endorse those related to migration and the special commission itself. On migration, Fr Mac Cuinnigeáin claimed that the idea would not be accepted in the Gaeltacht and that the cost would be exorbitant. While not opposing resettlement of individuals, he warned that 'there should be no general effort to transfer any large percentage of the inhabitants of the Gaedhealtacht, either as self-contained colonies, or as scattered units to districts, totally different from their own. I am convinced, this would mean so many Irish speakers ultimately lost to the Gaedhealtacht' (ibid.: 66). With regard to the future governance of Irish, Fr Mac Cuinnigeáin suggested a more robust model than that advanced by his fellow commissioners. He made far-sighted recommendations, suggesting a permanent board or commission to ensure implementation of the report, along the lines of the Congested Districts Board, but with a specific linguistic remit in addition to economic responsibilities. The members would be nominated by the President and represent various Gaeltacht areas, with a remunerated chairman based in Dublin with the support of staff. The commission 'should have an active and directive voice' (ibid.: 67) in relation to all government departments operating in the Gaeltacht, who would have to first submit their proposals to the commission for approval. It should also have 'full powers to develop the industrial life of the Gaedhealtacht in every respect, by setting up new industries, reviving, fostering and extending existing industries, opening up markets at home and abroad for the sale of Gaedhealtacht products, securing suitable transit facilities, etc.' (ibid.: 67). Fr Mac Cuinnigeáin said the commission:

> must be given a free and unfettered hand to spend, in the development of industries in the Gaedhealtacht, the monies and funds placed at its disposal by the Dáil … The funds of the late Congested Districts Board originally voted by the English

Parliament to solve the economic problem of the Congested Districts, should now be made available for a similar purpose in the Gaedhealtacht which is practically coterminous with the original Congested Districts and can surely lay claim, with all justice, to these funds as its own. (Ibid.)

In a separate addendum, Lawrence Moriarty, Secretary General of the Department of Fisheries, echoed Fr Mac Cuinnigeáin's concerns about the proposed advisory nature of the special commission, warning that it may become 'powerless' without a budget of its own. He recommended that the proposed commission be given an annual grant-in-aid of £100,000 for expenditure on the industrial development of the Gaeltacht, involving recoupment or repayment to the Land Commission, the Office of Public Works and the Department of Fisheries itself (ibid.: 68). The future role of the Department of Fisheries in Gaeltacht development is discussed below.

3.5 Public response

Several public meetings were held in the Gaeltacht in response to the Commission's report and community groups and branches of Conradh na Gaeilge around the country called for its recommendations to be implemented. A meeting in Donegal passed a resolution calling on the government 'to terminate their actual policy of neglect, and their oft-repeated promises of goodwill and support for the Gaeltacht. We are sick of these promises.' The resolution – copies of which were sent to President Cosgrave, Donegal TDs and the press – called for full implementation of the recommendations because of poverty, unemployment and the lack of industrialisation (MacNelis, 1926).

A special Christmas 1926 supplement of the Irish language newspaper *Fáinne an Lae* provides an interesting insight into reactions within the Irish language movement in Dublin to the Commission's report. *Fáinne an Lae* was by necessity bilingual as its readers spanned a wide spectrum of competence in Irish and it played an important propaganda role for the Revival among the broader population (Uí Chollatáin, 2004). With that audience in mind, the supplement is mostly in English and published an analysis of the report as well as detailed reports on the 'monster meetings in Dublin' held in the Mansion House in November (*Fáinne an Lae*, 1926: 7). A headline to the supplement urges the Executive Council to 'give full effect to the recommendations of the Gaeltacht Commission immediately' (ibid.: 7). It was reported that the event was broadcast by the nascent 2RN radio station and was held mostly in English, although some contributions were in Irish. The first speaker was co-founder of Conradh na Gaeilge, Douglas Hyde, who said that he would reluctantly speak English so that any non-Irish speakers ('Gaill'[23]) could understand what was being said. Hyde dismissed concerns about the financial implications of the report and said that any money spent on the Gaeltacht would not be wasted. Leader of the newly founded Fianna Fáil, Éamon de Valera presented a motion stating that it was 'a most urgent duty of the nation to foster and preserve the Gaeltacht, the true and only fountain-head of the tradition necessary for the resuscitation of the national language' (ibid.: 8), which was duly passed unanimously. Other leading figures to address the meeting included president of Conradh na Gaeilge, Cormac Breathnach, minister for Posts and Telegraphs J. J. Walsh, Leas-Cheann Comhairle (deputy speaker) of the Dáil Pádraic Ó Máille and Senator P. W. Kenny, chair of the General Council of County Councils. The supplement also includes the 'views of prominent Gaels' on the report and a resolution by Donegal County Council urging its full implementation (ibid.: 11, 17).

The 'Save the Gaedhealtacht' campaign held meetings across Donegal in 1927 and letters were sent from committees throughout the Gaeltacht. Resolutions were passed by the Irish language college in An Daingean and by a public meeting organised by the Irish language religious group, An Timire, in Tralee. Students attending Irish classes in Ballyhaunis, Co. Mayo, also called for the report to be implemented and a resolution was passed by the Civil Service Clerical Association. There were similar calls from branches of Conradh na Gaeilge in Cavan, Carlow, Mayo and Dublin and from the organisation's executive committee (for details, see NAI S7439). A public meeting in Galway in 1927 heard the Minister for Agriculture,

23   *Gall*, pl. *Gaill* also refers to 'foreigner'.

Patrick Hogan[24] describe the dire economic conditions in Connemara, west Mayo, west Donegal and part of Kerry as 'a blot on the country' that 'ought to be regarded as a national problem … It is a real and terrible problem' (*The Connacht Tribune*, 1927). The meeting was attended by public representatives and figures from Counties Galway, Mayo, Donegal, Clare and Kerry.

3.6 Government response

The government's response to the Commission's report was formulated over several months in 1926 and 1927 and illustrates at best caution about the proposals and at worst hostility to them.

3.6.1 Context

Before turning to the responses of individual departments, it is necessary to consider the broader context of governance of the new state and the role of Irish in it. Although the cabinet contained key advocates for Irish and senior civil servants counted some Irish speakers in their ranks, the hold of the dominant economic ideology over government restrained the extent to which the declared language policy could be carried out. Cosgrave was positive about Irish, had studied it as an adult and even sent his children to a Gaeltacht school for a period but had little ability in the language himself. If asked a question in Irish in the Dáil, another member of Cumann na nGaedheal would answer it in his place (Laffan, 2014: 184). Laffan believes that his tokenistic use of Irish was limited to his role as head of government and that he had mixed views about the core status of Irish in the education system. Another matter of concern was the potential negative impact of the language policy on reunification:

> The policy of Gaelicisation came into conflict with another of Cosgrave's objectives: the integration of southern unionists into the Free State … He was instinctively

---

24 This Patrick Hogan was a Cumann na nGaedheal/Fine Gael TD from east Galway and not the same person as the Pádraig Ó hÓgáin from Co. Clare who sat on the Commission. See Breathnach, Ciara, 2005: 172 and House of the Oireachtas, 2021.

> inclined towards reconciliation, and as soon as he achieved power he wanted the support of every possible group and individual. But such attitudes made it easier for republicans to brand Cumann na nGaedheal as 'West British'. (Ibid.: 185)

Of the Ministers formerly involved with Conradh na Gaeilge, Ernest Blythe was the most strongly committed to Irish and gave robust support to various initiatives, especially the publishing scheme An Gúm, which was also established in 1926. However, Blythe's dedication to the Revival caused tensions with senior officials in the Department of Finance, as outlined by long-serving civil servant León Ó Broin (Ó Tuathaigh, 2021: 11–13; see also Ó Broin, 1986). The Secretary of the Department from 1923, Joseph Brennan was from a comfortable background in Bandon, Co. Cork and had worked in Dublin Castle during British rule. Both he and his successor from 1927, J. J. McElligott, who was from Tralee in Co. Kerry (Lee, 1989: 74), were strict adherents to economic orthodoxy and committed to ruthless retrenchment for the new state. It has been claimed that their belief in fiscal rectitude led them to 'have an aversion to the working class in general' (ibid.: 108), a factor that must have weighed upon them when leafing through the recommendations of the Commission. The fact that both were from towns in the southwest located within, or adjacent to the Breac-Ghaeltacht may also have been a factor, as the middle class in such towns was less likely to have competence in, or affinity with Irish. Therefore, while Blythe, MacNeill and Mulcahy all played key roles in bringing the Commission into existence, Cosgrave's lack of engagement with Irish and the prevailing conservative economic philosophy at the heart of government were major restraining factors in developing a robust language policy.

The formidable Minister for Industry and Commerce (from 1927), Patrick McGilligan, was known for his harsh views on social policy, and his background as 'lawyer son of a comfortable Ulster businessman' (Lee, 1989: 127) has been noted. Infamously, he told a Dáil debate in 1924: 'People may have to die in this country and may have to die from starvation' (McGilligan, 1924, cited in Lee, 1989: 127). Lee argues that the cabinet's social policy was hostile to the poor, who were seen as authors of their own misfortune:

> The cabinet pursued a clear social as well as economic policy. It took the view that the poor were responsible for their poverty. They should pay for their lack of moral fibre. The existing distribution of income, and of opportunities, largely satisfied the demands of social justice. [Kevin] O'Higgins [Minister for Home Affairs, assassinated in 1927] had dismissed the part of the Democratic Programme dealing with natural resources as communism and the Proclamation of the Republic as poetry. The age of poetry was indeed dead. But there are many prose styles. Cosgrave's cabinet chose the iron style. The cabinet waged a coherent campaign against the weaker elements in the community. The poor, the aged, and the unemployed must all feel the lash of the liberators. (Ibid.: 124)

Such ideological currents did not augur well for comprehensive policy measures in support of the Gaeltacht. The influence of another civil servant, Gordon Campbell of the Department of Industry and Commerce, is discussed below.

3.6.2 Response of government departments

Following the publication of the Commission's report, Cosgrave's private secretary wrote to every member of the Executive Council, asking them to submit observations on it (Department of the President, 1926b). There were long delays in many responses and on 10th March 1927, the Seanad passed a motion calling on the Executive Council to introduce legislation to give effect to the report. Cosgrave's impatience was clear in a letter to the Department of Finance on the 21st of April: 'It is the President's wish that this matter be treated as one of extreme urgency' (Department of the President, 1927a).

When they came, departmental responses were lukewarm at best, and frequently rejected outright many of the Commission's proposals. Some departments, such as those of the President and External Affairs, claimed that the report had nothing to do with their work as they had little or no contact with the general public in Ireland (Department of the President, 1927d; Department of External Affairs, 1927). Lack of official terminology was advanced by Posts and Telegraphs and Finance as an excuse for not accepting proposals about official correspondence in Irish (Department of Posts and Telegraphs, 1926; Department of Finance, 1927a). Defence rejected the proposal for an Irish-speaking brigade in the Irish Army, but accepted recommendations that Irish be required by Army officers for promotional purposes and that one-third of vacancies be reserved for Irish speakers (Department of Defence, 1926).

Posts and Telegraphs was more positive than most, claiming that most of the recommendations regarding post offices were already in place. It described the Commission's report as 'a most admirable one the general principles of which should be adopted by the Executive Council as embodying a policy to be put into operation as circumstances admit'. This likely reflects the personal involvement of Minister J. J. Walsh and departmental secretary P. S. Ó hÉigeartaigh, both of whom were supportive of the Revival (Department of Posts and Telegraphs, 1926).

There was opposition, however, from several departments to proposals that Irish-speaking staff be redeployed to the Gaeltacht and non-Irish-speakers be transferred elsewhere. Posts and Telegraphs pointed out that use of these powers was normally a disciplinary matter and that policy should concentrate on new recruitment instead (Department of Posts and Telegraphs, 1926). Similarly, the Department of Fisheries raised the problem of '24 lady teachers and manageresses of Rural Industries centres in the Gaeltacht incapable of transacting their work in Irish. These must be gradually replaced by ladies so competent' (ibid.). The Department of Local Government and Public Health took fright at the recommendation to bring about the 'immediate disuse' of English by state officials and local authorities in the Fíor-Ghaeltacht, staying that the standard of local administration would deteriorate if business had to be conducted in Irish. It favoured some measures to strengthen bilingualism in the public service, however, supporting a language requirement for Irish for all officers employed by Galway Hospital and backing the proposal that Irish be required for all future permanent appointments to local authorities. Significantly, Local Government and Public Health supported the proposals for grants to improve the Gaeltacht's poor housing stock and to provide free school meals (Department of Local Government and Public Health, 1926). These were in fact among the proposals by the Commission that were clearly implemented by the enactment of the Housing (Gaeltacht) Act 1929 and the School Meals (Gaeltacht) Act 1930. The Housing Act remained on the statute books for decades and was an important financial support for Gaeltacht families.

In a similar vein, the Department of Justice opposed the transfer of Irish-speaking Gardaí to the Gaeltacht on the basis that there were not enough Irish speakers in the force to begin with. In fact, under article 6 (2) of the Garda Síochána Act 1924, Gardaí stationed in the Gaeltacht were supposed to be able to use it 'with facility' in the course of their duties but this was conditioned somewhat by the modifier 'so far as may be' and it was clear that the measure had not been successful. Justice argued that about 400 sergeants and ordinary Gardaí were stationed in the eighty or so stations serving the Gaeltacht but that the entire force contained only about 200 Irish-speaking members. It also claimed that if the 75 per cent quota of places for native speakers proposed by the Commission were adopted, the educational requirements would have to be significantly reduced or even abolished in order to fill the posts. Tellingly, it implied that the Gaeltacht was a dead end for talented members: 'Many men with a good working knowledge of Irish, now stationed in towns and cities which furnish opportunities for their abilities, would be to a considerable extent wasted as police officers if transferred to the Gaeltacht' (Department of Justice, 1927). Justice also opposed the proposal to give Gaeltacht-based Gardaí a pay bonus.

On the recommendation that District Courts in the Fíor-Ghaeltacht operate in Irish, Justice responded that the most that could be done was to provide Irish-speaking judges and clerks. It complained that while many Gaeltacht clerks could speak Irish well, most could not write it and were unfamiliar with legal terminology. It added that most clerks had kept their jobs because of competence in Irish, however incomplete, but that this had encouraged 'considerable sacrifice of efficiency with the result that the percentage of inefficient clerks in the Gaeltacht is higher than elsewhere'. In response to the recommendation that a District Court or other court official who is not capable of working in Irish would not be appointed in the Gaeltacht, Justice expressed concern about the lack of suitably qualified people to apply for such jobs (ibid.). Similarly, the Department of Agriculture and Technical Instruction feared that it would be challenging to find suitably qualified rates collectors who were also competent in Irish, referring to a recent competition where only one applicant out of forty-nine was so qualified. It also ruled out a land reclamation scheme in the Gaeltacht on the basis of expense (Department of Agriculture and Technical Instruction, 1927).

Some of the most strident opposition from government was to the dissenting opinion expressed by Fr Seán Mac Cuinneagáin from Donegal in favour of a permanent board or commission with executive powers that would ensure the implementation of the Commission's findings. It is clear that many departments, particularly Finance, did not want another execu tive body interfering with their work:

> The existing statutory framework of Government machinery provides for the admin-istration of all Government activities through the 11 Ministries. The operations of a Commission as suggested would cut right across that scheme. It would result in endless friction and do more harm than good ... In practice, Departments have to be trusted to carry out these regulations ... To set up another body to see that Departments are observing their Ministers' directions by carrying out the Government's policy in detail would hardly seem appropriate. It would look very like setting up a police force for the language. (Department of Finance, 1927a)

Unsurprisingly, Finance favoured the softer option proposed in the main body of the report, that a permanent advisory commission be established with no executive powers or budget. This should be attached to an ex-isting government department and Finance believed that the most appro-priate home would be Fisheries. Reflecting the influence of Finance on government, this was what transpired eventually and it reveals the extent to which the government viewed the Gaeltacht as essentially a regional development rather than a language problem. Finance opposed many other key proposals, describing bonuses for Irish-speaking staff as 'extra-ordinary' and 'bad psychologically', claiming that such a system would lead to 'mischievous results'. There was no need for bonuses because the position of Irish in the civil service was deemed to be improving rapidly. Senior officials of the department headed by Ernest Blythe were not con-vinced of the need for any preferential treatment for those civil servants proficient in Irish:

> It is difficult to see on what ground an officer in, say, a part of the west included in the Gaeltacht could claim a payment which would not be allowed to a brother official in an adjoining locality (outside the Gaeltacht) where the conditions affecting his service were little, if anything, different. Moreover, once the payment of bonuses were instituted, even with the intention of applying it to existing officials, it would be certain to create in the minds of all future officials in the Gaeltacht the feeling that they should get some preference in payment as compared with those elsewhere. (Ibid.)

Finance also opposed imposing a language condition on new civil service entrants under the age of 26. It claimed that the 'position cannot be far off when the force of circumstances in the service will operate even more effectively than a formal rule to induce existing officials to acquire a competent knowledge of the language ... The stage will be reached automatically by which promotion will only be obtained by people who have Irish.' In a later observation on the responses of various departments, Finance cast doubt on the validity of the Commission's work, claiming that the relationships between the various schemes proposed had not been thought through (Department of Finance, 1927b).

The response of the Department of Industry and Commerce is noteworthy because of its hostility to the notion that developing the Gaeltacht economically was even possible. Secretary General Gordon Campbell, a southern Unionist who transferred from London to Dublin when the Free State was founded, wrote the memorandum. He rejected the recommendation that companies be incentivised to employ Irish speakers, writing that 'in industry and commerce generally that qualification is not specially valued either by employers or by the trade unions ... A compulsory preference for Irish speakers would need legislation and is obviously impracticable.' He also argued, somewhat ironically, that the Gaeltacht was unfit for economic development because of its poverty, while leaving the door open to a targeted form of intervention. In response to Mac Cuinneagáin's statement, Campbell wrote that the proposal to set up a permanent board or commission 'is just as necessary for the industrial life of the Saorstat [sic] generally and seems likely to be affective only if undertaken as a special part, needing special adaptations, of a wider national policy with the same object' (Department of Industry and Commerce, 1926). Indeed, despite starting from a more *laissez-faire* position, Campbell became more convinced over time of the need for state intervention after doing the groundwork for the Shannon electrification scheme, which would become the hallmark of new minister Patrick McGilligan's term (Lee, 1989: 121–122). Campbell also changed his initial stance on the Gaeltacht, and by 1927 was arguing for greater intervention in its affairs (ibid.: 123). However, by that stage, the focus of his department was firmly on the hydroelectric scheme and not on the seemingly intractable economic problems of the Gaeltacht.

A large proportion of the Commission's recommendations (27 of 82) related to education. Given its key role in language policy in the formative years of the state, it is to be expected that the Department of Education responded in detail to the findings in the report. Although the new minister (since November 1925), John Marcus O'Sullivan, was less enthusiastic than his predecessor Eoin MacNeill, the submission was for the most part positive and endorsed many of the recommendations, but it criticised the Commission on a number of points. Justifying its attention to Gaeltacht schools since the foundation of the state, the memorandum argued that without supporting the Gaeltacht, the language Revival would have no foundation:

> At the same time it has always felt that the work done in the schools cannot have a permanent and enduring value if Irish should die as the ordinary speech of the Gaeltacht, since the language that would survive under these circumstances would be merely an artificial language without organic roots. The Department has therefore carried on the work of Gaelicising the schools to a much greater extent and with a much greater intensity in the Gaeltacht than in the non-Gaelic districts. (Department of Education, 1927)

The Minister for Education supported the implementation of most of the proposals, 'where practicable', but disagreed with the parts of the report 'which paint the educational condition of the Gaeltacht in terms of unrelieved gloom' (ibid.). The memorandum stated that the Minister took issue with the conclusions that primary education in the Gaeltacht led nowhere, had no clear objective and did not pave the way to higher education or employment. He rejected the claim that English was ousting Irish in primary schools throughout the Gaeltacht. In response to concerns about the lack of primary teachers fluent in Irish, Education believed that the new preparatory colleges would resolve the issue. It proposed setting up a new teaching training college with space for 200 students. However, it opposed the Commission's recommendation to remove teachers not competent in Irish, because of the large numbers involved (more than 1,200) and the risk of 'agitation' and 'serious opposition' that such a move would cause. Education favoured the payment of bonuses of 5 to 10 per cent to 'efficient' teachers in the Gaeltacht, in order to incentivise them to continue to work in remote districts (ibid.). This stood in contrast to the views of other departments, particularly Finance, which opposed remoteness as a justification of bonuses due to the knock-on effects throughout the civil service and the Gardaí.

Education clashed with the Commission over its proposals to develop secondary schools in the Gaeltacht and to oblige existing schools to switch to teaching through Irish (A-schools; see Chapter 3). It accused the commissioners of misunderstanding the fundamental nature of secondary education in Ireland, which was run almost entirely by private religious orders beyond the remit of the state. Reflecting the overwhelming power of the Catholic Church at the time, Education did not wish to spark conflict with diocesan authorities by attempting to 'produce sudden linguistic revolutions' in secondary schools run by religious institutions. It rejected a hybrid state-private model on the basis of cost, adding that it was difficult to entice parents in the Gaeltacht to keep their children at school beyond primary level: 'The people are on a poverty line which makes even free Secondary education a luxury in which they cannot indulge' (ibid.). Investing in technical schools at secondary level would be a better option as this would aid employability, concluded the Department, adding that another commission was considering the matter of technical education at that time and would be asked to consider the Gaeltacht in its work.

On other matters, Education rejected the Commission's proposal to reduce the entrance requirement to the civil service for native speakers of Irish on the basis that it 'would produce a general mistaken feeling in the Service that Irish and inferiority were closely connected ... the introduction of other reforms of the educational system will gradually supply the Service with a thoroughly competent Gaelic-speaking Civil Service' (ibid.). On a special commission or body to oversee implementation of the proposals, Education favoured a robust model with executive powers, in sharp contrast with other departments such as Finance. The Minister considered the Gaeltacht too important to be left to the 'ordinary activities' of government departments and feared that an advisory commission 'might develop the defects of an Opposition Party that could never hope to have the responsibility of having to carry out its own recommendations' (ibid.). The memorandum noted that the Gaeltacht problem was fundamentally economic and needed to be dealt with if gaelicising education and administration were to have meaningful impact. In what would turn out to be a prescient warning about the future governance of the Gaeltacht and the Irish language generally, Education urged the establishment of a single unitary authority, with executive powers and its own budget, to oversee all matters related to the Gaeltacht:

> The root of the situation therefore is that there should be in charge of this vital problem of the economic development of the Gaeltacht not a series of different Departments each with wide duties and responsibilities of which the Gaeltacht section is only a small and often unimportant part but one authority whose sole duty it will be to deal with the problem not piecemeal and in bits and snatches as at present but constantly, steadily and as a whole in such a fashion as to ensure that it is receiving the steady and unremitting attention that it needs. It is immaterial whether this authority should be one of the existing Departments, e.g. the Department of Fisheries or a special commission set up for the purpose. What is essential is that the development of the Gaeltacht should be its main if not its sole business and that for this purpose it should have wide financial and executive powers. (Ibid.)

The question of land redistribution and migration of population was discussed in detail in a memorandum from the Land Commission. Describing acute congestion as one of the biggest challenges facing the Free State, it said that the problem was particularly severe in the Gaeltacht. It calculated the approximate number of uneconomic holdings at 248,000, 64,000 of which were in the Gaeltacht. A shortage of available land meant that only about one million acres of land were available, whereas about 2.5 million would be needed in order to relieve such congestion. Estimating that about 20,000 of the 64,000 Gaeltacht 'congests' would need to be transferred elsewhere, the Land Commission budgeted the cost of such large-scale migration at £26 million involving 1.1 million acres. This would involve using up almost all of the available land in the state, thereby excluding all other groups living in congested conditions. The Commission said its estimate was based on the assumptions that all available land could be put to agricultural use, that all congests would be willing to move and that no other communities would oppose their re-settlement. In a telling insight into official ideology at the time, it pointed to what it saw as the pre-modern nature of Gaeltacht people:

> The small man, accustomed as he is to a very small way of life where farming and the standard of existence is extremely simple not to say primitive, takes alarm when he is asked to pay a higher rent or annuity for a holding three or four times better than his original one. He is not used to handling considerable sums of money and he feels unable to take on the responsibilities of conducting a good farm ... In addition, being accustomed to work on a light boggy soil, he feels completely at sea when asked to manipulate a holding comprised of fair heavy clay. The truth is that he is lacking in the necessary training and equipment for the proper working of a holding amongst a community where life is more complex than amongst his own. (Land Commission, 1927)

The Land Commission concluded that the large-scale migration plan proposed would lead to hostility in other parts of the county. It pointed to an ongoing migration scheme in Galway as a potential model for the type of transfer of population that could be undertaken in the future. Referring to an area of Connemara where 15,000 people lived on 3,000 uneconomic holdings, the Commission said it had acquired land in nearby valleys to resettle between fifty and seventy people. The Land Commission concurred with the Gaeltacht Commission's conclusions on the dire state of housing stock but fell short of endorsing the proposals on housing because of the large expense involving 'irrecoverable free grants' (ibid.). It supported reclamation grants, because of the relatively small cost, and investment in cottage industries.

3.6.3 Election 1927

In the run-up to the general election called for June 1927, a hint of the government's conservative response to the Commission came in a letter from Cosgrave to a priest from An Charraig in the Donegal Gaeltacht, warning about the financial implications of the report's recommendations:

> It must surely be clear that the financial effect is a matter of the greatest consequence to the nation as a whole, and it would be folly to embark upon an undertaking of the magnitude outlined in the report without the most careful examination of the financial liability which it involves ... In addition to this it will be perfectly evident to anyone who has studied the report that certain of the recommendations if carried out, would create very definite local difficulties. (Department of the President, 1927c)

The curt, parsimonious response could have been written by McElligott himself and gave no grounds for optimism to those who expected an interventionist response to the Commission's recommendations.

Cosgrave gave the public an insight into the direction of policy in an election leaflet from 1927. He began by warning of the 'heavy expenditure' and 'concentrated effort' that the measures would entail, 'spread over a considerable period of years' (Cumann na nGaedheal, 1927). Concern was expressed also about the many economic proposals that proposed to differentiate between people living in poverty based on their language, for instance the recommendation to provide a free meal to children in Gaeltacht schools: 'Now it is clear that in a manner such as this no differentiation can be made or should be made between the Irish-speaking child and the English-speaking child' (Cumann na nGaedheal, 1927: 12).

Cosgrave spoke of what his government had done already in relation to the Commission's report, focusing in particular on the programme to develop Irish in the schools. He referred to measures taken to increase numbers of Irish-speaking teachers in the Gaeltacht, increased grants for buildings and equipment and financial assistance for University College Galway. Other policy measures included the decision to make Irish essential for future entrants to the civil service, the appointment of Irish-speaking Gardaí in the Gaeltacht and the bilingual publication of government forms and notices:

> I may say at once that so far as the Government is concerned, they accept in principle the majority of the recommendations of the Commission in regard to these matters, and they will continue to push forward in every practical way to the realisation of the ideal that every officer of the State, central and local, will be qualified

to transact the business of the State with equal facility and with equal competence in the Irish and the English languages. They will as the material becomes available, make such administrative arrangements as the increase of qualified personnel will permit, to provide that State business in the Irish and partly Irish-speaking districts may be transacted through the medium of Irish alone. (Ibid.: 13)

However, alongside the apparent endorsement of the main aims of the report, Cosgrave signalled that the government would not accept many of the recommendations. He rejected the proposal that the training term of teachers competent in Irish should be shortened because of the negative impact on educational standards. Similarly, he opposed the recommendation that teachers not competent in Irish should be removed from the Gaeltacht, on the basis that the control was in the hands of managers and not the government. He was prepared to accept the principle of special recognition for teaching in Irish but added that such bonuses should not be extended in the public service as they would damage the 'cause of the Irish language itself' (ibid.: 13). Cosgrave also poured cold water on many of the economic recommendations, in particular those related to land resettlement and migration. This extract reveals an unwillingness to make distinctions based on language within the congested districts, all of whose inhabitants were deemed equally deserving:

[T]he economic problem in the congested districts cannot be dealt with in relation to the Irish language alone. It must be dealt with in relation to the entire population which inhabits these districts. ... We realise that it is a national duty to assist this area to raise itself to an economic level. (Ibid.: 14)

Rejecting the large-scale migration scheme proposed by the Commission, Cosgrave warned that there was not enough land available for redistribution and that migration, even if it did not spark hostility, was costly. Mentioning the more limited valley scheme as a model, Cosgrave said that much could be achieved 'by sane schemes of a migratory nature' (ibid.).

He also signalled a change in the governance of the Gaeltacht, referring to the difficulty of managing rural industries and schemes as they were currently the responsibility of various departments. Rejecting the final recommendation of a special commission, or body similar to the original Congested Districts Board, Cosgrave said such a proposal would cause friction in government. Instead, he proposed that all Gaeltacht schemes and industries would be co-ordinated by a single parliamentary head to ensure that there would be 'one definite policy running through all the projects which we propose to undertake for the restoration of this area' (ibid.). In August 1927, Cosgrave's office wrote to the Department of Fisheries formally transferring responsibilities for all matters related to the Gaeltacht Commission to it, including the preparation of the White Paper, the government's official response (Department of the President, 1927b).

3.6.4 White Paper

The White Paper, *Coimisiún na Gaeltachta: Statement of Government Policy on Recommendations of the Commission*, tabled on 15 February 1928, was an anti-climax as many of the measures had been signalled by Cosgrave during the election campaign the previous summer. Reflecting the conservative attitude of Finance, it repeated concerns about the implications for expenditure and the far-reaching nature of many proposals for all arms of government (Government of Ireland, 1928: 3).

A fatalistic attitude prevailed in relation to the complex economic problems of the Gaeltacht, including unproductive land and poor educational facilities and the daily challenges facing the population. These, the White Paper claimed, 'have made it impossible in many cases to devise remedies which would be at the same time effective and economically sound' (ibid.: 3). It was as if the government had no powers to act given the financial straightjacket it had donned on the back of non-interventionism. This was tempered by the remnants of the language ideology that had in brought the government to power, but even that was couched in the language of efficiency and economy:

> Having regard, however, to the exceptional circumstances of the districts in question, which form the last stronghold of Irish as a spoken tongue, the Government are prepared to adopt a number of exceptional measures which in other circumstances they would not feel justified in undertaking ... With a few outstanding exceptions, therefore ... the Government have decided to adopt and give effect to the recommendations of the Commission, either in their entirety, or with such modifications

as expert experience has shown to be necessary, or through the medium of alternative schemes designed to achieve in a more effective and economical manner the objects aimed at by the Commission. (Ibid.)

While this extract gives the impression that the government was prepared to endorse most of the proposals, it was disingenuous because a closer inspection of its formal response to the measures illustrates that a majority of them were either rejected outright or qualified in some way. Of the eighty-two recommendations, twenty-two were rejected without question. A further nineteen elicited ambiguous responses or were shunted off to other bodies for further consideration, eventually to be shelved completely: thirty were accepted, about 40 per cent of the total. Rejected measures included big-ticket items such as a large-scale migration and resettlement scheme, pay bonus for civil servants and Gardaí in the Gaeltacht, shortening the training period required for Gaeltacht teachers and a language requirement for promotion in the civil service and army. The government also opposed the development of Irish language schoolbooks by the Department of Education, the establishment of a Gaeltacht inspectorate, the roll-out of free secondary day schools and a schedule for existing secondary schools to switch to teaching entirely in Irish. It was deemed impossible to impose a condition that Irish would become the working language of Gaeltacht courts, a special employment bureau for the Gaeltacht was unnecessary given the work of the Department of Industry and Commerce and an agricultural college for Irish speakers was opposed.

The controversy over the nature of the special commission that was proposed by the Commission and two dissenting members was put to sleep finally by the government in its formal response. Rejecting all of the options presented, it nonetheless declared itself in 'complete accord' (ibid.: 30) with the objective that Gaeltacht matters such as land re-settlement, fisheries and rural industries, be co-ordinated by a central body. The government announced that the optimal arrangement to achieve this objective would be to give responsibility to the Minister for Fisheries to co-ordinate all Gaeltacht services in the future. It said that a purely advisory body would be ineffective and potentially clash with other departments and an executive agency would be costly and at risk of duplicating expense and effort.

The Land Commission had already been transferred to Fisheries and legislation would follow to bring about the other changes. The Executive
Council would continue to co-ordinate the work of other departments
in promoting Irish.

Issues kicked into the long grass included the thorny questions of
Gaeltacht teachers, Gardaí and officials not fluent in Irish and rural continuation and technical education. There were non-committal responses
to proposals about adequate school provision, university education, the
development of an Irish-speaking Army battalion, the use of Irish by court
clerks and the promotion of the language in the church, in private industry
and other professions.

Measures accepted included the division into Fíor- and Breac-
Ghaeltacht, which the government deemed 'convenient as a working arrangement' (ibid.: 3), although the categorisation was never confirmed in
legislation (Ní Bhrádaigh et al., 2008). Educational recommendations accepted included a requirement for primary school teachers in the Gaeltacht
to be fluent in Irish, an increase in teacher training provision, pay bonuses
for Gaeltacht teachers and a decision to keep qualified and fluent Gaeltacht
teachers in post over the age of 60. Administrative measures adopted included the duty of officials to work in Irish if they knew the language and
a language requirement for all new entrants and permanent appointments
to local government in the Gaeltacht. There would be increased recruitment of Gaeltacht teenagers as post office assistants, sub-postmasters would
continue to be required to know Irish and Irish-speaking Gardaí would be
transferred to the Gaeltacht. The government accepted the principle that
judges and court officials should have Irish competence, all civil service
examinations would be held in both languages and one-third of army officer posts would be reserved for candidates answering the paper in Irish.
However, in many cases the government qualified its response by warning
about issues of poor supply of Irish speakers or inserting escape clauses such
as the following in relation to the transfer of Gardaí: 'This is being done as
far as is practicable without imposing due hardship on individual members
or materially impairing the efficiency of the Force' (ibid.: 15). Economic
measures accepted included housing grants to improve Gaeltacht stock,
grants for land reclamation and the development of Gaeltacht industries

including textiles, kelp production and fishing. In relation to other professions, the government said that knowledge of Irish should henceforth be required for solicitors and barristers.

3.7 Discussion

The legacy of the Gaeltacht Commission has been assessed from various perspectives by historians, cultural geographers, economists and sociolinguists. Judgements of historians of twentieth century Ireland vary, with Laffan offering a generally positive view of the young state's efforts to promote Irish:

> The government might have had only limited success in tackling social and economic problems – problems that, it never tired of emphasising, had been compounded by the republican campaign of destruction during the civil war. But in areas such as 'Gaelicising' the state and making it conform more closely to Catholic ideals, projects already begun during its first term, it was able to implement changes that were largely to its satisfaction – and to the satisfaction of the powerful lobbies that advocated them. As befitted a co-founder of the Gaelic League, Eoin MacNeill was an enthusiast language revivalist ... minister for Finance, Ernest Blythe ... declared that he cared more deeply about Irish than about any other political question. This ensured that the language revival was funded more generously than many other government measures ... Elsewhere, he was more stringent. (2009: 392)

Noting that the government continued to support the Gaeltacht 'in a moderate fashion' following the Commission's report, Laffan also refers to Cosgrave's concerns that the financial implications might be too great. However, he claims that in general the government's initiatives on Irish were welcomed, referring to endorsement from *The Leader*, a newspaper that supported the Revival (ibid.: 259). Other historians such as Lee gave a more negative assessment of the Commission achievements:

> The Cosgrave government duly appointed a Gaeltacht Commission and duly sabotaged its report. Finance, though presided over by a language enthusiast in Blythe, took panic at the proposals. It had good reason to. The commission actually recommended free secondary school education in the Gaeltacht! The government rejected this heretical suggestion on the disingenuous grounds that parents were too poor

to avail of free secondary education because they had to send their children out to work at the age of twelve! ... It rejected on the same specious grounds a recommendation to increase scholarships among Gaeltacht children, though if the scholarships were not availed of, it is difficult to see how they would increase costs! It may be surmised that the real reason for the alarm among the mandarins of Finance was that it would be difficult to confine these policies to the Gaeltacht. Political pressure might compel their extension to the rest of the country. An approach towards equality of educational opportunity was too high a price to pay for the gaelicisation of Ireland. (1989: 134–135)

In her study of Cumann na nGaedheal, Meehan takes a similar view, describing the Commission as 'ill-fated' and repeating the claim that its report was sabotaged (2010: 9). She points to economic orthodoxy as a factor in the government's decision, saying that tightening the purse strings did Cumann na nGaedheal no favours electorally along the west coast (ibid.: 76). The perception that the Commission's work was scuppered gave ammunition to Fianna Fáil, then on the ascendancy following its foundation in 1926, who could claim to have a more pro-Irish policy (ibid.: 77; see also Whelan, 2009: 19). Although a majority of the Commission's proposals was repudiated, claims that the report was sabotaged do not stand up to scrutiny, given that about 40 per cent of the recommendations were accepted and certain important policy supports emerged from the Commission's work.

Other scholars with more detailed knowledge of the Gaeltacht focus on the ideological underpinnings of government policy in relation to Irish, and how this impacted on the state's perception of the Gaeltacht as an entity. In a commentary on the Commission's work, Ó Tuathaigh summarises the dominant social vision of the Gaeltacht at the time:

> An idealization of rural life, of 'traditional' life-styles in the Gaeltacht, an implicitly anti-industrial bias; an extraordinarily static vision of Gaeltacht society, timelessly in tune with the elemental values of the Irish people; the repository of the linguistic elixir of Irish nationhood; a vision encapsulated in the phrase 'tobar fíor-ghlan na Gaeilge' – the uncontaminated well-spring of the national language, from which the rest of the country could continue to draw sustenance. (1990: 11)

Another analysis by Ó Tuathaigh of the historical shifts in language policy points to the fact that the period in question was characterised by deep social conservatism. He argues that it was unfortunate for the language policy that many public intellectuals came to associate Irish with a censorious, philistine, anti-intellectual official culture, dominated by the Catholic Church. Some such criticism was exaggerated or unjustified, but the perception remained that the language itself was tainted by the dominance of the conservative political, social and cultural context (2011: 83).

On a quantitative track, the accuracy of the Commission's enumeration of the Gaeltacht has also been questioned. Pointing out that there were less Irish speakers in the entire Gaeltacht of 1925 (c. 257,000) than in Co. Cork in 1851, Ó Cuív refers to the 'illusory nature' of the statistics and contrasts the over-estimation of the 1920s with the under-estimation of Irish speakers in the mid-nineteenth century (1950: 29). Writing a quarter of a century after the Commission's work, he criticises the government for failing to adopt robust measures at the time:

> Even allowing that the Gaeltacht Commission was mistaken in its view as to the extent of the Gaeltacht, there was still a chance that vigorous and enlightened action would achieve some measure of success ... The problem was fundamentally an economic one, with a secondary factor of prestige; and what meagre measures were at length adopted were not adequate. (Ibid.: 29–30)

Ó Riagáin describes the Commission's statistical findings as 'inconsistent' compared to the 1926 census and concurs that the Breac-Ghaeltacht was larger and the Fíor-Ghaeltacht smaller than delineated (1997: 51; see also Hindley, 1990 & 1991). In his analysis of the history of economic policy towards the Gaeltacht from the foundation of the state until the late 1980s, Commins argues that the measures adopted amounted to little more than containing the economic problems of the Irish-speaking districts rather than a strategic development programme. This was reflected, he says, in the decision to transfer responsibility for the Gaeltacht to the Department of Fisheries, later Lands:

> The early policy measures of the new state were designed more for the containment or marginal improvement of a rural economy than for the development of a new economic base. (1988: 15)

In her analysis from the perspective of cultural geography, Johnson argues that many recommendations could have dealt with the Gaeltacht's problems but that the state failed to implement them. She highlights three main issues that were ignored: land resettlement, secondary education and an administrative structure to promote the language. This led to a failure to integrate language policy and economic policy:

> The Gaeltacht Commission Report suggested some solutions for the Gaeltacht's problems but the government's White Paper reflects a position which on the one hand eulogized the west as the cultural core of the nation yet separated its survival from the economic circumstances prevailing there. (1993: 167)

In another paper, Johnson highlights the implications for the Gaeltacht of the dominant ideology around the Revival, which saw the Irish-speaking districts as pre-modern and primordial. By prioritising cultural and ethnolinguistic arguments over social and economic ones, the state found itself in an ideological straightjacket preventing meaningful intervention in the economy of the Gaeltacht:

> The conversion of the Gaeltacht regions of Ireland into repositories of a primitive culture, and the attendant cementing of the nation's identity to discourses of premodernism and ethnic purity ... has had important consequences for state policy in the Gaeltacht, and for the response of Gaeltacht people to their assignment as traditional. (1997: 174)

The state saw the Gaeltacht areas as homogenous and therefore was unable to engage with them 'as modern and sustainable entities' (ibid.: 176). This tendency led it 'to fix the Gaeltacht in space' and 'to define socio-linguistic policy in static geographical categories' (ibid.: 183), a reference to the division of Breac- and Fíor-Ghaeltacht. Responding to the Commission's proposals, Johnson describes the recommendations on land resettlement as 'radical' because they linked cultural and economic policy (ibid.: 183) but notes that the Commission's main legacy was geographic and not economic. Its legacy was to define the boundaries of the Irish-speaking districts but not to deal with its economic problems, let alone expand its extent. The maps produced 'served, ironically, as the blueprint for monitoring the contraction of the Gaeltacht' (ibid.: 184). Johnson also describes the impact of the centrality of creating geographical boundaries both in political and psychological terms, noting that such an endeavour ignores the interconnectedness of the Gaeltacht with the rest of Ireland and indeed the world:

> While mapping has long preoccupied the state in its articulation of cultural policy, for the state the map has frequently acted as an archive to monitor decline and failure. The map then acts as a metaphor for a failed cultural project, a spatially defined society imploding under the strains of modernity. In this sense the map encloses as much as it discloses. A new map of the Gaeltacht, however, would extend beyond the boundaries of the West of Ireland or indeed of the state itself to include diaspora in Britain, the United States, Australia and beyond. (Ibid.: 187–188)

This keen analysis is a reminder that the cartographic approaches to the Gaeltacht over the past century have reified its borders in the public and official minds and overlooked the spatial reality of Irish elsewhere, including beyond the state's boundaries (for a discussion of this dynamic in Wales, see Jones & Lewis, 2019: 147–201).

4. Conclusion

Long before the concepts were developed and honed, the Gaeltacht Commission of the 1920s was an example of vertical top-down language policy by a highly centralised government finding its feet in the early years post-independence. That government, shaped by the values of the Revival period and containing some (but arguably not enough) strongly pro-Irish ministers, identified the decline of the Gaeltacht as a key challenge and set up a Commission to investigate the issue. The Commission's work was directed by the male middle class that accepted the Treaty, won the Civil War and committed to building the new twenty-six-county state. It consulted with people who were similar to its own membership, representatives of the middle classes from across the civil service and the Gaeltacht itself. Its sophisticated maps delineating Fíor-Ghaeltacht and Breac-Ghaeltacht laid down the blueprint for territorial concepts of the

Irish-speaking areas that continue to influence policy and perceptions around the Irish language. The Commission's recommendations were far-reaching and occasionally far-fetched, with little chance of political traction in the straightened economic and ideological climate, despite appearances.

Possessing more political sovereignty than other Western European regions where minority languages were spoken, the Irish state had the capacity to engage with language policy but was hamstrung by internal and external factors. Nationally, the state was floundering in its attempts to cement its precarious existence following a bitter civil war and continued political violence into the late 1920s, culminating in the assassination of the Vice-President of the Executive Council, Kevin O'Higgins in 1927. The idealistic romanticism of the Revival was tempered by the realpolitik of governing during economic and political crisis. Internationally, there was a lack of academic expertise in language policy, as the discipline would not emerge, as a sub-branch of sociolinguistics, for another 25–30 years. The global economic crisis sparked by the Wall Street Crash of 1929 caused officials to tighten public coffers further.

There were tensions between the three ministers most committed to Irish – Blythe, Mulcahy and MacNeill – and they found themselves on opposite sides during the period of the Commission and its aftermath. For Mulcahy, who lost his ministry following the Army revolt, taking the role of chair was a political consolation prize. Although MacNeill was strongly committed to Irish and occupied the key post of Minister for Education in the early years, he was distracted by his role in the Boundary Commission (1924–1925) and departed government in 1925 while the Commission was still doing its work. Blythe, despite his previous commitment to Irish and his influence in the establishment of the Commission, was hampered by the opposition of his officials in the Department of Finance to many of its findings. Cosgrave's support was lukewarm and his ability in Irish limited and he was not sufficiently engaged with the Revival aims to push for the acceptance of more recommendations. Meanwhile, the newly formed Fianna Fáil exploited the White Paper's weaknesses to question Cumann na nGaedheal's commitment to Irish, setting the scene for a new phase in language policy from the 1930s.

The Commission's work and the fallout from its report revealed ideological tensions between de facto and de jure language policy. The archives contain evidence of Cosgrave's pious endorsement of the classic revivalist rhetoric (that had to be translated into Irish in his letter to Mulcahy), the sincerely held beliefs of Mulcahy and commissioners strongly associated with the Revival movement, and others whose membership raised eyebrows. There were also clashes between government departments (i.e. Education and Finance) and outright hostility with some civil servants dismissing the problems of the Gaeltacht or rejecting even the possibility of ameliorating them. Some of the comments reek of an internal colonialism practised by the new English-speaking state against its Irish-speaking minority, despite the claim of gaelicisation. The evidence suggesting that native speakers were abandoning Irish in their droves heightens further the contradiction between the language's elevated constitutional status and its marginalised position in the Gaeltacht.

Hanging over the Commission's work is the stark challenge of dealing with severe underdevelopment and out-migration in the Gaeltacht within a centralised and conservative political culture and orthodox economic policy framework. Although many recommendations were impractical, the state missed a major opportunity in its decision to offload Gaeltacht policy to the politically unimportant Department of Fisheries (later Lands). The recommendation to set up a statutory, properly financed permanent commission, as proposed by Fr Mac Cuinnigeáin and others, would arguably have been possible even in straitened economic times and could have brought Gaeltacht policy closer to the centre of government in the following decades. Notwithstanding the lack of expertise in language policy nationally and internationally, the failure to create a powerful governance mechanism for the Gaeltacht in the early years, more than anything else, was the greatest missed opportunity related to the Commission's report. It would be 1956 before a dedicated central department was established and, as will be discussed in Chapter 3, it failed to carve out an authoritative space in government during the key policy shifts of the 1960s and 1970s.

The next chapter turns to another key plank of language policy, the position of Irish in education.

Education

1. Introduction

Chapter 3 analyses the position of Irish in the education system which is arguably the most significant and influential part of the language policy because it brings the vast majority of the population of the Republic of Ireland into contact with Irish throughout the entire schooling period. This is a significant policy prop for Irish and it gives considerable weight to the language policy. The chapter also reviews Irish in the growing all-Irish immersion sector and in Gaeltacht schools, before considering its more precarious existence at third level and particularly in Northern Ireland. The case study focuses on key policy shifts in relation to Irish in education in the decade c. 1965–1975 and analyses the pioneering work of the advisory body Comhairle na Gaeilge.

2. Language-in-education policy

The teaching of a language relates to the branch of language planning known as acquisition planning and the position of Irish as a core school subject, particularly outside the Gaeltacht, is a key part of such planning. It can also be interpreted as status planning, because the centrality of Irish in the curriculum sends a message that the state considers it important enough for all children to acquire during their schooling. As a result of the status of Irish in education, a large minority of Irish people (around 40 per cent) feel able to claim that they can speak it, although the census does not allow them to self-appraise their competence (Central Statistics Office, 2017c; see Chapter 1). The fact that only about 11 per cent of the population in Northern Ireland expresses some ability in Irish is linked to political tensions about the language but is also a direct effect of its more marginal role in schools north of the border (NIRSA, 2014). If Irish were to lose its elevated position in the Republic's schools, knowledge of the language among the general population would be far lower. Such a situation would likely have negative implications for other language policy measures that rely on evidence of strong public support for and reasonable knowledge of Irish. In this introduction, six main aspects of Irish in education will be discussed: Irish as a standalone subject, Irish as a medium of instruction outside the Gaeltacht, its position in Gaeltacht schools, Irish in higher education, its educational status in Northern Ireland and standardisation.

2.1 Irish as a standalone subject

The announcement by the Provisional Government that Irish was to become a core subject in every primary school and the medium of instruction in junior grades from St. Patrick's Day 1922 ranks among the most significant decisions taken in relation to language policy in the past century. Within six years, Irish was made a core subject for the Intermediate Certificate, became a required part of the secondary curriculum and became compulsory to pass the Leaving Certificate from 1934 (Mac Giolla Chríost, 2005: 117). Ó Buachalla (1994: 2) has described it as a 'megapolicy', one of the key measures that gave Irish a privileged position in the life of the new state, and Ó Laoire has argued that the schools were the government's main language planning agency (2019: 245).

The decision predated the foundation of the state by several months and was evidence of the importance of Irish to those who had negotiated the state's difficult birth. It also reflected the influence of Conradh na Gaeilge on education policy; the government adopted the organisation's existing programmes in relation to Irish in primary education, which included that it should be compulsory and used as the medium of instruction for at least an hour each day. Conradh na Gaeilge also favoured the 'direct method', by which teachers used Irish only to give orders or ask closed questions to teach certain grammatical rules. Ó Laoire argues that this limited real communicative interaction in Irish and despite many curricular revisions since, including the use of audiovisual materials and the introduction of communicative syllabi, the influence of the direct method can still be felt on the teaching of Irish (2019: 245–248). At secondary level, the emphasis was on literature and composition based on prescribed texts (from the 1940s), as it was taken for granted that children would acquire oral Irish at primary school. The Department of Education failed to strike a correct balance between oral and written aspects and was tardy in implementing the desire, as expressed in the 'Notes for Teachers' (Department of Education, 1933), that oral competence be emphasised in order to bring about the aim of making Irish a normal language of communication outside schools. One author critical of the core status of Irish claimed that this delay more than anything else led to the failure of the language policy:

> However, despite the repeatedly stated aim of reviving the language as a spoken tongue or a second vernacular, the emphasis in the schools, the primary instrument of the revival campaign, was on the written word. It was one of the great paradoxes underlying the revival policy and contributed greatly to the failure of the revival effort. The gap between the stated aim and what was actually being done in the schools in this respect is indeed surprising. (Kelly, 2002: 22)

An oral Irish examination at Leaving Certificate level was not introduced until 1960 and even then accounted for only one-sixth of the marks, sending out the message that written Irish was far more important (Ó Riain, 1994: 55). It would be the second half of the decade before greater emphasis was placed on spoken Irish in primary school in the form of courses based on Fr Colmán Ó Huallacháin's linguistic study of the corpus of spoken Irish (see below). The use of audiovisual methods to teach languages in other countries influenced the Irish context and such courses remained in place until the 1990s. The Committee on Irish Language Attitude Research found that there was widespread dissatisfaction with the teaching of Irish, even among those with favourable attitudes to the language and competence in it (Committee on Irish Language Attitudes Research [CILAR], 1975; see case study). In the same period (1973–1974), as a result of a successful campaign by the Language Freedom Movement (LFM), a sympathetic coalition government acceded to the demand that the Irish language requirement to pass the Leaving Certificate be removed. Irish was still a core subject and required for entry to the universities, but it was no longer essential to pass it in order to be awarded a Leaving Certificate (Rowland, 2014).

In the 1980s, the government's National Council for Curriculum and Assessment recommended the introduction of communicative syllabi along the lines of those of other European languages such as French, German and Spanish. Such new curricula for Irish came into effect in post-primary schools from 1989 and in primary schools from 1999 and were updated in 2017 and 2015, respectively. They were theoretically distinctive due to the centrality of the philosophy of the student as an active user and the emphasis on communication, sociolinguistic context and domain-based use of Irish in the community (Ó Laoire, 2002: 90–92; Ó Laoire, 2004). Since 2015, an integrated primary school language curriculum rooted in learning outcomes has linked the teaching of Irish and English, based on the principal that acquiring skills in one language will benefit the other. Although ostensibly welcome, Ó Laoire has warned that the greatest challenge is to ensure that teachers understand how to adopt the new approach as their role shifts from traditional tutor to facilitators of pedagogical interventions (2019: 254).

Despite the curricular revisions in the past thirty years, concerns remain about the acquisition of Irish in the education system. In large-scale national surveys conducted between 1985 and 2002, it was found that a significant minority of primary schoolchildren in mainstream English-medium schools failed to make meaningful progress in learning Irish and that standards have fallen sharply since the 1990s. There was a substantial drop in the percentage of pupils in such schools obtaining mastery in six out of seven listening objectives over the period in question (Harris et al., 2005: 35–36). In terms of speaking, the trend was similarly downwards with decreases in the percentages of pupils achieving mastery in all eight objectives. For instance, while in 1985 just over half of students mastered 'fluency of oral description' and 'communication', by 2002 this had fallen to less than a third (ibid.: 61). The surveys also found a drop in the percentage of teachers who were favourable to Irish being taught in schools and a large decline in the percentage of Irish teachers expressing satisfaction with teaching their subject during the period of study (ibid.: 130). There was also an increase in the percentage of teachers who believed that less time should be spent on Irish and a reduction in the percentage who believed that a correct amount of time was being spent. Large majorities of teachers in ordinary schools believed that pupils' ability to speak Irish had declined over the previous fifteen years (ibid.: 135). Harris warned of the negative implications of this for the entire language revival effort:

> Any state of affairs which results in substantial numbers abandoning the study of Irish at either primary or post-primary level – either formally opting out or, for all practical purposes, no longer engaging with the learning process – is a threat to a whole attitudinal basis for the national revitalization enterprise. In the Republic, for example, both individual attitudes to Irish and the strength of public support for various state efforts and institutions designed to maintain and extend the use of Irish depend crucially on the proportion of the population who have had a positive and successful experience of learning Irish themselves. Thus, it is important that the widest possible range of people study the language for long enough (i.e. at post-primary as well as primary) to acquire a worthwhile proficiency in the language. (Harris, 2008: 182–183)

The *20-Year Strategy for the Irish Language* made several proposals about Irish in mainstream schools, including developing partial-immersion education at primary level, beginning with the junior standards. This would require additional professional training for teachers and extra resources but little significant progress had been made at the time of writing (Government of Ireland, 2010: 12; Department of Culture, Heritage and the Gaeltacht, 2018: 24). The Department's action plan for the period 2018–2022 reported that trainee primary teachers now needed a higher entry level in Irish and that the length of their Gaeltacht placement had been increased (ibid.: 26).

2.2 Irish-medium education

The use of Irish as a medium of instruction in schools grew progressively from the foundation of the state until the 1950s but declined from then until the 1970s as doubts set in about the perceived failure of the Revival policy. Ó Laoire argues that the greatest flaw of the policy was to assume that knowledge of language and literacy in it would guarantee active use (2002: 86). Up to 1960, Irish was the medium of instruction in infant standards and first class in all primary schools. In 1928, for instance, the majority of primary schools were operating in Irish only or bilingually and following the election of Éamon de Valera in 1932, the policy was intensified. This was helped by the appointment of Tomás Ó Deirg as Minister for Education, who remained in power for the entirety of the Fianna Fáil government's tenure until 1948 (Kelly, 2002: 44–45). From 1928–1938, the number of 'A' schools – schools teaching entirely in Irish – grew to nearly 29 per cent of the total while more than two-thirds of other schools were teaching at least one additional subject through Irish.

Secondary education was less contentious as it was not yet under state control and involved only small numbers of pupils but from the 1930s on, opposition politicians and the Irish National Teachers' Organisation (INTO) began to question the policy in place at primary level (ibid.: 46–47). A report by the INTO in the 1940s found that most teachers were opposed to the immersion policy and academic studies in the 1950s and 1960s claimed that educational standards had suffered due to the emphasis on Irish (ibid.: 53–59). Ó Murchú points to the irony that just when the results of the language-in-education policy were beginning to take effect in the second half of the century, the state started to dismantle the measures it had hoped would work within a reasonably short period. The early cabinets had not recognised that language policy was a long, hard slog and would take generations rather than years to bring into effect, and Ó Murchú maintains that it would have been difficult politically for any modern democratic state to defend such a slow pace of change (2006: 3). A study by educationalist John Macnamara (1966) of 1,000 primary schoolchildren being taught through Irish claimed that their competence in English was compromised by gaining functional ability in Irish. This caused further damage to public attitudes towards immersion education and Mac Giolla Chríost refers to the period of the 1950s–1970s as one of 'de-institutionalisation', when the policy 'underwent substantial modification and in some respects … was reversed' (2005: 122). The 1970s was a low ebb for Irish in education. The Irish-medium schools sector all but collapsed and the government's decision to remove the Leaving Certificate requirement was a blow to the language's position, notwithstanding widespread public opposition to the original policy (Ó Riain, 1994: 194; 196–197).

Despite the negative situation overall, Ó Duibhir refers to research by Cummins (1977) critiquing the Macnamara findings and says that this reassured parents that immersion education was a viable option. The development of Irish-medium pre-schools (*naíonraí*) gained pace in the 1970s (Mhic Mhathúna & Mac Con Iomaire, 2022) and this led in turn to the development of Irish-medium primary schools (gaelscoileanna). The difference between such schools and the historical A-schools was that gaelscoileanna were the result of a parent-led movement rather than an initiative directed by the state. There has been exponential growth of the sector since the 1970s and there are now 255 such primary schools and 73 secondary schools in the Republic, compared to 11 primary and 5 post-primary in 1972. While the majority are standalone schools, some are Irish-language units within English-medium schools. Adding together Gaeltacht and non-Gaeltacht schools in the Republic with schools in Northern Ireland, 66,593 pupils attended all-Irish primary schools in 2020–2021. In the Republic, this amounts to 8 per cent of primary pupils (44,995) and 4 per cent of post-primary (15,483) (Ní Ghréacháin, 2021).

Surveys show that there is far more demand than supply in the Republic, with about one quarter of parents expressing their desire to send their children to all-Irish education. A large majority (72 per cent) of people in the Republic favours the government providing all-Irish schools where there is demand and even in Northern Ireland this figure reaches 63 per cent (Darmody & Daly, 2015: 82). The vast majority of pupils attending gaelscoileanna are from English-speaking backgrounds (Ó Duibhir, 2018: 15–18). Although there is some criticism of the type of Irish acquired by such pupils in immersion settings, research shows that they successfully acquire basic literacy and conversational skills, if lacking grammatical accuracy (Ó Duibhir, 2018: 15–19; see the detailed study of students' spoken Irish in the same volume).

Article 32 of the Education Act 1998 contained a number of important provisions about the Irish language. Primarily, it provided for the establishment of An Chomhairle um Oideachas Gaeltachta agus Gaelscolaíochta (COGG; Council for Gaeltacht and Irish Language Education) with responsibility for Irish language teaching resources, support services for Irish-medium schools and research into the sector. Since its establishment in 2002, COGG has commissioned a corpus of significant research on matters related to Gaeltacht and Irish-medium education.[1]

2.3   Gaeltacht schools

For most of the state's existence, no official attention was paid to the need for a separate syllabus for Gaeltacht pupils whose first language was Irish, despite the rhetoric about the importance of the Gaeltacht in the language policy. This changed between 2013 and 2017, during a lengthy consultative process about the Junior Certificate by the National Council for Curriculum and Assessment. As a result, it was decided to introduce two syllabi, one for schools teaching through Irish and another for English-medium schools. Ó Laoire points to the links between the new specification and other language policy measures such as the *20-Year Strategy for the Irish Language* (2010–2030), the Gaeltacht Act (2012) and the *Gaeltacht Education Policy* (2017–2022). He describes as significant the emphasis on the context for language learning and the proposal that pupils would be encouraged to participate actively in the language community (2019: 255–256). At the time of writing, a debate was continuing about the extension of differentiated syllabi for L1 (first language) and L2 (second language) Irish to Leaving Certificate level (Ó Caollaí, 2021).

In his study of Gaeltacht education since the foundation of the state, Ó Flatharta argues that although the curricula changed after independence to include Irish as a core subject, the governance of education remained largely

---

1   This is available at <https://www.cogg.ie/taighde-cogg/>.

unchanged since the period of colonial rule, including in the Gaeltacht. In 1926, the Department of Education established seven preparatory colleges, some in the Gaeltacht, aimed at fluent Irish speakers who would attend for four years before spending two years in a teacher training college to qualify. Within a decade, 600 pupils were attending the Colleges and while they succeeded in providing Irish-speaking teachers, there was opposition from those whose Irish was not as good but were otherwise qualified and claimed they were blocked from the training colleges. The Department of Education began to review the system and the preparatory colleges were closed eventually in 1960 (Ó Flatharta, 2007: 12–13; see also Kelly, 2002: 71–73).

In an analysis of seven reports from 1926 to 2004 in which Gaeltacht education is discussed, Ó Flatharta identified the themes of teaching and textbooks, curriculum, teacher training and provision, linkages with other elements of language planning and administrative structures (2007: 34–43). The fact that such themes emerged repeatedly proved that they had not been implemented and he criticised the paucity and temerity of recommendations about the structure of Gaeltacht education (ibid.: 43).

The Gaeltacht Commission report of 2002 pointed out that despite the existence of distinctive educational needs in the Gaeltacht, there was no separate policy for Gaeltacht education. It complained that teaching facilities or resources in Irish were inferior and that there was no distinctive curriculum for Gaeltacht schools. In order to prioritise Irish as L1, it recommended the provision of an entire education and training system at every level (Coimisiún na Gaeltachta, 2002: 17).

A report commissioned by COGG recommended reviewing the definition of 'Gaeltacht school' based on the educational models already in use (Irish-medium with Irish as L1, English-medium with English as L1 or Irish-medium with Irish as L2). The revised definition would be the future basis for the development of strategies and support services for Gaeltacht education. It also made other recommendations related to governance of and support services for Gaeltacht schools, development of a wide range of teaching resources and provision of teachers who were trained fully in Irish and prepared for teaching in Gaeltacht schools (Mac Donnacha et al., 2004: 124–138). Ó Flatharta recommended the establishment of a

Gaeltacht Education Board with full responsibility for Gaeltacht education and relevant statutory powers and resources to carry out its work. He further urged that responsibility for Gaeltacht and all-Irish education be given to a Minister of State in the Department of Education (2007: 65).

The *Comprehensive Linguistic Study of the Use of Irish in the Gaeltacht* recommended implementation of the report by Mac Donnacha et al. (2004) and said that COGG should be established as a statutory body with responsibility for all aspects of Gaeltacht education policy. It also recommended a Gaeltacht Education Board, language acquisition schools in Category A districts and an entry requirement that children already speak Irish for schools in these districts (Ó Giollagáin et al., 2007a: 43–44).

The Education Act 1998 emphasised the responsibility of schools in Gaeltacht areas to support the maintenance of Irish as the community language. As a result of the *20-Year Strategy for the Irish Language*, the Department of Education published a separate policy for Gaeltacht Education in 2016 which aimed to tackle the problem that not all Gaeltacht schools were in compliance with that provision of the 1998 act. At the time, 76 per cent of primary schools and 68 per cent of secondary schools in the Gaeltacht reported that they were working entirely through Irish (Department of Education and Skills, 2007: 7). A dedicated Gaeltacht Education Unit was established in the Department and schools were invited to submit expressions of interest in being recognised as Gaeltacht schools, on the basis that they would provide education through the medium of Irish. The policy seeks to extend full-immersion at primary and post-primary level on the basis of plans drawn up by schools and future resource allocation will be based on endorsement of the plans by the Department (ibid.: 9; see also Department of Culture, Heritage and the Gaeltacht, 2018: 23–24).

2.4 Higher education

Irish is offered as an academic subject in all seven universities[2] in the Republic and in both institutions in Northern Ireland. Its use as a medium

---

2   This does not include the recently designated 'Technological Universities', formerly

of instruction at third level is limited mostly to Galway, with more confined provision in Dublin and elsewhere. After designating Galway City as a 'Breac-Ghaeltacht' (partly Irish-speaking area) in 1926, the Gaeltacht Commission recommended that University College Galway be given responsibility for providing third-level education in Irish (Gaeltacht Commission, 1926: 26). This led to the University College Galway Act of 1929 which obliged the college to employ Irish speakers to lecturing positions where they were also suitably qualified academically. As discussed in the case study, there were difficulties with this policy from the outset and although Irish had a higher profile in Galway than in other universities, the campus never became truly Irish-speaking. In 2004, the renamed National University of Ireland, Galway, established Acadamh na hOllscolaíochta Gaeilge as a separate unit dedicated to providing university education in Irish both on the city campus and in three Gaeltacht satellite centres. In 2006, the employment requirement was scrapped in a revised act that instead obliged the university to include the provision of Irish language education in its strategic aims (Walsh, 2012: 273–274). Apart from Galway, the other main provider of university education through Irish is Dublin City University.

2.5 Irish in education in Northern Ireland

One of the greatest contrasts in language policy in the Republic and Northern Ireland is in the realm of education, as the language lacks core status north of the border. Despite the many challenges facing Irish in the Republic's education system (see the case study in this chapter), it is in a far stronger position and is widely accepted as a core part of the curriculum. In the North, Irish is taught both as a standalone subject but is optional and limited to Catholic schools and there is also a small but growing Irish-medium sector. Ó Murchú argues that Irish as a subject area has been particularly neglected historically, with Irish-medium education attracting more attention both in government and community circles

---

Institutes of Technology, that have little or no tradition of teaching Irish.

(2008: 327). Unlike Welsh in Wales, Irish is not part of the core curriculum in Northern Ireland and it was included only in 1989 after vigorous lobbying as an optional language alongside French, German, Italian and Spanish. The numbers studying languages increased in Northern Ireland and England over the following fourteen years and Irish became the second most popular language for the GSCE (intermediate) examination in Northern Ireland, after French, from 1988 to 2002. A revised curriculum (2003) replaced subjects with 'learning areas' focused on developing skills, interactive teaching methods and assessment for learning and in this context, less attention is paid to acquiring structures of language with a potentially deleterious effect on competence. The downgrading of languages in education in the UK over the past two decades has also had a negative effect. Since 2004, students only have to study a language for Key Stage 3 (11–14 years) and the requirement no longer applies to Key Stage 4 (14–16 years) (Mac Éinrí, 2019: 221). In Northern Ireland, the numbers studying Irish reached a peak of 2,641 in 2003 but have since declined subsequently. In 2016, 1,901 pupils sat the examination for GCSE in line with a fall in numbers studying languages in the UK generally. These include 369 pupils from gaelscoileanna, so the numbers taking Irish in English-medium schools are below 1,500 each year. 331 pupils took Irish at A-level (final examination) in 2015 (ibid.: 224–225).

Aligned with the changing political context, funding for Irish-medium schools in Northern Ireland increased in the 1990s (Mac Giolla Chríost, 2005: 137). In the Belfast Agreement of 1998, the British government committed to placing 'a statutory duty on the Department of Education to encourage and facilitate Irish-medium education in line with current provision in integrated education' (clause 4). Mac Éinrí argues that this prioritisation of the Irish-medium sector may in fact have marginalised further the teaching of Irish as a standalone subject (ibid.: 228). Although limited, Irish-medium education now exists at primary, post-primary and tertiary levels. In the school year 2020–2021, 6,115 pupils were in immersion education in Northern Ireland, 4,604 at primary level (thirty-five schools) and 1,511 at post-primary (five schools) (Ní Ghréacháin, 2021). There is a weak transfer rate from primary to post-primary level, which may reflect pupils' or parents' choices or the uneven provision of Irish-medium education across Northern Ireland (Mac Éinrí, 2019: 226–227). There has also been considerable change in the sociolinguistic make-up of schools over the past two decades with the arrival of many children speaking languages other than Irish or English. This greater diversity may have either positive or negative impacts on Irish: on the one hand, increased linguistic diversity may go some way towards reducing opposition to Irish, but the subject may find itself facing renewed challenges to its already marginal place in the curriculum (ibid.: 236).

The Belfast Agreement led to the creation of state-supported structures for Irish-medium education, Comhairle na Gaelscolaíochta (Council for Irish-medium education) and Iontaobhas na Gaelscolaíochta (Trust for Irish-medium education). Modules for students wishing to work in the immersion sector are available at St Mary's University College of Education in Belfast and a unit of that institution produces teaching materials (Ó Murchú, 2008: 331). Degrees in Irish as an academic subject are available at Queen's University Belfast and at the multi-campus University of Ulster.

Most schools in Northern Ireland are divided on religious grounds and provision of Irish is shaped by this. 'Controlled' schools operate under state management, have representatives from Protestant churches on their boards of management, contain mostly Protestant pupils and do not offer Irish. 'Maintained' schools are overwhelmingly controlled by the Catholic Church, contain Catholic pupils and may offer Irish. There are also integrated schools that aim to promote cross-community relations but Irish is only rarely offered in them (Mac Éinrí, 2019: 212–214). This historical legacy of a divided education system has created a situation where the exposure of children from Protestant or unionist backgrounds to Irish at school is minimal:

> There are very powerful structural reasons for the low incidence of Irish speakers amongst Protestants. The absence of the language from the curriculum of the state (almost wholly Protestant) educational system in the region and the very low status afforded to the language was the unionist-dominated government of NI seated at Stormont are probably the two main factors for the small numbers of Irish speakers recorded among Protestants. (Mac Giolla Chríost, 2005: 214)

In this context, the opening of a gaelscoil in a loyalist area of East Belfast in 2020 was a novel development that opens up the possibility of Irish being gradually extended on a cross-community basis (Simpson, 2021a). However, sustained unionist opposition to Irish-medium education and to other measures such as the Irish Language Act underlines the challenges involved.

2.6 Standardisation and education

Corpus planning is the aspect of language planning that refers to reform of the language itself, for instance, in terms of standardisation, spelling, dictionaries and terminology. When the Irish Free State was founded, there was no suitable standardised written form for Irish and the small number of people literate in the language tended to write an approximation of their own dialect, with the result that there was wide variation of spelling and grammatical forms. Early Modern Irish, in existence from approximately 1250 to 1650, was a standardised language used by bardic schools in Ireland and Scotland and was too far removed from the language of the early twentieth century to serve as a modern standard (Ó Murchú, 1985). The absence of a standard was problematic in the new domains in which Irish was being expanded, particularly education and public administration, and the need for textbooks covering specialised subjects and written in a standardised version was a major driver of linguistic modernisation in the decades after independence.

In 1941, Taoiseach Éamon de Valera announced a review of the spelling of Irish, which still contained historical consonant clusters no longer reflected in the phonology of any living dialect. This was followed by a review of the grammar and the publication in 1958 of a standardised written form, Caighdeán Oifigiúil na Gaeilge (Official Standard of Irish), for use in education, publishing and the media (Mac Mathúna, 2008). Despite complaints that regional dialects were being marginalised, the written standard has been widely accepted but efforts to introduce a spoken standard in the 1980s were less successful (Ó Baoill, 1986). The author of the spoken standard has complained that Irish language scholars have long paid excessive attention to dialectal differences and that the lack of a spoken standard is an obstacle to learners, most of them in schools (Ó Baoill, 2000). Dictionaries and terminology creation predate the foundation of the state (Mag Eacháin, 2014) but were developed significantly in the twentieth century in line with standardisation and the requirements of the education system (Nic Pháidín, 2008; Ní Ghallchobhair, 2014). One of the responsibilities of Foras na Gaeilge is to support corpus planning and milestones have been the creation of a national terminological database <www.tearma.ie> hosted by Dublin City University and the publication of a new English-Irish dictionary in written and online form in 2020. The status of Irish as an official EU working language (see Chapter 4) has also boosted terminology development across a range of domains with the result that Irish is well served by terminology in contrast to many other minoritised languages. The case study turns to key developments in education from the mid-1960s.

3. The work and legacy of Comhairle na Gaeilge

The 1960s and early 1970s were a crucial period for Irish in the education system, culminating in some of the most significant language policy retreats since the foundation of the state: the cancellation of the Irish language requirement for the civil service, and the removal of the requirement to pass it in order to obtain the Leaving Certificate. These were introduced by the 'National Coalition' government of the centre-right Fine Gael and centre-left Labour Party (1973–1977) who were less enthusiastic about Irish than their Fianna Fáil opponents. However, the origins of the shift can be traced back at least to the Fianna Fáil government's White Paper on Irish from 1965, which represented a retreat from the foundational rhetoric of gaelicisation. The decade 1965–1975 saw continued contestation and reshaping of language policy and was also characterised by increased professionalisation due to the emerging discipline of sociolinguistics internationally. This new scientific approach was noted by the government but, as the case study will reveal, it applied it only selectively. The policy was also influenced by the greater diffusion of decision-making, in line with the emergence of models of governance, and the government set up a number of advisory committees to report on different aspects of the question, including education.

3.1 Background

The change in government policy on Irish in the 1960s coincided with the liberalisation of economic policy after previous decades of protectionism. De Valera stepped down in 1959, marking the end of a long career in parliamentary politics and a change in direction for Fianna Fáil. The new Taoiseach, Seán Lemass, enthusiastically endorsed the *First Programme for Economic Expansion* (1959–1963), written by the dynamic Secretary of the Department of Finance, T. K. Whitaker, who took over a few years previously determined to depart from decades of economic orthodoxy (Lee, 1989: 342). The Lemass-Whitaker era was characterised by a move away from import-substituting industrialisation (ISI), which had stuttered to a halt by the 1950s, to export-led industrialisation (ELI), which embraced an expansive fiscal policy relying on foreign direct investment (FDI). De Valera's final policy initiative in relation to Irish as Taoiseach was to set up the Commission on the Restoration of the Irish Language in 1958. The Commission took five years to reach its conclusions, coinciding roughly with the entire Lemass-Whitaker economic programme, an indication of the glacial pace of language policy in contrast with development policy. By the time the Commission published its lengthy report in early 1964, Éamon de Valera had moved to the non-political role of the presidency and Ireland's new political leaders were open to challenging long-standing policy not only in economy but in language also. Liberalisation led to the growth of the private sector, opening up more employment opportunities where knowledge of Irish was no longer a potential barrier to advancement. As a result, instrumental or utilitarian reasons for achievement in the language declined, underlining the need for an overhaul of language policy if Irish was to make progress in the new economic era (Ó Riagáin, 1997: 216–239).

The link between language policy and development policy was Whitaker himself. Although a fluent Irish speaker, he did not support the Revival project unconditionally and was opposed to aspects of it. The Commission has been described as being steeped in the jaded ideology of early twentieth century cultural nationalism, offering no innovation in the philosophy underpinning the Revival despite the passage of decades (Ó Tuathaigh, 2011). Indeed, Whitaker's interpretation of the Commission's report was that it recommended the 'replacement' of English with Irish (Chambers, 2008: 340–342). He viewed such an approach as unrealistic and warned that it would 'sharpen the antagonism of those who see no point in preserving Irish, alienate the sympathy of those who cherish Irish but value the possession of English and discourage even idealists who recognise such an extreme aim to be unattainable' (Whitaker, 1983: 228 cited in Chambers, 2008: 341). There is no evidence that any Irish government ever seriously considered 'replacement' as its 'real' language policy but the perception that the aim was to marginalise English was gaining traction by this time. This was exploited enthusiastically by the Language Freedom Movement, who claimed regularly that the government intended to 'replace' English with Irish (Rowland, 2014). Possibly in response to such claims, the government reiterated in its first progress report on the White Paper that its policy was to 'extend and intensify the use of Irish', but in a context of bilingualism. It stated: 'It is not the Government's policy that the English language should be discarded but rather that the use of Irish should progressively be extended' (Government of Ireland, 1966: 34).

The shift in emphasis in language policy was also made possible by the lack of interest in Irish on the part of the new Taoiseach, Seán Lemass, compared to de Valera who was so strongly associated with gaelicisation (Garvin, 2009: 7 and 180). Whitaker's concerns about the Commission were shared by the Taoiseach, who asked his trusted Secretary of Finance to oversee personally the co-ordination of the government's response in the form of a White Paper (Chambers, 2008: 341–342). Interestingly, neither the newly established Department of the Gaeltacht nor the Department of Education – for so long associated with language policy – took leadership roles in the work. Having worked closely with Whitaker on the economic plan, Lemass wanted the country's most influential civil servant to mould the new language policy also. Conveniently, Whitaker was an Irish speaker but equally usefully, he was not associated with the language movement some of whose demands the government wanted to resist. Looking back with the benefit of twenty years' hindsight, a senior Irish-speaking civil servant working with Whitaker later described the White Paper as the 'new realism' (Ó Ciosáin, 1988: 266; for a discussion, see Walsh, 2021b).

3.2 White Paper

The *White Paper on the Restoration of the Irish Language* was presented to the Oireachtas on 15th January 1965. Published the following day, it sparked huge interest from the public and media and the print-run of 5,000 copies sold out within a week. The White Paper represented the most significant shift in policy in relation to Irish since the foundation of the state, marking the emergence of a discourse of bilingualism in place of the historical focus on gaelicisation. It shaped public policy on Irish, including in the education, for the next two decades and many aspects of that policy remain in place today. Although the White Paper did not make overt use of the concept of bilingualism, in its entirety it can be read as endorsing an approach to developing Irish within the context of English. For instance, it stated the aim in relation to Irish in the following terms:

> The national aim is to restore the Irish language as a general medium of communication. This aim will necessarily take much time and effort to achieve, notwithstanding the present state of knowledge of Irish and the goodwill which people in general feel towards it. (Government of Ireland, 1965a: 4)

Use of the adjective 'national' to qualify the aim reflects the earlier ideology of ethnolinguistic nationalism but this is further diluted by managing expectations in relation to the restoration of Irish. Rather than *the* general medium of communication, as inferred by the policy of gaelicisation, Irish would be *a* general medium of communication alongside English. To achieve this, the government proposed to implement the aim systematically through plans of action. Further tempering expectations, it added: 'Objectives will be set which are reasonable and realisable but which fix no boundary to progress' (ibid.: 6). The White Paper also dealt with the status of English in Irish society, a question over-looked in earlier iterations of formal language policy:

> Irish must have primacy as the national language and every effort will be made to extend and intensify its use. Nevertheless, for a considerable time ahead, English will remain the language chiefly used outside the Gaeltacht for various purposes. To assume otherwise would be unrealistic and would detract from appreciation of the effort needed to achieve the national aim in regard to Irish. (Ibid.: 6)

So in other words, the 'primacy' of Irish demanded the 'national aim' of restoration, but this was henceforth to be more aspirational and English would continue to be the country's dominant language for some time. Although the White Paper accepted the sociolinguistic reality in a more explicit way than previous governments, mere reference to the strength and relevance of English was a blow to those who viewed gaelicisation almost as an article of faith (e.g. Ó Fiaich, 1964). The White Paper contained further references to the importance of English for Ireland's economic and social development:

> It would also be unrealistic not to recognise that, because of our geographical position and the pattern of our economic and social relationships, a competent knowledge of English will be needed even in a predominantly Irish-speaking Ireland. English is of great value as an international language in communications, trade and tourism and as a means of participation in world affairs. It provides access to the knowledge and culture of the English-speaking countries as well as to the large body of literature written in English and to the prose, poetry, songs and speeches in which Irish national aspirations have to a large extent been expressed. Moreover, knowledge of English helps us to maintain our ties with the millions of people of Irish birth or descent living in English-speaking countries. (Ibid.: 10–12)

The reference to the importance of English, alongside the more familiar exhortations about the primacy of Irish, can be read as evidence of the 'real' language policy raising its head above the parapet (Shohamy, 2005). Although it hardly appears radical from the perspective of today, framing Irish in this way as a policy objective was a significant shift for an Irish government at the time. In a review published a year later, the government claimed that there was general agreement in the population with the policy aims (Government of Ireland, 1966: 4). Presumably, this was based on a subjective assessment of media and political commentary because it would be the best part of a decade before detailed sociolinguistic surveying of the population would begin. However, the government seemed to believe that it had given voice to those who favoured a more gradualist approach to the revival of Irish than had been the case in previous decades.

3.2.1 Educational measures in the White Paper

Section 4 of the White Paper dealt with education, covering primary, secondary, vocational and university education. Significantly, pre-schools were not discussed in depth in either the Commission's report or the White Paper, although they were dealt with by the advisory body Comhairle na Gaeilge a few years later (see below). Ó Riain identified the lack of adequate provision of pre-schools in Irish as a major weakness in language planning for education, because of the importance of prioritising language acquisition, particularly of phonology, in the early years (1994: 48–49). In its general comments on the educational system, the government defended the language policy in education to date and said it was essential that it succeeded in order to advance the position of Irish in other fields of life (Government of Ireland, 1965: 98). In a reflection of the bitter debates about 'compulsory Irish' that were ongoing, the White Paper criticised the parent or guardian 'who conditions the mind of a children by constantly associating the adjective "compulsory" with Irish'. This, it argued, was 'doing a disservice not only to that individual child but to other children and the nation in general' (ibid.: 98).

The government adopted a lacklustre approach to many of the Commission's recommendations on primary education, claiming that many of them were being implemented already, and rejected others. For instance, in response to the proposal that entrants to teacher training colleges should have a high standard of Irish, including oral skills, it responded that such entrants were required to have a Leaving Certificate honours grade and would also have to pass a special test administered by the teaching training college (ibid.: 100). It rejected a proposal to extend immersion so that all primary schools would use Irish to teach some subjects, increasing as the child advances to higher standards. The government maintained that such a plan was not appropriate 'until further investigation of the general effects of teaching through a language other than the home language of the child has been made' (ibid.: 106). Similarly, it rejected the recommendation to give special awards to schools using Irish socially among teachers and students and teaching at least half of the subjects through Irish. This was an interesting position as it contrasted with the emphasis in previous decades on gaelicising the schools and the significant growth of immersion or part-immersion until the mid-century. However, in response to the proposal that a scientific examination of the pedagogy of Irish as a spoken language be undertaken and an audio course prepared, the government said it had engaged a linguist (Fr Colmán Ó Huallacháin, see below) to prepare a new programme for teaching Irish in national schools (ibid.: 102).

There was a more positive response to the recommendations about secondary education, perhaps because of their general nature for the most part. In response to calls for further emphasis to be placed on spoken Irish, including introducing an oral examination at Intermediate Certificate level and raising the standard at Leaving Certificate, the government said the Minister for Education was in discussion with school authorities and teachers' unions about the matter (ibid.: 110). It endorsed a proposal to prepare an authoritative study of Irish in its historical context, explaining the reasons for language shift and the purpose behind the language policy (ibid.: 112). The government also accepted a recommendation by the Commission that a pass in Irish should remain essential to pass the entire Leaving Certificate but that those failing Irish should be given a second chance in a supplementary examination in the autumn (ibid.: 116–118). The debate about 'compulsory Irish' was yet to take off in earnest and the scant references to the issue in the White Paper stand in contrast with the publications of Comhairle na Gaeilge about education in the subsequent decade (see below). In the White Paper, the government did not endorse the recommendations that all secondary teachers of Irish should possess a degree in the language and that those not lacking such a qualification would have to prove their competence in Irish by other means. It declared itself 'satisfied that the vast majority of secondary teachers who are teaching

Irish are competent to do so' (ibid.: 118). The government endorsed in general terms the Commission's recommendations on vocational education, including a proposal to retain additional training for graduates of Irish who wished to become full-time teachers and another to improve the conditions and status of such teachers in vocational schools (ibid.: 120).

The government was decidedly lukewarm about the many recommendations made by the Commission about university education. These included placing additional emphasis on literary studies in academic Irish departments, requesting such departments to contribute to the creation of terminology, reforming the compulsory oral examination before graduation from the National University of Ireland and greater integration of Irish into life on campuses. It also recommended that further courses such as Celtic Studies, Arts, Commerce and Law be taught in Irish, that additional efforts be made at University College Galway and that the Higher Diploma in Education in Irish be made available more widely (ibid.: 128–136). The government offered a non-committal response to the list of demands, using the excuse of another commission on Higher Education to kick them into the long grass (ibid.: 136; Commission on Higher Education, 1967).

In its first progress report on the White Paper, the government reaffirmed the 'fundamental importance' of education for the language policy but added that any proposed changes to the teaching of Irish 'have to be viewed in the light of their effect on educational standards and attainments as a whole' (Government of Ireland, 1966: 24). This note of caution was in line with the revised tone of the new policy and introduced conditionality into what in previous decades had been overt support for the primacy of Irish over other subjects. However, the government pointed to progress with new research into spoken Irish at primary school and an experimental course aimed at testing the new methodology (ibid.: 24). At secondary level, the government reported that it had introduced an oral component to the Intermediate Certificate, as recommended by the Commission, and had arranged for a panel of scholars to deliver lectures on Radio Éireann about the decline and revival of Irish (ibid.: 26). There were no commitments on Irish at university level because the Commission on Higher Education was due to publish its report shortly, but the government both reaffirmed

its commitment to maintaining the core status of Irish and showed awareness of the importance of new scientific approaches to language pedagogy:

> The Government adhere to the view that no Irish child can be regarded as fully edu-
> cated if he grows up without a knowledge of the Irish language and that the edu-
> cational system will be seriously defective if it does not provide for the teaching of
> Irish to all children. As regards educational methods, the greatest promise of progress
> seems to lie in the scientific approach to language learning and teaching. (Ibid.: 36)

Individual government departments had responsibility for implementing
the decisions of the White Paper, but the Department of Finance was
given a general co-ordinating function, reflecting its central role in
shaping the document. The government also pledged to set up an advisory structure to aid policy development in the coming years, with a
special focus on extending the use of Irish in domains other than public
administration (Government of Ireland, 1965: 170). An increasingly
scientific approach to pedagogy, and broader insights from the emerging discipline of sociolinguistics, would form the basis of the work of
Comhairle na Gaeilge in the subsequent decade. References to the scientific approach in the White Paper are likely due to the influence of Fr
Colmán Ó Huallacháin, who had been appointed linguistic advisor to
the Department of Education. The next section considers the emergence
of a more scientifically informed approach to language policy and how its
development was impeded by bureaucratic inertia.

3.3 *Development of linguistics*

The period from 1965 to the early 1970s was characterised by movement
towards the professionalisation of language policy, especially in relation
to education, with engagement between the government and national
and international experts on linguistics and sociolinguistics. Although
this was in theory a positive development, academics were often frustrated by the slow pace of progress and poor co-ordination of policy.
Despite creating the appearance of engaging seriously with the issues,
the government favoured an approach of setting up advisory committees

whose findings could be quietly dropped instead of more robust structures such as statutory bodies with teeth.

The role of Fr Colmán Ó Huallacháin, a Franciscan priest trained in linguistics, was significant in this period. He brought clarity, expertise and urgency to the teaching of Irish but his negative experience of dealing with government exposed the deep faults in language policy, despite the illusion of change. Born into an Irish-speaking family in Dublin in 1922, Ó Huallacháin had lectured in Philosophy at University College Galway and was subsequently appointed Professor of Ethics in St Patrick's College, Maynooth. He later became interested in how emerging ideas about pedagogy of modern languages could be applied to the teaching of Irish and went to the US to study linguistics, graduating with an MSc in Applied Linguistics from Georgetown University in 1963. Ó Huallacháin was instrumental in setting up a language centre at the Franciscan College in Gormanston, Co. Meath, which would play a key role in the creation of modern teaching methods and resources for Irish and other languages. Evidence of the seriousness with which Ó Huallacháin approached the task is to be found in his remarks to the annual Georgetown roundtable on bilingualism in 1962, when he told delegates 'that the attempt to restore Irish as a means of ordinary communication all over the country would require at least as much expense, research and adjustment of administration as was provided for national defence, electrification, etc., but that nobody could seriously allege that such efforts had been made' (Ó Huallacháin, 1994: 165).

On his return to Ireland in 1963, Ó Huallacháin was appointed linguistics advisor to the Minister for Education, Patrick Hillery, to whom he recommended the recording and phonological analysis of native Irish speech. He conducted research on vocabulary, morphology and syntax of spoken Irish and produced an audiovisual course for primary schools, *Buntús Cainte*, which was piloted in at least 100 schools before being officially launched. *Buntús Cainte* provided a more uniform approach to the teaching of conversational Irish in primary school and was later adapted as a successful self-learning course for adults on radio and television. In 1965, invited by the Minister for Finance to submit his views on the White Paper, Ó Huallacháin proposed a plan of at least 15 years' duration to promote Irish, based on expertise in fields spanning communication, applied linguistics, sociology, culture, media, etc. He argued that this should be co-ordinated by a new state board for Irish, but warned that the endeavour would fail if it was not put on a firm scientific footing:

> Without such trained personnel, we are acting as though we thought that the development of the turf industry, rural electrification or tourism could be forwarded effectively by amateur common sense. If we continue our efforts at restoring the Irish language in such fashion, I am completely convinced – and I take this occasion to state as much formally – that the Irish language is doomed. (Ó Huallacháin, 1965 cited in Ó Huallacháin, 1994: 167)

Ó Huallacháin's views were submitted to Comhlacht Comhairleach na Gaeilge (the Consultative Council on the Irish Language), a body set up on foot of the White Paper to report to the Minister for Finance (Ó Riain, 1994: 20). Twenty-three members were appointed for a three-year term from March 1965 and in its first year, the Council held fortnightly meetings and submitted recommendations about education and the economic development of the Gaeltacht (Government of Ireland, 1966: 34).[3] After a year, however, the Council concluded that the White Paper was not being implemented and that there was no evidence of change of attitude within public administration because the language policy was not fully supported by the state. Reflecting the influence of Ó Huallacháin, the Council in 1966 strongly recommended the establishment of an executive

---

3   The government initially did not want more than fifteen members on the Council (Department of Finance, 1965). However, it became large and unwieldy, growing from 23 to 27 over time. During discussions about the membership, the Minister for Finance wrote to the Taoiseach expressing concern about the balance: 'This will leave the Consultative Council with four priests, one lady and one protestant [sic]. I think we will have to consider reducing the number of priests and increasing the number of ladies and protestants' (Ryan, 1965). A surprising addition to the membership was AJ (Tony) O'Reilly, then chief officer of An Bord Bainne (the dairy board), who would go on to become one of Ireland's most influential media tycoons (Government of Ireland, 1965b). Forty-four plenary meetings were held between March 1966 and June 1968 and the Council's sub-committees met forty-three times. Some meetings were attended by the Taoiseach and senior ministers and various questions were discussed with government departments and agencies (Comhlacht Comhairleach na Gaeilge, 1968: 2).

research agency involving a linguist, psychologist and sociologist as well as representatives of universities and teachers. At the end of its term in 1968, the Council repeated its conclusion that the state was not serious about the Revival by comparison with its efforts in other spheres such as provision of secondary education (Comhlacht Comhairleach na Gaeilge, 1968: 12). In the meantime, Ó Huallacháin consulted widely with experts on the study of bilingualism and pedagogy involving French, German and Welsh and proposed alternatives to the government. However, by taking over the direction and implementation of policy prematurely, Ó Huallacháin claimed that the Department of Education had marginalised expertise. For instance, his request that a linguist be appointed to a committee developing new primary and secondary courses for Irish was rejected (Ó Huallacháin, 1994: 164–170).

The establishment of the new Linguistics Institute of Ireland (Institiúid Teangeolaíochta Éireann, ITÉ) in 1967 and the frustrated role of Ó Huallacháin as Director, casts further light on the haphazard progress of language policy in this period. At a meeting with departmental officials in 1966, Ó Huallacháin urged progress on the recommendation that a research body into the teaching and learning of Irish be established. For him, such a mechanism was essential to implement the stated policy of strengthening the position of Irish in society:

> The success or failure of the programme for teaching Irish in the schools, at all levels, would be conditioned by the extent to which information, materials and guidance provided by such a body would make the speaking of Irish outside the schools possible and desirable, thus giving a social stimulus which would motivate an effective and conscientious effort on the part of all to get a proper grip of the spoken language. (Ó Huallacháin, 1994: 171)

He repeated his concern about the lack of expertise in the field, thereby underlining the need for a high-level research body (ibid.: 171). In 1967, the new Minister for Education, Donogh O'Malley, agreed to the establishment of the ITÉ and proposed that it be based at the Franciscan Centre in Gormanston, with Ó Huallacháin as Director. The role of ITÉ was to conduct scientific research on the teaching of Irish and other languages, including psychological and sociological aspects. In a reference to the growing controversy over 'compulsory Irish', O'Malley told the inaugural meeting of the ITÉ advisory committee that 'the whole position of the Irish language in our educational system and its place, so to speak, in the national ethos is being subjected to a great deal of critical examination' (ibid.: 173). Therefore, it was necessary to take advantage of scientific research on language teaching and learning in order to deal with the challenge of reviving Irish. He also referred to Ireland's impending membership of the European Economic Community and how it would be necessary to pay greater attention to other European languages in Irish schools.

Ó Huallacháin's papers provide a detailed insight into the failure of the Department of Education to grant adequate resources and status to ITÉ over the following five years. The Institute lacked a statutory basis, adequate grant-in-aid, academic status and senior staff and repeated attempts to resolve these matters fell on deaf ears. In 1969, Joshua Fishman, one of the founding fathers of sociolinguistics (see Introduction), visited Ireland at the invitation of ITÉ and met the Minister for Finance, Charles Haughey (ibid.: 175). In his recommendations to government, Fishman noted that despite increased activity around language policy, there was a lack of professionalism, which had led to the failure of many past initiatives. He referred to the absence of evaluation of previous successes or failures. To resolve this problem, Fishman suggested that ITÉ be expanded to a central government research and evaluation unit on language, based on a full-time staff, focusing initially on assessing current programmes to promote Irish in education, the media and public administration. Such a body should also engage in international benchmarking to assess Irish language policy in comparison with other bilingual jurisdictions. Fishman urged a clear distinction between research and policy and said that the latter should always be informed by the former. In response to what he saw as a widespread belief that the government was not doing enough for Irish, he believed that setting up such a high-level research agency would go a long way to dispelling such a view. Fishman concluded by summarising what he saw as the greatest administrative barriers to the success of Irish language policy:

[E]xcessive fractionalisation and bureaucratisation of effort, the absence of professionally competent supervision and revision of such projects as do get beyond the
'delaying stage', and lack of funds for serious and intensive efforts. It was his hope
that a central research unit would more quickly counteract all three of these lacks
than any other measure. (cited in Ó Huallacháin, 1994: 180)

Despite the concern of the advisory committee and Irish and international experts, there were still no senior appointments in ITÉ by 1971
and the situation had reached breaking point. In correspondence with
the Director, Fishman shared his concerns that the government was not
serious about putting ITÉ on a proper footing. He referred to the 'now
quite apparent delaying tactics whereby recommendations are neither rejected not implemented but simply surrounded by administrative silence
and inaction' and said that after four years advising the Irish government,
'I have not been used as a consultant but as an unwitting participant in a
master plan to do nothing.' Fishman continued: 'The institute has been
permitted to continue in a neither live-nor-dead state while policy has
continued to be merely verbiage' (ibid.: 186–187). Ó Huallacháin wrote
to the Minister for Education threatening to go public and, when no response was forthcoming, expressed his concerns in an address to teachers.
In response, the government undertook to reconstitute ITÉ as an independent company governed by a council of experts and terminated Ó
Huallacháin's contract a year before it was due to expire. Further bureaucratic problems meant that ITÉ was left without a Director until 1974.

In parallel with the ITÉ fiasco, however, another body was beginning its work on various recommendations in relation to language policy,
including education, some of which would have lasting impact. In 1969, yet
another advisory council was established, Comhairle na Gaeilge (Council
of Irish), which replaced the earlier Consultative Council. Ó Huallacháin
was worried that the new body risked duplicating the work of ITÉ and met
them to express his concern, particularly in relation to research, but the
bureaucratic quagmire into which ITÉ had sunk meant that no comprehensive research programme was possible anyway. It seemed that Comhairle na
Gaeilge reflected the government's penchant for 'excessive bureaucratisation', in the words of Fishman, but in fact the new advisory body succeeded
in making far-reaching proposals about language policy, the Gaeltacht and

Irish in education that would continue to reverberate in subsequent decades. It is to the work and legacy of Comhairle na Gaeilge, particularly in
relation to education, that we turn in the remainder of this chapter.

3.4   Comhairle na Gaeilge

As explained in the opening section, the most dramatic policy reversal
related to the status of Irish in the Leaving Certificate and the civil service
entry requirement in 1973–1974, but the decade also launched a broader
process of revision as a result of the work of Comhairle na Gaeilge. Its
function was to assist the government with reviewing the language policy,
produce research on policy and on measures to extend the use of Irish
(Comhairle na Gaeilge, 1970: v). Its inaugural meeting on 18 July 1969 was
addressed by Minister Charles Haughey, evidence that the most influential government department continued to take a leading role on language
policy instead of the Department of the Gaeltacht. As seen in the progress reports of the White Paper, the government was increasingly aware
of scientific research about language and Haughey asked the Comhairle
to prepare a study on the topic (Comhairle na Gaeilge, 1970: v).
     If its predecessor was unwieldy, the new Comhairle was considerably
bigger. Ten former members were reappointed along with twenty-seven
others from a variety of backgrounds spanning Irish language organisations, academics, educationalists and representatives of private business
and the public sector. The chairperson Noel Ó Maolcatha came from the
Irish Management Institute and had been seconded to the organisation
Gael-Linn, which had a particular interest in developing Irish language
business. He was also a lecturer in business administration in University
College Dublin. The membership included two Irish language academics
of note, Professor Seán Ó Tuama of University College Cork and Breandán
Ó Buachalla, a lecturer in Irish in UCD who would subsequently become a
renowned scholar in his field. Other notable members included the Director
General of RTÉ, T. P. Hardiman, and T. K. Whitaker, former Secretary of
the Department of Finance but who was now Governor of the Central Bank.
The single woman, Nóra de Buitléar, represented two organisations, the

educational body Foras Éireann and the Irish Countrywoman's Association
(Department of Finance, 1969). One newspaper article claimed that the
Comhairle was Fianna Fáil's challenge to the LFM and that the re-election
of a Fianna Fáil government shortly before the announcement showed
that most Irish people did not want Irish neglected (*The Irish Press*, 1969).

An occasional paper, *Language and Community* was prepared for
Comhairle na Gaeilge by Máirtín Ó Murchú, then a lecturer in Irish and
linguistics in Trinity College Dublin and an emerging authoritative scholar
in the sociolinguistics of Irish. The foreword referred to the 'new discipline'
of sociolinguistics, dealing 'specifically with the social aspects of language'
(Comhairle na Gaeilge, 1971c: v) and the paper cited the latest research by
sociolinguists such as John Gumperz and Joshua Fishman. While preparing
the paper, Ó Murchú discussed its contents both with leading figures in
Irish language academia and language organisations as well as officials from
the Department of Finance including T. K. Whitaker (ibid.: vii). The paper
defined foundational concepts such as language itself, speech community,
dialect, register, speech event, standard and code. Particular attention was
paid to the concepts of diglossia (a functional distribution of languages according to different domains) and bilingualism. Linguistic, psychological
and sociological approaches to language were also discussed. Of the four
scenarios for societal bilingualism and diglossia outlined, Ó Murchú said
that 'transitional bilingualism' or 'bilingualism without diglossia' was the
most familiar to people in Ireland and other Celtic countries. However, it
was important to realise that other forms of more stable bilingualism existed with diglossia present and that gaining a better understanding of these
was of major significance for Ireland in terms of language policy (ibid.: 22).
Having outlined the history of the diglossic relationship between Irish and
English, Ó Murchú recommended its adoption as a fundamental pillar of
the future language policy:

> [I]t is essential to our authenticity and self-confidence as a nation that the Irish lan-
> guage be re-established in a central rather than a marginal position in the commu-
> nicational matrix of our society. This, in effect, means setting as our immediate goal
> the attainment of an Irish-English diglossia in which Irish would have a significant
> part to play consistent with its function as the national language. Such a diglossia is
> not really new in our country: an Irish-English diglossia exists in the traditionally

Irish-speaking areas; an Irish-English diglossia, with, of course, a different domain configuration, exists in embryo in the rest of the country; and, historically, as we have seen, the distinctive speech pattern of Irish society from the seventeenth century to the cataclysmic events of the last was an Irish-English diglossia. (Ibid.: 32)

A framework for a language policy based on this theoretical foundation was produced by the Comhairle a few months later. *Towards a Language Policy* (1971d) defended the utility of diglossia by arguing that it could assist in analysing an existing linguistic situation, provide indications of public support for various measures and assist in defining new linguistic aims. This would lead to more clearly articulated aims and a pathway to achieving them, introducing a 'sense of purpose into language policy' (Comhairle na Gaeilge, 1971d: 2). The Comhairle noted that the Committee on Irish Language Attitudes Research (see below) had recently been established in order to assess current attitudes towards Irish and public support for various policy measures. This, the Comhairle said, would allow the identification of the domains most likely to be accepted by the public to extend the use of Irish. It also urged greater study of diglossic situations in Ireland, both in the Gaeltacht and elsewhere, including home-neighbourhood domains and schools, units of public administration and Irish-medium schools (ibid.: 6). Once the most favoured domains to promote Irish had been established, the Comhairle recommended using the mass media to inform the public and ensure its engagement in the process. The state should take a key role in introducing Irish to the new domains through, for instance, a marketing campaign encouraging bilinguals to use Irish according to the new patterns (ibid.: 4). Foregrounding its future work on education, the Comhairle underlined the importance of all levels of the system in the effort to develop stable diglossia throughout Ireland:

> Efforts to establish a new linguistic convention would need to be effectively supported by the educational system at all levels to ensure that the appropriate language facility was sufficiently developed for comfortable use in each domain. The evolution of the diglossia approach should go hand in hand with the development of language e.g., the elaboration and use of terminology. It obviously would entail a comprehensive programme for the development of teaching aids and specialised courses specifically designed to provide learners with the minimum facility of speech required by

the diglossia ... Thus the efforts of the educational system would be directed into a logical partnership with the efforts to change language use in the community at large. (Ibid.: 4)

Comhairle na Gaeilge also urged that particular attention be paid to stabilising existing diglossia that favoured Irish in the Gaeltacht, and that efforts be made to limit the development of English diglossia there. It also outlined the governance implications of implementing such a policy, and recommended the establishment of an adequately resourced planning and co-ordinating body to undertake the work. Such a body should have access to scientific expertise in the areas of linguistics and behavioural science as well as language activism. This first step, the Comhairle said, 'affords a new hope of enjoying in the foreseeable future the distinctive cultural and social benefits of a society in which Irish has been re-established in a central rather than a marginal position' (ibid.: 6).

Also in 1971, Comhairle na Gaeilge made detailed proposals about the governance of the Gaeltacht, covering the local government system, education, health and economic development policy. *Local Government and Development Institutions for the Gaeltacht* proposed a system of local government based on the recognition of Gaeltacht districts as electoral areas, each with its own local committee to which functions of County Councils would be transferred. Each committee would have its own office, conduct its business in Irish and act as an agency on behalf of state departments in its area. There would be a Central Council of Gaeltacht committees, providing a democratic voice for the Gaeltacht and representing its interests. The Comhairle also recommended the establishment of a Gaeltacht education committee with functions in respect of schools and that the local government system should also ensure the delivery of health services in Irish (1971b: 9–11). Significantly, it proposed that sociolinguistic considerations be built into the planning of economic development and that a Gaeltacht developmental body be established. Comhairle na Gaeilge recommended that the existing industrial development agency Gaeltarra Éireann lead a working party in association with the Shannon Free Airport Development Company (SFADCO), a successful local agency in Co.

Clare, and bring forward proposals on the future of Gaeltacht economic development (ibid.: 12–15).[4]

A year later, another landmark report from the Comhairle, *Implementing a Language Policy*, made two far-reaching recommendations that were adopted and remain in place, to varying extents, to the current day. It proposed that all functions related to the promotion of Irish in society should be transferred to a new statutory board called Bord na Gaeilge, whose work would include developing Irish language education (see below). It also recommended the establishment of a new statutory board for the Gaeltacht, Údarás na Gaeltachta, that would take over previous functions of Gaeltarra Éireann. Bord na Gaeilge was set up in 1975 and put on a statutory footing in 1978. Údarás na Gaeltachta was established in 1979 (see below). A third recommendation, a new government department called Roinn na Gaeilge (Department of Irish), was not accepted (Comhairle na Gaeilge, 1972: 18). An earlier proposal by the high-level Devlin review group on the future of the public service that a Department of National Culture be established subsuming Irish, arts, national heritage, cultural institutions and public broadcasting, was also rejected by the government at this time (Public Services Organisation Review Group, 1969: 311–315). However, since 1993, the Irish language has been included in a government department covering themes such as arts, culture and heritage and the present incarnation, which includes media, is strikingly similar to the Devlin proposals.

The Commission on Higher Education (1960–1967) said it received conflicting evidence in relation to the teaching of Irish at university level. Some submissions felt that universities' obligations to Irish were limited to promoting Irish Studies and that there was no demand for courses through the medium of Irish. Others argued that there was as much of a duty on third-level institutions to promote Irish as any other level of the education system and that its use should be extended in higher education

---

4   Detailed information about the work of Comhairle na Gaeilge in relation to Gaeltacht health services can be found in NAI FIN/2002/1/44. The Gaeltacht Sub-Committee of the Comhairle recommended the establishment of Gaeltacht Health Committees under the structure of new regional Health Boards established in the early 1970s (Comhairle na Gaeilge, 1971a).

(Commission on Higher Education, 1967: 97). The Commission noted the lack of engagement of universities in general with Irish, apart from University College Galway (ibid.: 107) and made recommendations about future provision for Irish at higher education level (ibid.: 712–722). Many of these proposals were later developed by Comhairle na Gaeilge.

Two seminal documents about education published by the Comhairle in the early 1970s will be examined in depth in the remainder of this case study. In 1970, when the battle over the core status of Irish was still raging, the Comhairle published *Submissions to the Higher Education Authority*, which was established that year to lead policy on the future of third-level education. As the country entered the new decade, there was an urgent need for a higher education policy because of the sharp increase in the numbers of students able to avail of secondary education since 1967. The status of Irish as a core subject of the Leaving Certificate was already a site of contention, but the Comhairle knew that its status at third level would soon become relevant for a large number of people and that was the principal focus of the 1971 paper. The second document, *Irish in Education*, set out the Comhairle's overview of the priorities for developing the status of Irish as a standalone subject, and as a medium of instruction, at all levels of education from pre-school to higher education. It was published after the government's decision to remove the core requirements for Irish in education and administration and reflects aspects of that debate. Taken together, these largely unstudied documents provide a valuable insight into the formation of Irish language policy in education in the modern era, many elements of which persist to the present day.

3.4.1 Submissions to the Higher Education Authority

The 1970 document began by outlining Comhairle's approach to teacher training, referring to progress in the scientific study of language and the consensus that the target language should be used in activities outside the classroom and in the teaching of other subjects if the pupils were to make real progress with it. This, it said, was recognised by the government in its progress report on the White Paper from March 1968. The salience of motivation in language teaching and learning was also highlighted:

It will not be sufficient, for the attainment of the national objective regarding the language, merely to teach Irish, or even to teach other subjects through Irish. The young person must be inspired and encouraged and the teachers themselves should be motivated through their training course. Therefore, Irish should be taught in the context of the whole culture. It is also necessary to provide teachers with a knowledge of the basic principles of linguistics and of the other related sciences. (Comhairle na Gaeilge, 1970: 5; see also Comhairle na Gaeilge, 1974: 3)

The document went on to make proposals in relation to Irish at pre-school, primary, secondary and university level. In terms of nursery schools, the Comhairle noted that although most such bodies were private or voluntary, it recommended an experimental course to attract teachers to this sector (Comhairle na Gaeilge, 1970: 5). It expressed concerns about falling standards of Irish among primary teachers and stated that all such professionals should be fully competent in Irish and trained to teach through the medium of it. A high standard of Irish from applicants to teacher training colleges was recommended, and such institutions were urged to employ native speakers to deliver courses in phonetics and idiom. All staff of such colleges, whether administrative or academic, should be capable of working in Irish and not receive permanent posts until they could prove their competence. The Comhairle recommended including linguistics and pedagogy in the curriculum, with a focus on teaching through the medium of a second language. It also proposed focusing on Irish in the context of culture, history, literature and 'the philosophy of the language restoration' (ibid.: 7). Part of university courses should be taught through Irish in order to ensure that student teachers did not lose contact with the language as their training advances.

At secondary level, the Comhairle recommended that every teacher of Irish should possess a degree in the language and a Higher Diploma in Education, including modules in linguistics and L2 pedagogy. It also proposed grants for Gaeltacht refresher courses and added that any new future teaching training college should use Irish as its working language. An enhanced system of higher education scholarships aimed at Gaeltacht or fluent Irish speakers was recommended (ibid.: 8–9) and proposals on improving the supply of Irish language textbooks were also made (ibid.: 10).

Submissions to the Higher Education Authority covered university education in depth, discussing the status of Irish in all universities and in particular University College Galway (UCG), which since 1929 had a special responsibility for promoting Irish. It noted the support given by the earlier Commission on Higher Education to the language policy, in particular its conclusion that teaching through Irish at university level was essential to develop Irish as a contemporary language (1967: 720). However, it criticised the Commission for failing to recognise the challenge of expanding university education in Irish outside UCG and made recommendations to develop Irish there. Options to enhance Irish-medium education outside Galway were presented, including teaching other subjects such as History, Geography, Maths, Archaeology, Linguistics, etc. through Irish and/or introducing a new course in Irish and Environmental Studies for the BA degree. The Comhairle proposed setting up Bord na Gaeilge[5] (the Irish language board) in every university, whose aim would be to expose as many students as possible to at least some Irish during their time at university (Comhairle na Gaeilge, 1970: 15).

The Comhairle also raised the problem of the falling number of A-schools and its impact on university education in Irish. It said that at UCG about 15 per cent of students took courses in Irish when available, the majority of whom were educated in A-schools or Gaeltacht schools. There were problems, however, with a lack of textbooks and grants no longer being competitive. It urged the Department of Education to bring forward a policy on the A-schools and to increase Gaeltacht scholarships (ibid.: 24).

Another recommendation was to radically expand university Irish departments as key elements of the promotion of the teaching and learning of Irish, including broadening the expertise base to include fields such as comparative literature, linguistics and cultural anthropology (ibid.: 15). The Department of Education in each university should also play a significant role in providing courses through Irish (ibid.: 26). The Comhairle also urged that the legislation establishing the HEA include an obligation on the authority itself and on third-level institutions to promote Irish and courses

---

5   The same name was adopted for the national Irish language board that was established in 1975.

through the medium of Irish (ibid.: 26). However, provisions about the promotion of Irish in the Higher Education Act 1971 were vague and did not place substantive obligations on the new body or on the universities in relation to the language. It was further evidence of the state's retreat from its foundational policy.

3.4.1.1 UNIVERSITY COLLEGE GALWAY

The Comhairle criticised UCG for failing to develop a strategy for teaching through the medium of Irish, despite its statutory responsibility to do so for the previous forty-plus years. It urged UCG to attend to a number of issues, including whether it should focus on the development of scientific and technical courses through Irish, the provision of units of certain subjects through Irish in later years on all courses or specialise in limited areas such as History where there was existing demand. It suggested that consideration be given to a new course through Irish in which there would likely be strong interest (for instance drama, communications and journalism). It also proposed a survey of existing students taking subjects in Irish in Galway and measures to develop the supply of textbooks. The Comhairle dwelt at some length on the issue of making Irish the dominant language of the campus, including boosting the influence of administrative and academic staff on language use, forging deeper links with the Gaeltacht and better supporting Gaeltacht students. Consideration should also be given to providing Gaeltacht scholarships to a larger cohort of students than before (ibid.: 16–17). The Comhairle recommended that the branch of Bord na Gaeilge to be established at UCG should go further than other institutions and set out a plan to develop the institution as 'an adequately bilingual university' (ibid.: 16).

The Comhairle's main recommendation was to establish a Residential Foundation at UCG to give greater prestige to Irish-speaking graduates and staff, which it claimed would enhance the public status of Irish and boost its place in higher education. It went into some detail about the structures of the proposed Foundation, whose purpose it said was to turn out an elite cadre of highly trained graduates in Irish, on the lines of the *École Normale*

Supérieure in France (ibid.: 18–24). Recommendations about third-level institutions other than universities were made in 1974 (see below).

3.4.2 Irish in Education

The first chapter of this report, 'Towards an Irish Language Policy in Education', was published as a standalone paper in 1973 and reproduced in the 1974 document with further commentary on the policy shift. The recommendations in *Irish in Education* concerned the governance of a language policy in education, teaching of Irish as a subject and teaching other subjects through Irish, a course of Irish studies, teacher training, nursery schools, third-level education excluding universities and publishing in Irish.

The Comhairle offered qualified support for the state's original language policy, saying that it did not wish to 'minimise the significant, though partial, success resulting from past programmes' as this 'would be unwarranted and ungenerous to the public, teachers, policy makers and administrators who displayed enthusiasm and commitment at a critical period of our history, in particular in the nineteen-twenties and thirties' (Comhairle na Gaeilge, 1974: 1–2). It pointed out that the policy had started from a very low base, with most teachers knowing little or no Irish, and in that sense could be considered 'a worthwhile achievement' (ibid.: 2). While census returns for Irish were healthy, showing an increase in the decades since independence, research was needed into why educational achievements had not been translated into greater community use. Comhairle na Gaeilge referred to its previous recommendation that language policy be based henceforth on the concept of diglossia. This it said would require both the development of Irish in the education system and a parallel community language programme. Bord na Gaeilge, a new state agency for Irish (and distinctive from the proposed Bord in each university in the 1970 paper), would be responsible for administering this (see Comhairle na Gaeilge, 1972).

The Comhairle set out its philosophical basis for the future language-in-education policy, objectives that it said were an essential element in any long-term plan for the teaching of Irish. In a reflection of the policy shift

contained in the White Paper that recognised the bilingual reality, it referred to the restoration of Irish as 'a general medium of communication'
(Comhairle na Gaeilge, 1974: 2), not *the* general medium. Its rationale for
the language policy rested on linking with heritage and forging community,
values that it said should be at the heart of education itself:

> Properly taught within the educational system, the Irish language opens up for Irish
> people, through Irish literature and history, some two thousand years of Irish life. It
> makes them conscious of that network of behaviour, thought and feeling which they
> share not only with the Irish community of the past but with most of the people of
> Ireland today, in the Gaeltacht and outside it. For Irish men and women an adequate
> knowledge of Irish is essential to that awareness of mind and feeling and to that inte-
> gration with community on which much individual development depends. This could
> be held to be one of the main objectives of education in its widest sense. (Ibid.: 3)

The paper added that teaching Irish 'as a second vernacular' would be a
wasted effort if it failed to achieve the general objectives by imparting
only a minimal amount of Irish that would not allow students to 'gain
real-life experience in it' (ibid.: 3). If students could not use Irish language
media, engage with Irish speakers or understand literature in Irish, the experience would not be educationally valid. It wished to ensure that a high
level of Irish would be acquired in the education system and that parallel
societal programmes would run alongside the schools to convert acquisition into use. In order to bring this about, a comprehensive plan covering
all levels of education was required.

Another key recommendation was that a plan for Gaeltacht education should be closely aligned with that region's socioeconomic needs. The
Comhairle also spoke optimistically about Irish accession to the European
Economic Community, expressing hope that increased exposure to multilingualism would have positive outcomes for the learning of Irish. It warned,
however, that promotion of other European languages in education should
not be used to marginalise Irish. In terms of governance, the Comhairle
recommended that a senior official in the Department of Education, reporting to the Secretary General, be given responsibility for co-ordinating
educational policy on Irish. Bord na Gaeilge would also have a key implementation role and take charge of research into the issue (ibid.: 14–15).

As stated previously, one of the milestones in language policy over the past century was the decision by the government in 1973–1974 to diminish the core status of Irish in education and public administration. When Fianna Fáil lost the general election of that year, the accession to office of the 'National Coalition' of parties less traditionally supportive of Irish, ensured that the change proposed before the election would become a reality. The policy shift was a result of the successful LFM campaign, elements of which overlapped with the ideology of elements of the main governing party, Fine Gael (Ó Riain, 1994: 194; Rowland, 2014). Presenting its recommendation before the government's decision, Comhairle na Gaeilge took a firm stance against the proposals. It disputed the idea that students voluntarily took on Irish when offered a choice, citing evidence from Northern Ireland showing only tiny percentages of children choosing Irish at school. It also disputed use of 'compulsion' to describe the status of Irish, arguing that English and Mathematics were compulsory in practice. Were the requirement to study Irish to be removed, there would be negative consequences for the language in the education system (Comhairle na Gaeilge, 1974: 5–6).

The Comhairle supported maintaining the core status of Irish in primary and post-primary level and endorsed the requirements that all pupils should take and pass the Leaving Certificate examination in Irish (ibid.: 6). It also recommended maintaining Irish as a requirement for the civil service general grades, arguing that it was a strong motivational factor for studying Irish at school (ibid.: 7). In Chapter 3, which was written after the government's decision, Comhairle na Gaeilge strongly opposed the change. It was a matter of deep concern that 'numbers applying themselves seriously to Irish in the schools in the future' might fall dramatically and therefore it was even more important than before to ensure a high standard of teaching in Irish, leading to a high competence among students. The Comhairle suggested additional 'special inducements' such as competitions between schools and publicity for students' achievements in order to boost motivation (ibid.: 8). The Comhairle's policy on teaching through Irish covered both Irish-medium schools and a part-immersion model where subjects other than Irish were taught through Irish. Supporting Irish-medium schools and ensuring their equal distribution throughout the country was one of the most important ways that the government could boost use of Irish in the community. It was a matter of great frustration to parents who supported the constitutional status of Irish that they could not access 'for their children the all-Irish education they regard as a right' (ibid.: 8).

The Comhairle recommended that a single body take responsibility for the strategic development of the all-Irish education sector, but advised that the government had a responsibility to stimulate demand if it was to achieve its own aims with regard to language policy (ibid.: 8). Placing excessive emphasis on all-Irish streams or units within mainstream schools was seen as misguided. The Comhairle documented the collapse in A-schools in previous decades, to the point that numbers were lower in 1974 than at any time since 1927. Many parts of the country had no provision at all; for instance, there were no A-schools in fourteen counties, nine of which were within Leinster (ibid.: 23–24). Maps of existing provision were provided and a suggestion made to establish about forty schools based in thirteen centres around towns, with better geographical distribution than at present (ibid.: 26–27). Bord na Gaeilge should establish existing demand in a given area and work to stimulate it further. Primary and secondary schools should be co-located, at least one other subject should be taught through Irish in other schools in the catchment area and Irish-medium options should be enhanced at regional third-level colleges (ibid.: 28).

Endorsing a recommendation in the White Paper, the Comhairle also recommended the introduction of part-immersion by teaching a subject or subjects other than Irish through Irish. This it saw as essential if the diglossia concept was to underpin the language planning effort, as it would associate Irish progressively with an expanding range of domains (ibid.: 5). It suggested environmental studies as an option for special development, but other choices could be music, art or physical education. The Comhairle accepted the challenges associated with such a change and foresaw that it would take some time to implement because of issues with availability of qualified teachers (ibid.: 31).

The Comhairle warned that failing to ensure basic fluency among primary school teachers and a sound understanding of pedagogy were impediments to the effective teaching of Irish. It welcomed the new primary school curriculum for Irish, which stipulated that a minimum of five hours per week be spent on the subject. However, it expressed concern that some schools could consider this a maximum, leading to a further fall in the standard. Anybody given responsibility for teacher training should investigate competence in oral Irish in schools (ibid.: 35). At post-primary level, it described the new Intermediate and Leaving Certificate syllabi as an improvement on their predecessors, but pointed to faults in the oral examination and a lack of supply of textbooks. The Comhairle also recommended the provision of optional post-school courses aimed at dealing with the 'slippage' in ability in later age cohorts (ibid.: 40).

To sweeten the bitter pill of the diminution of the status of Irish in 1973, the government had proposed a course in Irish Studies that would ensure that all students learn about Irish language, culture and heritage, rather than focusing exclusively on the language itself. Comhairle na Gaeilge welcomed such a proposal as an additional measure in the context of maintaining the core status of Irish, and expressed regret that it had not been a core part of the curriculum previously. It recommended that civics, then obligatory for post-primary pupils up to Intermediate Certificate, be replaced with Irish Studies, which would have a civics element. The course should be subject to examination and include written and oral Irish, and be made available as an option for the Leaving Certificate (ibid.: 41–42).

The Comhairle expressed concern that the status of Irish in teacher training colleges had fallen, leading to a decline in competence. However, primary teachers in particular should attain a high level of competence in order to teach the language. It warned about the small numbers of secondary teachers taking additional Irish training and pointed to a survey of teachers of A-schools that found that over 30 per cent required additional language training. However, no institution existed where such support was provided (ibid.: 45). The Comhairle suggested in-service training in pedagogy for Irish teachers in vocational schools in particular, who faced extra barriers to tenure than their counterparts in other subjects. There was an urgent need for more teachers capable of teaching all subjects through Irish in all-Irish schools and schools with an Irish stream. Comhairle recommended expansion of the Faculty of Education at UCG to allow greater numbers of teachers to do the Higher Diploma through Irish and receive training in teaching other subjects through Irish. Similar facilities in a university in or near Dublin should be expanded with the same aim, to ensure that a substantial part of the Diploma was available through Irish elsewhere. A resource centre based on a Welsh model was also proposed (ibid.: 49).

The benefits of pre-school education in minority language contexts such as Wales and Canada were discussed and the Comhairle recommended that an Irish-medium nursery school system be established. There were requirements in terms of suitable premises, qualified teachers and assistants and monitoring by the Department of Education. It recommended pilot schemes based on existing nursery schools associated with primary schools or a new system administered by a national organisation. Based on models in other countries, it proposed that the Department of Education should not be the lead agency with Bord na Gaeilge taking responsibility in co-operation with the Department. The Bord would then stimulate local demand for nursery schools, advise local groups on setting them up and establish local governance structures (ibid.: 51–53).

The Comhairle's main recommendations about university education in Irish were made in its 1971 submission to the HEA (see above). The principle proposal for other third-level institutions in the later document was that the new National College of Physical Education (NCPE) in Limerick would train teachers in teaching PE through Irish. It was strongly in favour of teaching PE through Irish because, it claimed, the average student enjoyed it, there were fewer communication problems and issues of terminology could easily be resolved. The Comhairle recommended that PE be taught through Irish as a matter of course and that the NCPE use Irish as its working language and teach most of its courses through Irish. However, it expressed concern that despite a commitment from the Department of Education, Irish was marginal in the new college and applicants did not require a pass in Irish in the Leaving Certificate to gain entry (ibid.: 55). The Comhairle also recommended the implementation of its HEA proposals in the new colleges of the National Institute for Higher Education and in the regional technical colleges serving the Gaeltacht, Galway and Letterkenny (ibid.: 57).

Finally, the document devoted considerable attention to the issue of publishing in Irish, based on a memorandum sent to the Minister for Finance and Education in 1972. It endorsed the recommendation by the

Commission on the Restoration of Irish more than a decade previously that a national publications board for Irish be established and that the lack of provision of textbooks in Irish be dealt with as a matter of urgency (ibid.: 58). The White Paper of 1965 had rejected that proposal and pledged instead to 'reorganize, co-ordinate and expand progressively the activities' of the various bodies that had responsibility for the matter (Government of Ireland, 1965a: 146). Despite a pledge by the Minister for Education in 1968 to introduce a new scheme, the Comhairle complained that the situation was still unsatisfactory and there was no progress in co ordinating and expanding the work of the various bodies involved. Based on its survey in 1971, the Comhairle concluded that there was not an adequate supply of texts and supplementary books for primary schools, texts and reference books for post-primary schools, university texts, books for children and teenagers and comics and general reading (Comhairle na Gaeilge, 1974: 63). It also complained that no planning was being done for the future nor market research into the extent of the problem (ibid.: 64). It suggested that Bord na Leabhar Gaeilge (the Irish books board) be strengthened considerably and established as an independent company, given a full-time staff and new terms of reference to co-ordinate publishing in Irish in association with the Department of Education's publication division An Gúm and private publishers, as well as doing market research. An Gúm should be removed from the civil service and established as a private company answerable to the Minister because the civil service was not a suitable environment for conducting a business (ibid.: 66).

3.5 Committee on Irish Language Attitudes Research

The Committee on Irish Language Attitudes Research (CILAR) was the most significant achievement of Comhairle na Gaeilge, as it oversaw and directed the first comprehensive sociolinguistic research project on Irish to be undertaken. Realising that it lacked basic data on various aspects of language policy, Comhairle na Gaeilge recommended that a separate committee of experts be established to investigate attitudes towards Irish and the language policy aims and the extent to which the public would support policy measures in pursuit of those aims. CILAR was established by the Minister for Finance and the Gaeltacht, George Colley, in September 1970 and comprised high-calibre Irish and international scholars in the fields of linguistics, sociolinguistics, sociology, planning, anthropology and psychology.

These included Patrick Commins (research sociologist, Agricultural Institute), Damian Hannan, (Professor of Social Theory and Institutions, University College Cork), Eileen Kane (Department of Anthropology, University of Pittsburgh), Máirtín Ó Murchú (Professor of Irish, Trinity College Dublin), Pádraig Ó Riagáin (Lecturer in Town and Country Planning, Queen's University, Belfast), Seán Ó Tuama (Professor of Modern Irish Literature, University College Cork) and Daithí Ó hUaithne (David Greene; Senior Professor at the Dublin Institute of Advanced Studies). Many such individuals would go on to dominate their academic fields over the coming decades and continue to contribute to research on Irish language policy. CILAR also contained a small number of civil servants, including Séamus Ó Ciosáin, then Assistant Secretary of the Department of Public Service, who had assisted T. K. Whitaker in co-ordinating the White Paper in 1964–1965. Eminent international members were leading figures in the new discipline of sociolinguistics: Joshua Fishman of Yeshiva University in New York, William Mackey, Director of the International Centre for Research into Bilingualism, Quebec and Jac Williams of the University of Wales in Aberystwyth. Fr Colmán Ó Huallacháin resigned his membership in 1971 following his public criticism of the government over ITÉ. CILAR assembled a team of research staff and begun a comprehensive research programme in 1972, investigating the current state of Irish, the degree to which the public supported it, attitudes to various policies and ability in and use of Irish among the general population. It addressed the following questions:

(a) What attitudes and beliefs are held by Irish people towards the Irish language and how are these inter-related?

(b) How are such attitudes distributed in the population and how can this be explained?

(c) What is the link between people's attitudes, abilities in Irish and communicative competence in the language?

(d) Has the position of Irish in education succeeded in allowing people communicative competence sufficient to allow people to speak Irish with others?

(e) What are the obstacles to converting competence into usage, especially in a context where English is dominant?

(f) Based on answers to the above, what policy measures are most likely to succeed and would they be supported by the public? (CILAR, 1975: 4).

An interim report was presented to the Minister for Finance in 1974, with a full version published in 1975. Stating that the development of detailed policy proposals should take place elsewhere, CILAR limited itself to the general implications of its findings. It said that its main contribution had been to inform the public about attitudes to, ability in and levels of use of Irish. It also aimed to explain how these were inter-related with each other and with broader social trends (CILAR, 1975: ii–iii). CILAR noted the establishment of Bord na Gaeilge and the reconstitution of ITÉ since it was established and expressed its hope that they, other research bodies and universities would continue the studies that had been suggested by its findings (ibid.: 5).

The extensive nature of CILAR is beyond the scope of this chapter, so the following section will focus on the most salient data in relation to Irish in education. CILAR found that a large majority – 68 per cent – believed that Irish should retain its core status as an obligatory school subject. A similar majority believed that more people would speak Irish if it was taught better in schools. A smaller majority – 58 per cent – favoured more expenditure on improving the methods of teaching Irish at school, suggesting a certain fatalism about reform (ibid.: 26). More detailed questions about education revealed very negative attitudes towards the transmission of Irish in the schools. 60 per cent of respondents believed that children studying through Irish did not do as well as those studying through English, 66 per cent agreed that most children resented having to learn Irish, 77 per cent agreed that many children fail exams due to Irish and the same percentage said that most children do not learn enough Irish to use it after school. A large minority – 46 per cent – agreed with the statement that there was too much punishment associated with Irish at school (ibid.: 30). Overall, only a small minority positively evaluated the teaching of Irish, with over 60 per cent expressing dissatisfaction (ibid.: 31). However, one quarter of respondents expressed more positive views about Irish now than when they were at school, compared to just 9 per cent of those who had a more negative view (ibid.: 32). CILAR concluded that the public's experience of the teaching of Irish at school was very negative, but that such attitudes recovered somewhat once people had left school for some time (ibid.: 33). Further questions about the teaching of Irish revealed more detailed information about attitudes to its core status. Between 65–77 per cent of respondents agreed that spoken or written Irish should be taught at primary or secondary school compared to almost 100 per cent for English. There was strong opposition to the requirement to pass Irish in order to obtain the Leaving Certificate, a policy that was about to be abandoned. Only 27 per cent of people agreed that written Irish should be required as a compulsory terminal Leaving Certificate examination subject while just 34 per cent believed that oral Irish should be required for this. In contrast, 80 per cent agreed that English should be compulsory to pass the Leaving Certificate (ibid.: 61). CILAR expressed concern about the potentially negative implications of the central status of Irish in education, focusing on its intersection with class as illustrated by strong resentment among working-class respondents:

> Irish has become rather more clearly 'marked' or salient as a subject than others, because of the central significance it has in schooling generally. As a result it appears to have become the object of attitudes which are as much concerned with children's educational progress generally as with the language itself. It is in this sense that most of working class resentment against the language – especially its perceived use as a block to examination success and entry into certain occupations – must be understood. An educational system which appears loaded against the educational progress of urban working-class children can easily generate attitudes which can settle on such a visible symbol. Seen in this light, it appears as a convenient if sometimes an unjustifiable focus of antipathy. There is, nevertheless, a very substantial reality to which the public is reacting. As became obvious from the data, the teaching of Irish does not generally succeed in yielding high verbal competence even after 12–14

years learning the language ... [F]or those who fail Intermediate or Group Certificate Examinations the language can be a salient object of their disaffection. (Ibid.: 295)

The class-based nature of opposition to Irish was a justifiable matter of concern for CILAR, whose members were committed to building broader social consensus around a comprehensive educational pro-gramme that would ultimately increase social use of the language across the population (see also Advisory Planning Committee, 1988: 66 and Ó Riagáin, 1997: 211–213). CILAR added that attitudes towards Irish in the education system were only weakly correlated with attitudes to public support for the language. In other words, those who supported Irish were almost as likely to have negative attitudes towards it as those who were uncommitted to its inclusion in education. Although current respond-ents tended to be more favourable now than when they were at school, CILAR professed itself 'to be disturbed by this remarkable consensus of dissatisfaction with the teaching of Irish in the schools' (ibid.: 295–296).

Limiting itself to only general policy proposals, CILAR said that its findings pointed to the need for reform of the curriculum with a greater emphasis on communicative competence. It pointed to disappointment among supportive respondents that so few students leaving school could speak the language, and to how this wasted effort fostered negative views (ibid.: 322). Noting that the current curriculum in English-medium schools was succeeding in achieving passive competence, CILAR expressed concern that it failed to engender effective communicative competence even among Leaving Certificate students. Suggesting that there was much to be learned from methods employed to achieve verbal competence among students of second languages in other countries, CILAR concluded:

> The view that it is impossible to teach children a second language at school in such a way that they will have adequate competence in speaking it is demonstrably unfounded; what is true is that the existing curriculum used for teaching Irish in English-medium post-primary schools in Ireland is not primarily directed to that goal. (ibid.: 322)

The stark conclusions of Comhairle na Gaeilge about the intersection of social class and language policy were concerning and are discussed further in the next section, which assesses the work and legacy of the body.

4. Discussion

The work of Comhairle na Gaeilge marked a turning point in the history of Irish language policy over the past century. After decades of wishful thinking about the Revival, the new scientific discipline of sociolinguistics was applied to the Irish situation and a structured approach to achieving a more sustainable version of societal bilingualism was advanced. Diglossia was the model to drive the expansion of Irish in certain domains, based on what attitudinal research would reveal as the most favourable options in the public's mind. The promotion of Irish in education would be a key domain itself, but suggestions spanning the range from pre-school to university education were aimed at developing Irish both inside and outside the classroom, an essential element of diglossia.

However, the fiasco surrounding Fr Ó Huallacháin and ITÉ suggests that the government was only prepared to go so far in its newfound interest in the language sciences and was reluctant to tie itself to permanent structures that would have real influence over policy formulation and implementation. It also highlights the limits to Fianna Fáil's stated aims in relation to the Irish language, which were allegedly only second to its support for Irish reunification (Whelan, 2009: 9). Rather than committing itself to the resources needed to set up a properly funded statutory research body, it was politically easier for Fianna Fáil to ask temporary consultative bodies to do some of the same work on an ad hoc basis. The political context is also salient: the activity of the late 1960s and early 1970s was a result of decisions made by Fianna Fáil whereas the subsequent National Coalition of 1973–1977 was less engaged with Irish and is remembered for giving in to demands to dilute its core status in education and public administration. Comhairle na Gaeilge was established by Fianna Fáil and its recommendation to establish CILAR in 1970 was also agreed to by that party. It was during the tenure of the Fine Gael-Labour coalition that Comhairle na Gaeilge was disbanded in 1974, but that government did move to establish Bord na Gaeilge in 1975, although on a non-statutory basis (it was put on a statutory footing by Fianna Fáil in 1978, after it returned to power again). CILAR was a critically important contribution to the sociolinguistics of

Irish and the most comprehensive survey conducted to date about competence in, use of and attitudes towards Irish among the general population.
Its findings that two-thirds of the population generally supported Irish but
that a similar percentage was unhappy with how it was taught in schools
underlined the pressing need for reform of the education system. Evidence
of working-class resentment against the language make for uncomfortable
reading and are a reminder that aspects of the language policy were too
often exclusionary and focused on high achievers. The failure to develop
out-of-school programmes to foster informal social use of Irish across the
population and its almost exclusive association with the classroom exacerbated this dynamic. It has been a retarding factor in the policy for most
of the past century.

   Because of its consultative nature, and given the long tradition of
inaction in language policy, it would be unrealistic to expect that all of
Comhairle na Gaeilge's suggestions would be accepted unconditionally,
but its impact on policy in the medium- and long-term was significant
nonetheless. There were short-term gains, particularly in relation to governance of language policy and education, while other measures took years
or even decades to come into effect. For instance, in 1973, the voluntary
organisation Gaelscoileanna was formed to lobby for the strategic development of Irish-medium primary and secondary schools. While not at-
tributable solely to the work of Comhairle na Gaeilge, the attention paid
by it to immersion education strengthened the rationale for a body to
lobby government for greater provision. A key aspect of governance that
also had its roots in the work of the Comhairle was the establishment of
Bord na Gaeilge in 1975 and although not given the wide educational
remit envisaged by the Comhairle, its range of promotional functions developed general conscientisation about the language. To co-ordinate the
development of the nascent nursery sector, a new voluntary organisation
Na Naíscoileanna Gaelacha (Na Naíonraí Gaelacha from 1979)[6] was established in 1974 under the auspices of Conradh na Gaeilge. A joint committee,
An Comhchoiste Réamhscolaíochta ('the pre-school joint committee'),
was formed by Bord na Gaeilge and Na Naíonraí Gaelacha in 1978 (Mhic

6   Both of these titles may be translated as 'Irish language pre-schools'.

Mhathúna & Mac Con Iomaire, 2022). Although it was replaced in 1999 under the new cross-border arrangements of the Belfast Agreement, some of Bord na Gaeilge's promotional work is carried on by its successor, Foras na Gaeilge. While Comhairle na Gaeilge's detailed recommendations about local government in the Gaeltacht were not adopted, Údarás na Gaeltachta was set up in 1979 as an industrial development agency for the Gaeltacht including a quasi-democratic function of elected members.[7] Údarás na Gaeltachta continues to function as a development agency for the Gaeltacht, with social and language planning functions added in recent years. These measures were far-reaching changes that shaped Irish language policy for a generation and while they fell short of the demands of campaigns in the Gaeltacht and among proponents of nursery education, the general policy context from which they emerged was sketched by Comhairle na Gaeilge.

In some ways, contemporary public demand can be seen to have anticipated the calls of the Comhairle fifty years ago. Despite little active stimulation by the Department of Education, demand for gaelscoileanna continues to outstrip supply and there has been exponential growth in the sector since the 1970s (Ó Duibhir, 2018). Although the Irish-speaking districts are grappling with advanced language shift, the *Gaeltacht Education Policy* of 2017 is a positive action that aims to consolidate the position of Irish in Gaeltacht schools. Further strategic development of the Irish-medium sector both within and outside the Gaeltacht has occurred due to the work of An Chomhairle um Oideachas Gaeltachta agus Gaelscolaíochta (COGG; The Council for Gaeltacht and Irish-Medium Education), a body established under the Department of Education in 1998. One of COGG's most important contributions has been to provide a full range of educational textbooks in Irish, a stark contrast with the dire situation in 1971. In terms of teacher training, there are now options for students wishing to qualify as teachers in Irish-medium primary and secondary schools. For instance, there has been strong demand for the Masters course in Irish-medium

---

7   From 1980 to 2005, regular elections were held in official Gaeltacht areas for members of the board of Údaras na Gaeltachta. This system was discontinued in 2011 as an economising measure due to the financial crash. In 2020, the government committed to reintroducing direct elections for Údaras na Gaeltachta members (Tuairisc.ie, 2021).

education at NUI Galway since its inception and successful graduates are strong contenders for employment in the sector. Progress on another key aspect of the Comhairle's recommendations – the teaching of another subject through Irish in every secondary school – has been much slower, but is reiterated in the *20-Year Strategy for the Irish Language* (Government of Ireland, 2010: 12). This proposal for part-immersion has far-reaching implications in terms of expanding Irish beyond certain domains, as argued by the Comhairle fifty years ago, but is still only at exploratory stage.

The recommendation to provide denominated degrees involving Irish was far-sighted and, if introduced, could have brought a much larger student cohort into contact with the Irish language than the small numbers in existing programmes. There has been modest progress at third level, concentrated in Galway as envisaged by Comhairle na Gaeilge, but the weak legislative provisions governing the universities prevent significant development. The situation was exacerbated in the mid-century period by the resolute opposition of Professor Michael Tierney as President of UCD from 1947 to 1964 to any expansion of teaching through the medium of Irish (see Chapter 2). Despite his proficiency in Irish and commitment to Irish folklore, Tierney did not support the Revivalist aim to expand the use of Irish in education and the absence of a pro-active stance in one of the state's largest and most prestigious universities was a major restraint on policy (Briody, 2007: 481–482). Nothing akin to an elite foundation is in existence, but NUI Galway in 2004 set up Acadamh na hOllscolaíochta Gaeilge (Academy for Irish-language university education), a structure that provides Irish-medium courses at diploma, graduate and postgraduate level in the university itself and in three Gaeltacht centres (Walsh, 2012: 273–274). Trainee teachers spend periods at these centres as part of their studies, and students of Irish from NUI Galway and other universities are located there for a semester. Since the enactment of the University College (Amendment) Galway Act 2006, NUI Galway has been obliged to provide education through Irish as one of its strategic objectives (e.g. National University of Ireland, Galway, 2020). However, teaching of mainstream subjects such as History and Geography on the main campus has contracted significantly in parallel with the expansion of the Acadamh and significant additional investment is required to make comprehensive university education through Irish a reality. Academic departments of Irish in other universities have diversified into new areas of expertise, including sociolinguistics and applied linguistics but apart from limited provision in Galway, the availability of other subjects through Irish in the sector is minimal in the extreme.

5. Conclusion

Clearly, the Comhairle failed in the short term in its aims to stimulate discussion about a national language policy. Despite the comprehensive survey of CILAR published in 1975, there was little movement on a national strategy until the Bord na Gaeilge action plans of the mid-1980s. Despite their detailed nature, these suffered once more from being merely advisory and were largely ignored by the state, which was in a particularly passive mode in relation to Irish at the time. It was not until the mid-2000s that work began in earnest on a national plan, culminating in the *20-Year Strategy for the Irish Language 2010-2030* (Government of Ireland, 2010). However, Ó Huallacháin in his efforts to establish ITÉ, Comhairle na Gaeilge and subsequently CILAR set down an important marker about the professionalisation of language planning and the need for evidence-based approaches to policy formation. In subsequent years, the reconstituted ITÉ produced valuable research on Irish and other European languages that influenced the policy framework, but it was closed in 2003, leaving another lacuna in sociolinguistic research. For the past two decades, sociolinguistic research has been conducted by the universities but as it celebrates a century in existence, the Irish state once again lacks a language research agency of its own, further evidence of the 'real' language policy at play.

Although Comhairle na Gaeilge and other Irish language bodies lost the battle around Irish in education in the early 1970s, the language retains much of that core status today, is still studied by most students to Leaving Certificate level (notwithstanding a discredited system of exemptions; SEALBHÚ, 2019) and remains an entry requirement for four of the seven universities in the state. However, as discussed in the introductory part of this chapter, there are well-documented concerns about poor competence of both teachers and pupils at primary and post-primary level in the mainstream English-medium sector. The lack of progress, or even decline, in teacher ability and student achievement is a matter of grave concern. It, more than anything else, is the most obvious element of the proposals by the Comhairle, ITÉ and others where implementation has failed. Unless the diglossia approach was actively pursued along the lines suggested, extending the use of Irish beyond its core group of speakers or active supporters was always going to be the greatest challenge to overcome. Irish language policy entered a period of severe retrenchment in the 1980s and the Comhairle's short-term achievements and long-term legacy should be assessed in that light.

Comhairle na Gaeilge represents a 'back-to-front' language policy because it developed an evidence base for policy recommendations up to a decade after they had been announced in the White Paper. Whereas the Commission of 1958–1964 largely restated the policy of the 1920s, the White Paper represented a retreat from overt gaelicisation, albeit with a scant research base and under the shadow of economic liberalisation. Pressure from Ó Huallacháin led to some changes in education policy but it was not until Comhairle na Gaeilge, and subsequently CILAR, that a robust basis for policy formulation was developed. The fact that both Comhairle na Gaeilge and CILAR were funded by the Department of Finance at the heart of government may go some way to explaining their relative success compared to the unhappy experience of ITÉ in its fractious relationship with the Department of Education. The next two chapters shift the focus to activism, beginning with the long campaign for an Irish language act in Chapter 4.

Legislation

1. Introduction

This chapter analyses the legal protection granted to Irish since the foundation of the state, a key policy measure that has underpinned many subsequent initiatives in favour of the language across a range of domains. The privileged constitutional status of Irish since 1922 paved the way for language policy interventions over the past century in the fields of public administration, education, broadcasting, the Gaeltacht and the planning system. The first section will provide an overview of the constitutional status in both 1922 and 1937, before turning to celebrated examples of case law that stem from both documents. It also reviews the Official Languages Act 2003 and the amended legislation enacted in 2021. The legal status of Irish in Northern Ireland and the implications of European Union membership for language policy are also considered. The case study focuses on the long campaign waged from 1977 to 2003 for a language act providing for public services for Irish speakers and conferring specific rights on them. It examines the ideological basis of the campaign, contrasts it with the resistance and frequent hostility of the state and tracks how positions on both sides shifted over time. This chapter, therefore, is an analysis of one of the higher props of language policy, legal status, and how it is shaped by civil society activism.

1.2 Constitution of the Irish Free State, 1922

In 1922, the Constitution of the Irish Free State declared Irish to be the
national language and both Irish and English to be official languages:

> The National Language of the Irish Free State (Saorstát Éireann) is the Irish language,
> but the English language shall be equally recognised as an official language. Nothing in
> this Article shall prevent special provisions being made by the Parliament of the Irish
> Free State (otherwise called and herein generally referred to as the 'Oireachtas') for
> districts or areas in which only one language is in general use. (Article 4, Constitution
> of Irish Free State)

In a study of the 1922 Constitution, Kohn remarked that Ireland was
unique among Commonwealth countries in having granted an elevated
status to a language other than English. He argued that the final part of
Article 4 was inserted to allow for the contingency of the reunification of
Ireland but added, tellingly, that it also aimed to 'preclude apprehensions
of a bilingual fanaticism, which might impede that much desired consum-
mation' (Kohn, 1932: 123 cited by Ó Máille, 1990: 3; see also Cahillane,
2016: 108). Article 42 of the Constitution related to the enactment of legislation. Following the passage of a bill by the Oireachtas and the assent
of the King to it, two copies – one in Irish and one in English – would be
made and one would be signed by the Governor General, which would
then have legal precedence in the case of a conflict. Kohn argued that as
all legislation was discussed and enacted in English, only the English version was submitted for signature, with the Irish version being translated
subsequently and published together with the original (Kohn, 1932: 211–
212, cited by Mac Cárthaigh, 2020: 46–47). Mac Cárthaigh points to the
tension between the constitutional status as proclaimed and the monolingual practice that was deeply ingrained, describing the legislative status
of Irish at the time as 'semi-official' (*leathoifigiúil*) (2020: 47). However,
Ó Tuathail argues that the aim of Article 42 was to ensure that English
and Irish versions of legislation would be available to the public simultaneously, in the expectation that the courts may need to use both languages.
This, he claimed, was achieved, with acts, statutory instruments, rules and
orders published in English and Irish as normal administrative procedure

until 1979 (2002: 10–12). Attempts were made by Conradh na Gaeilge in the 1930s to promote the enactment of legislation in Irish but these were rebuffed on practical and legal grounds. For instance, a campaign by Conradh na Gaeilge to have legislation enacted in Irish, in line with its constitutional status, ran into the mire. Solicitor Seán Ó hUadhaigh claimed that he had been promised by the Governor General that he would always sign the Irish version of a bill but the Department of the President rejected that approach:

> A bill which has been passed in English by both Houses of the Oireachtas – and that is the position in every case to date – must be signed in that form. The problem of enactment of Bills in Irish bristles with difficulties and is at the moment insoluble. (Department of the President, 1932)

There is a small corpus of judicial interpretations of Article 4 in relation to the use of Irish. Ó Máille notes that such case law is limited to the use of Irish in legal proceedings and does not assert a broader right to Irish language services, even if it is sometimes apparent that this is the basis for the judgement (Ó Máille, 1990: 5–6; Ó Tuathail, 2002: 14–20). In one such case (*Ó Foghludha vs. McClean*, 1934), Chief Justice Hugh O'Kennedy made important observations about the meaning of Article 4 that continue to reverberate in Irish language jurisprudence to this day. O'Kennedy ruled that the Constitution imposed positive obligations on the state in relation to Irish, as it obliged it 'to do everything within its sphere of action (as for instance in State-provided education) to establish and maintain it in its status as the National Language and to recognise it for all official purposes as the National Language' (*Ó Foghludha v. McClean* [1934], cited in Ó Máille, 1990: 8). For a more detailed analysis of the significance of *Ó Foghludha v. McClean*, see Mac Cárthaigh, 2020: 52–58.

1.3 Constitution of Ireland, 1937

The Constitution of Ireland dates from 1937 and was one of the crowning achievements of the early years of Éamon de Valera's leadership. Article 8 relates to the Irish language:

1. The Irish language as the national language is the first official language.
2. The English language is recognised as a second official language.
3. Provision may, however, be made by law for the exclusive use of either of the said languages for any one or more official purposes, either throughout the State or in any part thereof.

There was some opposition to the renewed designation of Irish as the 'national language' but this was rejected by de Valera on the basis that Irish was 'the language that is most associated with this nation; the language that is in accordance with the traditions of our people' (de Valera, 1937). John A. Costello, former Attorney General, Fine Gael TD and future Taoiseach questioned the language's status, objected to the use of 'Éire' (the Irish name of the state) in the English version of the Constitution and described as 'patent absurdity' the provision that the Irish text would prevail in the result of a dispute (McCullagh, 2010: 132–133).[1]

A briefing document in advance of a visit by Conradh na Gaeilge to de Valera in October 1958 contained the flimsy claim that Irish language services would automatically flow from the constitutional status. In response to a suggestion that departmental notepaper would include the statement 'Féadfair do ghnó a dhéanamh leis an Roinn i nGaeilge' ('You may do your business with the Department in Irish'), it was claimed that this was unnecessary because it was obvious from Article 8.1 of the Constitution that the public could conduct business in Irish (Department of the Taoiseach, 1958). The existence of case law in previous decades related

---

1   For an account of the how the Constitution, including Article 8, was formulated and received, see Keogh & McCarthy, 2007.

to attempts by Irish speakers to use Irish when dealing with the state refutes this simplistic claim.

Some of the case law related to Article 8 has concluded that it offered
greater status to Irish by comparison with the 1922 constitution in that
Irish was now designated the 'first official language' (Ó Máille, 1990: 15 &
19). However, problems arose from judicial interpretations of Article 8.3
because of the scope it granted to the Oireachtas to prioritise one official
language over another. In *Attorney General v. Coyne and Wallace* (1963),
related to a notice served in Irish about a road traffic offence, Mr Justice
Kingsmill Moore interpreted Article 8.3 to mean that either language could
be used until provision had been made by law that only one language was
to be used for official purposes (Ó Máille, 1990: 10–11). In a case related
to the non-possession of a television licence because of the lack of Irish
in programmes (*An Stát (Mac Fhearraigh) v. Neilan*, 1984), Mr Justice
O'Hanlon said that any District Court, where the case was initiated, could
issue summons in Irish or English as it pleased (ibid.: 13–14). Ó Máille refers
to the belief that Article 8.3, similar to the final part of the Article 4 in 1922,
was inserted in the hope that it might apply in the case of reunification,
with English becoming the only official language in what was previously
Northern Ireland. Alternatively, he said that it could facilitate legislation
to make Irish the only official language of the Gaeltacht (ibid.: 19). Such
a suggestion was made by Conradh na Gaeilge in 1958 when its Ard-Fheis
(assembly) passed motions to that effect, but these were rejected by the
Minister for the Gaeltacht who claimed that the language policy should
be based on enticement (*mealladh*) instead of compulsion (Department
of the Gaeltacht, 1958).

We saw that under the 1922 Constitution, the version of a bill signed
by the Governor General would have precedence in the case of conflict.
That situation changed under the 1937 Constitution, which stated, in
Article 25.6, that the Irish version would have the greater legal authority:

> In the case of conflict between the texts of a law enrolled under this section in both
> the official languages, the text in the national language shall prevail.

Ó Cearúil (1999) has conducted a detailed study of the Irish version
of the Constitution and refutes the common claim that it was merely a

translation (see, for instance, Keogh & McCarthy, 2007: 148–149). He questions whether the Irish and English versions are two versions of the same text, or amount to two separate constitutions (Ó Cearúil, 2002). Article 25.4 of the Second Amendment to the Constitution Act 1941 stipulated that all laws must be translated following their enactment:

> Where the President signs the text of a Bill in one only of the official languages, an official translation shall be issued in the other language.

Mac Cárthaigh analyses this provision in the light of the Irish version of Article 8, which refers to English as 'an teanga oifigiúil eile' (literally, 'the other official language'). He asks if Article 25 allows for only the enactment of bills in Irish or bilingually, as this would be more in line with the status of Irish as national and first official language (2020: 116). Be that as it may, no time period is stipulated in Article 25.4 and a significant backlog of untranslated legislation has developed, related particularly to the 1980s and 1990s. The Official Languages Act attempted to remedy this situation and Article 7 as enacted required that every act must be published simultaneously in both languages. However, a later amendment to Article 7 diluted this absolute requirement by permitting the publication of an act on the internet in one official language only. It is clear that this will facilitate electronic publication of legislation in English only, thereby further exacerbating the backlog in translations (Walsh, 2017).

1.4 Ó Beoláin vs. Fahy

A celebrated case related to the translation arrears in legislation began in the District Court in 1997. Séamus Ó Beoláin was accused of driving under the influence of alcohol but Irish translations of the relevant road traffic legislation or Rules of the District Court were not available. When the translations failed to materialise, Ó Beoláin took the case to the High Court as a judicial review and sought declarations that there was a constitutional obligation on the state to provide such documents. In 1999 in the High Court, Ms Justice Laffoy ruled that the state was obliged to provide an official translation of the Rules but that the passage of more than two years since they were published in English was not a 'reasonable period of time' to translate nearly 1,200 pages of text. Ó Tuathail criticised the judge's ruling that a 'reasonable period of time' was implied by Article 25.4 of the Constitution and argued that Ó Beoláin had several grounds for appeal (2002: 63). The Supreme Court appeal was heard in 2000 and in a majority judgement delivered in 2001, it agreed to the two declarations sought by Ó Beoláin. Both judges (McGuinness and Hardiman) made strong statements about the place of Irish in the Constitution and the duties that flowed from that. Mr Justice Hardiman said that it was completely contradictory to the bilingual policy to which the state was committed that laws would be provided in one language only and that it was essential that the rules of all courts be provided in both languages so that anyone taking a case could be equally effective in Irish as in English (ibid.: 64–5). He added that Irish, as the national and first official language, could not be excluded from any part of the official discourse of the state or from any official business of the state, could not be treated less favourably than the second official language and that those who wished to use it could not be disadvantaged (ibid.: 66). Ó Tuathail predicted that the Hardiman judgement would be drawn upon in future legal proceedings about language rights as a definitive judgement on the relationship that should exist between the two official languages (ibid.: 67). It was significant politically that the Ó Beoláin case was concluded around the same time that the government was preparing to publish legislation that would become the Official Languages Act, 2003 (see case study in this chapter). That legislation did not deal comprehensively with the translation of legislation, however. In 2010 in *Ó Murchú v. An Taoiseach*, the Supreme Court granted a declaration to the applicant that there was a constitutional duty to provide translations of all Rules of the Courts, including amendments, forms and indices, as soon as possible after their enactment (Mac Cárthaigh, 2020: 119–120).

1.5 Official Languages Act 2003

Eighty-one years after it was first granted official constitutional status, in 2003 the Oireachtas passed the Official Languages Act, the first piece of legislation to provide a framework for the delivery of public services in the Irish language. The background to the legislation, including the long civil society campaign for language rights, is discussed in the case study of this chapter. The Act consists of six sections related to general matters, organs of the state, public bodies, the language commissioner, placenames and general provisions. The general preamble states that the Act aims to promote the use of Irish for official purposes in the state and govern the use of official languages in the Oireachtas, legislation and the courts. It also covers the use of languages in communication by public bodies and in the provision of services and sets out the duties of such bodies in relation to Irish and English. Furthermore, the Act makes provision for the establishment of Oifig Choimisinéir na dTeangacha Oifigiúla (office of the Commissioner of official languages) and sets out its functions.

The Act is not cast in a rights framework and there are only two cases where a person has a direct right to use Irish: in the Oireachtas and in the courts. In Article 6, a member of either House of the Oireachtas has the right to use either official language in proceedings and committees. Similarly, a person appearing before either House or its committees may use either official language. However, while official reports are to be published in both official languages, contributions in either Irish or English may be published in the original language, so in effect, this amounts to reports almost exclusively in English. Article 7 states that after enactment, an Act will be published in both official languages simultaneously but as discussed above, this was amended subsequently to allow electronic publication in one language only. Article 8 states that any person may use either official language in court proceedings and cannot be placed at a disadvantage, inconvenience or expense for using one language over another. To avoid such disadvantage, the court must make arrangements for interpretation. Article 8.4 sets out provisions in relation to the use of official languages in civil but not criminal proceedings.

Articles 9 to 19 cover the use of official languages by public bodies. In
Article 9.1, the Minister is empowered to make regulations about the use
of official languages in oral recorded announcements, official stationery,
signage or advertisements. In 2008, the Minister made regulations covering
oral announcements, stationery and signage only. Article 9.2 stipulates that
correspondence in either official language with public bodies must be an-
swered in the same language and Article 9.3 obliges public bodies to use
both Irish and English when communicating with the general public or a
class of the public. This applies mostly to announcements of public policies
and/or consultations where the entire public or subgroups may be targeted
by the use of mailshots. Article 10 obliges any public body publishing
'public policy proposals', annual reports, financial statements, strategies or
other documents 'of major public importance' to be in Irish and English.

Articles 11 to 18 cover language schemes – internal language plans
developed and implemented by public bodies – that were intended to be
the central mechanism for the delivery of services in Irish. Under Article
11, draft schemes are requested by the Minister, setting out the services
that the public body will provide in Irish, in English and bilingually. The
body is also obliged to propose measures to extend the services it provides
in Irish. Article 12 provides for guidelines for preparing schemes. Article
13.2 relates to competence of Irish among staff of public bodies and the use
of the language in the Gaeltacht. Subsection (c) obliges a body to ensure
that it has adequate staff to provide services in Irish, subsection (d) obliges
it to ensure that it can provide services in Irish in the Gaeltacht and subsection (e) obliges it to ensure that Irish becomes the working language of
any Gaeltacht offices by a date to be determined by the Minister.[2] Article
14 stipulates that each scheme last for three years and should be replaced
by a new scheme following agreement with the Minister. Articles 15 and 16
set out the procedure for the review and amendment of schemes. Article
18 states that once agreed, a scheme must be implemented by the public

2   This date was stipulated in some language schemes agreed between the Minister
     and the public body but was not specified in the guidelines for preparation of
     schemes (Department of Community, Rural and Gaeltacht Affairs, 2004). I am
     grateful to Órla de Búrca, Oifig an Choimisinéara Teanga, for her assistance with
     this detail.

body. The language schemes were based on the system in place in Wales but became increasingly dysfunctional and discredited over time (Walsh, 2015). Articles 20–30 relate to the office of the language Commissioner, who is appointed by the President on the advice of the Oireachtas and is independent in their functions. Article 21 sets out the functions of the Commissioner, which include monitoring compliance by public bodies with the Act, investigating failures to comply, advising members of the public about their language rights, advising public bodies about their obligations and investigating possible breaches of other enactments mentioning Irish (see below). Article 22 outlines the powers of the Commissioner, which include the ability to require a person possessing relevant information to appear in front of them. If the person does not co-operate or otherwise hinders the Commissioner, they may be convicted of an offence and fined or imprisoned. Article 23 outlines the manner in which the Commissioner will conduct investigations into public bodies and Article 26 explains the procedure for reporting the result of such investigations including the making the findings and recommendations. Subsection 5 empowers the Commissioner to report a failure of a public body to comply with the recommendations of an investigation to the Houses of the Oireachtas. Article 28 allows a party to an investigation to appeal the findings and recommendations to the High Court on a point of law. Article 29 allows the Commissioner to publish commentaries on the Act and Article 30 covers the publication of the annual report and other reports as necessary.

Articles 31–35 relate to placenames. Under Article 32, the Minister may make a placenames order to confirm official Irish language versions of placenames, giving them the same legal force and effect as English versions. Under Article 33, the English version of placenames no longer have legal force in any act, on official maps or on road signs erected by local authorities. This led to a long controversy in the town of Dingle in Co. Kerry, where locals claimed that use of 'An Daingean' only on placenames and maps would lead to loss of tourist revenue (Walsh, 2017: 465).

1.6 Official Languages Act 2021

Eight years after a review of the legislation was announced and following criticism of two general schemes of bills in 2014 and 2017, the Official Languages (Amendment) Bill was published on the 11th of December 2019. While the new Bill was clearly an improvement on the existing legislation, there were concerns about the lack of specific aims and clear duties imposed on public bodies (Tuairisc.ie, 2019). Of the more than 300 amendments discussed, all 265 tabled by the opposition were rejected but more than 50 proposed by the Minister were accepted. Following almost two years of debate and the disruption to parliamentary business caused by the Covid-19 crisis, on the 6th of October 2021 the Bill was passed by Dáil Éireann (Tuairisc.ie, 2021b) and by Seanad Éireann on the 15th of December after additional amendments (Tuairisc.ie, 2021d). It was signed by the President and became law just before Christmas (Department of Tourism, Arts, Heritage, Gaeltacht, Sport and Media, 2021).

Section 9.2 of the original Act was expanded to include communication by social media in the requirement to respond to correspondence in either Irish or English with a public body in the same language. An amended Section 9.3 expands the scope of 'mailshots' beyond the existing requirement to provide information bilingually to marketing material also, with the proviso that text in Irish cannot be smaller than that in English. Five new sections (9A–9E) have been inserted after Section 9 covering names, addresses and titles in Irish, duties of public bodies regarding official forms and logos, names and logos of new bodies, and services provided on behalf of public bodies. Section 9A allows the Minister to require a body to ensure that its IT systems correctly record and use names, addresses and titles in Irish, including the use of the length accent (*fada*) in Irish text. Under Section 9B, the Minister may require a public body to comply with guidance regarding the content and layout of official forms in Irish or in Irish and English. Section 9C obliges a public body that is renewing or changing its logo to ensure that any text involved is in Irish or in Irish and English, with Irish first and no less prominent than English. Under Section 9D, the name of any new statutory public body should be in Irish and must adhere to the same rules about use of languages on logos. Section 9E covers 'public facing services' provided by third parties on behalf of public bodies and requires such bodies to take all appropriate steps to ensure that external providers adhere to other provisions in relation to Irish language services. A new Section 10A covers advertising in Irish by public bodies. It requires them to ensure that at least 20 per cent of their advertising each year is conducted in Irish and that at least 5 per cent of their annual advertising budget is spent on advertisements in Irish in Irish language media.

New Sections 18A–18F relate to new governance structures aimed at achieving the recruitment of more Irish speakers by public bodies. Article 18A obliges the Minister, no later than six months after the Act comes into effect, to establish an Irish Language Services Advisory Committee. Section 18B stipulates that the Minister will appoint a chairperson and between five and ten members representing the Department of the Gaeltacht, the Department of Public Expenditure and Reform, the Public Appointments Service, other public bodies and representatives of the Gaeltacht and other areas. Under Section 18C, the first function of the Advisory Committee is to prepare a National Plan for the provision of Irish language services within two years. The Plan, covering a six-year period, will identify services that should be provided in Irish, recommend if language standards (see below) should be applied to a public body and propose strategies for the better provision of services in Irish. Other functions of the Committee are to advise public bodies about the number and grade of staff who may be required to deliver Irish language services, to make recommendations about increasing the number of staff who can provide such services and about the level of competence required. It will also report every five years, providing information about competence in, use of and training in Irish within public bodies. Sub-section 18C (3) obliges the Advisory Committee to have regard to overarching objectives of increasing the provision of Irish language services in all three types of language planning district (see Chapter 2) and increasing the number of staff competent in Irish to 20 per cent of all recruits by 2030. Section 18E obliges the Minister, after submitting the National Plan to the government, to specify the date by which Irish will become the working language of an office of a public body in the Gaeltacht. It also requires the Minister to fix the date by which all services will be provided by a public body in Irish in the Gaeltacht, including services provided by public bodies from outside the Gaeltacht.

Sections 19A–19D relate to the introduction of language standards, a new mechanism aimed at ensuring the provision of Irish language services in place of the existing system of schemes. Section 19A allows the Minister to oblige public bodies to adhere to language standards. Such standards may include services to be included in Irish or in Irish and English, the level of competence of Irish required by staff and, if located in a language planning district, how the services may impact on the position of Irish there. The extent to which the body interacts with the public will also be considered when prescribing language standards. The Minister may consult with other Ministers and/or the Advisory Committee, publish draft standards and seek feedback from public bodies about them. Standards will be reviewed every five years. Section 19B stipulates that once agreed, a public body must comply with a language standard but Section 19C sets out in detail the grounds for seeking derogations from standards for up to three years, with an option of extending this for a further two years. Section 19D provides for the publication of guidelines for public bodies in relation to compliance with language standards.

Section 21 of the original Act is amended to expand one of the functions of the language Commissioner to allow them to monitor compliance of public bodies with other enactments mentioning the Irish language. Section 31 is amended to allow the establishment of a new Placenames Committee (new Sections 31A–31C), whose functions will be to advise the Minister about the making of placenames orders, to carry out research into the topic and to provide information about it as required.

Following a tortuous journey of a decade, a revised Official Languages Act was enacted at the end of 2021 and undoubtedly represents an improvement on the regime created by the 2003 legislation. There are advances in the areas of names and addresses in Irish, marketing by public bodies and advertising in Irish. Irish language groups robustly defended the overarching objective of 20 per cent of Irish-speaking recruits to public bodies and if implemented meaningfully, this is a far-reaching proposal. The new Advisory Committee and National Plan in relation to Irish language services will be capable of gathering data and making proposals in

relation to recruitment of bilingual staff to public bodies. The 20 per cent
objective has a clear timeframe and is required to be adhered to by law but
given the very low levels of Irish language ability in the public service at
present, it will be highly challenging for most bodies to attain such a level
of bilingualism within their staff.

An associated concern relates to competence itself, and there is a risk
that the lower levels of the Common European Framework of Reference
for Languages will be chosen when identifying 'Irish-language' jobs. The
language standards may be an improvement on the failed system of language schemes, but the scope given to the Minister in applying them selectively to public bodies risks delaying the provision of better service in
Irish. Furthermore, experience from Wales indicates that standards are
complex mechanisms imposing burdens on the civil servants responsible
for preparing them, so the question of administrative capacity arises (Mac
Giolla Chríost, 2016: 207–219). Of some concern is the detailed attention
paid by the Bill to the system of derogation under which a public body
could postpone its obligation to adhere to standards. Another cause of
disquiet is the absence of a date by which public bodies would be obliged
to provide all services in Irish in the Gaeltacht. For instance, Section 18E
is strikingly similar to the original Sections 11 (2) (d) and (e), which supposedly obliged public bodies in their language schemes to achieve the
same general objectives by 2020, a deadline that was missed in most cases.
It remains to be seen how effectively the new act will be implemented, but
the abject failure of the state to provide basic health information and services in Irish during the pandemic is an illustration of the challenge that
lies ahead (Walsh, 2021a).

1.7 Other enactments

As stated above, section 21 (f) of the Official Languages Act 2003 allows
the Commissioner to investigate a possible breach of other enactments
related to the official status of Irish. The Commissioner has the power:

> to carry out an investigation, whether on his or her own initiative, on request by the
> Minister or pursuant to a complaint made to him or her by any person, to ascertain

whether any provision of any other enactment relating to the status or use of an official language was not or is not being complied with.

The revised act will give the Commissioner the power to monitor compliance with other such enactments. Irish is mentioned in over 150 pieces of legislation since the foundation of the state and therefore, section 21 (f) is potentially wide in scope. Of the 156 acts identified in my analysis of the corpus of legislation, clear reference was made to the promotion or use of Irish in 197 sections or schedules covering general language policy, the Gaelacht, financial incentives, public sector employment, the legal profession, corpus planning, educational institutions, cultural institutions, broadcasting, placenames and the private sector. The study found that many of the provisions about language policy were vague and imprecise while others were conditional in some way, for instance that they were dependent on resources being made available. There were also substantive legislative provisions in relation to education, broadcasting, public service employment and road signage. Some legislative provisions in recent years attempted to limit the scope of language policy in relation to public employment provision and the Official Languages Act itself. Significantly, the private sector is almost entirely absent from the corpus, with only one long-forgotten act from 1936 placing limited Irish language obligations on insurance companies (Walsh, 2017).

1.8 Status of Irish in the European Union

When Ireland joined the then European Economic Community in 1973, the government sought a minimalist status for Irish, limited to translating the principal European treaties into Irish but denying the language the privileges of full working status. The secondary legislation, containing information of interest to the average person, would not be translated into Irish and Irish citizens would be denied employment opportunities in the European institutions due to the diminished status of Irish. Ó Tuathail argued that by prioritising English, the Irish government contravened Article 8.3 by failing to make provision by law (i.e. in the Oireachtas) for one language only to be used for official purposes (2002: 71–89). Mac

Cárthaigh described this 'semi-official' status (*leathoifigiúil*) as a new departure in European Union jurisprudence (2020: 81).

Following a vigorous campaign by Irish language groups, Irish became a working language of the European Union on the 1st of January 2007, although a derogation from translating all legislation was granted due to the need to train and employ qualified staff (a similar exception was granted to Maltese). This meant that the obligation to translate European Union law and European Court of Justice rulings was limited to regulations made by co-decisions of the European Council and Parliament. The Council reviewed the derogation in 2015 and decided that it would end entirely on the 1st of January 2022, thereby granting Irish complete working status for the first time from that date (Mac Cárthaigh, 2020: 83). Mac Cárthaigh said that no regulation made under European law comes into effect until it has been published in all official languages. He drew a distinction between the European linguistic regime – where all legislative proposals are introduced in multilingual versions, including Irish, to the European Parliament – and the Oireachtas, where the legislative process takes place in English only for the most part. Therefore, although all twenty-four versions of legislation carry equal legal weight in the European Union, in Ireland only the English text of Acts is authoritative with an official but secondary translation into Irish, although even this is not guaranteed (ibid.: 111–112). In this regard, the European Union is a good example of how supranational language policy can highlight inconsistencies and deficiencies in domestic regimes. The international status granted to Irish, particularly since the removal of the derogation on the 1st of January 2022, is also significant both in terms of linguistic development and attractive employment opportunities for Irish speakers in the European institutions.

Ó Máille raised the possibility of linguistic difficulties in relation to European community law and the free movement of workers, one of the fundamental objectives of the Union. He refers to the case of Anita Groener, a Dutch national who in 1984 applied for a permanent full-time post as a Lecturer in the National College of Art and Design, which was part of the Dublin Vocational Education Committee and therefore ultimately under the control of the Minister for Education. Ms Groener failed to be appointed because she did not pass an Irish language test, and she sought a judicial review of the Minister's decision on the basis that it contravened European law on freedom of movement of workers. The High Court raised three questions about the case with the European Court of Justice, one of which contained the kernel of the issue: should consideration be given to the Irish government's policy that a post holder required a knowledge of Irish even if such competence was not necessary to do the job itself? The Court ruled that the policy was justified because of the importance of education in supporting the government's language policy and due to the influence of teachers on young people. Therefore, it was reasonable that a teacher would be required to have some knowledge of Irish and this requirement was justified once it was imposed proportionately and in a non-discriminatory manner (Ó Máille, 1990: 38–39).

1.9 Legal status of Irish in Northern Ireland

In the Belfast Agreement of 1998, the British government committed to taking 'resolute action' on behalf of Irish in Northern Ireland, potentially ending decades of the language's marginalisation by the Northern authorities. As the Republic prepared to enact its own language legislation, attention moved to achieving a legal basis for the promotion of Irish in the North. Hopes were raised when the British government signed and ratified the European Charter for Regional or Minority Languages in 2001 and included Irish in Northern Ireland under Level 3 protection (the higher of two levels). In a submission to the Council of Europe about the Charter commitments on Irish, the non-governmental body POBAL criticised the lack of progress and pointed to the need for domestic legislation to protect Irish (POBAL, 2005). However, sensitivities around the Irish language in Northern Ireland and ongoing political instability in the Stormont institutions has meant that little substantive progress has been made on the legislative front over the past two decades.

In 2004, POBAL published draft legislative proposals based on expert opinion in other bilingual jurisdictions. In 2006, the British government in the St Andrews Agreement committed to legislating for the Irish language at Westminster but reneged on its promise (POBAL, 2006). Revised proposals were brought forward (POBAL, 2012) and these were followed by further consultation by the Department of Culture, Arts and Leisure in 2015. These proposals were in turn rejected by the Stormont Executive and POBAL lost its funding in a restructuring of the voluntary sector by Foras na Gaeilge. In 2017, a dispute about the Irish language and other issues between Sinn Féin and the Democratic Unionist Party led to the collapse of the Stormont institutions. Meanwhile, in 2017, Conradh na Gaeilge brought forward watered-down proposals for a free-standing Irish language act. The institutions remained closed and a possible breakthrough on language in 2018 came to nothing after a draft agreement was leaked to the media. In January 2020, agreement was reached between the parties in the form of *New Decade, New Approach* (NDNA), including proposals on Irish and Ulster Scots, and Stormont reopened. NDNA created no rights for Irish speakers but proposed the establishment of two language commissioners, one for Irish and the other for Ulster Scots. It further undertook to introduce language standards for public service provision, set up a central government translation hub and repeal the Administration of Justice (Ireland) Act 1737, which forbids the use of Irish in the courts. POBAL strongly condemned NDNA for failing to create a robust rights framework for Irish speakers and criticised the authorities for the lack of progress on implementing the agreement (for a detailed discussion, see Muller 2022). Meanwhile, forty Irish language groups pressurised the British government to introduce Irish language legislation in Westminster and attempts were made to internationalise the campaign, with Conradh na Gaeilge calling on the United Nations to support the immediate implementation of an Irish language act (Simpson, 2021b).

In parallel to its campaign for an act, Conradh na Gaeilge also sought a judicial review of the Northern Ireland Executive's failure to implement an Irish Language Strategy, in breach of article 28 (3) of the Northern Ireland Act, 1998. The Strategy was promised as part of the 2006 St Andrews Agreement between the British and Irish governments, which amended the 1998 act. As a result of the case taken by Conradh na Gaeilge, in 2017 the High Court in Belfast found that the Executive had failed to fulfil its duty under the act. Under NDNA the Strategy was to be brought forward within six months, but no such document was forthcoming. In 2021, after the Executive failed to respond to a legal notice from Conradh na Gaeilge, the High Court granted leave to the organisation to apply for a judicial review (Conradh na Gaeilge, 2021a).[3] One aspect of the legal context is now examined in greater detail, the campaign that led eventually to the Official Languages Act 2003.

2. Case study: The campaign for a language act

The case studies in this and the subsequent chapter move our analysis of language policy forwards in time to the 1970s and 1980s and focus on the role of activism in ameliorating the position of Irish in the domains of public administration and the media. This study examines the campaign for an Irish language act of almost thirty years' duration, which was born out of frustration at the policy retreats of the early 1970s as described in Chapter 3. The archival records reveal often sharp ideological contestation between voluntary organisations and the state as well as a professionalisation of activism and increased influences from similar campaigns for minority languages abroad. The analysis tracks how the campaign developed over time, became more broad-based and exploited wider changes in social attitudes and in the policy and governance context.

2.1 Context

In its 1968 report about the White Paper on the Restoration of the Irish Language, the government highlighted a speech by President Éamon de Valera on the fiftieth anniversary of the Easter Rising as its primary evidence of progress in relation to Irish in public administration. Two years earlier, de Valera had reminded people of the sacrifices made for the cause of independence and urged them to renew the spirit of 1916. This was

3   I thank Conchúr Ó Muadaigh of Conradh na Gaeilge for his assistance with this
     section.

cited as the first item in the section of the progress report dealing with public administration:

> The message stressed the vital role of the national language, the need to ensure that this generation will see to it that the language lives and the desirability that all who know the language should speak it and extend its use. (Government of Ireland, 1968: 4)

There was no obvious link between de Valera's jaded exhortations and improving Irish language public services and the ordering of priorities in the report exposed the threadbare approach of the government to the topic. Following the emergence of the LFM and in the context of broader questioning of foundational aims related to the language, Irish language civil society responded with a campaign to create a legal basis for Irish language services, thereby forcing the government to give practical effect to Article 8 of the Constitution. In 1973–1974, the government acceded to the LFM's demands and removed the requirement to pass Irish in order to be awarded the Leaving Certificate and the Irish language entrance examination for the civil service (see Chapter 3). Following these major policy retreats, Conradh na Gaeilge stepped up its efforts to codify rights for Irish speakers in a legal framework. It was a long and hard-fought campaign, with two high points: the late 1970s/early 1980s and the late 1990s when the government committed eventually to introduce language legislation. A campaign to achieve a bill of rights for Irish speakers gained pace from the mid-1970s and incorporated a symbolic declaration, a draft bill and a Rights Bureau within Conradh na Gaeilge to deal with complaints. The campaign lasted for at least a decade and was an important milestone in raising greater public awareness of the lack of public services in Irish. Although it would be 2003 until the enactment of the Official Languages Act, significant groundwork was done by activists in Irish language organisations in previous decades, including this campaign by Conradh na Gaeilge.

2.2 Rights Sub-Committee

In 1976, the newly formed Rights Sub-Committee of Conradh na Gaeilge began working on a declaration of rights and pledged to publish a draft bill by the following year. It also promised to publicise cases where members of the public had been insulted when seeking services in Irish (Mac Mathúna, 1976). One such case involved a member of Conradh na Gaeilge's Executive Committee Mairéad Uí Dhomhnaill who suffered verbal abuse and was threatened with detention at Glasgow Airport in 1977 because she used her Irish name, the only one by which she was known, to the Special Branch (Conradh na Gaeilge, 1977f & 1977g). Conradh na Gaeilge complained to the Department of Foreign Affairs and the British Home Office about the matter. Other cases highlighted included a Irish speaker from Donegal who was ordered to speak English to her son in Portlaoise prison, the refusal of a court case in Irish to a Donegal Gaeltacht man, a fine imposed on a Kerry priest for refusing to pay a parking ticket issued in English and the beating of a man by Gardaí for answering questions in Irish (Conradh na Gaeilge, 1976c). A briefing document claimed that basic civil rights were being denied to Irish speakers. It said that the campaign should ensure that no Irish speaker was obliged to use English in order to comply with the state's laws or use its services, that all services would be available in Irish and that state officials could not disparage Irish speakers (Conradh na Gaeilge, 1977e).

The Declaration of Rights for the Irish Language (*Forógra Cearta don Ghaeilge*) was published on 10th November 1976, containing five basic principles: (a) achieving equal rights and status for Irish; (b) giving every child the right to learn Irish; (c) ensuring that expansion of the Gaeltacht be adopted as a major policy; (d) ensuring that extension of the use of Irish be made a government policy and (e) offering justice and support to the world's minority languages (Conradh na Gaeilge, 1976b). An accompanying press statement said that the reason for the campaign was the retreat of the government from the aims of the Revival and the rejection of Irish by the Northern authorities. It also drew heavily on the recently published CILAR report (see Chapter 3), citing the high levels of support for language promotion, investment in the Gaeltacht, Irish-medium schools, Irish language textbooks and television programmes in Irish. Conradh na Gaeilge deplored the recent policy retreat in education and public administration and criticised the complete lack of support for Irish in Northern Ireland. It announced that it was working on a bill of rights for the Irish Language and had established a Rights Bureau in its head office to deal with complaints about public bodies. It also pledged to ensure compliance with a new statutory instrument mandating that road signs in Gaeltacht areas display placenames in Irish only (Conradh na Gaeilge, 1976a).

By July 1977, the Rights Bureau reported that it had dealt with seventy-five complaints, two-thirds of which had been satisfactorily resolved. In the absence of any legislative footing, the Bureau was operating purely on the powers of moral persuasion and goodwill on the part of state officials. A document from 1981 listed 360 complaints, including public, private and charitable bodies, almost 60 per cent of which had been resolved (Conradh na Gaeilge, 1981). The Bureau wrote to public bodies such as the train company CIÉ requesting that oral announcements be made bilingually and agreed to make a similar request to Northern Rail. Its members gathered data on the absence of Irish on signage at airports and ferry ports and contacted the banks asking them to accept cheques in Irish and provide other bilingual documentation. After an intervention from Conradh na Gaeilge, the Minister for Foreign Affairs, Garret FitzGerald, complained to the British Ambassador and Home Office in London over a case involving the delay of a man using an Irish name at Holyhead port (Conradh na Gaeilge, 1977e).

The Bureau dealt with a large range of bodies, private, public and voluntary during its existence. A correspondent from Dublin sent in a list of complaints about the postal service, including the lack of Irish in the 1985 telephone directory, the issuing of stamps in English only and English-only advertising. He believed that the state bodies and public institutions should not be allowed to discriminate against people who used the first official language of the state (Williams, 1985b). The postal service was also singled out for criticism for its English-only postcards featuring snakes wearing tricolour flags, issued on St. Patrick's Day (An Post, 1986). The telecommunications company Telecom Éireann features regularly in the archives, including a copy of a final warning, in English only, to Conradh na Gaeilge itself that its phone service would be cut if it did not pay the bill (it refused to pay as the bill was in English only) (Telecom Éireann, 1985). There were also references to pickets being mounted by Conradh na Gaeilge members on Telecom headquarters in response to telephone lines being cut off for non-payment of bills (Conradh na Gaeilge, 1987). A letter in Irish from Aer Lingus in 1987 expressed regret to a passenger that he had been unable to speak Irish to the airhostess on a flight from London. In a reflection of historical ideological framing of Irish, the Aer Lingus representative said that he understood why an Irish person living abroad would be disappointed at such an occurrence and that the company encouraged all its staff to speak Irish, 'our national language' (*ár dteanga náisiúnta*). However, he added that English was the international language of aviation and it was not possible to oblige all staff to speak Irish (Aer Lingus, 1987).

The private sector was targeted also. Writing from Connemara, a complainant expressed umbrage that Bank of Ireland posted English speakers to its travelling bank in the heart of the Gaeltacht (Williams, 1985a). A flyer in English distributed by a branch of First National Building Society in An Fál Carrach in the Donegal Gaeltacht prompted a complaint from a local person about the 'disrespect and insult shown to Gaeltacht building by English-language advertising' (*as an dhímheas [sic] agus as an mhasla atá imeartha ar phobal na Gaeltachta ag an fhógraíocht Bhéarla amháin sin*) (Mag Fhearraigh, 1987).

Not all correspondence was negative, however. The archives also contain examples of good practice in bilingual packaging or attempts to cajole public and private companies into introducing bilingual elements into advertising. In 1977, a campaign was launched to increase the use of Irish on the packaging of white foods such as milk and butter (Conradh na Gaeilge, 1977b). Evidence was gathered about the presence of Irish in Aer Lingus packaging and marketing, and the files contain a multilingual peanut package (Aer Lingus, n.d.) and a multilingual entry from the airline's inflight magazine *Cara* (Aer Lingus, 1982). In both cases, the text in Irish came first. There are bilingual receipts from supermarkets and bilingual forms from banks (Quinnsworth, 1984, Allied Irish Banks, n.d.). Examples of best practice from abroad were also kept and include multilingual packaging on Belgian chocolate bars (Toblerone, n.d.) and bilingual lottery tickets from Canada (Interprovincial Lottery Corporation [Canada], 1988). These were used by Conradh na Gaeilge as a campaign against the English-only approach of the Irish National Lottery when it was launched in 1986, and examples of the Canadian material were used in lobbying (see further examples in NUIG G60/29/2/2). There was correspondence with companies in the food, insurance and financial sectors encouraging them to use Irish in advertising and examples of positive responses from large private companies such as 7 Up (Seven-Up International, 1987) and FIAT (n.d.). A letter to the Electricity Supply Board entreats it to use some Irish in its newspaper and television advertising:

> Many common home life situations can be dealt with in adverts for electricity, and a phrase like 'cuir an citeal ar siúl' [put on the kettle] can be easily presented on TV. (Mac Fhearghusa, 1976)

2.3 Bill of Rights

The Bill of Rights for the Irish Language was first published in 1977, re-printed in slightly amended versions in 1978, 1979 and 1983 and formed the basis of the rights campaign for the best part of a decade (Conradh na Gaeilge, 1977b, 1977c, 1977d). It was based on information gathered internally and externally, including motions passed by the Ard-Fheis, the work of the Rights Sub-Committee and research into language legislation, actual or proposed, in other bilingual countries. The files include booklets about language data and legislation from Belgium and Luxembourg and letters to the Belgian, South African and Swiss embassy enquiring about the legal situation in those countries (Conradh na Gaeilge, 1975a, 1975b, 1975c). Information from Wales includes a copy of the Welsh Language (Equal Validity) Bill 1967, an attempt by Cymdeithas Yr Iaith Gymraeg (the Welsh Language Society, an equivalent to Conradh na Gaeilge) to expedite publication of a formal Welsh Language Bill that was enacted later that year. There were also draft articles of a putative Scottish Constitution published by the Scottish National Party in 1977, one of which promised official status for Gaelic, and a copy of the Gaelic (Miscellaneous Provisions) Bill 1981 (Scottish National Party, 1977 & 1981). Another file contains information about language requirements for the Brussels police (NUIG G60/29/4/6).

It was important for the organisation that the bill would bear the hallmarks of a legitimate document published by the Bills Office of the Oireachtas, which could then be used to lobby politicians to support it and initiate the formal legislative process. This would not have been achieved without the clandestine support of an unnamed official in the Bills Office who signed 'An Dréachtóir' (the drafter) on correspondence with Conradh in case of negative repercussions from superiors (An Dréachtóir, 1975). At one stage, the unnamed person ends a note with a warning: 'Think it over, & call me to an audience on the steps of you-know-where for further discussion. Don't forget to keep my name out of it all, so I won't end up in the breadline!' (An Dréachtóir, 1976). The correspondence with the drafter was in English, but it is clear that the person had a good command of written Irish, as they were capable of commenting on later translations of the draft. Having scrutinised international legislation sent by Conradh na Gaeilge, the drafter pointed to the fundamental difference between other bilingual jurisdictions and the Irish case: the 'constitutionally privileged position' enjoyed by Irish. They felt it would be constitutionally unsound and tactically unwise to bring forward a bill that would compel the state to provide services in Irish, because such services were already available theoretically under the Constitution. The problem was with the practice of those rights, and therefore what was needed was an act that would deal with the question of enforcement. The unnamed official suggested the Canadian Commissioner of Official Languages as a model to ensure that whatever theoretical rights already existed could be brought into effect. A handwritten translation of the bill was received from the Oireachtas Translation Section, with a note attached saying that the translator did not wish to risk having it typed in house (Ó Curraoin, 1976).

The bill was published in July 1977 and outlined the obligations of the government, ministers, departments and state-sponsored bodies to promote Irish. In particular, it would ensure that any citizens wishing to conduct their business in Irish with the state could do so without hindrance. Furthermore, the bill obliged all government departments and state bodies to provide their services entirely in Irish in the Gaeltacht. It proposed the

Office of Commissioner of the Irish Language to review the legislation and accept complaints from the public. The Commissioner would be empowered to apply to the High Court for an order against a minister if they failed to implement a provision of the bill (Conradh na Gaeilge, 1977d). In a letter sent in advance of the Seanad elections in 1977, Conradh na Gaeilge said that it intended to put the Bill before the Oireachtas and asked candidates to indicate whether or not they would support the Bill if elected (Conradh na Gaeilge, 1977c). A leaflet in English painted a picture of an organisation at war with the government on language policy. It claimed that the government was 'killing the Irish language. In spite of the stated aims of all the major political parties in favour of the Irish Language, the Government is actively and energetically persecuting Irish Speakers and discouraging the use of Irish in every walk of life. Irish Speaker[s] are for all practical purposes second class citizens in their own country' (Conradh na Gaeilge, c. 1977).

A handwritten note from former Secretary General Maolsheachlainn Ó Caollaí suggested that a delegation from Conradh should seek a meeting with the Taoiseach, Charles Haughey, to press the case. He mentioned the forthcoming Supreme Court appeal in the case of *Ó Monacháin vs. Ireland* in relation to Irish language competence of District Court judges in the Gaeltacht, and said that the Conradh should try to take advantage of its implications (Ó Caollaí, 1980). Political instability over the next two years, with three general elections held in an eighteen-month period in 1981 and 1982, prevented legislative progress on many fronts but Conradh na Gaeilge persisted with its campaign, distributing thousands of leaflets and urging the support of election candidates. It also met the main political leaders Charles Haughey of Fianna Fáil and Garret FitzGerald of Fine Gael to press the case with them (Mac Mathúna, 1986). FitzGerald, in coalition with Labour, won the November 1982 election and began a five-year term in office.

The fact that Conradh na Gaeilge was now dealing with the same parties that had overseen the major policy retreat a decade earlier may have fanned the flames on both sides. It issued a new version of the bill in 1983 and sent copies to all TDs and Senators, seeking their support. It distributed leaflets to the public explaining the gap between the constitutional status of Irish and the reality for many Irish speakers and adding that language legislation was the norm in many countries (Conradh na Gaeilge, 1983b). Another leaflet urged voters to contact their elected representatives and exert pressure on them to support the bill. Local authorities in Gaeltacht counties and in Dublin, as well as the GAA, traditional music body Comhaltas Ceoltóirí Éireann and Irish language bodies offered their support (Conradh na Gaeilge, 1983d). Public meetings were also held in the Donegal and Galway Gaeltacht to drum up support for the proposal (Conradh na Gaeilge, 1983a & 1983c). Secretary General Seán Mac Mathúna stood in the Seanad elections of 1982 and 1983 on the bill of rights issue and although not elected, gained further publicity for the campaign in the process (Mac Mathúna, 1986).

After a decade, the Conradh na Gaeilge campaign for the act was running out of steam. In a newspaper article, the Secretary General admitted that in spite of much effort, it had so far failed to generate enough political support and was switching attention to parties with large numbers of elected representatives (Mac Mathúna, 1986). The campaign seems to have petered out around this time as the question of Irish language media came more sharply into focus. The new independent broadcasting regime was another blow to the status of Irish, and Conradh na Gaeilge's energies became increasingly directed at the campaign for an Irish language television station (see Chapter 5).

2.4 Language planning activities by Bord na Gaeilge

The campaign of Conradh na Gaeilge may actually have been impeded at this time by the work of the new state board for Irish, Bord na Gaeilge (established on a statutory basis in 1978). The Bord published an *Action Plan for Irish 1983–1986*, which fell well short of endorsing the demand for legislation. The main weakness of the Plan, despite its many useful proposals, was its advisory status and as an arm of the state, there were obvious limits to how far the Bord could go with its demands. This cautious and mild rebuke of the state's approach to Irish stands in sharp contrast with the severe criticism meted out regularly by Conradh na Gaeilge:

It is widely perceived that in recent times the State has drifted towards a policy of relative neutrality in matters of language policy. It is imperative that State agencies see the encouragement and promotion of the language as one of their normal functions requiring planning, policy-making and implementation in the same way as other aspects of their affairs. A passive or 'arm's length' policy by the State towards Irish as a minority language in a system in which English is dominant, is not merely neutral but negative. (Bord na Gaeilge, 1983: 4)

Bord na Gaeilge made no direct proposals to provide Irish language services as a right, or on foot of a legislative requirement. Instead, it proposed a central development unit for Irish in the Department of the Public Service and the development of Irish language plans by departments and offices of state. Similar proposals were made for health boards and local authorities with the Bord urging the government to adopt Comhairle na Gaeilge's 1971 proposals on local government for the Gaeltacht (ibid.: 38–41; see Chapter 3). The only indirect reference to legislation was a call for the establishment of a review committee to consider the legal status of Irish (ibid.: 41).

The government hid behind the *Action Plan* in order to deflect the Conradh na Gaeilge campaign. In response to a Dáil question about the bill of rights, Minister for the Gaeltacht Patrick O'Toole said that he had no plans to introduce such a bill, as the *Action Plan* had just been published. The *Action Plan* proposed that government departments and state bodies would promote Irish and, according to the Minister, if that was successful, there might not be any need for a Bill (Dáil Debates, 1983). A terse letter from O'Toole to Ned O'Keeffe TD three years later indicated that the government had no intention of budging on the bill. O'Toole claimed that strenuous efforts were being made to increase the provision of services in Irish and that he hoped that the situation would improve significantly as a result (Ó Tuathail, 1986). In 1986, Conradh renewed its efforts, sending a new motion to town and county councils, TDs, political parties, trade unions, local GAA clubs and vocational education committees (Conradh na Gaeilge, 1986b).

Meanwhile, even Bord na Gaeilge's relationship with government could not conceal its disappointment at the pace of progress in its final report on the *Action Plan*. Funding had not been provided to finance the various measures proposed and the Bord chastised the state for failing to live up to its promises in relation to its own approach to Irish:

> The Government's assurance when the Action Plan was launched that 'a supportive environment' would be provided for all who wish to use Irish in their daily lives, has not been realised, and must be tackled with greater conviction and determination. Definitive guidelines must be laid down for State institutions and officials regarding their function in the context of the Action Plan. This would include specific directions regarding recruitment, training and deployment of staff, and also bilingualisation of forms, signs and other documentation. (Bord na Gaeilge, 1986: 25)

A significant development came under the chairpersonship of Helen Ó Murchú in the form of An Coiste Comhairleach Pleanála (Advisory Planning Committee) which produced valuable research analysing the main challenges facing Bord na Gaeilge as a language planning agency. The wide-ranging report *The Irish Language in a Changing Society* focused on the development of Irish in the media and public bodies and recommended the enactment of legislation along the lines of that already in place in Wales, the Basque Country and Catalonia (Advisory Planning Committee, 1988: 98). After over a decade of the campaign by voluntary bodies, the state's language planning agency was now seen to endorse the same demand for language legislation.

2.5 Office of the Ombudsman

Another impetus for an Irish language act came from the Office of the Ombudsman, an agency established in 1984 to handle complaints from the public about poor standards of public services. This created a more formal route than the Rights Bureau and the Ombudsman began to receive a small but steady stream of complaints each year. The first officer holder, Michael Mills – himself an Irish speaker – made a number of interventions about the issue, criticising in his annual reports the failure of the state to provide such services. In 1985, he told a seminar organised by Conradh na Gaeilge that if citizens wrote in Irish to a government department, they should receive a reply in the same language. He added that if people wished to complain to his office, the majority of staff were capable of dealing with enquiries in Irish (Mills, 1985). In 1996, the Ombudsman referred directly to the difficulties experienced in his office because of the lack of legislation: 'The recurring nature of these complains underlines the contribution which a Language Act could make to a more effective complaints examination system' (cited in Ó Cuív, 1998: 8). From the late 1980s on, there were regular references to lack of services for Irish speakers in the Ombudsman's annual report (Office of the Ombudsman, 1989; 1996: 22; 1997: 28; 1998: 25; 1999: 36).

2.6 Constitutional Review Group

A Constitutional Review Group was set up in 1995 to look at all aspects of the Constitution, including Article 8 in relation to Irish. Noting that Article 8 accorded primacy to Irish, it described the current wording as 'unrealistic, given that English is the language currently spoken as their vernacular by 98% of the population of the State'. Concluding that the constitutional status of Irish had brought little real change, it recommended changing the focus of the Article to promotional efforts in favour of the language, but it couched these in vague cultural terms:

> The designation of Irish as the 'national' and the 'first official' language is of little practical significance. The intention to give special recognition to the Irish language is understood and respected but it is arguable that this might be better achieved, while allowing both languages equal status as official languages, by including a positive provision in the Constitution to the effect that the State shall care for, and endeavour to promote, the Irish language as a unique expression of Irish tradition and culture. The Review Group considers that there is an implicit right to conduct official business in either official language and that the implementation of this right is a matter for legislation and/or administrative measures rather than constitutional provision. (Constitutional Review Group, 1996: 11)

The Review Group recommended a considerable dilution of Article 8, proposing that Irish no longer have special status as 'national' and 'first official' language:

1. The Irish language and the English language are the two official languages.
2. Because the Irish language is a unique expression of Irish tradition and culture, the State shall take special care to nurture the language and increase its use (ibid.: 15).

If implemented, the new Article would have negated decades of demand for rights-based legislation and possibly derailed the new campaign for a Language Act that was gaining ground at the time (see below).

2.7 Bord na Gaeilge in the 1990s

Following the call for legislation in the APC report from 1988, a more subtle strategy by Bord na Gaeilge kept the issue of language rights on the agenda in the 1990s. It set up its own version of the Rights Bureau, a mediation service to assist members of the public who had difficulties receiving services in Irish. This worked in co-operation with the Ombudsman and dealt with on average 100 complaints per year (e.g. Bord na Gaeilge, 1996b: 23).

In 1989, Bord na Gaeilge commissioned Tomás Ó Máille of the Law Faculty in University College Galway to write a study of the legal rights of citizens in relation to the Irish language. This was published in 1990 and is another milestone in the long and bumpy road to the Official Languages Act (Bord na Gaeilge, 1990: 9–11). In his introduction, Ó Máille highlighted the 'dearth of litigation on language-related issues' (1990: v), as evidenced by the paucity of reported case law in this area and by the fact that those who wished to assert their rights rarely took the legal route. He went on to describe the principles developed in Irish case law about the constitutional status of Irish and concluded that a number of key principles had emerged, based on the judgements of Mr Justice O'Hanlon in the High Court (see section 1.3 above). These were that a person who wished to conduct court proceedings in Irish had a constitutional right to do so, regardless of their knowledge of English, and that the state was bound to bear the costs of interpretation and/or translation. However, a person who wished to use Irish in such proceedings could not demand that another party do the same. Secondly, a person wishing to do business in Irish with the state should not endure additional effort or expense in doing so, for example, in bearing the cost of translation of forms, etc. Documentation regarding official or legal business in English must be made available in Irish as soon as possible (ibid.: 17). Ó Máille also analysed the provisions of international treaties related to language rights and considered the implications of European Community law on Irish language requirements in employment, including the Groener case (1990: 38–39). Although not referring specifically to the case for a Language Act, he called for the establishment of a legal information centre within Bord na Gaeilge and for further research into the topic internationally (ibid.: 42). Ó Máille concluded that although Article 8 of the Constitution is not framed as a right, case law had concluded that important rights flowed from it and that this must be taken seriously:

> They are legitimate claims which the citizen can make upon the state; and the state owes reciprocal duties to the citizen. No right is absolute and a balance must inevitably be struck between competing rights when a conflict occurs. But given the fundamental importance of the human right to communicate, it is essential that we give much further thought to the rights of those who wish to communicate in the first national language. (Ibid.: 42)

The Bord's annual report for 1990 bemoaned the continued absence of progress on public services in Irish, criticising in particular a decision by the government to minimise the advantage of Irish language competence in internal promotion in the civil service. It complained of a lack of planning to ensure Irish language services, which was causing problems to Irish speakers in the Gaeltacht and elsewhere, and concluded that a comprehensive state policy on Irish was urgently needed (Bord na Gaeilge, 1990: 11). In 1993, a new coalition government of Fianna Fáil and Labour asked Bord na Gaeilge to prepare directives for action plans that would be implemented by government bodies and state agencies (Department of Arts, Culture and the Gaeltacht, 1993). The Bord issued such directives and also prepared guidelines for the public service on providing services in Irish (Bord na Gaeilge, 1993b). Over 5,000 copies of the guidelines were issued and the Bord organised a seminar entitled 'A Bilingual State', which was attended by over sixty state bodies (Bord na Gaeilge, 1993c: 17–18). Its high-profile chairperson, Micheál Ó Muircheartaigh, made presentations regularly to various state bodies and local government to promote the expansion of bilingualism (see for instance, Bord na Gaeilge, 1994: 21).

In 1995 and 1996, Bord na Gaeilge commissioned research about the availability of Irish language public services as part of its review of the guidelines to the public sector. The research found that Irish language service in most state bodies was extremely deficient. Levels of bilingual competence were as low as 2 per cent in some organisations or units and the existing guidelines about recruitment and training in relation to Irish were not being adhered to. Only 17 per cent of the organisations surveyed stated unequivocally that they provided an Irish language service and many claimed there was no demand for such a service. Bord na Gaeilge interpreted this as silence from a community that would use an Irish language service if available but was not willing to seek it out in the absence of information about how it may be accessed. Some progress was reported, however: 42 per cent of organisations did business in Irish with the public at least once a month and 17 per cent advertised actively that such a service was available. 52 per cent included bilingual competence in recruitment policy and 83 per cent gave some support to staff with Irish, for instance by providing terminology or special leave to learn the language. 89 per cent of organisations had Irish language or bilingual nameplates in their offices, 42 per cent had Irish language signage and 42 per cent used bilingual advertising (Bord na Gaeilge, 1995 & 1996a).

The Bord, in conjunction with Údarás na Gaeltachta, commissioned University College Galway to research the provision and use of such services in Co. Galway. The report found of all the organisations surveyed, the Bord's guidelines were being implemented satisfactorily in only the Department of Arts, Culture and Gaeltacht (as it was known at the time) and Údarás na Gaeltachta, which were already operating in Irish. It praised the efforts of other bodies such as Galway County Council, the Gardaí, the Department of Justice, An Post, the ESB and RTÉ, however it said that most state bodies ignored the guidelines. Heads of department in only nine organisations had copies of the guidelines. The report concluded that a substantial number of Irish speakers and Gaeltacht people conducted their business in English with state bodies because the Irish language service was unsatisfactory. The Irish language community had little confidence in the state to serve it in its own language and the state bodies displayed a lack of engagement with the issue. For instance, few bodies stipulated a bilingual requirement in recruitment and only four organisations required an Irish examination for applicants. Lack of fluency in Irish among staff was cited as the main reason that public bodies did not provide services. Other reasons included lack of demand, lack of knowledge of the guidelines, a perception that it was easier to do business in English and that Irish was unsuitable for technical tasks and a general belief that the public service operates in English. Another finding was lack of advertising that Irish language services were available through, for instance, signage in public offices (Ó Cinnéide & Ní Chonghaile, 1996).

A third report on the topic was published by Bord na Gaeilge in 1998 and found that only 44 per cent of organisations had an action plan in place, only 14 per cent had a list of bilingual services available, only 43 per cent used bilingual stationery and only 27 per cent of forms were available in both languages. However, it also reported some progress on 1993–1994, with an increase in the number of organisations that advertised the availability of Irish language services, an increase in the percentage of the public conducting business in Irish and an increase in the number of local authorities attaching an Irish language requirement to recruitment (Bord na Gaeilge, 1998a: 29–30).

Another important contribution by Bord na Gaeilge to the debate on a language act was its hosting of a public lecture on language rights delivered by Niamh Nic Shuibhne, an Irish legal scholar based at the University of Edinburgh. Taking a human rights approach, Nic Shuibhne reviewed Article 8 of the Constitution and the absence of explicit rights in it as well as the case law that had accorded implicit rights to Irish speakers over the decades. She argued that the courts had not considered the full implications of Article 8 but that the proposed legislation could address the problem:

> The state must assess the needs of Irish speakers and establish the necessary structures so that these needs can be accommodated. It is important that these needs be assessed

realistically [and] that the State's plans are not over-ambitious. If the philosophy of the new Bill is to be grounded on concern for the future of the Irish language in the abstract, then it falls within the domain of linguistic survival; any costs or other implementative requirements will be difficult to justify; in particular they cannot be justified on the basis of human rights. (Nic Shuibhne, 1998: 16)

She cautioned that the recommendations of the Constitution Review Group (see above) would not provide a robust basis for the legislation as the proposed constitutional amendment would have based state duty on 'the aesthetic and abstract grounds of culture and tradition' related to the language itself rather than on 'any concern for the rights of its speakers' (ibid.: 16). Instead, Nic Shuibhne recommended that the government base the new Act 'on the fundamental human rights of speakers of the Irish language', which would 'place a firm responsibility on the state for ensuring the effective implementation of the rights to be detailed by the Act' (ibid.: 16–17).

2.8 Renewed campaign for a Language Act

The umbrella body for the Irish language voluntary sector, Comhdháil Náisiúnta na Gaeilge, took a leading role in a renewed campaign for language legislation in the 1990s. It represented a range of voluntary language organisations, so brought a broader base of support to the campaign than the efforts of the 1970s and 1980s. Comhdháil developed a key role in ensuring that Irish language considerations were included in the legislative process and its director Peadar Ó Flatharta lobbied politicians on the issue of a language act. As representative of the Irish committee of the European Bureau for Lesser Used Languages in Brussels, Ó Flatharta was also able to avail of expertise from other minority language regions such as Wales, the Basque Country and Catalonia. The election of Éamon Ó Cuív to the Dáil in 1992 as Fianna Fáil TD for Galway West, covering the country's largest Gaeltacht area, was another key development due to his personal commitment to language rights. Ó Cuív, a grandson of former Taoiseach and President Éamon de Valera, was raised in an Irish-speaking family in Dublin but moved to Galway in the 1970s to manage a

Gaeltacht co-operative. Since joining the Oireachtas as a Senator in 1989, as a backbench government TD from 1992 to 1994 and as an opposition TD from 1994 to 1997, Ó Cuív strongly supported Comhdháil's campaign for a language act (Mac Donnacha, 2021). Looking back at his term in office many years later, he ranked the Official Languages Act as his greater achievement (Ó Cuív, 2021).

The general election in 1997 was a game changer in achieving language legislation because the new coalition government led by Fianna Fáil committed in its programme of work to enacting legislation to grant rights to Irish speakers. In addition to renewed lobbying by the voluntary sector, another likely influence was the expansion of the equality agenda, with public discourse and policy throughout the 1990s showing greater support for increased protection for minority groups. Although language did not become a protected characteristic in equality legislation, the greater political attention to and public awareness of minority rights was an advantage to the Irish language organisations. The establishment of the Irish language television station TnaG (TG4) in 1996 was framed consistently in terms of language rights by the Minister for the Gaeltacht, Michael D. Higgins (e.g. Higgins, 1996), and the development of the Northern Ireland peace process was also a factor, with greater attention being paid by both the Irish and British governments to language rights. The result of these changes was that twenty years after Conradh na Gaeilge launched its rights campaign, the need for statutory provision for Irish language services was finally accepted by the state. The chief executive of Bord na Gaeilge described the development as 'the central and most fundamentally radical commitment to the language in the Government programme' (Bord na Gaeilge, 1998b: 3). The appointment of Éamon Ó Cuív as Minister of State in the Department of Arts, Heritage, Gaeltacht and the Islands was another important step, and his promotion to senior Minister in 1999 marked another milestone in the process.

In response to the government's commitment, Bord na Gaeilge and Údarás na Gaeltachta jointly published a policy document *Gníomh don Ghaeilge* (Action for Irish), calling for urgent action to strengthen the statutory basis for the language rights of the public. It requested that the legal position of Irish be strengthened under the Constitution and in equality legislation and that Irish be given full status as a working language of the European Union. After fifteen years of failed action plans and non-binding guidelines, it urged that language planning in relation to the state sector be put on a statutory basis and that an executive unit to carry out the measures be established at a senior level in the civil service. It also called for specific attention to the needs of the Gaeltacht in a proposed new decentralisation policy and urged that the maintenance of Irish be made a criterion when assessing planning applications in the Gaeltacht (Bord na Gaeilge, 1998b).

2.9 Legal opinions

A compendium of essays by legal scholars and practitioners in Ireland, Wales and Canada was published in order to lay out possible parameters for the future legislation (Mac Cárthaigh, 1998). In a paper on the legal status of Irish, Nic Shuibhne noted that the constitutional provisions made Irish the first official language in theory only and that greater importance attached to how such provisions were interpreted and implemented by the courts over the decades. Although the High Court judge Mr Justice O'Hanlon had attempted to provide a comprehensive overview of Article 8 in his 1983 judgement in the case *An Stát (Mac Fhearraigh) vs. Mac Gamhnia*, it was not possible for him to deal with all of the obstacles placed on Irish by the state. Although the courts have since agreed with the 1934 Kennedy judgement in the *Ó Foghludha vs. McClean* case – that the state should do everything necessary to ensure that Irish is the national language in reality and not in the Constitution alone – it was clear that the state had failed to implement the right to language choice in reality (Nic Shuibhne, 1998: 3). While the courts had proven themselves willing to deal with individual cases, they did not want to make a general judgement about the duty of the state to provide services in Irish. Nic Shuibhne went on to underline the problems with relying on a general constitutional provision in this regard:

> Ach is foráil leathan í Airteagal 8, agus níl aon treoirlíne ag na cúirteanna ón Oireachtas ar an ábhar sin. Caithfidh siad focail an Airteagail a phlé in aghaidh fhuarchúis an phobail ar thaobh amháin, agus díograis an mhionlaigh ar an taobh eile. Is léir go

ndearna na cúirteanna iarracht teacht ar chomhghéilleadh: níor phléigh siad dualgas ginearálta an Stáit, ach, i gcásanna aonair, thug siad faoiseamh do shaoránaigh ar theasaigh uathu gnó oifigiúil a dhéanamh trí mheán na Gaeilge. Ach ní dhéanfaidh beartas meata cosúil leis sin an gnó: caithfear glacadh leis an dualgas atá ar an Stát mar chomhthoradh ar chearta teanga an tsaoránaigh agus ar stádas dlíthiúil na Gaeilge mar theanga náisiúnta agus príomhtheanga oifigiúil an Stáit. Sa tslí sin ní fhanfaidh beartais an Rialtais maidir le húsáid oifigiúil na Gaeilge ar pháipéar amháin, ach cuirfear i bhfeidhm iad. (Ibid.: 6)[4]

As a first step, Nic Shuibhne said it was necessary to ensure that Irish speakers would have a right to deal with the state in Irish if they so wished. The constitutional status of Irish and related case law gave us a 'rough map' (*garbhléarscáil*), but it was necessary to go further and consider theories from sociolinguistics and minority rights and to learn from the successes and failures of other jurisdictions (ibid.: 7).

In the same volume, a barrister pointed to the ambiguities created by Article 8.3 as evidenced by various court cases, which he said allowed the state to do as little as possible in relation to Irish. More was needed to promote Irish than the principled statement of Mr Justice Kennedy in 1934 and he favoured an amendment to Article 8.3 that would not allow the state to choose one official language in its dealings with the public. Furthermore, a future act should provide a broader definition of the language rights of people wishing to do business in Irish and penalise the state in the form of damages if it refused to provide such services (Ó Sé, 1998: 52–53). However, another barrister cautioned against rights-based legislation, arguing that such laws often led to a minimalist approach because creating a right to use something also created an opposing right not to use it. He argued against

---

4   But Article 8 is a broad provision, and the courts have no guidelines from the Oireachtas on that subject. They have to discuss the words of the Article against the apathy of the public on the one hand, and the diligence of the minority on the other. It is clear that the courts tried hard to reach a compromise: they did not discuss the general duty of the State, but, in individual cases, they granted relief to citizens who wish to conduct official business through Irish. But a cowardly policy such as that is not good enough: the duty on the State must be accepted as a consequence of the language rights of the citizen and of the legal status of Irish as national language and first official language of the State. In that way Government policies on the official use of Irish will not remain on paper only, but will be implemented.

a minority strategy on the basis that large numbers of Irish speakers did not feel that their rights were being denied or that they were under pressure. There was more understanding of the language itself being under pressure as a vernacular and therefore the legal strategy should focus on an act that impacts on life in general rather than drawing on the theory of rights. He proposed legislation that contained clear targets in relation to Irish language services (Ó Dúlacháin, 1998: 56–57). He concluded by stating that he did not wish to dismiss or marginalise the philosophy of language rights but that a comprehensive legal strategy consisted of more than general legislation or individual acts and should draw on all branches and aspects of the law (ibid.: 61).

2.10 Proposals of voluntary sector

The voluntary sector also presented new proposals following the announcement of the government's commitment. Comhdháil Náisiúnta na Gaeilge was requested by Minister of State Ó Cuív to prepare a detailed submission about a language act, and in 1998 it held a series of meetings in Dublin, Cork, Belfast and the three main Gaeltacht regions to seek public views on the proposed legislation. A comprehensive discussion document outlining the rationale for, and scope, structure and implementation of the act was published. Stressing that simply introducing legislation would not suffice, the document paid considerable attention to the 'structural changes necessary to provide a comprehensive service on a continuous basis to Irish speakers' (Comhdháil Náisiúnta na Gaeilge, 1998b: v). Arguing in favour of the necessity for an act, Comhdháil referred to a widespread perception among Irish speakers in the Gaeltacht and elsewhere that it was impossible to do business in Irish with the state because it was not committed to providing such services. The implications of such a failure, it added, were that other influential sectors of society could not be expected to follow suit if the state did not take a clear leadership role in this area (the example given was the impact of the paucity of Irish programmes on RTÉ on the independent broadcasting sector; see Chapter 5). The absence of services in Irish created a sense that

Irish speakers did not enjoy 'parity of esteem' (itself a phrase used in the course of the Northern Ireland peace process) and this fostered cynicism towards Irish in the community and added to the pressure on parents to speak English to their children. Describing the efforts of Bord na Gaeilge in the early part of the decade as 'inconsequential', it stated that a statutory basis was needed to ensure a robust language rights framework (ibid.: 1).

Comhdháil divided services for Irish speakers and Gaeltacht communities into three categories: (1) the provision of general services through Irish by state bodies (the translation of forms, brochures, correspondence, etc.); (2) services aimed specifically at Irish speakers (for instance health services, education and social services provided by specialists) and (3) services providing for the specific needs of Irish speakers (for instance dedicated institutions in media and education, computer software and family support services) (ibid.: 2–3). In its review of Irish language services provided to date, Comhdháil reported that the only successful model was organisations aimed specifically at Irish speakers such as Údarás na Gaeltachta, Raidió na Gaeltachta or the Department of the Gaeltacht (ibid.: 4). The discussion document made sophisticated arguments about demand for services in Irish, pointing out that citizens generally sought a service and the organisation providing it generally dictated the language in which it was available. Therefore, Gaeltacht residents did not normally demand to be served in English but it was standard administrative practice by state bodies to provide them with forms, etc. in English. The public sector, as the service provider, had the capacity to change the language of service rather than the public and therefore it was essential that the public sector should develop and offer services in Irish to give a true choice to all citizens. 'There is a long-established public perception that the norm for conducting business with public sector organisations is through the medium of English', Comhdháil said, adding that many Irish speakers felt that it was not feasible to seek services in Irish due to extra effort, delays, additional expense or dealing with poorly translated documents. It said that the public would not demand a service if they knew that it did not exist and that many people would not want to risk antagonising a public servant in a situation where they were dependent on the service (ibid.: 6).

Comhdháil recommended that the scope of the act deal primarily with public sector organisations but that it be extended to parts of the private sector also, given that the state had already assigned it particular responsibilities. Private or other non-state bodies that should fall under the act included banks and other financial institutions, the churches, media and information technology providers. It was also proposed to introduce a right to Irish-medium education at all levels, to include Irish as a planning criterion in the Gaeltacht and to establish the Gaeltacht as a separate region with its own local authority. Other proposals related to the provision of services in Irish abroad by the diplomatic service and the introduction of an explicit right to use Irish in the courts (ibid.: 9–11). Reflecting its European connections, Comhdháil framed its demand for an act in international terms, referring to the instruments such as the Universal Declaration of Human Rights and the European Charter for Regional or Minority Languages. It also situated its campaign in the context of constitutional rights, not only Article 8 but also other articles related to equal rights, personal rights, the rights of the family, etc. (ibid.: 12–16).

Proposals related to the structure of the legislation were made, with Comhdháil suggesting a tripartite approach comprising (1) a general definition of the state's duties in relation to Irish (based on Conradh na Gaeilge's original Bill of Rights for the Irish Language), (2) a provision that the Minister for the Gaeltacht would be responsible for ensuring that the Act was implemented and (3) a provision for an interdepartmental committee to co-ordinate all aspects of the state's work in relation to Irish (ibid.: 17–18). The document proposed a language rights basis for the legislation, suggesting the following definition setting out the basic rights of every citizen:

> No citizen will be placed at a disadvantage as a result of having Irish as their first language or as their language of choice. Therefore, every citizen and every organisation has the right to obtain all the services of every state organisation and every state-funded organisation through Irish, free from any impediment or extra cost to themselves and that those services shall be of equal standard and congruent with similar services provided through English. (Ibid.: 18)

Reference was made to specific rights related to correspondence in Irish from the state, conducting business with public sector organisations,

using Irish before the courts, obtaining health, education and social services in Irish, and a right to compensation when denied such services
(ibid.: 18–19). The document also made proposals about the duties to be
placed on public bodies in relation to services in Irish, including specific
provision for Irish speakers and Gaeltacht communities. It recommended
that strategic plans of such bodies contain details about services in Irish
and that each organisation ensure that it had enough staff to cater for
Irish speakers and the Gaeltacht. Any staff member taking up positions
dealing with Irish speakers would have to obtain a certificate of compe-
tency in Irish and any offices situated by public bodies in the Gaeltacht
would have to be staffed by fluent speakers. The document proposed that
each government department or public body appoint a senior official to
ensure the delivery of services in Irish (ibid.: 19–20).

In order to ensure the smooth operation of the legislation, Comhdháil
proposed the appointment of an Irish Language Ombudsman to deal with
complaints from the public and an Irish Language Commissioner ('Oifig
Choimisinéir na Gaeilge') to monitor the quality and provision of Irish
language services and the appropriateness of the governance structures for
ensuring the Act's implementation. The Commissioner was to be a powerful
office with a wide range of responsibilities and functions related to various
aspects of Irish language policy. The post holder should be guaranteed independence and be appointed by the President on the recommendation
of the Houses of the Oireachtas, place an annual report before the Dáil,
report on other topics as deemed necessary, and conduct a major review
of the legislation every three years. The Commissioner would also have
the power to seek a High Court order to oblige a public body to comply
with the Act. Their main functions would be to ensure that public services
are provided in Irish, to monitor the effectiveness of the Act, to monitor
provision of Irish language services and to conduct a language audit of all
public bodies every three years. They would agree a language plan with
each public body setting out a timetable for delivery of Irish language services, ensure that each organisation implements a language charter, draft
a Gaeltacht development plan in association with Údarás na Gaeltachta
and assess the impact of housing developments on the use of Irish in the
Gaeltacht. The Commissioner would provide information to the public

about the functioning of the Act and establish public hearings on language matters as necessary (ibid.: 23–25).

2.11 Conference on language legislation

An international conference on language legislation was held by Comhdháil Náisiúnta na Gaeilge in Dublin in the autumn of 1998 and was attended by researchers and practitioners from various bilingual jurisdictions including Norway, Bolzano/Bozen, the Basque Country, Galicia, Wales, Scotland, Catalonia and Canada. Canada's Commissioner of Official Languages was among the high-profile international speakers. The conference aimed to study language legislation in other countries, to examine the structures of state bodies responsible for the implementation of such legislation and to assess its effectiveness in order to make recommendations about the most suitable system for Ireland (Comhdháil Náisiúnta na Gaeilge, 1998a: i). The keynote address was by Minister Ó Cuív, who told delegates that his officials were in the process of preparing a Language Bill and outlined the background to the issue, referring to the gap between constitutional status and the lack of services in Irish. He said that in the absence of legislation, it was difficult to convince state bodies that people had a right to service in Irish. He highlighted the lack of a process for implementing such services, referring to the failure of the Bord na Gaeilge guidelines and the 'lukewarm' approach of public bodies to Irish language services. Ó Cuív framed the need for legislation in a rights perspective, reflecting the influence of the campaign of the previous two decades, which had brought a rights-based approach centre-stage. He said that he was seeking equality between Irish and English, a position that would cause problems down the line (see below):

> It is extremely important that the Bill will contain a clear statement in regard to the language rights of the citizen. One of its provisions must grant the Irish speaker the right to carry out his business through Irish. Although I have used the word *rights* what I really mean is *equality*. Citizens should have a choice of language. In accordance to the principal of equality people may choose Irish or English and that is how

it should be. At present what is offered is normally a service through English. (Ó
Cuív, 1998: 9, emphasis in original)

The Minister said that his aim for the Bill was that a statutory obligation
would be placed on public bodies to provide the same level of services in
Irish as they currently did in English. He referred to the Welsh system
of language schemes or plans and said that he intended to introduce a
similar approach in Ireland (ibid.: 9–10). There would be specific provisions related to the Gaeltacht and each public body operating in that
district would have to prepare a plan. Rather than introducing a comprehensive act dealing with every aspect of the question, Ó Cuív signalled his
intention to develop enabling legislation under which the Minister would
have the power to make regulations in relation to signage, advertising,
forms stationery, etc. (ibid.: 10). He set out a number of options in relation to implementation and monitoring, adding that he felt it important
that the Minister would have a role in approving plans of public bodies. If
Bord na Gaeilge was to become responsible for implementation, Ó Cuív
said that there could be conflict between its existing promotional role
and its new role. He raised the possibility of charging another agency,
possibly a Language Commissioner, with monitoring and implementation. Ó Cuív concluded by tempering expectations in relation to the
legislation, warning that the situation would not change overnight and
that the Act would be the first to ensure basic rights for Irish speakers.
Addressing those both within and outside government who opposed the
move, he said that the government did not wish to oblige any civil servant
to conduct their business through Irish but to ensure that services would
be made available in Irish on a basis of equality (ibid.: 11).

A parallel development that transformed the nature of all-Ireland governance may have influenced the progress towards a Language Act. The
Good Friday Agreement of 1998 led to new legislation that wound up Bord
na Gaeilge and replaced it with An Foras Teanga (The Language Body), a
cross-border institution with two parts, one of which would promote Irish
and be called Foras na Gaeilge. Bord na Gaeilge was dissolved on the 2nd
of December 1999 and its staff, assets and functions transferred to Foras
na Gaeilge (Bord na Gaeilge, 1999: 4). The establishment of a cross-border
body for language promotion was a major shift in language governance

and arguably helped to focus attention on achieving the language act. It was not an uncontroversial decision, however, with a leading sociolinguist criticising the Irish government for relinquishing control of its sovereignty over Irish language policy in favour of an untested governance structure requiring the agreement of the British authorities to make decisions (Ó Murchú, 2006: 15). The vicissitudes of the peace process over the past two decades have underlined the far-sightedness of this prescient observation. With active progress occurring on the language legislation front, Foras na Gaeilge did not continue Bord na Gaeilge's function of mediation with members of the public. Its final intervention on the matter was to make a submission to Minister Ó Cuív about the Official Languages (Equality) Bill of 2002 and declare itself satisfied with the progress to date (Foras na Gaeilge, 2002: 18).

2.12 *Official Languages (Equality) Bill 2002*

The publication of the Official Languages (Equality) Bill was another milestone on the journey towards the desired legislation, but it was not without its problems and failed to gain universal approval from those concerned about language rights. The first challenge related to the title, as it implied equality between Irish and English, a claim that was contradictory to the constitutional status set out in Article 8. This was acknowledged by Minister Ó Cuív in a Dáil debate on the second stage of the Bill in May 2003. Despite his earlier desires to achieve equality between Irish and English, the Minister explained the problem:

> Is iad na príomhcheisteanna a bhí romham agus mé ag cur an Bhille seo in eagar ná aitheantas cuí a thabhairt do sheasamh bunreachtúil na Gaeilge mar an príomhtheanga [sic] oifigiúil gan aon ghearradh trasna a dhéanamh ar an seasamh bunreachtúil sin agus, ag an am céanna, feabhsaithe [sic] praiticiúla ar staid lag na Gaeilge sa saol poiblí a bhaint amach, go háirithe ó thaobh seirbhísí poiblí trí Ghaeilge a chur ar fáil. (Ó Cuív, 2003, cited in Mac Giolla Chríost, 2005: 192–193)[5]

5 These are the main questions which were in front of me as I presented the Bill; thus, to give appropriate recognition to the Irish language in its constitutional position as the main official language without interfering with or contradicting that

Ó Cuív said that he had wanted to include 'equality' in the title because he felt that 'it would capture the public imagination' (*go mbéarfadh sé ar intinn an phobail*) due to greater public awareness of the importance of equality but that it was improper for any legislation to confer equality on the Irish language in the light of the Constitution. He stood by his amendment removing references to equality, arguing that they did not diminish the status of Irish or remove anyone's constitutional rights. Mac Giolla Chríost summarises the problem as Irish being de jure more equal than English but de facto less than equal (2005: 193).

2.13   *Analysis of legislative process*

The sociologist Pádraig Ó Laighin, who spent years working in Montreal, Canada before returning to Ireland, wrote a sharp critique of the Official Languages Bill as it was approaching the end of the legislative process. In an analysis of the bill at the committee stage, Ó Laighin described the background to a fundamental change in the bill's provisions and character that occurred since it was initiated in 2002: the removal of the philosophy of equality between Irish and English. Ó Laighin argued that when initiated, the bill was entitled the 'Official Languages (Equality) Bill, 2002' and proposed 'to promote equality of status and equal rights and privileges as to their use' in parliamentary proceedings, legal affairs and communications between citizens and public bodies. He argued that the equality aspect was more prominent than the constitutional provision of Irish and the absence of references to the Gaeltacht in the bill reflected this tendency. In this respect, the bill bore a resemblance to the philosophy underpinning the Canadian Official Languages Act, 1985. Describing 'equality of opportunities' as a powerful social good that would be difficult to oppose, Ó Laighin argued that the Bill as initiated confused equality of status with equality of opportunities. Given the constitutional position, it would be impossible to introduce legislation granting equality of status to Irish and English but instead of framing the bill in terms of equality of opportunities, the government removed all references to equality. From then on in the process, Ó Laighin argued that this was an Irish language rather than an equal opportunities act and that the most important aspect had been destroyed:

> Le himeacht an chomhionannais, bhain an tAire amach as an Acht an t-alt ba lárnaí ann a dheimhnigh comhionannas deiseanna – an t-alt a dhearbhaigh go bhféadfadh an duine aonair cumarsáid a dhéanamh le haon eagras stáit nó comhlacht poiblí, agus seirbhísí a fháil uathu, i gceachtar den dá theanga oifigiúla (alt 8, mar a tionscnaíodh é). Ba é an t-alt sin croílár an Achta. Nuair a baineadh amach as an mBille é, criogadh an tAcht ar fad. (Ó Laighin, 2003: 5)[6]

Ó Laighin also made observations about weaknesses in the provisions concerning the use of official languages in the Houses of the Oireachtas. Under the Irish bill, only members of the Oireachtas (i.e. Teachtaí Dála and Senators) would have the right to use Irish in the Houses of the Oireachtas. However, an equivalent provision in the Canadian act allowed any *person* to use either English or French in any parliamentary events (so held either inside or outside the parliament building itself), thereby giving it a wider application. Ó Laighin argued that this article, as initiated, could lead to a situation where there would be no right for members of the public to use Irish at an Oireachtas hearing held in the Gaeltacht (ibid.: 7). He also pointed to differences between the Canadian and Irish acts in terms of provision for simultaneous interpretation for parliamentary proceedings. Such interpretation between English and French is available in both directions under the Canadian legislation but practice in the Oireachtas is to interpret only from Irish to English. Ó Laighin criticised the absence of a reference to simultaneous interpretation in both directions in the Irish bill (ibid.: 8). He also criticised the conditionality of article 7 as initiated, that acts would be printed and published bilingually *as soon as possible* after their enactment, in contrast to Canada when an act cannot be enacted until it is available in both

---

6   With the departure of equality, the Minister removed from the Act the most central paragraph that guaranteed equality of opportunities – the article that confirmed that an individual could communicate with any state organisation or public body, and receive services from them, in either of the official languages (article 8 as initiated). That article was the heart of the Act. When it was removed from the Bill, the Act was completely destroyed.

French and English. Ó Laighin pointed to the long delays in translating legislation in the Irish Statute Book and said that the bill represented no progress in this regard. He recommended that the phrase 'as soon as possible' should be removed from the Bill (ibid.: 9).

In terms of the administration of justice, Ó Laighin said that the provisions in the Irish bill were similar to those in Canada and were strong and clear. However, he argued that the Irish bill did not oblige the courts to provide interpretation at the request of one of the parties and pointed to the fact that the Irish Bill did not require a judge to have competence in the official language(s) chosen by the parties to the case (ibid.: 11–12). Ó Laighin also discussed provisions in relation to the provision of services by public bodies, noting that the bill as initiated had proposed to grant an individual the right to communicate in either official language with public bodies and that a concomitant duty would be imposed on such bodies to communicate and provide services in both languages. Article 8 as initiated stated that an individual may communicate with any public body and receive services from them in either official language, according to any scheme that was in place in relation to that company. Furthermore, the individual's ability in either official language could not be questioned. Article 9 provided that public bodies would ensure that any individual could communicate with it and obtain services from it in either official language, again in accordance with the scheme in place. Comhdháil Náisiúnta na Gaeilge requested that the reference to 'schemes in place' be removed in case it diluted the individual's right to obtain a service but instead, the Minister removed articles 8 and 9 entirely. Ó Laighin described this as a 'lightning bolt' (*caor thintrí*) that reduced the power of the bill significantly and he recommended that it should not be enacted without it (ibid.: 14).

Ó Laighin dwelt at length on the provisions in relation to language schemes for public bodies. Apart from the right to receive an answer to correspondence in the same official language as it was written (article 10.2), he pointed out that the bill contained no reference to any other right in dealing with public bodies and did not impose any significant duty on such bodies in relation to services in Irish. The provisions on language schemes were based to a large extent on the Welsh Language Act but Ó Laighin described them as a 'cuckoo's egg in a blackbird's nest' (*ubh cuaiche i nead*

céirsí), pointing out that after removing the original articles 8 and 9, there
was little option but to include them instead. He criticised the conditionality of the system of language schemes, pointing in particular to the fact
that the Minister's only power in relation to the failure of a public body
to prepare or implement a scheme was to report it to the Houses of the
Oireachtas. Ó Laighin referred to the stronger nature of the original article 13, which established a system of language schemes that would ensure
that anyone wishing to access services in either official language would
be treated on an equal basis. Instead, the new article 9 was 'unclear, ambiguous and weak, and its wording was self-contradictory and internally
confusing' (*doiléir, débhríoch, agus lag, agus tá comhbhréagnú nó trasnaíocht
inmheánach i gceist ina fhoclaíocht*) (ibid.: 19). The reason for the criticism
was the requirement that a public body specify the services that it intended
to provide in Irish only, English only or in both languages and the measures that it would take to ensure that any services not currently in Irish
would be so provided in the future. Ó Laighin argued that if services were
to be made available in English only, it was impossible to provide them
in Irish at the same time and that this amendment represented another
dilution of the equality aspect (ibid.: 19–20). Furthermore, referring to
the Kennedy judgment of 1934, he added that any public body providing
services in English only could be brought before the courts on the basis
that it was in contravention of the Constitution (ibid.: 20). Mac Giolla
Chríost similarly pointed to the absence of a legal commitment to equality
and its potential implications both within and outside the Gaeltacht. He
added that the principle of territoriality overtook the principle of person-
ality during the redrafting process, meaning that recognition of language
rights in relation to the Gaeltacht as a district defined by law became more
important than rights conferred on individual speakers, regardless of location (ibid.: 195–196).

Describing the process for agreeing draft schemes with public bodies
as 'complicated, awkward, and misleading' (*casta, amscaí, agus éidreorach*)
(ibid.: 22), Ó Laighin said that it appeared the central purpose of the bill
was to delay the provision of services in the official language chosen by
the individual and that if such action was taken in order to ease its birth
pains, it was a mistaken decision. He compared it to the voluntary system

of guidelines initiated by Bord na Gaeilge a decade earlier as well as other similar schemes since the foundation of the state. Ó Laighin recommended including additional guidelines and targets in relation to schemes in the bill itself and reinserting the principle of equality as a public good. While praising Minister Ó Cuív's commitment and ability, he warned that someone with less interest and even with no competence in Irish could be appointed to the post in the future, and that the act should be robust enough to weather such a storm (ibid.: 22–23).

Ó Laighin also criticised article 31 as initiated, which prevented an individual from taking a court case if a public body failed to implement a language scheme. He contrasted this with the Welsh Language Act 1993, under which the Secretary of State was empowered to seek a mandamus from a court in order to oblige a public body to comply with the legislation, and the entire section of the Canadian act that was devoted to court proceedings. He questioned Minister Ó Cuív's claim that it would be too complicated to ensure specified sizes for Irish and English text on signage and proposed a wording that would require that all signs were in Irish, or Irish and English, with Irish either larger or both texts the same size. Criticising the current practice to place the Irish placename in italics on road signs, he said that there was no provision in the Bill to deal with this anomaly and cited various examples of equal treatment in bilingual signage from other jurisdictions (ibid.: 33–35). He welcomed the proposal to establish a Commissioner of Official Languages in Ireland, referring to how successive Canadian commissioners managed to influence reluctant public bodies.

Ó Laighin concluded his commentary by referring to Ó Cuív's commitment as Minister of State to enact an act that would grant rights to Irish speakers, grant them equality of opportunity to obtain services in Irish and rectify the historical injustices done to them, particularly in the Gaeltacht (see above). However, he said that the current offering fell well short of that vision, and that there was no value to an act that did not give citizens the right to deal with the state in the official language of their choice. Neither was there value to legislation that did not impose duties on public bodies to provide services in both languages to all on a basis of equality. Calling for substantial amendments to be made to the bill, Ó Laighin ended his analysis with a cutting reference to the primacy of economic considerations in public discourse in the 'Celtic Tiger' era:

> Agus ní haon mhaith Acht Teanga nach gcuireann i gcuimhne dúinn ar fad gurb í an Ghaeilge an teanga náisiúnta, nach bhfuilimid ag caint ar mheán cumarsáide amháin, ach ar shaibhreas Éireannach agus Eorpach nach féidir a chur i dtaisce sa bhanc. (Ibid.: 42)[7]

Ó Laighin wrote his critique from the perspective of someone who had spent many years in Canada, where the significantly stronger social position of French ensured that it had greater protection in law than what was proposed for Irish. While his criticisms are of merit when considered in an equality framework, they are less persuasive in the context of the much lower starting point for Irish and its marginal position in Ireland's political culture. Despite Ó Laighin's reservations, the Official Languages Bill received unanimous assent in the Oireachtas and was signed into law by the President on the 14th of July 2003. All provisions of the act not already covered by ministerial order came into effect three years later, on the 14th of July 2006. The first Commissioner, Seán Ó Cuirreáin, was appointed on the 23rd of February 2004. He resigned ten years later on the 23rd of February 2014 in protest at government inaction on language policy and was replaced by Rónán Ó Domhnaill, who is currently midway through his second term.

3. Conclusion

The road to an Irish language act was a long and tortuous process lasting almost thirty years. Born out of frustration at the major policy retreats of the early 1970s, it drew on the discourse of language rights that had emerged a decade earlier on the back of agitation by minorities and

---

7 And there is no worth in a Language Act that does not remind us all that Irish is the national language, that we are not just referring to a medium of communication, but to an Irish and European wealth that cannot be deposited in the bank.

under-represented groups throughout the western world. It was also motivated by increasing impatience at the gaping chasm between the elevated constitutional status of Irish and its legal status in reality, as illustrated by the small number of Irish speakers who over the decades had
to rely on the courts to clarify their rights. As we have seen, many such
judgements were narrow in scope and did not apply to the broader questions of the provision of state services in Irish, although they provided
moral fodder for campaigners. The dedication of Conradh na Gaeilge in
developing the campaign of the late 1970s, culminating in the publication of a Bill of Rights in 1977, was crucial in raising greater public and
political awareness of the problem. The role of an insider, 'An Dréachtóir',
in providing a professionally produced 'bill' based on best practice, gave
the campaign additional credibility. Despite many setbacks, hostile responses and ongoing political instability, the campaign continued for a
decade, when the focus of the voluntary sector switched to the demand
for Irish language television. It was revived in the late 1990s and involved
a broader coalition of organisations, led by the co-ordinating body for the
voluntary sector, Comhdháil Náisiúnta na Gaeilge. The ascent to ministerial office of Éamon Ó Cuív was a game changer, as he was one of Dáil
Éireann's most committed Irish speakers and strongly supportive of the
legislation. However, by framing the bill within the equality discourse,
Ó Cuív unwittingly created a constitutional difficulty and was forced to
water down the proposals as a result. Despite the misgivings of Ó Laighin,
the act was nonetheless a major step forward as it provided a legal framework for the delivery of public services in Irish, for the first time since the
foundation of the state.

The campaign for the Official Languages Act is a good example of
how one of the higher props of language policy – legal protection – is formulated through the political process. Spolsky's framework of language
policy is again useful here as it helps us understand how ideological contestation played out during the campaign, leading eventually to a new
form of language management. On the one hand was an overwhelmingly
English-speaking political establishment where ideologies towards Irish
ranged from the generally supportive to the outright hostile. This contained plenty of contradictions between overt language policy as declared

by the state itself or individual political parties and the de facto policy as carried out in practice within government departments and state bodies. On the other hand was Irish language civil society, led in the first phase by Conradh na Gaeilge, which adopted a rights discourse to pursue its aims and consulted widely with other bilingual jurisdictions to hone its case. This transnational element was a significant factor throughout the campaign and emerged again in the late 1990s when more widespread legal protection was in place for minority languages in Western Europe. Such developments were ably exploited by Comhdháil Náisiúnta na Gaeilge and the Irish act bore the hallmarks of Canadian and Welsh influences (the Commissioner and system of language schemes, respectively). Changes in the national context – for instance the establishment of TG4 in 1996 and the support offered to Irish by the Belfast Agreement in 1998 – may have played a positive role by enhancing the profile of Irish more broadly. Although the legislation as passed was not based on a rights framework, growing awareness of the diversity agenda and of the needs of minorities was also a likely factor. The complex status of Irish as simultaneously official, national and minoritised was also at play: the campaign was prompted by the fact that the status of Irish as first official and national language was not being implemented, yet the activities and statements of campaigners were framed by a discourse of minority rights. The proposal as early as 1977 to create a Language Commissioner was a reflection of the increased complexification of government and a harbinger of models of diffused governance that would gain ground in the 1980s. Even as a renewed Official Languages Act comes into force in 2022, the key question of implementation is a concern, and it remains to be seen how less than favourable ideology towards Irish within the state system and other structural problems may impede the ambitious target of achieving 20 per cent of recruits with competence in Irish by 2030.

The final thematic chapter looks at another aspect of activism over the past fifty years, campaigns for Irish language community media on both sides of the border.

CHAPTER 5

Broadcasting

1. Introduction

This chapter analyses the role of the Irish language in radio and television broadcasting as a policy pillar since the foundation of the state. It begins by surveying the marginal place of Irish in state-controlled media, Radio Éireann (established as 2RN in 1926) and subsequently on the television channel, Telefís Éireann (established in 1961). The campaigns for separate radio and television services for the Gaeltacht are also discussed, as is the exclusion of Irish from radio and television in Northern Ireland until relatively recently. In the case study, I focus on the history of Irish in community media and its role in two volunteer-led radio stations in Dublin and Belfast.

1.1 Irish on national radio

The relationship between broadcasting and Irish language policy in the twentieth century reveals complex ideologies around identity construction and language policy since independence. Licensed radio broadcasting in the Irish Free State began in 1926 and was immersed in debates about language and identity from its inception (Cormack & Hourigan, 2007; Pine, 2007). Radio was a mass medium entering its golden age and would exert a potent influence on the general public during the first half of the twentieth century. Therefore, it played an important role in moulding attitudes towards the language policy.

The fledgling radio station 2RN, broadcasting to the Dublin area only, was launched almost entirely in Irish in 1926 by the former president and founder of the Gaelic League, Douglas Hyde, who stressed the importance of an Irish radio station for bolstering national identity (Watson, 2003). Hyde began with a few sentences in English 'for any strangers who may be listening in' but then turned to Irish to 'address my own countrymen', a potent illustration of his ideological stance that all Irish people could (or should) understand what he was saying (Clarke, 1986: 42). The socio-linguistic reality was far removed from Hyde's belief, however, with the Census of 1926 recording that only 18.3 per cent of the population could speak Irish, the vast majority of them in areas where 2RN could not be heard (Department of Industry and Commerce, 1932: 1).

This set the scene for radio broadcasting to become an ideological battleground in Irish language policy, with an expectation by the authorities that the station would broadcast material in Irish but a contrasting desire among the public that more programmes should be in English. In reality, the dichotomy was not so clear-cut: although political pressure for more Irish came from some quarters, the Department of Posts and Telegraphs was decidedly lukewarm to the idea of a considerable amount of Irish on 2RN and Radio Éireann as it was to become in 1937. For instance, a proposal in 1939 by Conradh na Gaeilge to Taoiseach Éamon de Valera that Radio Éireann increase its programmes in Irish to 50 per cent of total output was rejected by the Department on the ground that listeners would abandon the station for the BBC, which could be received clearly in the eastern part of Ireland (Conradh na Gaeilge, 1939).

The pinnacle of Irish language output was reached in the 1940s and 1950s, but even then only about ten per cent of programmes were in Irish (Watson, 2003: 26). The language policy of the station was two-pronged, reflecting the dual national policy of maintenance in the Gaeltacht and revival elsewhere (described as the 'preservation' and 'restoration' policies, respectively, by Watson). Both approaches are based on the notion of Irish as the 'national language' but in different ways. The restoration policy rests on the premise that the 'national language' belongs to all and subsequently that the national radio station has a duty to propagate it. According to the preservation policy, there should be a service for native speakers who use the 'national language' on a daily basis: they already embody what the rest of the country is supposed to achieve and therefore deserve their own special programmes in a prominent place on the country's sole radio station. Listeners who did not know Irish could switch off Radio Éireann during the programmes aimed at the Gaeltacht, but with limited radio choice for most of the population, they could not fail to be aware of the special treatment afforded to native speakers of Irish.

The history of Radio Éireann from its inception to the present day is marked by tensions between these two ideological poles and reflects the ambiguities at the heart of language policy since independence. In the early years, the service prioritised native speech and at a later stage began focusing on learners but even these programmes were based on instruction by native speakers (Walsh, 2018). A further ideological tension has emerged since the 1960s and 1970s: the shift from the notion of Irish as a national language to that of a minority language (Mac Giolla Chríost, 2005: 176), represented by the establishment of Raidió na Gaeltachta and the further marginalisation of Irish on the existing radio and television services.

1.2 A radio station for the Gaeltacht

Despite demands for a separate radio service for the Gaeltacht as early as 1926 at the inception of 2RN, none was forthcoming until 1972 and only after a pirate station began broadcasting in Connemara. During the intervening half century, a separate Gaeltacht channel was ruled out repeatedly on grounds of expense, technical challenges and even the promotion of English itself. Rejecting calls for an all-Irish station, a report by the Department of Posts and Telegraphs expressed concern that the more widespread availability of radio in the Gaeltacht could lead to greater consumption of stations in English, presumably Radio Éireann itself and overseas stations that could be received on medium wave, particularly at night (Department of Posts and Telegraphs, 1945, reproduced in Watson, 2003: 129–139). The report recognised the sociolinguistic reality of the Gaeltacht, which by the 1940s had become increasingly bilingual with an ever-expanding familiarity with English, although not bidialectal (that is to say, other dialects were not easily understood), creating additional challenges in the absence of an oral standard for Irish. As outlined in a detailed technical addendum, there were sound engineering and financial reasons to rule out the establishment of a separate station for the Gaeltacht in the 1940s. However, at the same time that it was ruling out a separate Gaeltacht channel, the Department of Posts and Telegraphs – at the behest of de Valera – was embarking on plans for an expensive high-powered shortwave station aimed at the Irish diaspora in the United States. Such a channel was due to be launched in 1947 and subsequently delayed only to be cancelled by the inter-party coalition that came to power in 1948 (for an analysis of that government, see McCullagh, 1998). Originally conceived as a means of combatting anti-Irish propaganda in the British and American media, the shortwave station was de Valera's attempt to present a uniquely Irish message to the world but the considerable time and financial investment in it distracted from consideration of a Gaeltacht station. Indeed, it raises questions about de Valera's commitment to Irish in that large sums of money were invested in the failed shortwave station while the Gaeltacht service had to wait until the 1970s (for further information see NAI S9092). It has been argued that the failure to establish a separate station in the 1940s was ideological: by maintaining a respectable amount of Irish on Radio Éireann, the government bolstered its own ideological stance that Irish was the national language and that the Revival was already underway with the help of radio, similar to Hyde's sentiments when he opened 2RN (Horgan, 2001: 18).

The establishment of Raidió na Gaeltachta reflected an ideological turn in the history of language policy. After decades of radio's lip service to the notion of Irish as the 'national language' which was to be realised through limited programmes for both learners and native speakers, the new television channel, Telefís Éireann, was less concerned with the historical ideology and broadcast only minimal amounts of Irish after its launch in 1961 (see below). The demand for a separate Gaeltacht radio service emerged from a civil society campaign that drew on a discourse of minority rights, in parallel with other ethnic, linguistic and social minorities throughout the western world. While invoking the constitutional and legal status of Irish as the 'national language', the campaign positioned itself as protecting Irish speakers as a minority within their own state: they deserved separate treatment as a minority, but as a special kind of minority due to their historical status (Hourigan, 2003: 97–118). While the percentage of time devoted to Irish on Radio Éireann held its own during the 1960s, the greater cultural influence of a largely monolingual Telefís Éireann was such that it sparked demands among Irish speakers in the Gaeltacht for their own separate media. A Gaeltacht television channel would have been an impossible demand politically and technically in the 1960s, so the focus instead turned to the more realistic aim of achieving a radio station. RTÉ objected on technical and financial grounds, even drawing on some of the same arguments made in the 1945 departmental report, but eventually the government yielded after a campaign of civil disobedience culminating in the establishment of Saor-Raidió Chonamara ('Free Radio Connemara'), a pirate radio station (Ó Glaisne, 1982: 21–26; see 2.1 below).

Raidió na Gaeltachta began broadcasting on Easter Sunday, the 3rd of April 1972 from studios in Connemara and subsequently established headquarters in other Gaeltacht areas. From the outset, the station adopted an essentialist approach to covering Gaeltacht life: traditional speakers were favoured, folkloric material in traditional dialect was recorded and songs with lyrics in English were prohibited until 2005. Despite the closure of some regional studios, the station has endeavoured to represent all Gaeltacht areas and has covered Gaeltacht cultural and sporting events in detail throughout its existence. Delap argues that in contrast with other Irish-language media, Raidió na Gaeltachta has strong roots in the Gaeltacht and has been accepted by the community there but he refers also to debates about inherent tensions between the radical nature of its roots and the conservatism of much of its output (2012: 16; see also Ó Ciosáin, 1998). The ban on English lyrics in its output was exploited by the new community station, Raidió na Life in Dublin in 1993, which prized itself on the range and diversity of its musical programming in English and other languages (see the case study below).

Ironically, the failure to create Raidió na Gaeltachta until the 1970s may in fact have contributed to greater public consciousness about the role of the Gaeltacht in national identity. During the fifty years that Radio Éireann was the sole licensed broadcaster in the country, its Irish language

content formed part of the range of state initiatives that cemented the perception that the Gaeltacht was the wellspring upon which the revival of
Irish could be built. This proposition was by no means met with universal
approval but successive surveys since the 1970s indicate that a majority
favours supporting the Gaeltacht as an Irish-speaking area, even if they do
not have active competence in Irish (e.g. Mac Gréil & Rhatigan, 2009: 6–7,
12).[1] Had Raidió na Gaeltachta been established in the 1920s or 1930s, it is
likely that Irish would have become even more marginal on Radio Éireann
as tended to be the case when specialist Irish language channels were established. Despite persistent complaints from Irish language organisations
that Radio Éireann was not doing enough for Irish, by the standards of
today the station broadcast a significant amount of original material on a
wide range of genres during what are now primetime hours. The foothold
of Irish in the national consciousness, and subsequent awareness of the
special status of the native speaker, may have been a lot weaker had it not
been for the unifying and nation-building force of Radio Éireann in the
early- and mid-twentieth century during the golden age of the medium.
However, the establishment of Raidió na Gaeltachta coincided with an
increasing diminution of Irish language programming on Radio Éireann,
or RTÉ Radio 1 as it became after 1979.

Today, Irish has a minimal presence (about 2 per cent of total output)
on the country's independent commercial and community radio stations,
reflecting the vague provisions of broadcasting legislation enacted since the
late 1980s (Walsh et al., 2018; Walsh, 2021c). RTÉ Raidió na Gaeltachta, as
it is now known, is a full-time station available nationally on FM, focusing
on the language, culture and music of Gaeltacht communities. There are
two community radio stations broadcasting in Irish on FM locally, Raidió
na Life in Dublin and Raidió Fáilte in Belfast, and an online pop-music
station Raidió Rí-Rá. The role of Irish in community radio is considered
in detail in the case study in this chapter.

---

1   A recent survey found that maintaining Irish-speaking households in the Gaeltacht
    was deemed the second most important policy initiative, with 43 per cent of re-
    spondents in the Republic choosing this option (Darmody & Daly, 2015: 84).

1.3 Irish on television

In an interim report in 1959 as preparations for Telefís Éireann were underway, the Commission on the Restoration of the Irish Language argued that television should be used to support the Revival. It said that that a 'satisfactory percentage' of the schedule should be in Irish, with the majority of children's programmes in Irish. The working language of the new station should be Irish and permanent appointments should be conditional upon Irish language competence (Bowman, 2011: 11–12). The American Director General of Telefís Éireann, Edward Roth, made little secret of his disinterest in Irish, provoking alarm among language organisations who expected that the new station would become an arm of the Revival policy. In an interview published just before the station's launch, Roth said that minorities – presumably including Irish speakers – should be looked after 'in a minor way'. In response to a question about Irish, he said that Telefís Éireann would give the Irish people the service that they wanted while complying with statutory requirements (ibid.: 12). The umbrella group for the voluntary sector, Comhdháil Náisiúnta na Gaeilge, met Telefís Éireann management within a few months of the station's launch to express its concern about lack of provision for Irish (ibid.: 60–63).

Telefís Éireann faced the same dilemma in relation to Irish as Radio Éireann in the 1930s: as the country's sole domestic television service, it had to cater for everyone as well as promote Irish in an ill-defined framework, while always cognisant of competition from British television widely available in the eastern part of Ireland. In the absence of progress on Irish in the 1970s, the campaign for Irish language television began in earnest, comprising two often separate and sometimes mutually antagonistic elements. In Connemara in particular, there were demands for a local, community television service for the Gaeltacht but others prioritised the creation of a national television service in Irish. Inspired by successful agitation for minority language media in other countries, Conradh na Gaeilge embarked on a long campaign for Irish language television, emphasising the need for a national service for Irish speakers everywhere (see NUIG G60/36/3). Íte Ní Chionnaith, who would go on to become the organisation's president, was herself imprisoned in 1977 following a prosecution for failing to buy a television licence as a protest against the lack of Irish on RTÉ. In total, fifteen Irish language activists spent periods in prison between 1977 and 1992 for the same reason (Ní Chionnaith, 2008: 28–30). The establishment of the second national television channel, RTÉ 2 in 1979, raised hopes that Irish might finally gain a central place in the schedule but these were dashed (Ó Gairbhí, 2018: 11) and Conradh na Gaeilge boycotted the opening broadcast in Cork as a protest (Conradh na Gaeilge, 1978).

Meanwhile, a group of activists from Connemara visited the Faroe Islands to examine the practicalities of a local television service broadcasting in a lesser-used language to a small population. This led in 1987 to a pirate television station, Teilifís na Gaeltachta, which like its unlicensed radio predecessor broadcast from Connemara. The Taoiseach Charles Haughey was also Minister for the Gaeltacht at the time and requested Údarás na Gaeltachta to prepare a report about the possibilities of a Gaeltacht television service. In a far-sighted move that anticipated political developments in the 1990s, Údarás na Gaeltachta invested in training courses in all aspects of television production (Ó Gairbhí, 2018: 20–26). Debates continued between those in favour of additional Irish on RTÉ, a local Gaeltacht service and a national Irish language channel (Hourigan, 2002: 97–118). However, in 1990, a national campaign was established, Feachtas Náisiúnta Teilifíse (FNT; National Television Campaign), which gained broad backing and lobbied politicians, culminating in support from every political party in the general election of 1992 (Ó Gairbhí, 2018: 35–71).

The personal commitment of two senior Irish-speaking politicians was crucial to the government decision: the Minister for Communications, Máire Geoghegan-Quinn (1992–1994), herself from the Connemara Gaeltacht, and the Minister for the Gaeltacht, Michael D. Higgins (1992–1997), a long-standing TD for Galway West. In the end, the government decided to establish a national station under the auspices of RTÉ, with its headquarters in the Gaeltacht. There was strident opposition from journalists, mostly associated with Independent Newspapers, to the project on the spurious grounds that it was economic folly, with sustained personalised attacks on Minister Higgins (Ní Chionnaith, 2008: 31–33; Ó Gairbhí, 2018: 72–101). Teilifís na Gaeilge (TnaG) eventually came on the air as the third national channel in a blaze of publicity on the 31st of October 1996 from its studios at Baile na hAbhann in Connemara. Similar to S4C in Wales, it would commission most of its content from independent production companies, spawning a small Irish-language television industry in the Gaeltacht and elsewhere (Ní Bhrádaigh, 2008c; Mac Murchú, 2008).

1.4 From TnaG to TG4

TnaG faced enormous challenges in the initial few months that damaged its credibility as a national media outlet. Due to transmission difficulties, up to 25 per cent of the population, including some pockets in the Gaeltacht, could still not receive it at the end of 1996. New equipment that had not been tested adequately frequently failed, causing breaks in transmission and its audience did not rise above 0.5 per cent in the first few months, well short of a target of 3 per cent. The meagre budget fell far short of what was required to run a national television station and there were claims that TnaG was ignoring the quality of Irish and making excessive use of English. After a short honeymoon in the aftermath of the station's promising launch, journalists resumed their attacks and morale at the station was low by the beginning of 1997 (Ó Gairbhí, 2018: 166–178). Content Manager, Alan Esslemont was instrumental in a rebranding exercise that led to a change of name to TG4 in 1999. 'TG' referred to Teilifís na Gaeilge and '4' signalled that it was the fourth national channel (the independent commercial station TV3 had gone on air in 1998). Esslemont argued that 'TG4' gave the station a 'national resonance' instead of the niche market inferred by the name TnaG (Ó Gairbhí, 2018: 212; see also Ó Ciardha, 2008: 18). From an audience point of view, the rebranding was successful, with TG4 doubling its viewership within a few months, albeit from a very low base. Despite opposition from RTÉ, in 2007 TG4 achieved its long-term objective of independence as a separate public service broadcaster, allowing it to take greater control over its own destiny (ibid.: 254).

TG4 achieved its highest ever audience share, 3.2 per cent, in 2005 but has struggled since to maintain its audience in the increasingly fragmented digital media landscape. For the past decade, it has been stuck at around 2 per cent, making it the sixth most watched television station in Ireland (Ó Gairbhí, 2018: 372). When he took over as Director in 2016, Alan Esslemont announced a 'twin-pole' audience strategy with Irish language programmes in the genres of current affairs, drama, documentary and entertainment aimed at its 'core' audience and sport, music and programmes in English aimed at the national audience (ibid.: 356–360).

Since its inception, TG4 has faced criticism from Irish speakers about the use of English in the schedule, both in programming entirely in English and in the use of English in programmes that are supposed to be in Irish (see the detailed discussion in Ó Gairbhí, 2018: 277–322). While accepting that producing original television content in Irish is expensive, it has been claimed that the excessive presence of English contradicts TG4's foundational aim as a television station aimed at Irish speakers (Ní Chionnaith, 2008: 33–37). Another aspect relates to the omnipresence of open (i.e. burnt-in) subtitles in English on programmes in Irish, reinforcing the sense of an English-language experience (O'Connell et al., 2008: 13–14). Other variations on this theme have been that TG4 was established not as a television station but in pursuit of a language planning aim (Mac Donnacha, 2008: 103) and that downtime in its schedule should be filled by programmes in immigrant languages rather than English (Ní Ghallachair, 2008: 117–122). Referring to a finding by consultants Crowe Horwath in 2013 that over half of the population never watched TG4, Ó Gairbhí asks why the station expends so much effort trying to attract such people. Accepting that TG4 has contributed to more positive attitudes towards Irish among the general population, he argues for the station to focus more on its core Irish language audience in the future (2018: 373).

TG4 has been restricted by a lack of funding since its launch but its support from the exchequer has been increased in recent years to €38.3 million in 2020 (TG4, 2020: 35) with an additional €4.2 million committed in 2021 (TG4, 2021). Along with other broadcasters, the station also benefits from the Sound and Vision scheme of the Broadcasting Authority of Ireland, which funds original content in Irish and other genres, and the Irish Language Broadcast Fund in Northern Ireland. By comparison, the

Welsh language broadcaster S4C received £96.4 million (€113.3 million) from the British exchequer in 2020–2021 (S4C, 2021).

1.5 Irish language broadcasting in Northern Ireland

As is to be expected, provision of Irish language broadcast media has been far more limited in Northern Ireland, reflecting the marginalisation of the language there. In contrast to the BBC in Wales and Scotland, which broadcast programmes in Welsh and Gaelic from the 1920s, no Irish was heard on BBC Radio Ulster until 1981 and television programmes followed only a decade later. Output was just fifteen minutes per week at first and described memorably by one activist as 'somewhere in the no-man's land between minimalist and undetectable' (Mac Póilin, 2003a: 88). The Belfast Agreement of 1998 contained provisions related to the development of Irish language broadcasting and film and following its ratification of the European Charter for Regional or Minority Languages in 2001, the British government signed up to additional commitments. However, Muller notes that there is no statutory provision for Irish language broadcasting in the North, in contrast with Welsh in Wales and Gaelic in Scotland. She points to considerable disparities between expenditure on public service broadcasting in the three Celtic languages (2010: 100–102). The failure to include the Irish language in a White Paper on a new UK Communications Bill in 2000 caused tensions between the Irish and British governments and was condemned by Irish language groups. In 2003, a joint declaration about the peace process by both governments included a commitment to establishing an Irish language film and television production fund and improving reception of TG4 in the North (ibid.: 104–106). The Irish Language Broadcast Fund, as it was called, began distributing funding to media production companies in 2005 (ibid.: 113–118). The BBC's Irish Language Unit now produces approximately 260 hours of Irish radio programmes per year, which is augmented at times by additional programming about Irish language cultural or musical events. Up to twenty-six hours of new television content in Irish is created annually, in partnership with the Fund (Kirby, 2021).

The history of the Belfast community radio station Raidió Fáilte is discussed in the case study.

2. Case study: Irish language community media

This case study focuses on the position of Irish in community media over the past fifty years. Unlicensed pirate radio stations were set up in response to the lack of Irish on RTÉ, taking advantage of a loophole in outdated broadcasting legislation. Drawing on a rights discourse similar to that discussed in Chapter 4, some such stations focused solely on providing services for the Gaeltacht, but there was also an attempt to set up a pirate radio station in Irish in Dublin. Irish was largely marginal in the commercial pirate radio explosion of the 1980s although some unlicensed community stations gave it a place in their schedules and went on to apply for licenses in the new independent radio regime after 1989. The case study concludes with an analysis of the two community radio stations broadcasting in Irish, Raidió na Life (literally 'Radio of the Liffey') in Dublin, and Raidió Fáilte ('Radio of welcome') in Belfast. In that way, it gives us an insight into the intersection of media activism and language policy on both sides of the border.

2.1 Saor-Raidió Chonamara

The 1960s in Britain witnessed the greatest shake-up in the radio industry since its inception four decades earlier when Radio Caroline and other pirate stations took to the air from ships off the coast just outside UK territorial waters, taking advantage of a loophole in the broadcasting legislation. Irishman Ronan O'Rahilly was the most famous pirate, establishing Radio Caroline on a boat off the Essex coast and broadcasting pop music and commercial advertising to millions of young listeners bored with the staid diet of the BBC. As a result of the phenomenal success of Caroline and other pirates, the British Labour government in 1967 introduced the Marine and Broadcasting Offences Act. Although the legislation was meant to silence the pirates, Caroline famously continued to broadcast after the midnight deadline on 14 August and continued in various guises until the early 1990s. However, the government also moved to re-organise the BBC to establish a pop music station, local BBC opt-outs and commercial radio (Chapman, 1992). The success of the British pirates spawned the Irish pirate radio industry and while most stations were motivated by the commercial ethos of Caroline, some people in the Gaeltacht saw the unlicensed airwaves as an opportunity to promote Irish. The Irish language activist and intellectual Máirtín Ó Cadhain recommended that the Irish language movement should consider a 'secret radio station' (*stáisiún rúnda raidió*) of its own (Ó Glaisne, 1982: 24). A leading figure in the Gaeltacht Civil Rights Movement, Seosamh Ó Cuaig, visited Derry during the 'Battle of the Bogside' in 1969 and heard the pirate Radio Free Derry, which was broadcasting at the time. He used his newspaper column to advocate for a similar service for the Gaeltacht:

> Radio fíor-Ghaelach a bheadh ann; bheadh ceoltóirí, aisteoirí, cainteoirí, srl. as an gceantar ag soláthar ábhair dó agus, de réir a chéile, b'fhéidir, dhéanfadh sé freastal ar Ghaeilgeoirí ar fud na tíre ar fad ... Sílim go gcaithfear a admháil go bhfuil dochar mór á dhéanamh ag radio agus teilifís Éireann do shaol Gaelach Iarchonnacht le blianta anuas. Chriog an dá cheann acu an amhránaíocht ar an sean-nós anseo, mar shampla, chabhraigh siad go mór le dul i léig na cuartaíochta agus thacht siad beo beathaíoch na scéalaithe. (Ó Cuaig, 1969, cited in Ó Glaisne, 1982: 24)[2]

Ó Cuaig added that transmitters cost very little, would operate over an area of 20 miles and a request could be made to use a vacant frequency already allocated to Radio Éireann:

> Mura dtabharfaidís an cead, bheadh orainn 'dul ar an run', mar adéarfá: an 'transmitter' a iompar ó áit go háit; fear amháin a choinneáil ag obair; fear eile ag plé leis na ceirníní; agus duine nó beirt ag bailiú nuachta agus ábhair de gach cineál. Bhraithfeadh

---

2   It would be a fully-Irish radio station; musicians, actors, speakers, etc. from the area would supply material to it and eventually, perhaps, it would serve Irish speakers all over the country ... I think it has to be admitted that national radio and television has caused great harm to the Irish language world in west Connacht in recent years. They both killed off *sean-nós* [traditional] singing here, for example, they really helped wipe out the tradition of visiting each other's houses and they strangled the storytellers completely.

dul ar aghaidh na scéime cuid mhór ar chomhoibriú an phobail, ach tá mé cinnte go mbeadh sé ar fáil, tríd is tríd. Seans, ceart go leor, go mbeadh corrdhuine measúil ag seasamh amach ar chnocán agus ag rá gur scabhtaeracht a bheadh ann, ach thiocfadh ciall dóibh sin de réir a chéile. (Ibid.: 26)[3]

A student from Cork, Micheál Ó hÉalaí – who was involved in a pirate station in that city – had read Ó Cuaig's article and offered to help the Connemara group with equipment. It was decided that the station would broadcast from Ros Muc for symbolic reasons; one of the executed leaders of the 1916 Rising, Patrick Pearse, had stayed in a house in the area learning Irish and at one stage the group considered setting up the station in the same building. Eventually, a caravan was bought, equipment installed in it and Saor-Raidió Chonamara went on the air on Saturday, the 28th of March 1970 on 1484 kHz (202 metres). Ó Cuaig described the drama of the moment:

> Ag leathuair tar éis a cúig shroich me an carabhán. Chuaigh mé suas an cnoc agus trainsistear agam. Ansin a chuala mé túschraoladh an chéad raidió lán-Ghaelach sa domhan. (Ibid.: 29)[4]

An unnamed man who witnessed the event said that the caravan moved to An Cheathrú Rua because of fears of a raid, but by its final day it announced its location on air, invited people to a 'saor-chéilí'[5] outside the caravan and took a roving microphone into the crowd. The event proved, he said, that there were people in the Gaeltacht with the technical knowledge to put a radio station on air and that there was huge public interest in the broadcasts (ibid.: 29–30). The newsletter of the Gaeltacht Civil

---

3   If they didn't give permission, we'd have to go "on the run": carry the transmitter from place to place, keep one man working; another managing the records; and one or two gathering news and all kinds of material. The progress of the scheme would depend to a large part on the co-operation of the community, but I'm sure that it would be available for the most part. There is a chance that the odd respectable person would stand on a hillside and say that we were up to no good, but they would come to their senses gradually.

4   At half past five, I reached the caravan. I went up the hill with a transistor. Then I heard the first broadcast of the first all-Irish radio station in the world.

5   Literally a 'free céilí', referring the traditional form of céilí (traditional) dancing.

Rights Movement, *Tuairisc*, urged readers to write to the Minister for Posts and Telegraphs to demand a licence for the station (ibid.: 32). A letter to the Minister said that the station should be operated by a local radio committee and have nothing to do with RTÉ. George Colley, Minister for Industry and Commerce and for the Gaeltacht, said that he favoured a Gaeltacht radio station and the Gaeltacht Civil Rights Movement continued to lobby him and other politicians for a station under community control (ibid.: 35–36). In October 1969, Saor-Raidió Chonamara returned to the air that autumn as part of a local festival Oireachtas na nGael,[6] itself a protest against the fact that the main Irish language festival Oireachtas na Gaeilge was being held in Dublin instead of the Gaeltacht. This time, it was based above a shop in the village near where most of the festival was taking place. Ó Glaisne claims that while the local Garda sergeant was ordered to raid the studio, he refused because of fears that such an action would provoke a riot. The second broadcast was more professional than the first and convinced many people that a Gaeltacht radio service was a legitimate demand (ibid.: 5152).

Despite its short existence, Saor-Raidió Chonamara upped the temperature of the campaign and within two years, Raidió na Gaeltachta went on the air on Easter Sunday, the 3rd of April 1972. However, a key demand of the campaigners was rejected: the station was under the control of RTÉ, whose poor provision for the Irish language on its radio and television services had led to the pirate station in the first place (ibid.: 103–114). Meanwhile, Irish language groups outside the Gaeltacht were also looking at the potential of pirate radio to get their message across.

2.2 Raidió an Phobail

Conradh na Gaeilge's broadcasting sub-committee exerted a significant influence on various campaigns for Irish language radio and television in the 1970s and 1980s. Established in 1973 as a reaction to the proposal

6   Literally, 'assembly of Irish speakers', distinguishing itself from the official Oireachtas na Gaeilge ('Irish language assembly') event.

by former Minister for Posts and Telegraphs Conor Cruise O'Brien to rebroadcast BBC television throughout Ireland instead of establishing a second RTÉ channel, it was chaired by former president Maolsheachlainn Ó Caollaí. Ó Caollaí had spearheaded reforms in Conradh na Gaeilge from the 1960s and internationalised the debates about Irish by linking them with social and linguistic issues in other countries. The sub-committee promoted an alternative vision of media, drawing on ideo-logical currents such as cultural anti-imperialism, anti-commercialism and participatory communication. As pirate radio began to take off in Dublin in 1978, Ó Caollaí said that Conradh na Gaeilge would set up its own station:

> There seemed no reason why the Irish Language Movement should not set up its own radio station to broadcast Irish news, and uncensored opinion in Irish during the times of day and night when RTÉ and Radio na Gaeltachta are failing to offer a service for Irish speakers or for Irish music lovers. (*The Irish Times*, 1978)

The station was originally to be called Radio na nGael (literally 'radio of Irish speakers') and launched in March 1978 but this was delayed. As the second television channel RTÉ2 in 1979 approached, the sub-committee campaigned to ensure that the new station would have an adequate Irish language output, and its own pirate radio station was part of that cam-paign (*The Irish Independent*, 1978).

In May 1978, the Executive Committee of Conradh na Gaeilge passed a resolution to establish its own pirate radio station over which it would have exclusive control. At a meeting on the 6th of October 1979, final de-cisions were made about the station, to be known as Raidió an Phobail ('radio of the community'), just before it took to the airwaves. An AM transmitter on 1500 kHz (200 metres) was bought for £670 from another pirate station Independent Radio Galway, which had closed down earlier in the year. Despite a low output of 50 watts, the radius was estimated op-timistically at 10 miles, giving it coverage of the city centre. It was agreed that no English would be used except to give information about classes, that there would be a ban on music with English lyrics, that the station would broadcast outside the hours of Raidió na Gaeltachta and that it would not accept commercial advertising (Conradh na Gaeilge, 1979a).

A press release was issued on the 16th of October, the day of the launch, explaining that no part of the state grant for Conradh na Gaeilge had been used to fund any part of the radio's activities. Raidió an Phobail was funded solely from subscriptions from branches of Conradh na Gaeilge and from individuals and groups who were invited to make their own programmes. The press release explained that Raidió an Phobail was founded as a protest against the failure of RTÉ to adequately serve Irish speakers and the 'Anglo-American domination of RTÉ programming'. Broadcasting hours would be from 9–10 p.m. each night and the service would consist only of music and information about Irish language events until a longer-term arrangement was made. Music in Irish and music from other countries would be broadcast and the station hoped to become a link between listeners and 'the non-Anglo-American world which is so ignored by RTÉ'. Raidió an Phobail would not accept advertising, because this was the 'fundamental cause of RTÉ's Anglo-Americanism and its anti-nationalism'. Commenting on the burgeoning pirate radio scene in Dublin at the time, Conradh na Gaeilge argued that Raidió an Phobail was as legal as any other pirate station and that any attempt to close it down without dealing with all unlicensed stations would be discriminatory. It saw itself as both an Irish-medium station and 'a challenge to the established commercial concepts and objectives of the broadcasting system in Ireland' (Conradh na Gaeilge, 1979b).

There was extensive press coverage of the new station in both Irish and English. A representative of the station claimed that the government had shown itself to favour commercial independent radio and that Raidió an Phobail was a stance against that. It was also a 'propaganda coup' (*buille bolscaireachta*) against RTÉ and a new means of communication that would encourage an *esprit de corps* among the young people involved in Conradh na Gaeilge (*Inniu*, 1979b).

Technical difficulties with the transmitter and mast meant that the radius of the station in the first few weeks was limited to a few miles and the station suffered from co-channel interference from a European station on the same frequency, a regular occurrence in the unregulated world of pirate radio. Equipment was basic but the message was clear: on the wall of the rudimentary studio was a poster featuring the slogan 'Impiriúlachas

cultúir' (*cultural imperialism*) and showing a group of people chained to a
television wearing a hat bearing the American stars and stripes (Conradh na
Gaeilge, n.d.). Asked about the possibility of applying for a licence should
the government enact new broadcasting legislation, Ó Caollaí said: 'We
possibly would be interested, but it's not really our business. Basically we
are aiming to show what the official station should be doing and we hope
to go out of existence eventually' (O'Rourke, 1979). Technical improvements increased the radius of the station within a few weeks and ten volunteers were involved in producing and presenting the nightly programme,
which included interviews with Irish language groups and discussion of
the Oireachtas festival (*Inniu*, 1979c). Later in the year, Raidió an Phobail
broadcast for two weeks from the Mayo Gaeltacht as a protest against the
failure of Raidió na Gaeltachta to set up a studio there (*Inniu*, 1979a). The
station planned to broadcast results of the elections to the newly established
Údarás na Gaeltachta as Raidió na Gaeltachta's signal was barely audible
in the area (*Mayo News*, 1979).

Raidió an Phobail planned to return in 1980 with a 500-watt transmitter made by an amateur radio technician, of whom there were many
in Dublin serving the pirates. Ó Caollaí reported that technical difficulties with the aerial delayed the start of programmes as the crowded city
centre site was not a suitable location from which to broadcast on medium
wave. Although the station's initial aims were more political in nature, Ó
Caollaí felt that Raidió an Phobail should henceforth be used to publicise
the work of Conradh na Gaeilge and to encourage Irish speakers in the
city to become involved (Ó Caollaí, 1979). The station was heard again in
October of that year on a new frequency of 1413 kHz (212m) over a wider
area than previously (*Inniu*, 1980) but seems to have petered out after that.

2.3 Attempts to license independent radio

The first of four attempts to bring forward legislation to regulate the
independent radio sector was made in 1979 when a bill was published
by Fianna Fáil. RTÉ expressed an interest in running community radio
at this time but Irish language organisations were concerned that they

would not win the franchise to operate such stations, because of a commitment in the bill to establish an independent broadcasting authority. A memorandum from the co-ordinating body for the voluntary Irish language sector warned of the negative implications of commercial interests getting involved in local radio and urged groups to develop a policy on the matter (Comhdháil Náisiúnta na Gaeilge, 1980).

The broadcasting sub-committee of Conradh na Gaeilge took an active role in developing such a policy throughout the 1980s. In a memorandum, Maolsheachlainn Ó Caollaí warned that commercial radio could do permanent damage to the position of Irish and that the movement needed to mobilise behind a positive but alternative policy. Describing commercialism as one of the most powerful forces shaping RTÉ, the paper warned that a further expansion of the commercial ethos was proposed. Ó Caollaí put forward various counter-arguments to the legalisation of commercial pirate stations. He rejected the argument that RTÉ was not playing pop music and opposed the view that initiative shown by the pirates should be rewarded, describing their operations as 'anti-communitarian' (*frith-chomhdhaonnach*). In response to the view that increased competition would force RTÉ to improve its standards, history showed that additional services would cause convergence and reduce choice. In response to freedom of speech arguments, Ó Caollaí said what was proposed was allowing commercial interests to profit from one-way communication. The paper also referred to the 'gombeen nature' (*nádúr gaimbíneach*) of the pirates, a reference to their supposed interest in making a quick profit (Ó Caollaí, 1982).

Conradh na Gaeilge condemned the 1983 Local Radio Bill, claiming that it amounted to a licence to print money for commercial interests and would force RTÉ to become more commercial. It argued that no commercial system would treat the Irish language fairly (Conradh na Gaeilge, 1983g). The organisation wrote to Taoiseach Garrett FitzGerald and leader of Fianna Fáil Charles Haughey urging them not to succumb to commercialism in local radio. In an article published after the publication of the Local Radio Bill 1983, Ó Caollaí accused RTÉ of being 'the leading promoter of cultural alienation' in Ireland because of its heavy reliance on imported television material (Ó Caollaí, 1983). This was linked to colonialism and a world-view hostile to languages other than English and it was claimed that it resulted in the marginalisation of the Irish language and culture. However, the situation was unavoidable because despite its statutory aims in relation to Irish language and culture, RTÉ was obliged to sell its services to listeners and viewers in competition with British channels. As a result, minority programming including Irish was shunted to the sidelines with minimal resources and small audiences (ibid.: 9). Ó Caollaí condemned government inaction on the expanding pirate radio sector and blamed neo-liberal influences from Thatcher's Britain for the demeaning of the public service in favour of private gain. The newly published bill proposed to set up local community radio stations that would be operated by RTÉ. While Ó Caollaí was concerned about the implications of commercialism for such an arrangement, he deemed it preferable to a fully commercial model where private gain would be the only objective: 'Will it copperfasten the anti-Irish, alienating nature of broadcasting or will it represent the begin-ning of a new era in which broadcasting will become an instrument for real national development?' (ibid.: 11).

A submission by Conradh na Gaeilge about the 1983 bill to the Joint Oireachtas Committee on Legislation distinguished between two types of broadcasting: the public service approach and the commercial approach, coming down firmly in favour of the former. Describing Irish as having 'suffered so greatly at the hands of RTÉ', it argued that two groups needed to be targeted in different ways, Irish-speaking communities and 'recep-tive bilinguals and learners' (Conradh na Gaeilge, 1984). A detailed letter from Ó Caollaí to opposition communications spokesman Terry Leyden in 1986 referred approvingly to the New International Information Order, a movement to protect against cultural domination supported by UNESCO and many voluntary bodies (MacBride, 1980). Ó Caollaí also appealed to traditional nationalist concerns in Fianna Fáil and urged it to reverse its policy in favour of commercial local radio. He claimed that the Irish mass media was the most dominated of any state in the world due to saturation of British television and press, while commercial radio (mostly pirates) were described as 'carbon copies of Anglo-American models' broadcasting 'the most banal mid-Atlantic rubbish' that had no regard for the Irish lan-guage. In the context of ongoing attempts to legalise independent radio,

Ó Caollaí urged the development of a national broadcasting policy recognising the central importance of the media as a leading cultural agency with enormous influence on the population, including in matters of language. (Conradh na Gaeilge, 1986a).

After almost a decade of failed attempts to regulate independent radio, two pieces of legislation – the Broadcasting and Wireless Telegraphy Bill and the Radio and Television Bill of 1987 – marked the beginning of the end of the pirate radio era. The unlicensed stations would have to close down by the end of 1988 and this would be followed by a local radio licensing process, but with a focus on commercial activity. Similar to its response to other bills, Conradh na Gaeilge reacted with dissatisfaction, claiming that the new law was 'a retrograde step' as it would create a profit-based model for private business and not serve the public interest, including the promotion of Irish. Unlike the 1983 bill, RTÉ was not to be allowed participate in the new system, leaving it open to fully commercial interests. Conradh na Gaeilge urged that Raidió na Gaeltachta should be expanded in anticipation of the new stations and a percentage of the profits made by the commercial sector set aside for developing public service broadcasting in Irish (Conradh na Gaeilge, 1988). Comhdháil Náisiúnta na Gaeilge similarly opposed the new bill and urged that at least 15 per cent of broadcast time on each station be given over to Irish (Comhdháil Náisiúnta na Gaeilge, 1987a).

After the short-lived experiment of Raidió an Phobail, Conradh na Gaeilge developed links with non-commercial pirate radio stations operating around the country. While many pirates of the decade 1978–1988 were avowedly commercial in outlook, often generating huge profits despite the recession, some stations adopted the AMARC (World Association of Community Radio Broadcasters)[7] principles on community radio and developed local services based on voluntary effort and community participation. Eleven such stations formed the National Association of Community Broadcasting (NACB) and most broadcast regular programmes in Irish, in contrast to commercial pirates that avoided specialist programming that might narrow their audience. There was some Irish on some of the bigger pirates – for instance ERI in Cork and

---

7   Known in French as *Association mondiale des radiodiffuseurs communautaires*. See <https://amarceurope.eu/>.

KISS FM in Dublin, a specialist offshoot to the highly successful Radio Nova –
but in general, community radio was a more likely home for Irish programmes
(Walsh & Greene, 2020). The Conradh na Gaeilge archive contains bilingual
documentation from the unlicensed Concord Community Broadcasting Co-
operative in Dublin and a list of names of people involved in the NACB in
Dublin. Letters in Irish from Concord urged Irish language organisations to
participate actively in its work and in other NACB stations, suggesting that
they make their own programmes, take part in interviews or provide news and
information (North Dublin Community Radio, 1983). The NACB Charter
outlined the principles of community radio, including democratic ownership
and control, non-commercialism with any profit invested in community development, two-way communication of diverse opinions, training of local
people, encouraging participatory democracy and promoting the Irish language (Concord Community Radio, c.1983). There were also contacts with
pirates in places such as Tipperary and Mayo, some of whom sought Conradh
na Gaeilge's input into applications for licences when these were announced in
1989 (Independent Radio Mayo, 1988; Conradh na Gaeilge, 1989b; Premier
County Communications, 1989). Despite these contacts and its own dabble
with piracy in the form of Raidió an Phobail, the philosophy of community
radio does not seem to have exerted a deep influence on Conradh na Gaeilge's
policy. This may have been due to the organisation's suspicion of the commercial pirates or the realisation that only a small number of community pirates
existed and therefore lacked influence.

    Comhdháil Náisiúnta na Gaeilge praised the efforts in favour of Irish
by pirate Bray Local Broadcasting (BLB) in Co. Wicklow in a statement
opposing the commercially oriented 1987 local radio bill. In a 1988 circular
on the new legislation that seemed to recognise the commercial reality,
Comhdháil stated that Irish speakers could either enter partnerships with
private companies to ensure a percentage of airtime or to form alliances
with other cultural bodies such as the GAA and traditional music organisation Comhaltas Ceoltóirí Éireann. Noting that community radio was
a possibility from 1990 under the new legislation, Comhdháil outlined
the case for an FM station serving Irish speakers in Dublin and reminded
members that the NACB was actively seeking the involvement of Irish

speakers in radio co-operatives that could apply for licences (Comhdháil Náisiúnta na Gaeilge, 1987b; Ó Murchú, 2018).

2.4 Licensed independent radio

Given the commercially driven legislation, it was to be expected that Irish language bodies would be bitterly disappointed by the new broadcasting landscape that emerged from 1989. The first battle was over the new commercial national radio station Century Radio, which Conradh expected to 'include in its schedules a broad range of programmes which would cater for the Irish-speaking community and learners of Irish' (Conradh na Gaeilge, 1989a). Given that its decade-long campaign to halt the commercialisation of radio had failed, and following the enactment of vague provisions about Irish, it was an unrealistic expectation and it was duly smashed when Century announced its programmes at the end of August: only one hour per week was to be Irish on the new national station. A flurry of letters followed to the Minister, the Independent Radio and Television Commission (IRTC) and to Century investor, businessman Oliver Barry (Conradh na Gaeilge, 1989c, 1989d & 1989e). The IRTC's response revealed the reality of the weak legislation: it agreed that one programme was not enough and said that it had told Century previously that it must also provide an Irish-language news service and that it was complying with that request. The IRTC also referred to other unspecified plans to develop Irish language output and said it would be in touch with Century from time to time about the matter (Independent Radio and Television Commission, 1989). In other words, because of the vagueness of the new legislation, there was nothing concrete that the Commission could do about the lack of Irish on Century Radio. There was similar disappointment about commercial local radio; for instance in 1990, the Mayo branch of Conradh na Gaeilge organised a public meeting to air concerns about the failure of the new licensed Midwest Radio to live up to its promises to broadcast Irish language programming (Conradh na Gaeilge, 1990b). A Conradh na Gaeilge branch in Co. Meath complained to the IRTC about the lack of Irish on the new local station LMFM

(Independent Radio and Television Commission, 1990). The booklet of Conradh na Gaeilge's annual Ard-Fheis (assembly) in 1990 described the state of Irish on local radio as 'dreadful' (*go hainnis*) and said that the level of provision to Irish speakers was very low. It also referred to a survey of sixteen stations conducted by the IRTC that found that only four were broadcasting programmes in Irish, three of which were aired after 7 p.m. (Conradh na Gaeilge, 1990a).

The pirates that had pioneered community radio in Ireland lost out badly in the new regime after 1989. Of the twenty-five local licences, former community stations succeeded in a small number of areas but most failed after a short time (Walsh & Greene, 2020). It was hoped that specific community licences would be made available shortly after the roll-out of commercial radio and contacts were made between community groups and Irish language organisations about this after the new legislation came into effect. Comhdháil Náisiúnta na Gaeilge wrote to its members urging them to consider buying shares in licensed community radio stations in order to ensure Irish language output (Comhdháil Náisiúnta na Gaeilge, 1989). A letter to Conradh na Gaeilge from the successor organisation to former pirate North Dublin Community Radio said that it had strongly emphasised the Irish language and culture in its application for a community licence. It requested the cooperation of Irish language organisations in providing presenters, contributors and material for programming and advised setting up a formal link with the NACB to co-ordinate programming and training for volunteers (Dublin North-East Community Communications Co-operation Society, 1989).

The emphasis of the licensing process was commercial and no specific community licences were issued, leading radio co-operatives around the country to put their plans on ice. Following pressure from the NACB, various groups were invited to combine their efforts in one Dublin-wide community station that was supposed to cater for all groups in all areas, an impossible task and a contradiction of the localness of the community radio ethos (Day, 2021). Anna Livia FM came on the air as a 'community-of-interest' station in 1992 and aired a nightly Irish language programme and news headlines (Conradh na Gaeilge, 1992). No other local community stations began full-time broadcasting until 1995, when a change of policy was announced by the new Minister for Communications, Michael D. Higgins. Meanwhile, Irish language organisations were preoccupied with two other important media projects: the campaign to establish an Irish-language community station in Dublin and the push for an Irish language television channel.

2.5 Establishment of Raidió na Life

With the exception of Raidió na Gaeltachta, broadcast media content in Irish was very limited at the beginning of the 1990s, despite hopes that the new licensing regime would address the issue. In fact, there was little more than symbolic or tokenistic use of Irish on over thirty commercial and two public service radio stations and the putative Irish-language television channel was still years away. Irish speakers in Dublin in particular were dissatisfied with the state of affairs as they felt unserved by Raidió na Gaeltachta, which had been set up for those living in the Irish-speaking districts. Only limited programming was aired from Dublin and the station focused almost exclusively on the speech and culture of rural Gaeltacht communities. A group of young Irish speakers in Dublin, some of whom were raising their children with Irish, came together to form Comharchumann Raidió Átha Cliath (Dublin Radio Co-operative), with the aim of establishing a full-time Irish language station for the city. They were concerned at the lack of Irish in mass media and wanted a radio station for those like them who were young Irish speakers based in Dublin. The aim of the co-operative was to provide 'a comprehensive Irish language radio service on an educational and community basis'. It was argued that this was 'an essential cultural service' and that it would build good will for the language in Dublin (Raidió na Life, 2021).

One of the station's founders, Éamon Ó Ciosáin explained how the community radio ethos was at the heart of the co-operative's aims:

Bhí gluaiseacht raidió pobail, sórt comharchumainn, gluaiseacht mar a déarfá ón mbun aníos nach raibh dírithe go hiomlán ná mórán ar chor ar bith ar díreach a bheith ag casadh ceoil agus ag fáil fógraíocht isteach agus ag déanamh airgid mar a bhí go leor, cuide de na stáisiúin bhradacha mar a deirtí ag an am, agus bhain Raidió

na Life is dóighe leis an ngluaiseacht sin. Bhí daoine i gceantracha éagsúla sa tír ag
iarraidh a dhul i gcion ar an rialtas le ceadúnais a thabhairt amach sa gcaoi is go
bhféadfaí raidiónna pobail a bheadh ag freastal ar an bpobal agus ag soláthar oiliúint
raidió [a bhunú]. Is cuid d'idé-eolaíocht forbartha phobail a bhí i gceist sa rud seo
mar a déarfá, ba chuid de chur chuige níos leithne ná cúrsaí raidió amháin a bhí sna
comharchumainn raidió seo a bhí ar bun ag an am. (Ó Ciosáin, 2018)[8]

Meetings of the radio co-operative were held in 1989 to discuss the possibility of applying for a licence for the Dublin area. It was expected that
an application would be made that year but correspondence from the
co-operative indicated delays in hearing applications on the part of the
IRTC (Comharchumann Raidió Átha Cliath, 1989). In 1990, it was announced that the station was to be called Raidió na Life and would apply
for the city's sole 'special interest' licence. It would broadcast a range of
programmes for Irish speakers in the Dublin area and there would be
120–150 volunteers, many of them already trained by the co-operative or
in other radio stations (presumably the pirates of the 1980s). The project had received support from all Irish language organisations and had
sold £7,000 in shares to date, with an aim to increase that to £12,500 in
time for the application (Comharchumann Raidió Átha Cliath, 1990).
In a direct link to the 1980s pirate scene, a publicity leaflet stated that
Raidió na Life would operate according to the charter of the NACB.
It would be aimed at Irish speakers in Dublin, Gaeltacht people living
in the city, students of gaelscoileanna, members of youth Irish language
organisations and anyone wishing to hear programmes about Dublin
in Irish (Comharchumann Raidió Átha Cliath, c. 1990). Although the

8   There was a sort of community radio movement, a co-operative movement you
     could say, coming from the bottom-up, that was not fully focused, nor even at all,
     on just playing music and getting advertising in and making money as many were
     doing, as some of the pirate stations were, at the time, and Raidió na Life was, I
     suppose, part of that movement. People in different areas in that movement were
     trying to put it up to the government, to get a license so that community radio sta-
     tions could serve the community, and provide community radio training. That is
     part of the ideology of community development that was central to this thing they
     were doing, it was part of that approach – a wider approach than just radio, radio
     matters only – that was in the radio co-operatives that were being set up at the time.

special interest licence was awarded to an English-language consortium, the Raidió na Life application was not in vain, as it helped them prepare their case and prove that an Irish language community station was possible (Nic Eoin, 2021). Raidió na Life received a temporary licence to broadcast during the Oireachtas na Gaeilge festival in Clondalkin in Dublin in 1991 (Nic Eoin, 2018) and continued to campaign for a fulltime licence. A sample programme schedule showed the diversity of the proposed offering: an events and music programme each evening, news headlines, specialist programmes each night including traditional music, women's affairs, environmental matters, a book programme, a schools' programme, a show for teenagers and a weekly interview. There would also be a nightly magazine programme covering arts, culture and current affairs and a nightly specialist music programme featuring a different genre each evening (Comharchumann Raidió Átha Cliath, c. 1992).

Raidió na Life was awarded a full-time licence in 1992 and announced its intention to launch on St. Patrick's Day 1993 (Comharchumann Raidió Átha Cliath, 1992), but the launch was put back until the autumn because of a delay in awarding a frequency (Comharchumann Raidió Átha Cliath, 1993). Nic Eoin recalls how members of the group used their contacts to drum up moral, financial and technical support, including public meetings, a lottery in association with a Gaeltacht co-operative in Co. Meath, sponsorship and assistance with transmission from commercial station Clare FM (Nic Eoin, 2021). The support of the Irish language sector was crucial: Comhdháil Náisiúnta na Gaeilge looked after publicity, Gael-Linn provided £30,000 for studio equipment and Bord na Gaeilge provided another £40,000 (Gael-Linn, 1993). On the day of the station's launch, the 29th of September 1993, Bord na Gaeilge described Raidió na Life as 'one of the most significant Irish language developments in the capital in recent times. There is a sizeable pool of Irish competence in Dublin and Raidió na Life offers a range of programmes in Irish designed for a contemporary urban audience' (Bord na Gaeilge, 1993a). An innovative and diverse launch event was held on a bridge over the River Liffey, including music spanning rock, classical, hip-hop and a group of singers from South America. The Minister for Culture, Michael D. Higgins, launched the station and spoke in Irish, English and Spanish:

Tá an dóchas agus an fhealsúnacht ar a bhfuil an tseirbhís sainspéise raidió seo bunaithe an-ghar do mo chroí féin ... agus tá moladh ar leith ag dul do na daoine óga uile ar éirigh leo an misneach, an t-idéalachas agus an dóchas sin a cheangal le hobair, le fuinneamh agus le dúthracht chun an tseirbhís nua raidió seo, Raidió na Life, a chur ar an aer. (Raidió na Life, 1993: 1).[9]

Raidió na Life received a mostly warm welcome from reviewers in the media. The Irish language newspaper *Lá* in Belfast said that Raidió na Life had 'shocked' those involved in Raidió na Gaeltachta in Dublin[10] and that it would earn listeners that the Gaeltacht station would never have (Gearóid Ó Cairealláin, *Lá*, 20 January 1994, cited in Raidió na Life, 1994). Many English-language reviewers seemed surprised at the station's innovative approach to broadcasting and singled out its diverse musical offering. For instance, *The Irish Times* said that 'the Irish language station has brought a sense of adventure back to music programming' (Michael Cunningham, 'Radio Highlights', 22 January 1994, cited in Raidió na Life, 1994). The tabloid *Sunday World* summed up the positive mood:

> Maria is the radio queen of Gaelic rap ... her Tuesday night show is about the only slot on the official[11] airwaves that you're likely to hear the hottest rap, grunge, techno, raga, hardcore, trash and industrial music ... to prove just how difficult they are to tame down at Raidió na Life. 'Radio Fiáin', or 'Wild Radio' goes out on Saturday nights. This show broadcasts the booming sounds played by the DJs in Club Wild late night in the Irish Film Centre – the first link up of its kind in the city. (*Sunday World*, 27 February 1994, cited in Raidió na Life, 1994)

One of the station's early volunteers, Fachtna Ó Driseoil – now with RTÉ Raidió na Gaeltachta – described the arrival of Raidió na Life as a 'small revolution' (*réabhlóid bheag*) and focused again on the music policy.

---

9   The hope and philosophy on which this special interest radio service is based are very close to my own heart ... and particular praise is due for all of the young people who managed to link confidence, idealism and hope with work, energy and dedication to put this new radio service, Raidió na Life, on the air.

10 'Tá Raidió na Life i ndiaidh croitheadh a bhaint astu siúd a bhaineann le Raidió na Gaeltachta sa phríomhchathair'.

11 This is a reference to the fact that many pirate stations returned to the air in Dublin in the early 1990s, broadcasting specialist music genres.

He pointed out that this was the first time that a full range of contemporary music with English lyrics was presented in Irish and argued that this contributed in part to changes in Raidió na Gaeltachta in the 1990s (Ó Drisceoil, 2007: 174). However, despite the fanfare about musical diversity, financing even a station operated mostly by volunteers was a constant challenge from the outset. Raidió na Life employed a marketing manager and produced professionally designed brochures extolling the benefits of advertising in Irish, with endorsements from leading figures in the world of business (Raidió na Life, c. 1993). Although it received sponsorship from public and private companies in the early years, as a non-commercial station, it was prohibited from broadcasting advertising and businesses in particular were reluctant to spend advertising budgets on an Irish language station in the absence of accurate audience figures (Raidió na Life, 1993: 2).

2.6 Analysis of Raidió na Life

In research on the early years of Raidió na Life, it was concluded that the station avoided the common tendency in minority language contexts to adopt a preservationist approach. It was argued that Raidió na Life defied expectations in relation to Irish language media by focusing on revitalisation of the language in urban contexts and giving access to the airwaves to speakers with varying levels of Irish (Cotter, 1999: 135). On the occasion of the twenty-fifth anniversary of the station in 2018, I decided to conduct new research on the station in association with one of its founders, Rosemary Day, now also an academic. This recent research (Day & Walsh, 2020; Walsh & Day, 2021), has focused on two axes: (a) the extent to which volunteers in the station saw themselves as language activists and/or were building a language community and (b) their views on linguistic prescriptivism on and off air. It was decided to take stock of the station's development from sociolinguistic and community development perspectives by probing the extent to which it was achieving its primary aim of building a community of Irish speakers in Dublin. The sociolinguistic aspect drew on work from minority language media (MLM) studies which is distinguished from mainstream media studies by its focus on how media support minority languages. The work of Cormack (2007; 2013) and Browne (1998) on the benefits of MLM is well known and outlines a number of advantages conferred by the media outlet on speakers of the language and broader society including symbolic power, positive representation, economic opportunities, linguistic development and fostering in-group cohesion. The socialisation aspect of media – either in physical or virtual spaces – has been shown to have an influence on language revitalisation in that it provides opportunities for informal use of the language to people who may not be able to speak it regularly due to the sociolinguistic environment. Other studies of how practitioners' involvement in MLM influences their use of and attitudes towards the minority language were also relevant. The sociolinguistic element was also enriched by work on 'new speakers' of minority languages (see Introduction).

The community development perspective refers to the ownership, control and management of the media outlet by members of the community. Community media aims to empower those involved by tackling marginalisation and disenfranchisement in the community, building links between people and training them in media literacy (Day, 2009). Clearly, a study of an MLM outlet operating in a minority language such as Irish needed to draw on both approaches to analyse all angles of the challenge and how it was being met. Therefore, certain questions loomed large: how was a community radio station broadcasting in Irish achieving its aim of building a community of Irish speakers in Dublin? To what extent did volunteers participate in and commit to the project? What was their understanding of the station's aims, who was their community and how did they relate to it? By contributing to a public media space in Irish, did they see themselves as language activists or simply broadcasters who happened to be using Irish?

The methodology consisted of a focus group with a sample of about 10 per cent of Raidió na Life volunteers (seven people), an interview with another volunteer and interviews with management, as well as analysis of a documentary broadcast to mark the anniversary. Volunteers were mostly in their 20s and 30s and one was aged around 50. All were currently presenting programmes ranging from music to speech content and most had been with the station for some time. Everyone in the group was at ease with spoken Irish and had no difficulty taking part in the discussion and while two of the eight had more limited competence, they were still capable of presenting live radio programmes. Transcripts were coded, pseudonyms assigned to participants and salient themes identified related to language background, motivations for involvement, influence of involvement on language use, appraisal of media content, relationship with listeners, understanding of community development, attitudes to language revitalisation and linguistic prescriptivism. With the participants' permission, a provisional analysis of the transcripts was shared with management and feedback sought, which was then incorporated into the discussion.

2.6.1 Language background and influence of Raidió na Life on Irish

In terms of language background, all of the participants could be described as 'new speakers', as they fitted the profile of Irish speakers who had acquired the language for the most part outside the home. Five out of the eight volunteers had attended gaelscoileanna in Dublin and six out of eight had studied Irish at university, or some aspect of their degree involved Irish. Before joining Raidió na Life, five of the eight reported that they had spoken Irish regularly in their daily lives. For instance, Roibeárd (in his 30s) had always used Irish socially but was not involved in any formal Irish language organisation:

> Nuair a thosaigh mé ag obair bhínn de shíor ag lorg deiseanna chun Gaeilge a úsáid agus bhí úsáid shóisialta á bhaint agam aisti ar feadh blianta sular thosaigh mé anseo *so* bhí sí lárnach i gceart cé nach raibh sé mar theanga baile agam. Ní raibh mise bainteach le saol na Gaeilge mar dhea, cé go raibh mé ag úsáid Gaeilge gach lá. Níor bhuail me le haon dream Gaeilge aon áit sular tháinig mé isteach anseo go Raidió na Life.[12]

---

12   When I began working I was always looking for opportunities to use Irish and I was using it socially for years before I came here so it was really central although it wasn't my home language. I wasn't involved in the so-called Irish language world, although I was using Irish every day. I didn't meet any Irish-speaking group anywhere until I came in here to Raidió na Life.

The remainder said that their level of competence was declining over time, a common occurrence in the age cohorts after compulsory education. Áine, in her 30s, had been abroad and lost the habit of speaking Irish, despite gaining fluency when she attended a gaelscoil in her childhood. All said that Raidió na Life had a positive influence on their use of Irish, with every volunteer agreeing that they now spoke the language more regularly in the station itself, with each other and with a broader population of speakers. They felt part of a social network of volunteers associated with the station itself and had deepened their relationships with other Irish speakers through cultural events they had attended in Dublin. This theme was explored by Naoise (in his 20s):

> Bhí mé ag labhairt cuid mhaith Gaeilge sular thosaigh mé ag obair le Raidió na Life ar chor ar bith. Ach *yeah*, d'fhéadfainn a rá go raibh tionchar aige orm. Is dóigh go labhraím b'fhéidir daichead faoin gcéad Gaeilge, seasca faoin gcéad Béarla nó rud eicínt mar sin mar ní bheadh focal Gaeilge ag duine ná deoraí as mo chairde ón mbaile ach tá aithne agam ar i bhfad níos mó daoine a bhfuil an Ghaeilge acu anois *so* is dóigh go mbíonn níos mó seasanna agam an Ghaeilge a úsáid.[13]

Another volunteer, Uinsionn (in his 20s), spoke about how Raidió na Life had helped him meet new friends when he came to Dublin:

> Úsáidim níos mó Gaeilge ó thosaigh mé le Raidió na Life toisc go bhfuil aithne agam ar níos mó daoine le Gaeilge agus má fheicim iad in áit ar bith bím ag labhairt i nGaeilge leo. Mura raibh mé le Raidió na Life b'fhéidir nach mbeadh aithne agam orthu agus dá bharr sin ní bheinn ag labhairt as Gaeilge.[14]

For some participants, presenting on Raidió na Life had given them exposure to new registers of Irish, thereby boosting their confidence and competence in the language. For those whose experience of Irish was more

---

13   I was speaking a good deal of Irish before I started working with Raidió na Life at all. But yeah, I could say it influenced me, I suppose I now speak maybe 40 per cent Irish, 60 per cent English or something like that because my friends from home wouldn't have a word of Irish. So I suppose I have more opportunities to use Irish.

14   I use more Irish since I started with Raidió na Life because I know more Irish-speaking people and if I see them anywhere I speak Irish to them. If I wasn't with Raidió na Life I might not know them and then I wouldn't be speaking in Irish.

limited to an educational setting, socialising in Irish at the radio station was a new linguistic experience in contrast with the more rigid language of the classroom. This also worked in the other direction as illustrated by this exchange between two volunteers, both in their 20s, who worked on news programmes. They described how they had become more familiar with formal terminology since taking up that duty:

> DOIREANN: Bhí mé díreach ag iarraidh a rá, is dóigh liom go gcabhraíonn sé leat do chuid Gaeilge a fhorbairt chomh maith, *like* nuair atá tú ag déanamh scéalta éagsúla a scríobh agus mar sin de caithfidh tú foclóir eagsúil a úsáid *like*-
>
> NAOISE: -teanga teicniúil agus mar sin de-
>
> DOIREANN: -mar bíonn an nuacht ag athrú i gcónaí *so* bíonn do chuid foclóir ag athrú i gcónaí.[15]

Áine was one of the two participants whose Irish was less fluent, in her case due to a long period abroad. Now working as a teacher in a mainstream English-medium school, she had few opportunities to use Irish at work, but joining the radio both improved her Irish and gave her a new social circle of Irish speakers:

> Bhí sé go hiontach, *just* an deis é a labhairt agus an taighde a rinne mé don chlár agus ag teacht isteach ansin agus ag caint le daoine agus ag cur agallaimh ar bannaí nó ceoltóirí, *yeah* bhí se iontach an deis *just* í a labhairt. Ach anois tá mé ag múineadh i scoil Béarla faoi láthair agus níl mórán deis agam an Ghaeilge a labhairt seachas nuair a thagaim isteach chuile Aoine *so* tá sé brónach.[16]

---

15   DOIREANN: I just wanted to say, I think that it helps you develop your Irish as well, like when you are writing different stories and so on you have to use different vocabulary, like-
     NAOISE: -technical language and so on-
     DOIREANN: -because the news is always changing so your vocabulary is always changing.
16   It was great, just the opportunity and the research, the chance to speak it and the research I did for the show and coming in then and speaking to people and interviewing bands or musicians and it was great [to get] the opportunity just to speak it. But now I am teaching in an English-language school at the moment and I don't have much chance to speak Irish other than coming in here every Friday so it's sad.

Áine's reference to the absence of Irish in her normal working week reflects the language's marginal position in the sociolinguistic context of Dublin and in her case, the station played an important role in maintaining contact with Irish. For those with higher levels of competence, it was clear that becoming a volunteer had at least increased their opportunities to speak Irish but for others, it allowed them valuable exposure to the language and a pathway to building confidence.

2.6.2 Community building

Volunteers' motivations for becoming involved in the work of Raidió na Life were also examined, in order to probe the extent to which the station's aims of building an Irish language community had influenced them. No-one mentioned this aim directly and instead volunteers identified love of radio, love of the Irish language, the ability to practice and socialise in Irish and the possibility of gaining paid media work as motivations. The social aspect was particularly salient and it was clear that volunteers looked forward to the opportunities to meet each other in the station and enjoyed participating in the broader social networks that they had created. This comment from Áine was typical:

> Rinne mé ceann des na cairde is fearr liom, bhí sí mar chomhláithreoir ar mo chlár ceoil. *Just* is breá liom teacht isteach, is féidir leat Gaeilge a labhairt agus tá craic iontach againn agus faighim preas pasanna isteach ag *gigs* [gáire] agus rudaí simplí beaga agus táim cairdiúil le go leor bannaí agus ceoltóirí atá an-mheas agam orthu. Anois tá aithne agam orthu, deir siad 'Dia dhuit Áine', *you know*? Agus is breá liom sin agus tá se iontach nuair a thagann bannaí isteach chun seinnt beo ar mo chlársa, tá siad os mo chomhair ag canadh *just* dom féin [grúpa ag gáire]![17]

17   I made one of my best friends, she was a co-presenter on my music show. I just love coming in, you can speak Irish and we have great craic [fun] and I get press passes to gigs [laughter] and simple little things and I'm friendly with lots of bands and musicians who I respect. Now I know them, they say "Hello Áine", you know? And I love that and it's great when bands come in to play on my programme, they're in front of me singing just for me [group laughter].

The enthusiastic endorsement of this comment by the group suggests that the ability to enjoy themselves through Irish is a major motivation factor for these community radio volunteers. Much language policy focuses on the 'harder' aspects such as government strategies, legislation and education but the importance of the informal social realm in language revitalisation tends to be overlooked. Some recent exceptions in the case of Irish include Moriarty (2015) and Kelly-Holmes (2011) who have studied the use of comedy and hip-hop to promote Irish and Seoighe (2018) who has investigated the informal social gatherings of the 'Pop-Up Gaeltacht', an impromptu meeting of Irish speakers held in various pubs. MLM is potentially a fruitful field for further work in this area.

Volunteers were asked about their understandings of the aims of the Raidió na Life: why it was established and what was it trying to achieve? The original aim of building a community of Irish speakers in Dublin did not feature in the responses of the majority of participants. Most identified providing opportunities for young people to broadcast or to broadcast through Irish and other languages as the primary aims (a small percentage of programmes are in immigrant languages; see below). Another saw the main aim as building an Irish language *radio* community as opposed to an Irish language community, perhaps based on her experience of expanding her own social network within the station. Only one identified explicitly the aim of building the Irish-speaking community although another seemed to endorse this indirectly by saying that she believed Raidió na Life was set up to make the language more 'sociable'. The group agreed with this stance and it prompted the following comment:

> Tá sé tábhachtach le taispeáint go bhfuil an teanga beo agus le clos agus in úsáid taobh amuigh den Ghaeltacht. Tá a fhios agam go ndéanann Raidió na Gaeltachta é sin ar bhealach ach is féidir le duine ar bith siúl isteach i Raidió na Life agus ceapaim go dtugann an mothúchán sin an chaoi go nglacann siad le gach éinne le fios, *you know*, ní linne amháin an teanga, is linn uilig í ar bhealach (Uinsionn).[18]

---

18   It is important to show that the language is alive and is to be heard and is in use outside of the Gaeltacht. I know that Raidió na Gaeltachta does that in a way but anyone can walk into Raidió na Life and I think the way that they accept anyone lets people know that the language isn't just ours, it belongs to everyone in a way.

After some prompting, the group endorsed the founding aim and agreed that Raidió na Life would not exist without the Irish language, but they did not seem to accept personal responsibility for implementing that goal. While Irish was agreed to be important, volunteers were unanimous that content was king, especially the alternative music offered by the station in contrast to the non-stop pop diet of commercial radio. They identified this alternative offering as the primary reason for the station's success, not the fact that it was in Irish, and they were very proud of its distinctiveness in the mediascape and its ability to attract listeners with little or no Irish:

> Tá ardéisteacht ar na cláracha ceoil, toisc an caighdeán. Ó thaobh na cláracha ceoil tá a fhios againn níos mó ná aon rud eile mar tá aithne pearsanta agam ar dhaoine a éisteann le Áine, le Billy Ó hAnluain ar an Satharn, le Jama, le cláracha eile. Tá cáil éigin i mBaile Átha Cliath bainte amach ag na cláracha sin. (Roibeárd)[19]

In fact, the volunteers rejected the idea that Raidió na Life was a station for Irish speakers only and it was clear that they did not position themselves as language activists with an explicit responsibility to build the community of Irish speakers, in line with the station's founding aims. One participant saw the station as serving a broader audience than fluent Irish speakers alone, by acting as a space for those with more limited Irish and even those speaking other languages:

> Stáisiún pobail a dhéanann iarracht freastal ar ghrúpaí nach bhfuil freastal á dhéanamh orthu ag na stáisiúin eile – sin é an bealach a smaoiním air agus ní chuirim an Ghaeilge san áireamh ann *really*. Deirimse go n-úsáidtear go leor Gaeilge ar an stáisiún ach ceapaim go bhfuil sé an-tábhachtach go bhfuil daoine nach labhrann mórán agus ansin daoine a labhrann trí theangacha éagsúla [seans]. (Alison)[20]

19   There's a really high listenership for the music programmes, because of the standard. With regards to the music programmes, we know, more than anything else, because I personally know people who listen to Áine, to Billy Ó hAnluain on Saturday, to Jama, to the other programmes. Those programmes have earned a certain fame in Dublin.

20   A community radio station that makes an effort to serve groups that no one else is serving – that's how I think of it [Raidió na Life] and I don't really count the Irish language as part of that really. I say that we use a lot of Irish on the station but I think it's very important that people who don't speak much Irish, and then people who speak different languages get a chance.

The station manager expressed surprise initially at this finding but on reflection remembered that his own initial motivation as a volunteer was based more heavily on love of music rather than simply a desire to promote Irish. He thought that the greatly enhanced media landscape for Irish in the past thirty years was also a factor in the apparent lack of overt concern about the language:

> B'fhéidir go bhfuil an drochriocht a bhí ar chúrsaí sna 1980í agus sna 1990í nuair a bunaíodh an stáisiún, go bhfuil sé sin athraithe agus go díreach don dream atá ag fás aníos le fiche bliain anuas nach cuimhin leo gur mar sin a bhí agus nach bhfeiceann siad go bhfuil aon fhadhb. (Ó Fiannachta, 2017)[21]

Seen through the prism of the 'discourse of endangerment' (Duchêne & Heller, 2007), this approach could be interpreted as denying or downplaying the severity of the challenges facing Irish as a community language in the Gaeltacht and elsewhere, as has been highlighted extensively over the past two decades in particular (e.g. Ó Giollagáin et al., 2007a). However, despite the desires of the station's founders, it is not realistic to expect that everyone involved in cultural production through a minority language will see themselves as activists. Raidió na Life has undeniably created a permanent public social space for Irish in the crowded mediascape in Dublin and continues to contribute positively to building the community by drawing together disparate Irish speakers from across the city. The socialisation and engagement of volunteers in this space have resulted in stronger binds within that network and beyond to other Irish speakers of variable levels of competence. The net result is arguably the attainment of the original aims, although this appears to have happened in a spontaneous rather than a planned fashion on the part of the volunteers.

The extract from Alison above introduced linguistic prescriptivism to the analysis, an issue that emerged as one of the most salient themes in the data.

---

21 Perhaps the bad state of affairs in the 1980s and 1990s when the station was founded has changed and that simply for those who grew up in the last twenty years, they don't remember that that was how it was and they don't see that there's a problem.

2.6.3 Linguistic prescriptivism

Since its inception, Raidió na Life has been the target of criticism in other
media and in popular discourse for its alleged failure to ensure that 'correct' Irish is used on air. This is not a surprise, for as long as mass media has
existed, it has been accused of promoting sloppy use of language (Cotter,
1999). The situation is arguably more marked in the case of MLM because
of the weak status of the languages in question and the prevalence of
translanguaging practices in the community. It is a well-attested fact that
informal registers of speech in the Gaeltacht and among Irish speakers
generally are marked by the influence of English, as is to be expected give
the sociolinguistic context and the uneven balance of power at play. This
is not a new phenomenon (Mac Mathúna, 2007), although it has gained
pace given the increased pace of language shift over the past sixty years.
Therefore, to expect Raidió na Life (or even RTÉ Raidió na Gaeltachta)
to be immune from such processes is unrealistic, regardless of the efforts
of management to curtail it. The situation is complicated further by the
fact that as a community station, Raidió na Life relies entirely on volunteers to provide a schedule, most of whom are 'new speakers' with varying
degrees of competence in Irish, and its listeners can be said to fit a similar
profile. In 1996, one of the station's founders Máirín Nic Eoin wrote an
article for the Irish language press defending the station's linguistic standards against the allegation that it was promoting a 'pidgin' type of Irish.
She said that this was an attack on the varieties of Irish spoken by the
young people to be heard on Raidió na Life who came from different linguistic backgrounds including the Gaeltacht itself, Irish-speaking families
in Dublin and English-speaking backgrounds (Nic Eoin, 1996). Looking
back from the perspective of today to the early days after the foundation
of the station, Nic Eoin recalls how the committee was cognisant of the
linguistic question from the outset and took a pro-active approach by
providing Irish language workshops and cassettes to support the young
volunteers (Nic Eoin, 2021).

Prescriptivism reared its head regularly in the research, and many
volunteers felt the need to be defensive about the standard of Irish to be

heard on Raidió na Life. For instance, Alison referred to her memories of studying Irish at university where criticism of the station was commonplace:

> Bíonn drochmheas ar Raidió na Life ag grúpaí áirithe, daoine áirithe agus cloisim sin, cloisim gearáin agus fiú nuair a bhí mé san ollscoil is cuimhin liom a bheith le mic léinn agus déarfadh siad 'ó ní éistfinn leis sin, *like* tá an Ghaeilge go hainnis', daoine a bhí líofa nó líofa go leor iad féin. *So* bíonn drochmheas acu ar an stáisiún agus mar sin déanann siad cinneadh gan éisteacht leis mar gheall air sin agus breathnaíonn siad air ar bhealach eile.[22]

However, the imperfect linguistic standards of Raidió na Life were worn as a badge of honour by the volunteers. Everyone in the group accepted that a range of ability could be heard on air but this was seen as a positive and welcoming policy to allow everyone to participate. A regular contrast was drawn between RTÉ Raidió na Gaeltachta, which was seen as prescriptive in showcasing native Gaeltacht speech and demanding a high standard, and the more liberal and flexible approach of Raidió na Life. Alison claimed that contributors to Raidió na Gaeltachta would be nervous in case they made a mistake, whereas the opposite would be the case in Raidió na Life. Similarly, Roibeárd praised the presenters of specialist music programmes – seen as having the weakest ability in Irish, limited to short links between tracks – for their efforts. Any linguistic deficiency was more than compensated for by the innovation and originality of the content:

> Tá idir lag, an-lag agus níos laige ach ó shin ar aghaidh go dtí líofacht. Tóg mar shampla anocht, tá Executive Steve ag dul a bheith ar an raidió agus níl Gaeilge ag Executive Steve, foghlaimíonn sé cúpla nath cainte ach tá clár den scoth aige. Foghlaimíonn sé cúpla nath ach seachtain agus ní labhrann sé Béarla ar bith ar an gclár ... Bíonn idir ard agus íseal ó thaobh caighdeán na Gaeilge de. Tá ardchaighdeán ag roinnt mhaith, formhór de na cláracha cainte, bíonn siad go maith ó thaobh caighdeáin de

---

22   There is disrespect for Raidió na Life among certain groups, among certain people and I hear that, I hear complaints and even when I was at university I remember being with students and they'd say 'oh I wouldn't listen to that, like the Irish is awful', people who were fluent or fairly fluent themselves. So they disrespect the station and therefore decide not to listen to it because of that and they look at it in a different way.

agus bíonn tacaíocht ann i gcónaí ón meitheal lánaimseartha chun feabhas a chur ar an nGaeilge.[23]

In what may be a reflection of 'the *cúpla focal* ideology' – the idea that a limited amount or few words (*cúpla focal*) of Irish will suffice as a marker of support for the Revival policy (O'Rourke & Walsh, 2020) – what matters here is that an English speaker makes an effort to learn and use incidental Irish in order to satisfy the requirements of an Irish-language radio station but concentrates on playing the best music possible in order to please his audience. Executive Steve may be a rare example of a presenter whose Irish is at the rudimentary extreme of the station's spectrum, but the argument points to a broader belief that prescriptivism is not the most important issue for Raidió na Life volunteers.

A similar observation can be made about the overwhelmingly positive attitude of the group to the tiny minority of Raidió na Life programmes broadcast in languages of other minority groups in Dublin such as Portuguese, Catalan, Spanish and Polish at various times over the years. There was unanimity that this was an important aspect of the station's work and a worthwhile aim, although it amounts to only about 2 per cent of output. Such programmes are presented in the original language, but presenters use a few phrases of Irish at the beginning and end, a practice praised highly by the volunteers as an acceptance of the station's language policy. Therefore, any effort to use Irish, no matter how imperfect or limited, either by Executive Steve or the Catalan show *Electricitat*, was valorised by volunteers as a key part of the station's open linguistic policy. There were limits to this openness, however, as use of English was not accepted as a valid part of Raidió na Life's linguistic repertoire, an aspect of the policy that had clearly been internalised by volunteers. It may also reflect their experience of Irish-only policies in certain domains such as immersion education and

---

23 There's weak, very weak and weaker again but from that up to fluency. Take, for example, tonight, Executive Steve is going to be on the radio and Executive Steve doesn't speak Irish, he learns a few phrases but he has a great programme. He learns a few phrases every week and he doesn't speak any English on the show ... There is both a high and low standard of Irish. Some, most of the talk shows, have a good standard and there is always support from the permanent staff to improve Irish.

Gaeltacht summer colleges, where use of English is prohibited so that the minority language can develop. In sum, the attitudes position volunteers in favour of linguistic diversity, both within Irish itself and including other minoritised languages in the overwhelmingly English-speaking context of Dublin, but excluding English.

The station manager was surprised at the salience of programmes in other languages as they were not part of the original plans for Raidió na Life but developed organically over the years. He referred to station manuals emphasising linguistic correctness and said that he had always tried to discourage presenters who spoke no Irish at all but were of the view that they could simply learn a few phrases to get on air. He was uncomfortable with this aspect of the station and would prefer if presenters had a higher standard of Irish, but had gradually made peace with the fact that Raidió na Life was a reflection of the messy reality of Irish as it is spoken in Dublin:

> Is dócha go hidéalach go mbeadh Raidió na Life b'fhéidir áit éigin idir an cruth reatha atá ar Raidió na Gaeltachta agus an cruth atá orainn féin. Go hidéalach b'fhearr liom go mbeadh seirbhís teangan níos fearr le cloisteáil ar Raidió na Life ach táimid inár scáthán ar phobal na Gaeilge i mBaile Átha Cliath agus is dócha go bhfuilimid mar scáthán freisin ar an speictream den nGaeilge atá le cloisteáil i mBaile Átha Cliath. B'fhéidir gur mar sin atá. Arís, b'fhearr liom dá mbeadh an caighdeán níos saibhre agus sílim gur ceist thábhachtach í go dtugtar cineál dlisteanacht teangeolaíoch go huathoibríoch don mhéid a chloistear ar stáisiún raidió. Glacfaidh níos mó agus níos mó daoine leis go bhfuil rud inghlactha má chloistear minic go leor é agus is dócha, is gá cothromaíocht éigin a aimsiú ansin ionas gan dlisteanacht fhoirmeálta nó leathfhoirmeálta a bhronnadh ar dhroch-Ghaeilge nó fíor-dhroch-Ghaeilge agus ag an am céanna gan cosc a chur ar dhaoine dul ar an aer toisc nach bhfuil a gcuid Gaeilge thar mholadh beirte. (Ó Fiannachta, 2017)[24]

24   I suppose ideally Raidió na Life would be somewhere between the current state of Raidió na Gaeltachta and our own state. Ideally a better linguistic service would be heard on Raidió na Life but we are a mirror of the Irish language community in Dublin and I suppose we are a mirror also of the spectrum of the Irish that is heard in Dublin. Maybe that's the way it is. Again, I would prefer if the standard was richer and I think that an important issue in this regard is that that which is heard on a radio station is automatically lended a certain degree of linguistic legitimacy. More and more people will accept that something is acceptable if it is heard often enough and I suppose, some sort of balance has to be struck there, in order to avoid inadvertently lending formal or semi-formal linguistic legitimacy to poor or

The fact that Ó Fiannachta albeit reluctantly accepts the sociolinguistic reality of speaking a minority language in Dublin points to more fluid attitudes to prescriptivism generally and aligns with the convergence of media into formats that bypass rules and regulations entirely and allow people to create their own media content unimpeded (for a discussion of youth media identities in Basque, see Elordui, 2018).

Translanguaging is a sensitive topic when applied to minority languages, as it can be interpreted as disregarding legitimate concerns about the future social sustainability of languages with weak social status, caught in the unbalanced power dynamic of language shift (Singleton & Flynn, 2021). However, by downplaying the preservation of individual lexical or grammatical features in favour of 'translanguaging practices that the community finds valuable' (Otheguy et al., 2015: 299), it points to new possibilities for MLM serving post-traditional communities such as Raidió na Life. Having robustly defended the mixed and imperfect linguistic practices of the station, volunteers did not report any dissatisfaction on the part of their loyal listeners and this draws attention to the adjective 'valuable' in the above extract. Although further research among volunteers and audience is needed, based on our sample it appears that both presenters and listeners are satisfied with the linguistic output and therefore we can conclude tentatively that the station's translanguaging practices are 'valuable' for those most closely involved.[25]

2.6.4 Discussion

In conclusion, Raidió na Life provides a broad alternative public space for Irish in Dublin, by providing a platform for people of varying linguistic ability to improve their Irish, to join a social network based around the station and to deepen relationships with broader networks within the city. Although volunteers do not spontaneously identify with the station's

---

severely incorrect Irish, while at the same time not preventing people from having a voice on air just because their level of Irish isn't the best.

25   By explicitly excluding the use of English, however, volunteers are in fact restricting translanguaging practices as presenters are unable to draw upon their full linguistic repertoires.

founding aim, they contribute to it indirectly through socialisation in and engagement with the space provided. They are less concerned with linguistic correctness than with the communicative function of Irish and the innovative content of Raidió na Life trumps any concerns about pre-scriptivism. Their belief that the language policy is open and fluid aligns with the community radio philosophy of encouraging all members of the community to become involved, despite reservations of the management over language standards. Such tensions will always exist in MLM but en-suring ongoing engagement with such media outlets into the crowded future of media convergence will remain as key a challenge in the future as building the language community itself.

2.7 Raidió Fáilte

Raidió Fáilte was founded as a pirate station in west Belfast in 1985 and was part of a local media infrastructure that included the Irish language newspaper *Lá* ('day'). It broadcast sporadically without a licence for the best part of twenty years, aimed at the west of the city where most Irish speakers are located. Licensed by the UK communications body OFCOM in 2006, Raidió Fáilte now broadcasts on a community radio licence over a ten-mile radius of the centre and west of the city and hopes to expand its coverage area on FM. It also plans to participate in small-scale DAB (digital audio broadcasting) multiplexes that would give it coverage in other areas. From humble origins on the Falls Road, its impressive stu-dios are now located close to the city centre and are arguably the best community radio facility in all of Ireland, having received £1.5 million in funding from Belfast City Council, the Department of Communities, an Irish language investment fund for capital projects and Foras na Gaeilge. Raidió Fáilte employs ten staff members and about eighty volunteers pre-sent programmes, ranging in age from the teens to the 80s. It has four broadcast studios, a production studio, a recording studio and meeting rooms. The building also houses an Irish language café and an event space where music, book launches and exhibitions are held or where panel dis-cussions can be arranged.

2.7.1 History

Belfast's Irish language community station Raidió Fáilte emerged from
language activism in the nationalist west of the city in the 1980s. A group
of people led by Gearóid Ó Cairealláin wanted to develop Irish language
cultural activities and media based on a strong community development
ethos. Another leading member of the group Eoghan Ó Néill, now a
well-known journalist with the station, said that they all shared that philosophy, sometimes unconsciously. Ó Cairealláin had been influenced by
earlier Irish language initiatives such as the social club in Cluain Ard and
the micro-Gaeltacht on the Shaw's Road (Gaeltacht Bhóthar Seoighe; see
Chapter 1). They were cognisant of how these campaigns had strengthened the Irish-speaking community and served some of their needs and
saw the establishment of local media as part of the Revival (Ó Néill,
2021). Members of the group had in 1984 moved into the old Ardscoil
(high school) building on the Falls Road and established the daily newspaper *Lá* and an Irish language bookshop. Both initiatives operated on an
entirely voluntary basis and with no state support, unsurprising given the
repression of Irish in the North at the time, and were infused with a spirit
of youthful idealism:

> Go leor againn tharla muid ag obair leis na fiontair seo cionn is gur daoine óga muid a
> bhí gan obair bhuan agus thaitin sé linn, mar is nós le daoine óga, tabhairt faoi rudaí
> nua, rudaí dodhéanta, rudaí a bhí beagánín ar an imeall. Cúiseanna teibí is dócha.
> Cén dochar do lá a chaitheamh ag cur aithne ar dhaoine óga eile, ag cleachtadh/
> foghlaim na Gaeilge agus ag déanamh rud fiúntach don teanga agus lucht a labhartha?
> (Ó Néill, 2021)[26]

Ó Néill and Ó Cairealláin were aware of previous pirate stations in Belfast,
particularly Radio Free Belfast that was established by Republicans in the

---

26   Many of us happened to be working with these projects because we were young
     people without permanent work and as happens with young people, we enjoyed
     taking up new things, impossible things, things that were a bit edgy. Abstract causes
     I support. What harm was there spending your day getting to know other young
     people, practising/learning Irish and doing something useful for the language and
     its speakers?

Falls area at the start of the Troubles (Bohan, 2021). They also had information about Saor-Raidió Chonamara from 1970, but the main reason for Raidió Fáilte was to build the community projects already in existence, particularly *Lá* and the bookshop. Ó Néill explained that there were a number of factors in their favour already: community support for Irish language initiatives, an Irish-speaking contact who could build a transmitter but most importantly, an ethos to get things done without waiting for grants or government approval (ibid., 2021). Once *Lá* was on a more stable footing, in 1985 Ó Cairealláin began pushing the idea of a pirate radio station. Their contact built an AM transmitter and a simple audio mixer was constructed with the aim to begin broadcasting either on St. Patrick's Day or Easter 1985. The date was advertised in local press but on the appointed day, the transmitter malfunctioned. Once it was repaired, they resumed broadcasting on a trial basis without any publicity and Ó Cairealláin and Ó Néill drove around the Falls area to gauge reception. A fire in the high school in April 1985 destroyed the radio equipment and forced the other projects into various temporary locations. After an all-Ireland cycle trip to raise money, the group moved into new accommodation in the Conway Mill building on the Falls Road in 1986 or 1987. They immediately began re-establishing Raidió Fáilte and acquired an AM transmitter from one of the many pirate radio stations in Dublin. Bringing broadcasting equipment across the border was challenging given the legal and political context but the transmitter eventually arrived in West Belfast. Another complicating factor was the location of Conway Mill opposite another converted mill building on North Howard Street where British Army soldiers were based. Ó Néill recalls the risk that they took to erect the aerial on the roof:

Bhí radharc ag na saighdhiúirí ar gach a bhí ar bun againn nach mór. Bhí muid ag cur an aeróg ar an díon nuair a nocht péas agus ochtar saighdiúir ar an díon in aice linn. Cheistigh siad muid agus dúirt go raibh an t-ádh orainn nár scaoil an *sentry* in North Howard Street muid cionn is go bhfaca sé beirt fhear ar an díon agus rud ar nós raidhfil acu. D'amharc duine de na saighdiúirí ar an tarchuradóir agus ar seisean: 'cad é sin, sibh ag cur sin in airde do chomhlacht tacsaí an ea?' 'Díreach é', arsa Barry, 'don *depot* suas Bóthar na bhFál ansin!'. (Ibid., 2021)[27]

Ó Néill recalls the symbiosis between the various community projects and how a pool of people could contribute to one initiative or another, depending on their skills or the requirement. Often, people from the newspaper would be asked to present a radio programme or act in a play, while actors would contribute articles or assist with Raidió Fáilte also. The station broadcast on a regular basis at this time and forged its own musical style that emphasised links with the Gaeltacht and other minority languages. Ó Néill recalls buying cassettes of the Scottish Gaelic band Runrig on a trip to the Isle of Skye and playing them on the station. Raidió Fáilte also regularly played music by Na hAncairí, a country music band from Connemara, emphasising links with the Gaeltacht. Ó Néill said that they were unconcerned about the station's illegality from the outset:

> Bhí muid maíte ar na rudaí seo a chur ar fáil do phobal na Gaeilge agus go pointe glacadh lenár eascair as sin. Ina dhiaidh sin bhí muid buartha go ndéanfadh na péas nó saighdiúirí ruathar ar an fhoirgneamh agus muid sa Mhuileann. Chuige sin dhruid muid geataí agus dorais an chuid sin den mhuileann a raibh muid lonnaithe ann fad is go mbíodh muid ag craoladh. Bhí muid ar an tríú urlár agus thógfadh sé cúpla uair a chloig go fiú ag saighdiúirí gearradh tríd na geataí agus teacht a fhad linn. (Ibid., 2021)[28]

27   The soldiers had a view of nearly everything we were doing. We were putting the aerial on the roof when a policeman and eight soldiers turned up on the roof beside us. They questioned us and told us we were lucky that the sentry in North Howard Street didn't shoot us because he saw two men on the roof with something that looked like a rifle. One of the soldiers looked at the transmitter [mast] and said: 'What's that, are you putting that up for a taxi company?' 'Exactly', said Barry, 'for the depot up there on the Falls Road!'

28   We were determined to provide these things for the Irish language community and to a point what emerged from that was accepted. However, we would worry that the police or soldiers would raid the building when we were in the Mill. Therefore, we closed the gates and doors of the part of the mill where we were based when we were broadcasting. We were on the third floor and it would take a few hours even for soldiers to cut through the gates and reach us.

Raidió Fáilte moved into the new Irish language cultural centre, the Cultúrlann, on the Falls Road in 1991. A milestone in Irish language development in the North, the centre housed a number of important initiatives including Raidió Fáilte, *Lá*, an Irish-medium secondary school and other drama and cultural groups. The broadcasts were sporadic at this stage but Raidió Fáilte returned on a more regular basis in the mid-1990s and benefited from a larger group of volunteers and a new FM transmitter. By this time, the UK communications regulator OFCOM had introduced temporary community radio licences but these were not of interest because they were limited to one month only and not open to the pirates. Recordings from the early 2000s show that Raidió Fáilte was broadcasting for several hours a day from the Cultúrlann during that period. Ó Néill recalls that there was considerable interest in Irish language media around the new millennium: the Good Friday Agreement had gone some way towards supporting Irish, more Irish than before was being broadcast on BBC Radio Ulster and the 2001 census showed an increase in the number of Irish speakers (see Chapter 1). This strengthened the case for services for Irish speakers and there was an opportunity to develop the media. Ó Néill recalls rumours that the Stormont authorities were trying to find a way of bringing Irish language media into the system. He also believes that the Irish government played a role, as there were regular visits by officials from Dublin to the Cultúrlann to investigate what was happening on the ground and see how Irish, including media, could be promoted. Ó Cairealláin was also aware of developments in Britain with the introduction of full-time community radio licences from OFCOM (ibid., 2021).

2.7.2 Analysis of Raidió Fáilte

Published research on Raidió Fáilte is limited and the following section is based on observation of programming, analysis of strategic documents and interviews with station staff. I visited the station's impressive new headquarters in west Belfast on a number of occasions in 2019 and 2020 and observed a full day's programming, which revealed a wide variety of topics and programme genres. As well as an hourly news bulletin, these included hate speech on social media, the UK election in Belfast, a local youth history project, a new programme by the Cultúrlann, a review of local GAA fixtures and interview with a camogie player, the fiftieth anniversary of the west Belfast 'Gaeltacht' and a local cultural festival. There were also features about teaching Irish to Unionists and the Orange musical tradition was showcased in a programme presented by an Irish speaker from a Unionist background (field notes, visit to Raidió Fáilte, 2 December 2019). Journalist Eoghan Ó Néill emphasised the importance of the station's new building, saying that the massive investment was a sign of the changing fortunes of the Irish language in Northern Ireland. Irish was moving more towards the centre and while opposition and hostility still existed, more people were becoming more open to the language. The investment signalled acceptance by the authorities that Raidió Fáilte was of benefit to the entire population of the city, whether or not they wanted to speak Irish (Ó Néill, 2019).

In 2022, the station published a new strategic plan, declaring that its mission is 'to promote the Irish Language by providing comprehensive, inclusive community radio and media services through Irish'. Its core values reflect a mixture of language promotion, equality and community development perspectives in the context of Northern Ireland. Raidió Fáilte has also committed to promote Irish and give access to high-quality radio services through Irish, to act as ambassadors and advocates for the language and to be non-discriminatory and inclusive in its approach. It will also contribute to quality of life in areas of socioeconomic deprivation and engage with stakeholders on a cross-community basis (Raidió Fáilte, 2022).

2.7.3 Listenership of Raidió Fáilte

Asked what community the station felt it served, the station manager said it provided a service to the entire community regardless of background and also welcomed other minority groups to use its space:

> An phríomhsprioc atá againn ná cur chun cinn na Gaeilge agus gach seirbhís atá againn a sholáthar trí mheán na Gaeilge. Anois go bhfuil an foirgneamh seo againn tá muid ag dúil ní amháin go mbeidh muid inár n-áit le haghaidh craoltóireacht raidió ach go mbeidh muid ann mar mhol na meán Gaeilge amach anseo. Is don

phobal ar fad muid, níos mó ná pobal labhartha na Gaeilge. Bhí an t-ádh orainn go raibh cúpla comhtionscadal againn i mbliana le grúpaí ón taobh amuigh. Bhí grúpa amháin ann Belfast Printworks, grúpa ealaíne agus bhí ealaíontóirí ann ó thíortha eile agus bhí muid ag obair le baill ó na grúpaí mionlaithe. Tá daoine a thagann chugainn ní amháin ó thíortha eile ach ó phobal eile ar leith, mar shampla an pobal aerach.[29]

Asked how this aligned with the station's objective to promote Irish, the manager said that they would work with anyone well disposed towards the language to increase the level of competence:

Ní stopfaidh an obair sin, beidh muid ag iarraidh an Ghaeilge a chur chun cinn. Níl muid ag dul duine ar bith a chur ó dhoras, oibreoidh muid leo le cibé leibhéal Gaeilge atá acu a ardú agus achan rud mar sin.[30]

Ó Néill said that the audience was both local but increasingly international due to streaming technology. What linked listeners to the station and to each other were shared values about the Irish language and the station prided itself in providing a Belfast perspective on the world and 'talking in a Belfast accent' both linguistically and culturally. Although linked to the broader Irish-speaking community and sharing a common perspective on the language, the station wanted to be distinct from other media outlets based in Dublin or Galway. He also spoke of the importance of recognising in programming the links between the Irish-speaking community in Belfast and the Gaeltacht in Co. Donegal. Since the late nineteenth century Revival period, there have been strong connections

---

29   Our main aim is to promote Irish and provide all of our services in Irish. Now that we have this building, we hope not only to be a place for radio broadcasting but that we will become an Irish language media hub in the future. We are for all the community, more than Irish speakers. We were lucky to have a few projects this year with groups from outside. There was one group, Belfast Printworks, an arts groups and there were artists from other countries and we were working with members of minoritised groups. There are people who come to us not only from other countries but from specific communities, for instance the gay community.

30   That work will not end, we will be attempting to promote Irish. We are not going to turn anyone away, we will work with them to improve whatever level of Irish they have and everything like that.

between both areas and many Irish speakers in Belfast have a special respect for Donegal's language and culture (Ó Néill, 2019).

Former manager Fergus O'Hare said that the accessibility of the
building was a key factor in connecting with listeners, particularly those
wishing to learn Irish. He stressed the central location and social space
provided and said that it embodied the idea that Irish belongs to everyone
who wants to access it. Asked about the balance of programming for people
with different levels of Irish, O'Hare said that the emphasis was on fluent
speakers but that learners could benefit from the station also:

> So it's for people who are fluent and who are learning and we find that that's our
> major audience. So it works for fluent speakers and for learners. We do some classes
> but we want to be sure that people who are already fluent aren't getting turned off.
> It works very well for those who are fluent and those we are learning and I suppose
> at the end of the day sure we're all learning! (Ibid.)

The emphasis on learning is significant as it reflects the fact that the
Irish language community in the North consists almost entirely of 'new
speakers', people who were not socialised with Irish in early childhood and
learned it in most institutional settings. The former manager sees himself
as much a part of that group as anyone else and most of those involved in
the station are from a similar background. The station's website also contains a section of podcasts aimed specifically at learners, distinguishing it
from Raidió na Life which does not target such a group directly. There are
also plans to develop high-quality audio material for learners (Breatnach,
2021). This is also a reflection of the distinctive socio-political and sociolinguistic context, where Irish is associated almost exclusively with one
part of the community and more marginalised in state policy.

2.7.4 Community development and Raidió Fáilte

The station's co-ordinator Máire Nic Fhionnachtaigh also emphasised
the community development aspects of the project, referring to the deprived area in which the station is now located. The following exchange
illustrates the salience of this question in the station's existence:

MÁIRE: There certainly is a large aspect of community development in what we do and I guess we're funded to do a lot of that work and the basis on which we were able to secure the funds to construct this building was around the regeneration of the local area. The building is built on a site that was previously problematic in terms of anti-social behaviour and all of those things so we're in an area of high levels of deprivation and we see ourselves as contributing a lot to the regeneration of our community and that is what really matters. We're an Irish language project but a community development project as well.

JOHN: And a radio station?

MÁIRE: Of course [laughter] (Nic Fhionnachtaigh, 2019).

It is noteworthy that Nic Fhionnachtaigh overlooked the radio aspect in her comments until prompted, underlining the fact that community radio is often more a tool to drive community development than a radio service alone. In this case, the Irish language and the community came first, with radio literally an after-thought. The question of community development raises the issue of unionist involvement with Raidió Fáilte. During one of my visits, a group of Protestant/loyalist learners of Irish from the Turas project in East Belfast was visiting the building (field notes, visit to Raidió Fáilte, 6 July 2019; see also Simpson, 2021a). Some of the volunteers are from a unionist background, including the well-known author and journalist Ian Malcolm. Ó Néill acknowledged that while there was some representation of this community on Raidió Fáilte, it was important not to overstate it as work remained to be done (ibid., 2019).

2.7.5 Motivation of volunteers

One long-time volunteer, referred to here as Jamie, recalled his motivations for becoming involved in Raidió Fáilte and his understanding of its aims. He began while still at school, when the radio operated from the Cultúrlann on the Falls Road and continues to broadcast with the station today. Similar to many volunteers in Raidió na Life, music rather than overt language activism was his initial motivation:

Nuair a bhí an deis ann clár de mo chuid féin a dhéanamh bhí suim agam sa cheol agus ardán [a bheith agam]. Mheall sin go mór mé, is cuimhin liom go maith gur shíl mé gur rud measartha *cool* a bhí ann. Is cuimhin liom go raibh daoine thart fán am sin, daoine atá i ndiaidh méid áirithe a bhaint amach i saol na Gaeilge agus bhí dream ann istigh ansin sa raidió cheana féin agus ba chlár ceart a bhí ann agus is cuimhin liom *just* ag smaointiú, *you know*, go raibh sé go maith. Déarfainn gur ábhar misnigh a bhí ann go dtí pointe a bheith sa chomhluadar sin. (Anonymous, 2020)[31]

This extract displays a sense of youthful admiration of others who had already been successful as Irish speakers, potentially inspiring Jamie to have more confidence in his own identity, but it did not yet amount to overt language activism at that stage in his life. During his early time at Raidió Fáilte, he said that the station helped broaden his horizons beyond the narrow confines of his experience of Irish up to then:

> Ar dtús báire áit raidió a bhí ann ina raibh mé féin ábalta clár ceoil agus clár s'agam féin a chur amach agus ansin anuas air sin go raibh daoine ann a bhí leathanaigeanta ó thaobh domhan beag Gaeilge s'agam féin, ag dhul go rudaí san áit chéanna agus go raibh mise mar chuid de sin. Sílim gur mhothaigh mé b'fhéidir go raibh giota den *milieu* sin ann.[32]

This extract emphasises the importance of such spaces in contexts where the social use of Irish is very limited and how they can support young people in particular in building new senses of identity. Jamie recalled how his relationship to Irish changed over time and he was now far more engaged politically with the language. The conscientisation process was deepened further in 2014 following the emergence of a protest movement for Irish language rights in the North, An Dream Dearg ('the red group', see also Chapter 4), in response to the failure to bring forward an Irish

---

31   When I had a chance to do a programme of my own I was interested in music and [having] a platform. I remember that that really attracted me because I thought, you know, that it was pretty cool. I remember people around that time you know who had achieved a certain amount in the Irish language world and they were in the radio already and they had a proper programme and I remember just remembering, you know, that it was good. I'd say it was a source of confidence for me to be in that company.

32   In the first place it was a radio space where I was able to do my own music programme and also that there were people who were open-minded in terms of my own little Irish language world and they were doing things in the same place and I was part of that. I think I felt that perhaps there was a bit of that *milieu* there.

language act. After attending a protest march, he realised that the radio could be an important tool to bring about social change around the status of Irish:

> Bhí sé go hiontach ar fad agus daoine ag plé gnéithe éagsúla ó thaobh na polaitíochta de agus na Gaeilge de agus cúpla mí ina dhiaidh sin tháinig an deis a bheith ag obair leis an raidió agus bhí mé ag rá liom féin is rud é sin ba chóir domh a dhéanamh, *you know?* Deis a bheith mar chuid den phobal arís agus thiocfadh leat é a dhéanamh go deonach. Dúirt mé 'thig leis an domhan mór fostaíochta fanacht, thig liom cineál mé féin a phréamhú b'fhéidir sa phobal rud beag'. Bheadh deiseanna agallaimh ann, bheadh deiseanna a dhul amach ag imeachtaí, bheadh deiseanna ann ardán a thabhairt do rudaí, rudaí éagsúla *so* an t-am sin bhí sé coinsiasach. (Anonymous, 2020)[33]

Asked about his understanding of the station's aims, Jamie said that it was first and foremost established to serve the Irish language community but that it had to balance the Irish language and community aspects. Raidió Fáilte was similar to a pendulum swinging back and forth and attempting to serve both sides of the equation, but the need to serve the Irish language community was paramount and that meant striking a challenging balance between participation, standards and relevance. Building community confidence and providing a platform or voice for people could only come about after sustained effort. Resources were needed to communicate but frequently these were in the hands of multinational corporations that increasingly control the commercial media. Jamie also spoke about the challenges facing community media to gain control of their own resources in a sector overwhelmingly reliant on state support. Irish language organisations including Raidió Fáilte faced the dilemma of depending on grants from Foras na Gaeilge, which had potential implications for their independence. He was convinced of the role of culture

---

33   It was really fantastic and people were discussing various aspects of politics and the Irish language and so then a few months later a chance came up to work with the radio and I said to myself this is something I should do, you know? A chance to be part of the community again and you could do it in a voluntary way. I said "the big world of employment can wait, I can kind of put down roots in the community". There'd be a chance to do interviews, there'd be opportunities to go out to events, there'd be a chance to give things a platform, various things so that time it was conscious.

in bringing about radical social change and he believed that Raidió Fáilte could be a part of that process.

2.7.6 Discussion

Research on Raidió Fáilte is limited and my plans to spend more time at the station were derailed by Covid-19. The analysis presented here is preliminary and requires further work with volunteers and staff to tease out understandings of Raidió Fáilte's role in relation to Irish and community. Some trends can be detected at this early stage, however, that are distinctive from Raidió na Life in Dublin. Obviously, the political contexts are entirely different, but Raidió Fáilte draws more overtly on its role as a community development project in an area marred by severe socioeconomic disadvantage. Such marginalisation has been intertwined with issues of identity for more than half a century and this has allowed Irish to emerge as an important tool to mark the area's distinctiveness within Belfast. We saw in Chapter 1 that although percentages of speakers are much lower than in the Republic, some of the greatest concentrations are to be found in West Belfast, Raidió Fáilte's franchise area. The station's radical past as a pirate appears to have left a mark also, as there are references to alternative, grassroots-led media in the discourse of some of those involved. The cross-community element, while underdeveloped so far, is another distinguishing dimension as is the overt open-door policy by Raidió Fáilte staff to those with limited or even no Irish.

3. Conclusion

This chapter analysed latter-day media activism that drew heavily on the rights discourse emerging from the mid- to late 1960s, leading to large parts of today's Irish language mediascape. Following a review of the philosophy and methods of engagement within Conradh na Gaeilge from the 1960s, the organisation began to reframe its demands in a rights discourse influenced by minority language movements elsewhere. As part of this process, the organisation's broadcasting sub-committee engaged critically with new theoretical thinking about communication and the mass media as defined by the New International Information Order. This was used to link the ongoing marginalisation of Irish with advancing commercialism in RTÉ and the increasingly neoliberal nature of broadcasting policy.

While mostly avowedly commercial in outlook, pirate radio was a reaction to the state's failure to legalise local radio and Conradh na Gaeilge exploited the legal loophole by setting up its own station for a time. However, its suspicion about the commercial ethos of the pirates impeded engagement with those unlicensed stations that adhered firmly to community radio principles and supported Irish. Meanwhile, in the Gaeltacht, similar arguments about minority rights were mobilised by the Gaeltacht Civil Rights Movements, one of whose key aims was a Gaeltacht radio service. The pirate Saor-Raidió Chonamara also took advantage of the lax broadcasting law and led to the establishment of Raidió na Gaeltachta two years later. This was a difficult compromise for the campaigners as the new station was under the auspices of RTÉ, a governance structure that they had rejected out of hand. While the station went on to serve the Gaeltacht well, its perceived conservatism and localism sparked demands for a separate station catering for Irish speakers in Dublin. Changes in national media policy and the licensing of local radio meant that the pirate route was no longer the only option. However, an analysis of the establishment of Raidió na Life reveals the deeply commercial ethos underpinning the new system for licensing local radio, confirming the fears of Conradh na Gaeilge a decade earlier as the tortuous legislative journey to licensing got underway.

This chapter has also highlighted the contrasts in language and media policy in the Republic and Northern Ireland, and the influence of the distinctive ideological contexts on the campaigns for Irish language community media in Dublin and Belfast. The Northern context was more avowedly activist and radical in the face of the absence of even minimal provision for Irish speakers by the BBC. The freewheeling pirate radio spirit suited the 'just do it' mentality of Irish language activists in West Belfast and the widespread availability of cheap equipment kept the unlicensed Raidió Fáilte on air for many years. Later, the relative normalisation of Irish following the Belfast Agreement led to belated engagement with the authorities and, ironically, one of the best resourced community radio stations in Ireland. In the Republic, the campaign was motivated by resentment at the blatantly obvious 'real' language policy, as the newly licensed independent sector failed to provide anything more than symbolic amounts of Irish.

This analysis of both stations, while not exhaustive, has highlighted similarities and differences, partly reflecting the distinctive political and sociolinguistic contexts. In Raidió na Life, there appears to be a gap between the aims of the station founders – to build the community of Irish speakers in Dublin – and the motivations of volunteers who see the station more as a platform for alternative music that happens to be in Irish. Despite the lack of an overt interest in building community, however, volunteers appear to achieve this indirectly by cementing relationships among themselves and with other Irish speakers in the city through their work and socialisation. Raidió Fáilte is more conscious of its links with an economically deprived community in West Belfast and sees itself as much a community development as an Irish language project. While Raidió na Life management is more prescriptive in its views about standards of Irish, volunteers are more relaxed and see the wide spectrum of Irish used as evidence of the station's inclusivity. In contrast, Raidió Fáilte more overtly welcomes people with limited or even no Irish into the station, once they show a positive attitude towards it.

Both stations are undoubtedly sites of Irish language revitalisation and create important urban spaces, both physical and digital, in which mostly new speaker populations can socialise and create media in Irish. This final thematic chapter, therefore, links us back to Chapter 1 where speakers of Irish were discussed. Informal social outlets such as media platforms may not hold the same status in language policy as higher props such as laws and the education system, but they are essential to link and develop the Irish-speaking communities and networks of the future. Such media are challenged to hold their own in the increasingly fragmented digital media landscape and require both major funding and renewed strategic thinking by civil society and state alike. The final chapter draws together the book's conclusions and identifies patterns that are common to all five thematic analyses. It offers an assessment of the past century of Irish language policy and highlights key issue of concern for the future.

Conclusion

1. Introduction

When the Irish state came into being in December 1922, it faced an unusual sociolinguistic conundrum. As a newly independent state in a western European context, Ireland was exceptional because it had experienced a drastic language shift from Irish to English in the previous two centuries, resulting in almost the loss of Irish. By the time the Free State came into existence, Irish was in a very weak position demographically, limited to impoverished districts mostly along the western seaboard and suffered from a low status among its dwindling native speaking population. Other countries that gained independence around the same time, such as Norway and Finland, faced linguistic challenges of their own, but were starting from a stronger social base. Nationalist movements in sub-state entities such as Wales, Scotland and the Basque Country were decades away from gaining political power and were deeply embedded in centralised, monolingual and majoritarian state systems. Therefore, although 'reversing language shift' in Ireland, to use the Fishmanian term, was a formidable problem, the new Irish state possessed far greater political agency to do something about it than the weaker authorities in other comparable situations. Having analysed a century of language policy covering the themes of speakers, the Gaeltacht, education, legislation and broadcasting, this chapter reviews the findings, identifies patterns and trends that are shared across domains and assesses the achievements and failures of the policy. It also highlights key policy challenges for the future in a vastly changed world from that of 1922.

2. Understanding a century of Irish language policy

The thematic analysis of this book began in Chapter 1 with a discussion of the changing nature of Irish-speaking communities and their relationship to language policy over the historical arc. The rhetoric of the overt or de jure language policy was to maintain Irish as the vernacular of the Gaeltacht and revitalise it elsewhere, with the Irish speaking districts seen as a cultural wellspring from which the Revival would emanate. However, the delineation of the 'Breac-Ghaeltacht' as a hybrid linguistic space was an early acknowledgement that the Gaeltacht was far from uniform linguistically and a study of this area of Co. Waterford in the 1930s served as a microcosm of the ideological contestations between Irish speakers, activists and the state. The folklore collector whose diaries were analysed was a prototypical language manager in his community, making keen observations about language practice and ideology and nudging individuals to share cultural lore under the preservationist shadow of the Irish Folklore Commission.

The analysis of the contemporary language planning process in west Waterford revealed a more explicitly localised form of management attempting to influence language practices and ideologies. Although a strong local cultural identity was seen as a stabilising factor, the work of language planning officers was characterised as underfunded and lacking control over broader societal issues, i.e. housing. This is a common challenge to all aspects of the language planning process and is ultimately a question of governance and political power. Considerable additional resources and strategic thinking are required if the state is to support Irish speakers more actively and robustly in increasingly diversified geographical communities and online spaces.

The nature of Irish 'speakers' has been transformed since the foundation of the state, and while rhetoric about the pre-eminence of the Gaeltacht remains influential, the geography of the Irish language has become much more diffuse. Research on 'new speakers' of Irish has highlighted new spaces of language socialisation outside the Gaeltacht and the language planning process itself recognises this territorial diffusion in the new linguistic categories of Gaeltacht Service Towns and Irish Language Networks. The promotional work is more decentralised and focused geographically as a result of changes in governance, but lacks political power and authority both in the Gaeltacht and elsewhere. The historical grand narrative of ethnolinguistic identity underpinning the early decades of language policy has been eroded but it is not clear what has replaced it. Discourses of political nationalism have retreated in the ideational foundation of language policy but it cannot be stated with certainty that a model of civic nationalism is being actively pursued, as has been identified in language policy in Catalonia (Woolard, 2016).

Having considered Irish speakers from the perspective of the community, Chapter 2 turned to state policy on the Gaeltacht, taking as its case study the seminal work of the Gaeltacht Commission of the 1920s. This initiative, the first large-scale state intervention aimed at the Gaeltacht after independence, adopted a top-down approach and was infused by the dominant ideology of ethnolinguistic nationalism. The analysis highlighted the contested ideological terrain at play with different elements of the elite taking opposing sides in relation to Irish and tensions emerging between various profiles of speakers and learners. Although proponents of Irish within government played key roles in supporting the Commission, they were too few to ensure that more robust policy measures would be adopted in the long term.

Many of the Commission's recommendations were rejected and the highly centralised nature of government militated against the establishment of a more powerful statutory structure that would have ensured greater attention to the governance of Irish. The broader conservative political system and ideology of economic retrenchment within government acted as another restraining factor while recent experience of the Civil War and continued anti-Treaty agitation threatened the stability of the state. The 'real' language policy during these years is apparent in the lukewarm or even hostile responses contained in internal documents from government departments, often standing in stark contrast to the proclaimed revivalist aims as contained in the 1922 constitution and elsewhere.

The Commission was concerned with the economic problem of the Gaeltacht but many of its recommendations to ameliorate this – for instance, large-scale population resettlement – were unrealistic and un-enforceable. The government saw the Gaeltacht as a regional issue and allowed it to languish in the politically weak Department of Fisheries and Lands, but failed to bring forward a broader economic strategy dealing with underdevelopment in the Irish-speaking districts. The Cumann na nGaedheal agricultural development policy of 'comparative advantage' was underpinned by a laissez-faire philosophy and this did not bode well for the Gaeltacht with its distinctive needs. Some changes in Gaeltacht policy came about after 1932 due to the 'developmental nationalism' pursued by Fianna Fáil, but there was no significant shift until the establishment of separate Gaeltacht institutions in the 1950s (Kirby, 2010). The work of the Gaeltacht Commission should also be seen against the backdrop of a lack of scientific knowledge of the complex linguistic issues related to language shift. The development of sociolinguistics and language policy as distinct academic disciplines was still decades away and this lack of expertise would have hampered even a more engaged government. The Commission and its legacy should also be considered in the context of a perceived link between conservative social norms, Catholic ideology and language promotion, a belief that did no favours for the Irish language.

   Chapter 3 examined another central plank of language policy over the past century, the Irish language in the education system. Moving forward in time from the period of the Commission, it considered the decade of key policy shifts from the mid-1960s to the mid-1970s. Significant progress was made with Irish in education during the first three decades after inde-pendence, as evidenced by the high percentage of schools teaching partly or fully through Irish by the middle of the century. As argued by Ó Murchú (2006), however, just as the language-in-education policy was beginning to bear fruit, the state took fright and retreated from the foundational aims. This was partly due to ignorance of the complexity of language policy and to impatience with the slow nature of progress. Salient domestic influences were a questioning of the ideals of the 1916 Rising, including the Revival policy, centred around its fiftieth anniversary in 1966, and the switch from protectionism to free trade. The policy of economic liberalisation was in line with external shifts in models of governance in Western Europe and

North America in particular, and the changed structures influenced language policy also.

During this time, the government showed awareness of emerging scientific developments in applied linguistics and sociolinguistics, revealing the influence of both the professionalisation and internationalisation of language policy on Ireland. However, the calamity surrounding the foundation of the Linguistics Institute of Ireland and criticism by respected academics of the slow pace of change revealed the limits of the government's engagement. The decision to accede to the LFM demands to reverse major policy positions on education and public administration was a major blow to the Irish language movement, even if the Leaving Certificate policy in particular was very unpopular with the public. The period was also characterised by a tendency to establish advisory committees to work on various issues including education, with a result that some of the more difficult questions were kicked to touch. However, one high-level committee, Comhairle na Gaeilge, made sophisticated and far-reaching recommendations that continue to reverberate today in education policy and beyond.

The work of Comhairle na Gaeilge and the milestone survey of CILAR signalled the diffusion of the policymaking process further away from the locus of power, as stakeholders were given greater input into decisions. It represented an advancing horizontal process of governance of language policy – rather than a vertical approach of government but of note also was the central role of the Department of Finance, not the Department of the Gaeltacht. Many recommendations in the realm of education were not accepted but another salient restraining factor was the change of government in 1973 when parties less traditionally supportive of Irish came to power and weakened existing policy measures. However, evidence of the calibre of the Comhairle na Gaeilge proposals is provided by the fact that many of them were accepted in subsequent years and decades. Education remains a key language policy plank because of the status of Irish as a core school subject. This is of crucial importance to the language policy as a whole, as it ensures that almost the entire population is exposed to Irish for several years, notwithstanding concerns about standards of teaching and a discredited system of exemptions. Maintaining and developing this status into the future is among the greatest challenges for the Irish language movement.

The final two chapters turned to the role of activism in shaping language policy in two realms, legislation and broadcast media. In both cases, Irish language civil society exploited gaps in current policy provision, often from a radical perspective, and made significant gains by achieving new institutional structures to promote Irish. In Chapter 4, the long war waged by Conradh na Gaeilge and others in favour of an Irish language act was studied in depth. The context for the campaign was the policy retreat of the early 1970s, when the Irish language requirement to work in the civil service was removed, thereby undermining further the already weak provision of services. In its campaign, Conradh na Gaeilge showed perseverance and doggedness in the face of official responses that ranged from apathy to hostility. Further professionalisation of activism was evidenced by the involvement of an anonymous parliamentary drafter who secretly drew up a model bill of rights in order to aid the campaign. Meanwhile, Conradh na Gaeilge established a Rights Bureau to advocate for those who had experienced difficulties receiving Irish language services. This was a precursor to the statutory mechanism of the language Commissioner that would eventually be established in 2004. There were also contacts with campaigners in other jurisdictions such as Wales, Belgium and Scotland about language laws in place there.

The changing shape of governance in the 1990s helped push the issue further, particularly with the creation of a cross-border body for Irish, Foras na Gaeilge, under the Belfast Agreement. An increased awareness of minority rights generally may also have been beneficial and a change in government in 1997 was crucial as it led to the appointment of a strongly supportive and engaged Irish speaker as Minister, Michael D. Higgins. Further international influences came into play as campaigners invoked developments in legal protections for minority rights in other bilingual jurisdictions, including Canada and Wales. In the end, a rights framework was ruled out and the Official Languages Act was based more on placing obligations on public bodies than on creating justiciable rights for citizens. This did not please everyone, but the act was a significant advance on the vacuum of previous decades and was a significant victory for campaigners after almost three decades.

The study of the campaign for the Official Languages Act highlighted the complexities of achieving policy change and the sustained engagement and commitment required by activists to make progress. It also emphasised the importance of the national and international political context, ranging from the ideological complexion of the government, to the presence of key individuals in it, to broader international developments in minority and language rights. Ultimately, it was an attempt to reshape the language management of the state and bring it closer to the overt language policy, but like many campaigns, ultimately it had to compromise and the 2003 act fell short of the original demands. However, both it and the revised Official Languages Act 2021 were arguably the best deals that could be struck in the circumstances of the time and the focus of activists must now shift to implementation.

Chapter 5 analysed key developments in Irish language media over the historical arc and focused on latter-day campaigns for dedicated community radio stations. Similar to the campaign for an Irish language act, the activism that led to community media in Irish was prompted by the failure of both the British and Irish states to provide adequate broadcasting time for Irish speakers. With origins in the freewheeling pirate era of the 1970s and 1980s, the campaigns were born of frustration with domestic language and media policy and influenced by broader radical ideological strands such as the New International Information Order. In Belfast, the pirate years of Raidió Fáilte gained an additional edge from the local philosophy of self-reliance in the face of repression suffered by the nationalist community from the unionist establishment and British government. The creeping neoliberalism of broadcasting policy in the 1980s was challenged by Conradh na Gaeilge, which again internationalised the campaign by co-operating with media activists in contexts such as Wales and the Basque Country.

The result was not the mainstreaming of Irish in English-language media but the creation of functionally complete niche services serving Irish speakers. On the one hand, this may be interpreted as the increased minoritisation of Irish in media generally when seen against the backdrop of vague legislative provisions that have allowed independent commercial media to avoid any stringent Irish language requirements. On the other hand, these new services have created significant spaces of socialisation for mostly young Irish speakers in the challenging sociolinguistic contexts of Dublin, and more particularly Belfast, where knowledge and use of Irish is weak in the general community. The stations are also important sites of language revitalisation populated mostly by new speakers of Irish and function as what can be seen as 'safe spaces' for post-traditional linguistic production (O'Rourke & Walsh, 2020: 154–156). Niche services such as Raidió Fáilte and Raidió na Life are also increasingly in line with international trends in media consumption which tend towards individualisation and specialisation. However, greater support is required to consolidate and promote both digital and physical spaces for socialisation of Irish speakers in the future, requiring major funding from the state and more strategic thinking by activists.

The campaigns for community media in Ireland are also marked by important distinctions between north and south. In Dublin, the founders of Raidió na Life challenged the neoliberal broadcasting policy that prioritised commercial radio in English and the backdrop of positive attitudes and long-standing promotional policies for Irish allowed them to achieve their goals within a short period (1989–1993). The challenges facing Raidió Fáilte were much greater, as the station spent years broadcasting illegally in the face of outright hostility to Irish in the North in the 1980s and more stringent broadcasting laws than in the Republic. It was only with the consolidation of the peace process and commitments by the British government to support Irish language broadcasting that the station could come in from the cold and apply for a licence. Through different forms of activism in distinctive contexts, both stations have reshaped language management in relation to media as practiced by both governments. The fact that they are funded by the cross-border body Foras na Gaeilge is an indication of how key shifts in the governance of Irish have recently gained an all-Ireland dimension.

3. Patterns across a century of language policy

Having examined the development, implementation and contestation of language policy across five interlinked themes, a number of key patterns common to all domains can be observed.

3.1 New modes of governance

The case studies highlight the transformation of the governance of Irish over the decades. Language policy was initially highly centralised and top-down, as was the case with the Gaeltacht Commission, and lacked a central government department that would assume strategic control. This changed in the 1950s with the establishment of separate Gaeltacht institutions, but these were seen as remote from the public they were supposed to serve. In later years, a diffuse and complex model of 'partnership' has emerged between the state and voluntary sector, with the latter in a potentially vulnerable position. Irish in Northern Ireland was the victim of a non-policy for decades: nevertheless, the North-South dimension has transformed the way in which it is governed there. In sum, the proliferation of agencies, state and voluntary, in broader and thinner modes of language governance throughout Ireland has created significant challenges to the implementation of Irish language policy.

3.2 Role of civil society

Relatedly, the case studies of legislation, media and to a lesser extent, speakers, point to the crucial importance of maintaining a critical Irish language civil society sector with as much operational and strategic independence as possible. This book contains examples of voluntary language organisations achieving significant policy gains, and yet the sector faces many challenges in the future due to its almost total reliance on the state through Foras na Gaeilge. An aggressive restructuring of the sector in 2014 led to some long-standing organisations being extinguished, re-sulting in a loss of decades of valuable expertise (Ó Murchú, 2014; Muller, 2022). The Irish language voluntary sector must strive to diversify its fi-nancial base and avoid excessive or sole reliance on the state, constantly learning from similar movements in other jurisdictions and advocating for improved governance structures that reduce the vulnerability of the sector.

3.3 Internationalisation and professionalisation

This book has also illustrated that international trends have influenced the development of Irish language policy over time. This has ranged from contacts between Conradh na Gaeilge and similar organisations in Wales, Scotland and the Basque Country, to the enactment of international legal protection for minorities as invoked during the later stages of the cam-paign for an Irish language act. Developments in pedagogy and socio-linguistics played a key role from the mid-1960s as they revealed to the Irish government that academic research was engaged with these issues and that governments elsewhere were grappling with similar challenges. Notwithstanding the weaknesses in current policy, there is increased awareness in the Department of the Gaeltacht (if not in more powerful government departments) of the broader global context and the need for evidence-based interventions. The period from the 1960s has also witnessed a more professional approach by activists, again influenced by international developments. We have seen how campaigns for language rights elsewhere and critiques of the prioritisation of commercial over community media were adopted by Irish language organisations at dif-ferent times in the last fifty years.

3.4 New spatiality of speakers

The shifting spatiality of Irish speakers in the past century is a recurring theme in this book. All chapters touch on the often-fraught relationship between the Gaeltacht and learners or new speakers of Irish elsewhere. In common with international trends due to ongoing socioeconomic transformation, language shift persists in Gaeltacht communities and loose networks of Irish speakers continue to emerge elsewhere with each generation. Not all speakers, whether in the Gaeltacht or elsewhere, are equally committed to Irish and there is huge variation in competence, as an analysis of the headline census figure of c. 40 per cent illustrates. Uncertainty and insecurity about the extent of a core community committed to speaking Irish has been a recurring refrain in language activism over the past century. Consolidating the weak base of Irish speakers and increasing levels of competence and use among those already engaged with the language remain major challenges for future policymakers. These challenges are also related to economics and additional career pathways involving Irish need to be explored and promoted further. It remains to be seen if the new 20 per cent requirement for the public service will change attitudes in this regard, but any such shift will require genuine engagement by the state, well beyond the confines of the Department of the Gaeltacht, to be successful.

3.5 *Public vs. private*

In this regard, a striking feature of all of the case studies is the dominance of the state and voluntary sectors over the private sector. We have seen that Irish language policy is almost entirely reliant on the state for survival, although this is facilitated by public support for moderate promotional measures over several decades. The private sector has barely featured at all in this book, mainly because very little economic activity is conducted in Irish, with the exception of some companies in the Gaeltacht and a handful of language-related enterprises elsewhere. As economic instrumentalism will continue to be an important factor in language acquisition and use, this is a pressing challenge for the future. The difficulty is more acute in Northern Ireland where Irish is far more contested and opposed aggressively by a significant proportion of the unionist community.

3.6 Vulnerability

Vulnerability is the final pattern common to all of the case studies. Since the 1920s, there has been a sense of foreboding among Irish speakers and activists about the future viability and sustainability of the language. From the Gaeltacht Commission of the 1920s, to the policy shifts in education and public administration in the 1960s and 1970s, to the media and rights campaigns of the 1980s and 1990s and right up to the current language planning process, concerns are expressed that Irish faces an existential threat as a spoken language. There is plenty of evidence to support this concern, and studies of language shift in the Gaeltacht in particular have sparked justifiable fears. It is important to remember that Irish in the Republic benefits from significant policy supports only dreamed of by other minority language communities: its own media, legal protection, core status in education, a central if symbolic presence in the public imagination and dedicated state and voluntary institutions. Yet it is precisely these governance arrangements that provoke concern, because despite the proliferation of organisations promoting Irish, there remains an absence of engagement with the language at the heart of government and a concomitant lukewarm engagement by most of society.

Convincing recent evidence for this proposition is provided by the three anecdotes presented in the Introduction, and in the utter failure of the state to provide basic public health information and interactive services in Irish throughout the pandemic. The case studies also highlight how language policy is vulnerable to the vagaries of changes of government and officials or ministers ranging from MacNeill and Mulcahy in the 1920s, to Whitaker and Lemass in the 1960s, to Ó Cuív in the 1990s. At the beginning of 2022, the Minister with responsibility for Gaeltacht Affairs was Catherine Martin of the Green Party; it was under her watch that the long-awaited revised Official Languages Act was finally enacted, but it remains to be seen if her positive engagement with the Irish language to date can ensure its effective implementation. In Northern Ireland, while Irish has in some ways gained from the all-island dimension of Foras na Gaeilge, that same body was responsible for closing the voluntary body POBAL, which did pioneering work on an Irish language act for two decades. The absence of progress on an Irish language act for the North and the deeply entrenched views held by many unionists about it are a reminder of the vulnerability of Irish speakers there.

4. Language policy in the next century

The four key questions for future analysis of language revitalisation and social transformation presented in the Introduction are worthy of being restated here, as they allow us sketch some of the future challenges facing Irish language policy as it enters its second century. The first question related to the transformation of intergenerational transmission and the nature of families. Research on Irish-speaking families in the Gaeltacht and elsewhere indicates that, regardless of location, they will all require enhanced and targeted initiatives in order to support their efforts and guard against demoralisation. This challenge is acute in the Gaeltacht, where such families amount to less than a quarter of the total, but it is also urgently required elsewhere where Irish-speaking families may feel particularly isolated in the absence of community supports. Recognition of the increased diversification of the family is also crucial, as different combinations of caregivers and children need to feature in a reconfigured support programme.

The second question covered mobility, community and language use, and points to the need for greater investment in micro-level initiatives in physical locations as well as digital spaces. The language planning process is severely underfunded and requires further strategic investment, particularly in the Gaeltacht, in line with public support for the maintenance of Irish there. The glacial pace of implementation elsewhere is also noteworthy; a decade after the process was launched, it is a matter of concern that only five Irish language networks have been recognised nationally. This question also draws attention to the importance of a sociolinguistics of mobility, as seen in the discussion of migrants as new speakers in the Introduction. The failure of Irish government to develop an awareness programme about Irish for immigrants is a significant policy weakness given the relatively

large population (c. 17 per cent) not born in Ireland and is a missed opportunity to develop a more civic model of nationalism. The increasing
mediatisation of society (Hjarvard, 2013) draws attention to the need for
greater state investment in the Irish language media as part of its broader
language policy.

The third question related to globalisation and the economy and highlights the need, as expressed above, to develop a more meaningful and
extensive Irish language economy where linguistic skills can be converted
into economic capital. The Gaeltacht economy has been transformed in
line with broader national and international trends in recent decades and
requires careful management to balance regional development and language
maintenance. Údarás na Gaeltachta has been stymied by severe disinvest-
ment over the past decade and requires additional support so that it can
develop a sustainable regional development model based on Irish, as has
been proposed at various times over the past three decades. Elsewhere, the
development of a commercial Irish language sector needs to go beyond the
well-worn model of bilingual shopfronts and menus that has been practiced
for the past few decades, arguably with little linguistic impact.

The fourth question about governance and policymaking reminds us
that one of the greatest challenges of all is to embed Irish language considerations in all aspects of government policy, in contrast to its current
precarious position on the margins in a politically unimportant corner
of a crowded government department. This was supposed to happen in
the *20-Year Strategy for the Irish Language* but more than ten years later,
progress has been uninspiring outside those divisions that also had direct
responsibility for the language such as the Department of Education and
the Department of Tourism, Culture, Arts, Gaeltacht, Sport and Media.
Irish language civil society needs to monitor closely what is happening in
other comparable contexts internationally, learn from successful models
and lobby to achieve similar structural changes in Ireland. It is instructive
to analyse what has been achieved at sub-state level by non-sovereign governments such as in Wales and the Basque Country.

Other future challenges include the opportunities and threats presented by automation and artificial intelligence, which have far-reaching
implications for the provision of commercial and public services. The

climate emergency ignores borders and languages but risks being particularly acute in coastal Gaeltacht communities that may be submerged by
rising waters. Mitigating the worst effects of climate change will also have
implications for physical planning, land use and public services in rural
areas, including the Gaeltacht. Greater linkages between language planning
and land use planning in the Welsh policy framework are pertinent in this
regard (Jones, 2022). Relatedly, the Irish language voluntary sector could
learn a lot from the environmental movement about how to build broader
alliances in relation to shared concerns. The rise of extremism online and in
physical spaces threatens all minorities, including Irish speakers, and risks
provoking the election of far-right parties that could reverse decades of
hard-won progress. We have seen in Ireland that even parties with minor
ideological differences can make substantive changes to language policy
and the entrenched opposition to Irish in Northern Ireland is a reminder
of how meaningful language policy measures can be blocked by one side
of the community. Finally, the implications of Brexit and increased talk
about a United Ireland introduce an additional conundrum. If reunification is to come about, will the Irish language, for instance in the education
system, be sacrificed in the name of greater 'inclusivity' in a new thirty-
two-county state? There has been surprisingly little discussion about this
to date by civil society and political groups engaged with the question of
unification, which is revealing in itself.

5. Conclusion

The past century of Irish language policy has been characterised variously
by idealism, naivety, dedication, enthusiasm, hypocrisy, apathy and hostility. Looking back from the perspective of 2022, the last 100 years of
the Revival have been neither an unmitigated disaster nor a roaring success and they have seen both significant wins and bitter setbacks. To use
the Spolsky framework, in terms of language management and language
ideology, Irish appears to be in a relatively good place in the Republic of
Ireland. Institutionally, it enjoys considerable protection across a range

of domains, particularly education, at least for the moment. Most Irish people support its promotion in general terms, even if they do not speak it very well or at all. The language has a rich cultural tradition and a small but vibrant publishing sector produces books of calibre on a range of topics each year. Irish is standardised, has developed an extensive technical vocabulary and has full official status as a working language of the European Union, where it paradoxically enjoys a higher legal status than at home. In terms of language practices, however, Irish as a vernacular language in community settings is in a much weaker position. Although it continues to be spoken as a community language and in networks in every county in Ireland and further afield, the percentage of people who use it for everyday interactions is very small, at around 2 per cent of the population. The language management side of the equation is not without its complications either, because despite the significant institutionalisation of Irish, disjointed policy and the marginalisation of the language within central government have had an ongoing negative impact on policy implementation throughout the decades. This has been exacerbated by increasingly diffuse models of governance in parallel with the disengagement of the Irish state from the Revival project over the past fifty years. While there is potential for development through cross-border arrangements, Irish is in a more precarious position in Northern Ireland with even lower levels of use, weaker ideological support and fragmented and piecemeal policy supports.

There are grounds for hope and opportunities for growth. This book has shown how Irish language groups can shift policy direction, not always in line with their original aims, but nonetheless achieving significant change. Given that governments tend to be reactive rather than pro-active, language activists need to constantly up their game, learn from other contexts and present new solutions and strategies that can earn broader community support and lead the way for future changes in policy.

Bibliography

Archival collections

National Archives of Ireland (NAI). Departments of the Taoiseach (President), Finance, Communications (Posts and Telegraphs): FIN/2002/1/44, S11197A, S11197B, S13756, S3532/1, S3717, S5111, S7439, S7440A, S7440B, TAOIS/2000/6/440, TAOIS/2000/6/536, TW9546 and TW49040/64.

National Folklore Collection (CBÉ): 205, 294, 382.

National University of Ireland, Galway (NUIG). Conradh na Gaeilge Collection: G60/7/4/4/3, G60/29/2, G60/29/3, G60/36/10, G60/36/12, G60/36/12, G60/36/12, G60/36/3/2, G60/36/6/1, G60/36/6/2, G60/36/6/3, G60/36/11/1, G60/36/11/1, G60/29/4/2, G60/29/4/3, G60/29/4/4, G60/29/4/5, G60/29/4/6, G60/29/4/7, G60/29/4/8, G60/29/4/9, G60/29/2/1, G60/29/2/1, G60/29/2/1, G60/29/2/2, G60/29/2/3.

Legal sources

Legislation (UK)

Administration of Justice (Language) Act (Ireland), 1737. Richmond: HMSO. Available at: <https://www.legislation.gov.uk/aip/Geo2/11/6>.

Marine and Broadcasting Offences Act, 1967 (UK). Richmond: HMSO. Available at: <https://www.legislation.gov.uk/ukpga/1967/41/enacted>.

Northern Ireland Act, 1998, c. 47. Richmond: HMSO. Available at: <https://www.legislation.gov.uk/ukpga/1998/47/contents>.

International law and agreements

Agreement between the Government of the United Kingdom of Great Britain and Northern Ireland and the Government of Ireland ['Belfast Agreement'], 1998. Available at: <https://www.britishirishcouncil.org/about/britishirish-agreement>.

European Charter for Regional or Minority Languages, 1992 (CETS No.: 148). Available at: <https://www.coe.int/en/web/european-charter-regional-or-mi-nority-languages/text-of-the-charter>.

St Andrews Agreement between the British and Irish governments and Northern Ireland parties, 2006. Available at: <https://www.gov.uk/government/publi cations/the-st-andrews-agreement-october-2006>.

European Court of Justice

Groener v. Minister for Education and the City of Dublin Vocational Education Committee. Case 379/87, [1989] ECR 3967.

Legislation (Ireland)

Broadcasting and Wireless Telegraphy Act, 1988. No. 19/1988. Dublin: Stationery Office. Available at: <https://www.irishstatutebook.ie/eli/1988/act/19/enact-ed/en/index.html>.

Constitution of Ireland, 1937. Dublin: Stationery Office. Available at: <https://www.irishstatutebook.ie/eli/cons/en/html>.

Constitution of the Irish Free State (Saorstát Éireann) Act, 1922. No. 1/1922. Dublin: Stationery Office. Available at: <https://www.irishstatutebook.ie/eli/1922/act/1/enacted/en/print>.

Education Act, 1998. No. 51/1998. Dublin: Stationery Office. Available at: <https://www.irishstatutebook.ie/eli/1998/act/51/enacted/en/index.html>.

Gaeltacht Act, 2012. No. 34/2012. Dublin: Stationery Office. Available at: <https://www.irishstatutebook.ie/eli/2012/act/34/enacted/en/index.html>.

Gaeltacht Areas Order, 1956. SI No. 245/1956. Dublin: Stationery Office. Available at: <https://www.irishstatutebook.ie/eli/1956/si/245/made/en/print>.

Gaeltacht Areas Order, 1967. SI No. 200/1967. Dublin: Stationery Office. Available at: <https://www.irishstatutebook.ie/eli/1967/si/200/made/en/print>.

Gaeltacht Areas Order, 1974. SI No. 192/1974. Dublin: Stationery Office. Available at: <https://www.irishstatutebook.ie/eli/1974/si/192/made/en/print>.

Gaeltacht Areas Order, 1982. No. 350/1982. Dublin: Stationery Office. Available at: <https://www.irishstatutebook.ie/eli/1982/si/350/made/ga/print>.

Gaeltacht Industries Act, 1957. No. 29/1957. Dublin: Stationery Office. Available at: <https://www.irishstatutebook.ie/eli/1957/act/29/enacted/en/html>.

Gaeltacht Industries Act, 1965. No. 18/1965. Dublin: Stationery Office. Available at: <https://www.irishstatutebook.ie/eli/1965/act/18/enacted/en/index.html>.

Garda Síochána Act, 1924. No. 25/1924. Dublin: Stationery Office. Available at: <https://www.irishstatutebook.ie/eli/1924/act/25/enacted/en/html>.

Garda Síochána Act, 2005. No. 20/2005. Dublin: Stationery Office. Available at: <https://www.irishstatutebook.ie/eli/2005/act/20/enacted/en/index.html>.

Higher Education Authority Act, 1971. No. 22/1971. Dublin: Stationery Office. Available at: <https://www.irishstatutebook.ie/eli/1971/act/22/enacted/en/html>.

Housing (Gaeltacht) (Amendment) Act, 2001. No. 10/2001. Dublin: Stationery Office. Available at: <https://www.irishstatutebook.ie/eli/2001/act/10/enacted/en/index.html>.

Housing (Gaeltacht) Act, 1929. No. 41/1929. Dublin: Stationery Office. Available at: <https://www.irishstatutebook.ie/eli/1929/act/41/enacted/en/index.html>.

Housing (Gaeltacht) Act, 1934. No. 29/1934. Dublin: Stationery Office. Available at: <https://www.irishstatutebook.ie/eli/1934/act/29/enacted/en/index.html>.

Institute for Advanced Studies Act, 1940. No. 13/1940. Dublin: Stationery Office. Available at: <https://www.irishstatutebook.ie/eli/1940/act/13/enacted/en/index.html>.

Local Offices and Employments (Gaeltacht) Order, 1928. SI No. 33/1928. Dublin: Stationery Office. Available at: <https://www.irishstatutebook.ie/eli/1928/sro/33/made/en/print>.

Ministers and Secretaries (Amendment) Act, 1956. No. 21/1956. Dublin: Stationery Office. Available at: <https://www.irishstatutebook.ie/eli/1956/act/21/enacted/en/index.html>.

Official Languages (Act), 2003. No. 32/2003. Dublin: Stationery Office. Available at: <https://www.irishstatutebook.ie/eli/2003/act/32/enacted/en/index.html>.

Official Languages Act 2003 (Section 9) Regulations 2008. SI No. 391/2008. Dublin: Stationery Office. Available at: <https://www.irishstatutebook.ie/eli/2008/si/391/made/en/print>.

Official Languages (Amendment) Act, 2021. No. 49/2021. Available at: https://www.irishstatutebook.ie/eli/2021/act/49/enacted/en/index.html

Placenames (Ceantair Ghaeltachta) Order, 2004. SI No. 872/2004. Dublin: Stationery Office Available at: <https://www.irishstatutebook.ie/eli/2004/si/872/made/ga/print>.

Planning and Development Act, 2000. No. 30/2000. Dublin: Stationery Office. Available at: <https://www.irishstatutebook.ie/eli/2000/act/30/enacted/en/index.html>.

Radio and Television Act, 1988. No. 20/1988. Dublin: Stationery Office. Available at: <https://www.irishstatutebook.ie/eli/1988/act/20/enacted/en/index.html>.

School Meals (Gaeltacht) Act, 1930. No. 23/1930. Dublin: Stationery Office. Available at: <https://www.irishstatutebook.ie/eli/1930/act/23/enacted/en/index.html>.

Second Amendment of the Constitution Act, 1941. No. 2/1941. Dublin: Stationery Office. Available at: <https://www.irishstatutebook.ie/eli/1941/ca/2/enacted/en/index.html>.

Údarás na Gaeltachta Act, 1979. No. 5/1979. Dublin: Stationery Office. Available at: <https://www.irishstatutebook.ie/eli/1979/act/5/enacted/en/html>.

Universities Act, 1997. No. 24/1997. Dublin: Stationery Office. Available at: <https://www.irishstatutebook.ie/eli/1997/act/24/enacted/en/index.html>.

University College Galway Act, 1929. No. 35/1929. Dublin: Stationery Office. Available at: <https://www.irishstatutebook.ie/eli/1929/act/35/enacted/en/index.html>.

University College Galway (Amendment) Act, 2006. No. 1/2006. Dublin: Stationery Office. Available at: <https://www.irishstatutebook.ie/eli/2006/act/1/enacted/en/index.html>.

Wireless Telegraphy Act, 1926. No. 45/1926. Dublin: Stationery Office. Available at: <https://www.irishstatutebook.ie/eli/1926/act/45/enacted/en/index.html>.

Bills (Ireland)

Broadcasting and Wireless Telegraphy Bill, 1979. No. 12/1979. Dublin: Stationery Office. Available at: <https://www.oireachtas.ie/en/bills/bill/1979/12/>.
Broadcasting and Wireless Telegraphy Bill, 1985. No. 25/1985. Dublin: Stationery Office. Available at: <https://www.oireachtas.ie/en/bills/bill/1985/25/>.
Broadcasting and Wireless Telegraphy Bill, 1987. No. 49/1987. Available at: https:// data.oireachtas.ie/ie/oireachtas/bill/1987/49/eng/ver_b/bills1988-1h-04.pdf
Independent Local Broadcasting Authority Bill, 1983. No. 14/1983. Dublin: Stationery Office. Available at: <https://www.oireachtas.ie/en/bills/bill/1983/14/>.
Independent Local Radio Authority Bill, 1981. No. 17/1981. Dublin: Stationery Office. Available at: <https://www.oireachtas.ie/en/bills/bill/1981/17/>.
Local Radio Bill, 1985. No. 24/1985. Dublin: Stationery Office. Available at: <https://www.oireachtas.ie/en/bills/bill/1985/24/>.
Official Languages (Amendment) Bill, 2019. No. 104b/2019. Dublin: Stationery Office. Available at: <https://data.oireachtas.ie/ie/oireachtas/bill/2019/104/ mul/ver_b/b104b19.pdf>.
Official Languages (Equality) Bill, 2002. No. 24/2002. Dublin: Stationery Office. Available at: <https://data.oireachtas.ie/ie/oireachtas/bill/2002/24/eng/ initiated/b2402s.pdf>.

Case law (Ireland)

Attorney General vs Coyne and Wallace [1963]. 101 ILTR 17.
Ó Foghludha vs McClean [1934]. IR 469.
Ó Monacháin vs An Taoiseach [1986]. ILRM 660.
Helen Ó Murchú vs Cláraitheoir na gCuideachtaí agus an Aire Tionscail agus Tráchtala [Registrar of Companies and the Minister for Industry and Commerce]. High Court, 20 June 1988.
An Stát (Mac Fhearraigh) vs Mac Gamhnia. High Court, 1 July 1983.
An Stát (Mac Fhearraigh) vs Neilan. High Court, 1 June 1984.
Ó Beoláin vs Fahy [2001]. 2 IR 279.
Ó Murchú vs An Taoiseach [2010]. 4 IR 484.

Case law list based on Ó Máille, 1990 and Mac Cárthaigh, 2020.

Other printed sources

Advisory Planning Committee, 1988. *The Irish Language in a Changing Society: Shaping the Future*. Dublin: Bord na Gaeilge.

Aer Lingus, 1982. 'Fáilte/Welcome/Bienvenue/Willkommen'. *Cara*, July/August, 13. NUIG G60/29/4/6.

Aer Lingus, 1987. Letter from M. Gannon to P. Ó Conchúir, 25 September. NUIG G60/29/2/2.

Aer Lingus, n.d. Multilingual (GA/EN/FR/DE) peanut package. NUIG G60/29/2/2.

Allied Irish Banks, n.d. Bilingual lodgement and withdrawal slips. NUIG G60/29/4/6.

AMARC Europe, 2019. 'AMARC Charter'. Brussels: AMARC Europe. Available at: <https://amarceurope.eu/who-we-are/amarc-charter/>.

An Comhchoiste Sealadach Feidhmiúcháin [Provisional Implementation Committee], 1964. Letter from Chairman Fr Tomás Ó Fiaich to Taoiseach Seán Lemass, 24 November. NUIG G60/29/4/2.

An Dréachtóir, 1975. Letter to P. Ó Snodaigh, 28 August. NUIG G60/29/4/7.

An Dréachtóir, 1976. Letter to unnamed person, 27 January. NUIG G60/29/4/7.

An Post, 1986. 'Happy St. Patrick's Day: Love and hisses'. Postcard, 17 March. NUIG G60/29/2/1.

Anonymous, 2020. Interview with 'Jamie', Raidió Fáilte, Belfast, 25 January.

Armstrong, T. C., 2012. 'Establishing new norms of language use: The circulation of linguistic ideology in three new Irish-language communities'. *Language Policy*, 11, 145–168.

Augustyniak, A. and Higham, G., 2019. 'Contesting sub-state integration policies: Migrant new speakers as stakeholders in language regimes'. *Language Policy*, 18, 513–533.

Bermingham, N. and Higham, G., 2018. 'Immigrants as new speakers in Galicia and Wales: Issues of integration, belonging and legitimacy'. *Journal of Multilingual and Multicultural Development*, 39 (5), 394–406.

Blythe, E., 1924. 'Appointment of Commission on the preservation of the Gaeltacht'. Memorandum to government, 17 December. NAI S3717.

Bohan, E., 2021. Interview with Eddie Bohan about Belfast pirate radio. *The Pirate.ie Podcast #7*, 16 July. Available at: <https://pirate.ie/archive/the-pirate-ie-podc ast-7/>.

Bord na Gaeilge, 1983. *Plean Gníomhaíochta don Ghaeilge 1983–1986/Action Plan for Irish 1983–1986*. Dublin: Bord na Gaeilge.

Bord na Gaeilge, 1986. *Tuarascáil 1985–86: Plean Gníomhaíochta don Ghaeilge 1983–86/1983–86 Action Plan for Irish: 1985–86 Report.* Dublin: Bord na Gaeilge.

Bord na Gaeilge, 1990. *Tuarascáil Bhliantúil 1990.* Dublin: Bord na Gaeilge.

Bord na Gaeilge, 1993a. Ábhar/Subject: Raidió na Life 102 FM'. Press release on launch of Raidió na Life. 29 September. NUIG G60/36/11/1.

Bord na Gaeilge, 1993b. *Leathnú an Dátheangachais: Treoirlínte don Earnáil Phoiblí do Chláracha Gníomhaíochta/Expanding Bilingualism: Guidelines for Action Programmes in the State Sector.* Dublin: Bord na Gaeilge.

Bord na Gaeilge, 1993c. *Tuarascáil Bhliantúil 1993.* Dublin: Bord na Gaeilge.

Bord na Gaeilge, 1994. *Tuarascáil Bhliantúil 1994.* Dublin: Bord na Gaeilge.

Bord na Gaeilge, 1995. *An Dátheangachas san Earnáil Phoiblí: Ceistneoir faoi Fheidhmiú Polasaí 1994–1995/Bilingualism in the State Sector: Questionnaire on Policy Implementation 1994–1995.* Dublin: Bord na Gaeilge.

Bord na Gaeilge, 1996a. *An Dátheangachas san Earnáil Phoiblí: Anailís ar Fhreagraí Cheistneoir 1995/Bilingualism in the State Sector: Analysis of 1995 Questionnaire Responses.* Dublin: Bord na Gaeilge.

Bord na Gaeilge, 1996b. *Tuarascáil Bhliantúil 95–96 Annual Report.* Dublin: Bord na Gaeilge.

Bord na Gaeilge, 1998a. *Dul Chun Cinn Dátheangach san Earnáil Phoiblí i rith 1996/Bilingual Progress in the State Sector during 1996.* Dublin: Bord na Gaeilge.

Bord na Gaeilge, 1998b. *Tuarascáil Bhliantúil/Annual Report 1998.* Dublin: Bord na Gaeilge.

Bord na Gaeilge, 1999. *Tuarascáil Bhliantúil Bhord na Gaeilge 1999/Bord na Gaeilge Annual Report 1999.* Dublin: Bord na Gaeilge.

Bowman, J., 2011. *Window and Mirror – RTÉ Television: 1961–2011.* Cork: The Collins Press.

Braun, V. and Clarke, V., 2006. 'Using thematic analysis in psychology'. *Qualitative Research in Psychology*, 3, 77–101.

Breathnach, Caitríona, 2019. 'Tábhacht na féiniúlachta agus na hoidhreachta cultúrtha i nGaeltacht na nDéise: dearcthaí a nochtadh sa phróiseas pleanála teanga'. *An Linn Bhuí: Iris Ghaeltacht na nDéise*, 23. Crosspatrick and Dublin: Leabhair na Linne, 122–135.

Breathnach, Ciara, 2005. *The Congested Districts Board of Ireland, 1891–1923.* Dublin: Four Courts Press.

Breathnach, D. and Ní Mhurchú, M., 2021a. 'MAC COLUIM, Fionán (1875–1966)'. *Ainm.ie.* Dublin and Indreabhán: Dublin City University and Cló Iar-Chonnacht. Available at: <https://www.ainm.ie/Bio.aspx?ID=28>.

Breathnach, D. and Ní Mhurchú, M., 2021b. 'MAC MEANMAN, Seaghán (1886–1962)'. *Ainm.ie.* Dublin and Indreabhán: Dublin City University and Cló Iar-Chonnacht. Available at: <https://www.ainm.ie/Bio.aspx?ID=158>.

Breathnach, D. and Ní Mhurchú, M., 2021c. 'MAC SEÁIN, Pádraig (1895–1981)'. *Ainm.ie*. Dublin and Indreabhán: Dublin City University and Cló Iar-Chonnacht. Available at: <https://www.ainm.ie/Bio.aspx?ID=653>.

Breathnach, D. and Ní Mhurchú, M., 2021d. 'Ó CADHLA, Pádraig (1878–1948)'. *Ainm.ie*. Dublin and Indreabhán: Dublin City University and Cló Iar-Chonnacht. Available at: <https://www.ainm.ie/Bio.aspx?ID=181>.

Breathnach, D. and Ní Mhurchú, M., 2021e. 'Ó CEALLAIGH, Seán 1872–1957'. *Ainm.ie*. Dublin and Indreabhán: Dublin City University and Cló Iar-Chonnacht. Available at: <https://www.ainm.ie/Bio.aspx?ID=0388>.

Breathnach, D. and Ní Mhurchú, M., 2021f. 'Ó FOGHLUDHA, Risteard (1871–1957)'. *Ainm.ie*. Dublin and Indreabhán: Dublin City University and Cló Iar-Chonnacht. Available at: <https://www.ainm.ie/Bio.aspx?ID=75>.

Breathnach, D. and Ní Mhurchú, M., 2021g. 'Ó hEOCHA, Séamus (1880–1959)'. *Ainm.ie*. Dublin and Indreabhán: Dublin City University and Cló Iar-Chonnacht. Available at: <https://www.ainm.ie/Bio.aspx?ID=743>.

Breathnach, D. and Ní Mhurchú, M., 2021h. 'Ó hÓGÁIN, Pádraig (1885–1969)'. *Ainm.ie*. Dublin and Indreabhán: Dublin City University and Cló Iar-Chonnacht. Available at: <https://www.ainm.ie/Bio.aspx?ID=343>.

Breathnach, D. and Ní Mhurchú, M., 2021i. 'Ó LOINGSIGH, Fionán (1889–1966)'. *Ainm.ie*. Dublin and Indreabhán: Dublin City University and Cló Iar-Chonnacht. Available at: <https://www.ainm.ie/Bio.aspx?ID=528>.

Breathnach, D. and Ní Mhurchú, M., 2021j. 'Ó SCANAILL, Tadhg (1883–1967)'. *Ainm.ie*. Dublin and Indreabhán: Dublin City University and Cló Iar-Chonnacht. Available at: <https://www.ainm.ie/Bio.aspx?ID=0111>.

Breathnach, D. and Ní Mhurchú, M., 2021k. 'Ó SIOCHFHRADHA, Pádraig (1883–1964)'. *Ainm.ie*. Dublin and Indreabhán: Dublin City University and Cló Iar-Chonnacht. Available at: <https://www.ainm.ie/Bio.aspx?ID=783>.

Breathnach, M., 1966. *Cuimhne an tSeanpháiste*. Dublin: Stationery Office.

Breathnach, M. S., 2021. Personal communication with Máire Seó Breathnach, Irish Language Officer, Waterford City and County Council, 3 September.

Breathnach, T., c. 1937. Untitled handwritten notebook containing English medical terms and Irish equivalents. 'Tomás Breathnach's Téarmaí Leigheas [sic]'. NUIG G5/1.

Breatnach, C., 2021. Interview with Cillian Breatnach, manager, Raidió Fáilte. Online. 15th November.

Breatnach, N., 1998. *Ar Bóthar Dom*. An Rinn: Coláiste na Rinne.

Breatnach, R. B., 1961. *Seana-Chaint na nDéise II*. Dublin: Dublin Institute for Advanced Studies.

Briody, M., 2007. *The Irish Folklore Commission 1935–1970: History, Ideology, Methodology*. Helsinki: Finnish Literature Society.

Briody, M., 2010. 'Ceapadh chéad Choimisiún Béaloideasa Éireann, 1934–1935'. *Béaloideas*, 78, 168–186.

Browne, D., 1998. 'Talking the talk on indigenous radio'. *Cultural Survival Quarterly Magazine*, June. Available at: <https://www.culturalsurvival.org/publicati ons/cultural-survival-quarterly/talking-talk-indigenous-radio>.

CAAS (Environmental Services), 2001. *Ring-Helvick-Old Parish Area Action Plan 2001*. Dublin: CAAS.

Caglitutuncigil, T., 2018. 'Beween myth and reality: Language classrooms in Spanish and Catalan social integration programmes'. *Journal of Multilingual and Multicultural Development*, 39 (5), 431–444.

Cahillane, L., 2016. *Drafting the Irish Free State Constitution*. Manchester: Manchester University Press.

Central Statistics Office, 2004. Small Area Population Statistics (SAPS) for the Gaeltacht (1981, 1986, 1991, 1996, 2002). Purchased from CSO.

Central Statistics Office, 2017a. 'Irish Language and the Gaeltacht'. *Census of Population 2016 – Profile 10: Education, Skills and the Irish Language*. Cork: Central Statistics Office. Available at: <https://www.cso.ie/en/releases andpublications/ep/p-cp10esil/p10esil/ilg/>.

Central Statistics Office, 2017b. *Census 2016 Summary Results – Part 1*. Cork: Central Statistics Office. Available at: <https://www.cso.ie/en/media/csoie/newseve nts/documents/census2016summaryresultspart1/Census2016SummaryPa rt1.pdf>.

Central Statistics Office, 2017c. *Census of Population 2016 – Profile 10: Education, Skills and the Irish Language*. Cork: Central Statistics Office. Available at: <https://www.cso.ie/en/releasesandpublications/ep/p-cp10esil/p10esil/>.

Chambers, A., 2008. *T.K. Whitaker: Portrait of a Patriot*. Dublin: Transworld Publishers.

Chapman, R., 1992. *Selling the Sixties: The Pirates and Pop Music Radio*. London: Routledge.

Clarke, Paddy, 1986. *'Dublin Calling': 2RN and the Birth of Irish Radio*. Dublin: RTÉ.

Coilféir, M., 2020. 'Breithiúna agus breithiúnais sa Ghúm'. In: Coilféir, M. (ed.) *An Scéim: An Gúm 1926–2016. Cnuasach Aistí*. Dublin: An Gúm, 49–62.

Coimisiún na Gaeltachta, 2002. *Tuarascáil/Report*. Dublin: Coimisiún na Gaeltachta.

Coimisiún um Athbheochan na Gaeilge (Commission on the Restoration of the Irish Language), 1963. *Summary, in English, of Final Report, 13th July, 1963*. Dublin: Stationery Office.

Coimisiún um Athbheochan na Gaeilge, 1963. *An Coimisiún um Athbheochan na Gaeilge: An Tuarascáil Dheiridh*. Dublin: Stationery Office.

Comhairle na Gaeilge, 1970. *Submissions to Higher Education Authority/Meabhráin don Údarás um Ardoideachas*. Dublin: Stationery Office.

Comhairle na Gaeilge, 1971a. 'Seirbhísí Sláinte na Gaeltachta'. Unpublished report of Gaeltacht Sub-Committee. Undated but accompanied by hand-written note from 20/10/71. NAI FIN/2002/1/44.

Comhairle na Gaeilge, 1971b. *Local Government and Development Institutions for the Gaeltacht/Institiúidí Rialtais Áitiúil agus Forbraíochta don Ghaeilge*. Dublin: Stationery Office.

Comhairle na Gaeilge, 1971c. *Occasional Paper No. 1: Language and Community/ Páipéar Ócáideach Uimh. 1: Urlabhra agus Pobal*. Dublin: Stationery Office.

Comhairle na Gaeilge, 1971d. *Towards a Language Policy/I dTreo Polasaí Teanga*. Dublin: Stationery Office.

Comhairle na Gaeilge, 1972. *Implementing a Language Policy/Feidhmiú Polasaí Teanga*. Dublin: The Stationery Office.

Comhairle na Gaeilge, 1974. *Irish in Education/An Ghaeilge sa Chóras Oideachais*. Dublin: Stationery Office.

Comhairle Pobail na Rinne, 2005. 'Moltaí Chomhairle Pobail na Rinne i leith na Gaeilge agus Plean Forbartha an Chontae 2005–2011'. Submission to Waterford County Council on County Development Plan.

Comharchumann Raidió Átha Cliath, 1989. Letter from M. Nic Eoin, 13 December. NUIG G60/36/11/1.

Comharchumann Raidió Átha Cliath, 1990. Publicity letter from M. Nic Eoin, 13 June. NUIG G60/36/11/1.

Comharchumann Raidió Átha Cliath, 1992. Letter from Máirín M. Nic Eoin, 9 December. NUIG G60/36/11/1.

Comharchumann Raidió Átha Cliath, 1993. Letter from M. Nic Eoin, 18 August. NUIG G60/36/11/1.

Comharchumann Raidió Átha Cliath, c. 1990. 'Raidió na Life – an spéis leat raidió nua?' Bilingual leaflet. NUIG G60/36/11/1.

Comharchumann Raidió Átha Cliath, c. 1992. Clárscéideal – Programme Schedule. NUIG G60/36/11/1.

Comhdháil Náisiúnta na Gaeilge, 1980. 'Raidió áitiúil'. Letter from E. Ó Néill to S. Mac Mathúna, 17 August. NUIG G60/36/6/2.

Comhdháil Náisiúnta na Gaeilge, 1987a. 'Do chomhaltaí na Comhdhála: Raidió áitiúil'. Letter to members, 7 December. NUIG G60/36/6/2.

Comhdháil Náisiúnta na Gaeilge, 1987b. 'Raidió áitiúil'. Letter to all voluntary organisations, 7 December. NUIG G60/36/3/2.

Comhdháil Náisiúnta na Gaeilge, 1989. Letter from C. Ó Dúlacháin, 8 July. NUIG G60/36/6/2.

Comhdháil Náisiúnta na Gaeilge, 1998a. *Comhdháil Idirnáisiúnta ar Chearta Teanga/International Conference on Language Legislation/Conférence internationale sur la législation de la langue: Tuarascáil ar Imeachtaí na Comhdhála/ Conference Proceedings/Compte-rendu de conférence.* Dublin: Comhdháil Náisiúnta na Gaeilge.

Comhdháil Náisiúnta na Gaeilge, 1998b. *Pléchaipéis – Towards a Language Act: A Discussion Document/Pléchaipéis maidir le hAcht Teanga.* Dublin: Comhdháil Náisiúnta na Gaeilge.

Comhlacht Comhairleach na Gaeilge, 1968. *Tuarascáil don Tréimhse 1 Aibreán, 1966 go dtí 14 Meitheamh, 1968.* Dublin: Stationery Office.

Commins, P., 1988. 'Socioeconomic development and language maintenance in the Gaeltacht'. *International Journal of the Sociology of Language*, 70, 11–28.

Commission on Higher Education, 1967. *Commission on Higher Education 1960– 1967: II Report (Volumes 1 & 2).* Dublin: The Stationery Office.

Committee on Irish Language Attitudes Research [CILAR], 1975. *Tuarascáil arna chur* [sic] *faoi bhráid Aire na Gaeltachta, Deireadh Fómhair 1975/Report as Submitted to the Minister for the Gaeltacht, October 1975.* Dublin: Government Publications.

Concord Community Radio, c. 1983. 'Concord Community Broadcasting Co-operative'. Bilingual leaflet about station including National Association of Community Broadcasting Charter. NUIG G60/36/6/1.

Conradh na Gaeilge, 1939. 'Meamram ó Choiste Gnótha Chonradh na Gaeilge chuig an Taoiseach Éamonn (sic) de Vailéara do réir do mar a d'iarr an Taoiseach ar an gCoiste Gnótha a leithéid a cheapadh agus a chuir chuige'. Estimated date 14 March. NAI S11197A.

Conradh na Gaeilge, 1975a. Letter from S. Mac Mathúna to Embassy of the Republic of South Africa, London, 8 August. NUIG G60/29/4/4.

Conradh na Gaeilge, 1975b. Letter from S. Mac Mathúna to Embassy of Belgium, 8 August. NUIG G60/29/4/4.

Conradh na Gaeilge, 1975c. Letter from S. Mac Mathúna to Embassy of Switzerland, 15 August. NUIG G60/29/4/4.

Conradh na Gaeilge, 1976a. 'Cáipéis eolais don phreas-agallamh ar Fheachtas Cearta na Gaeilge, Dé Céadaoin, 10 Samhain, 1976'. Press release. NUIG G60/29/4/2.

Conradh na Gaeilge, 1976b. 'Forógra Cearta don Ghaeilge'. Leaflet. NUIG G60/ 29/4/2.

Conradh na Gaeilge, 1976c. 'Ráiteas ó Sheán Ó Drisceoil, Cathaoirleach, An Fochoiste Cearta ag preas-agallamh, 10 Samhain, 1976'. NUIG G60/29/4/2.

Conradh na Gaeilge, 1977a. 'An Fochoiste Cearta: Cruinniú, Dé Sathairn, 12 Márta, 1977, 7.00pm'. Minutes. NUIG G60/29/4/3.

Conradh na Gaeilge, 1977b. 'Bán-bhianna'. Documents about white foods. NUIG G60/29/2/2.

Conradh na Gaeilge, 1977c. 'Bill of Rights for the Irish Language'. Letter to Seanad candidates, 20 July. NUIG G60/29/4/2.

Conradh na Gaeilge, 1977d. 'Bille Cearta don Ghaeilge'. Leaflet. NUIG G60/29/2/2.

Conradh na Gaeilge, 1977e. 'Conradh na Gaeilge's campaign of rights – Report on work of the Rights Bureau'. Press release, 1 March. NUIG G60/29/4/5.

Conradh na Gaeilge, 1977f. 'Preas Ráiteas'. Press release, 10 October. NUIG G60/29/3.

Conradh na Gaeilge, 1977g. 'Preas Ráiteas'. Press release, 8 October. NUIG G60/29/3.

Conradh na Gaeilge, c. 1977. 'A Bill of Rights for the Irish language'. Undated leaflet. NUI G60/29/4/5.

Conradh na Gaeilge, 1978. 'Call for boycott of RTÉ 2's opening ceremony'. Press release, 31 October. NUIG G60/29/18/2.

Conradh na Gaeilge, 1979a. 'Cruinniú faoi Raidió an Phobail, Dé Sathairn, 6 Deireadh Fómhair 1979'. Minutes, NUIG G60/36/10.

Conradh na Gaeilge, 1979b. 'Press release, Raidió an Phobail, 16 October 1979'. NUIG G60/36/10).

Conradh na Gaeilge, 1981. 'Líon na ngearán a sásaíodh'. List of complaints. NUIG G60/29/2/3.

Conradh na Gaeilge, 1983a. 'Bille Cearta don Ghaeilge, Siompóisiam, An Cheathrú Rua'. Poster, 29 October. NUIG G60/29/4/5.

Conradh na Gaeilge, 1983b. 'Bille Cearta don Ghaeilge: éilímis ár gcearta teanga'. Flyer. NUIG G60/29/4/5.

Conradh na Gaeilge, 1983c. 'Cruinniú Poiblí, Na Doirí Beaga'. Poster, 2 May. NUIG G60/29/4/5.

Conradh na Gaeilge, 1983d. 'Eolas faoin mBille Cearta'. Campaign leaflet. NUIG G60/29/4/5.

Conradh na Gaeilge, 1983e. 'Proposed local radio legislation condemned – Statement from Conradh na Gaeilge, 12 August'. Press release, NUIG G60/36/6/2.

Conradh na Gaeilge, 1984. 'Local Broadcasting: Submission from Conradh na Gaeilge to Joint Oireachtas Committee on Legislation'. *Rosc: Iris Dhátheangach Chonradh na Gaeilge*, 33: 1, 11–22. 10 Aibreán, NUIG G60/36/3/2.

Conradh na Gaeilge, 1986a. Letter from M. Ó Caollaí to T. Leyden, 23 April. NUIG G60/36/3/2.

Conradh na Gaeilge, 1986b. Various letters to local authorities and voluntary organisations. NUIG G60/29/4/8.

Conradh na Gaeilge, 1987. 'Telephone line is disconnected – The result of corresponding with Telecom Éireann in Irish'. Press release, 11 November. NUIG G60/29/2/2.

Conradh na Gaeilge, 1988. 'Sound Broadcasting Bill 1987'. Press release, 5 January. NUIG G60/36/3/2.

Conradh na Gaeilge, 1989a. 'New national radio station – Call for contractual obligations for Irish language programmes'. Press release, 20 January. NUIG G60/36/12.

Conradh na Gaeilge, 1989b. 'Suirland Radio'. Note about new radio service, author unknown. NUIG G60/36/6/2.

Conradh na Gaeilge, 1989c. Letter from S. Mac Mathúna to O. Barry, 31 August. NUIG G60/36/12.

Conradh na Gaeilge, 1989d. Letter from S. Mac Mathúna to R. Burke, 29 August. NUIG G60/36/12.

Conradh na Gaeilge, 1989e. Letter from S. Mac Mathúna to S. Henchy, 29 August. NUIG G60/36/12.

Conradh na Gaeilge, 1990a. 'Leabhrán Ard-Fheise 1990'. NUIG G60/36/6/3.

Conradh na Gaeilge, 1990b. 'MWRFM agus an Ghaeilge'. Flyer, 10 November. NUIG G60/36/6/3.

Conradh na Gaeilge, 1992. 'Leabhrán Ard-Fheise 1992'. NUIG G60/36/6/3.

Conradh na Gaeilge, 2021a. 'High Court grants leave for Irish Language Strategy judicial review against Executive'. Press release, 10 June. Available at: <https://cnag.ie/en/news/1491-high-court-grants-leave-for-irish-language-strategy-judicial-review-against-executive.html>.

Conradh na Gaeilge, 2021b. Polasaí Náisiúnta do Phleanáil Tithíochta sa Ghaeltacht: Moltaí/National Policy for Housing Planning in the Gaeltacht: Recommendations. Available at: <https://cnag.ie/images/30DF2020_Polasai%CC%81_Na%CC%81isiu%CC%81nta_don_Phleana%CC%81il_Tithi%CC%81ochta_sa_Ghaeltacht_1.pdf>.

Conradh na Gaeilge, n.d. 'Impiriúlachas cultúir'. Poster, NUIG G60/7/4/4/3.

Constitutional Review Group, 1996. *Report of the Constitution Review Group*. Dublin: Stationery Office.

Corcoran, D. P., 2013. *Freedom to Achieve Freedom: The Irish Free State 1922–1932*. Dublin: Gill and Macmillan.

Cormack, M., 2007. 'The media and language maintenance'. In: Cormack, M. and Hourigan, N. (eds) *Minority Language Media: Concepts, Critiques and Case Studies*. Clevedon: Multilingual Matters, 52–68.

Cormack, M., 2013. 'Concluding remarks: Towards an understanding of media impact on minority language use'. In: Jones, E. H. G. and Jongbloed, U. (eds)

Social Media and Minority Languages: Convergence and the Creative Industries.
Bristol: Multilingual Matters, 255–268.

Cormack, M. and Hourigan, N. (eds), 2007. *Minority Language Media: Concepts, Critiques and Case Studies.* Clevedon: Multilingual Matters.

Cotter, C., 1999. 'Raidió na Life: Innovations in the use of media for language revitalization'. *International Journal of the Sociology of Language*, 140, 135–147.

County Councils' General Council, 1924. Letter to President Cosgrave, 12 January. NAI S3717.

Cumann na nGaedheal, 1927. *Programme of the Cumann na nGaedheal Party by President Cosgrave, June 1927.* NAI S7440B.

Cummins, J., 1977. 'Immersion education in Ireland: A critical review of Macnamara's findings'. *Working Papers on Bilingualism*, 13, 121–127.

Cunningham, J., 2012. '"Something that is new and strange": The 1911 Irish Trade Union Congress in Galway'. *Journal of the Galway Archaeological and Historical Society*, 64, 169–182.

Cymdeithas Yr Iaith, 1967. Welsh Language (Equal Validity) Bill 1967. Draft bill. NUIG G60/29/4/4.

Dáil Éireann, 1983. Questions to Minister for the Gaeltacht, P. Ó Tuathail, 9 November, 1820–1822. NUIG G60/29/4/5.

Darmody, M. and Daly, T., 2015. *Attitudes towards the Irish Language on the Island of Ireland.* Dublin: ESRI/Foras na Gaeilge. Available at: <https://www.esri.ie/system/files/publications/BKMNEXT294_Vol%201.pdf>.

Day, R., 2009. *Community Radio in Ireland: Participation and Multiflows of Communication.* Cresskill, NJ: Hampton Press.

Day, R., 2011. 'Radio and the Irish Language'. In: Howley, K. (ed.) *Media Interventions.* New York: Peter Lang, 210–224.

Day, R., 2021. Interview with Rosemary Day, Department of Media and Communication Studies, Mary Immaculate College, University of Limerick. Online, 15 November.

Day, R. and Walsh, J., 2020. 'Building a language community through radio in the age of social media: The case of Raidió na Life'. *Radio Journal: International Studies in Broadcast and Audio Media*, 18 (1), 79–94.

de Paor, E., 2000. 'An Seana Phobal: Déise Mumhan'. In: Ó Tuathaigh, G., Ó Laoire, L. and Ua Súilleabháin, S. (eds) *Pobal na Gaeltachta: A Scéal agus a Dhán.* Indreabhán: Cló Iar-Chonnacht/Raidió na Gaeltachta, 637–650.

de Valera, É., 1937. 'Bunreacht na hÉireann (Dréacht) – Coiste'. Dáil debates, 67 (8), 25 May. Available at: <https://www.oireachtas.ie/en/debates/debate/dail/1937-05-25/13/>.

Delap, B., 2012. *Ar an Taifead: Fís, Fuaim, Focal.* Dublin: Cois Life.

Department of Agriculture and Technical Instruction, 1927. Response to Gaeltacht Commission, 15 January. NAI S7440A.

Department of Arts, Culture and the Gaeltacht, 1993. *Leathnú an Dátheangachais i Sochaí na hÉireann: Treoirlínte don Earnáil Phoiblí do Chláracha Gníomhaíochta/Expanding Bilingualism in Irish Society: Guidelines for Action Programmes in the State Sector*. Dublin: Department of Arts, Culture and the Gaeltacht.

Department of Community, Rural and Gaeltacht Affairs, 2004. *Treoirlínte faoi Alt 12 d'Acht na dTeangacha Oifigiúla 2003/Guidelines under Section 12 of the Official Languages Act 2003*. Na Forbacha: Department of Community, Rural and Gaeltacht Affairs.

Department of Culture, Heritage and the Gaeltacht, 2018. *20-Year Strategy for the Irish Language 2010–2030: Action Plan 2018–2022*. Na Forbacha: Department of Culture, Heritage and the Gaeltacht.

Department of Defence, 1926. Response to Gaeltacht Commission. 30 September. NAI S7440A.

Department of Education and Skills, 2016. *Polasaí don Oideachas Gaeltachta 2017–2022*. Dublin: Department of Education and Skills.

Department of Education, 1927. Response to Gaeltacht Commission, 25 February. NAI S7440A.

Department of Education, 1933. *Notes for Teachers: Irish*. Dublin: Department of Education.

Department of External Affairs, 1927. Response to Gaeltacht Commission. 2 May. NAI S7440A.

Department of Finance, 1927a. 'Observations on the recommendations of the Gaeltacht Commission affecting staff'. NAI S7440A.

Department of Finance, 1927b. Observations of Finance on Local Government, Justice, Lands and Agriculture, 2 May 1927. NAI S7440A.

Department of Finance, 1965. Note on 'Consultative Council on the Restoration of the Irish Language' from S. Ó Ciosáin to Department of the Taoiseach, 12 January. NAI TAOIS/2000/6/440.

Department of Finance, 1969. Press release by Minister for Finance Charles Haughey accompanied by list of members of Comhairle na Gaeilge, 14 June. NAI TAOIS/2000/6/440.

Department of Fisheries, 1927. Response to Gaeltacht Commission, 20 October. NAI S7440A.

Department of Industry and Commerce, 1926. Response to Gaeltacht Commission, 11 November. NAI S7440A.

Department of Industry and Commerce, 1932. *Roinn Tionscail agus Tráchtála, Saorstát Éireann. Census of Population 1926: Volume VIII, Irish Language with*

Special Tables for the Gaeltacht Areas. Dublin: Stationery Office. Available at: <https://www.cso.ie/en/media/csoie/census/census1926results/volume8/C_1926__Vol_8_entire.pdf>.

Department of Justice, 1927. Response to Gaeltacht Commission, 16 April. NAI S7440A.

Department of Lands, 1938. *Seirbhísí na Gaeltachta (Roinn Tailte): Tuarasgbháil na mBliadhain 1935/36 agus 1937/38/Report of the Gaeltacht Services Division of the Department of Lands for the Years 1935–36 and 1937–38.* Dublin: Stationery Office.

Department of Local Government and Public Health, 1926. Response to Gaeltacht Commission, 11 November. NAI S7440A.

Department of Posts and Telegraphs, 1926. Response to Gaeltacht Commission, 23 September. NAI S7440A.

Department of Posts and Telegraphs, 1945. 'Report of the Departmental Committee to consider the question of special station/stations for broadcasting in Irish'. 8 August, NAI S13756.

Department of the Gaeltacht, 1958. Letter to Department of the Taoiseach, 8 September. NAI S11197B.

Department of the President, 1924. Memorandum to government about Gaeltacht, 29 March. NAI S3717.

Department of the President, 1926a. 'President Cosgrave's broadcast, 17th March 1926 on 2RN'. NAI S5111.

Department of the President, 1926b. Letter from M. McDunphy to every member of Executive Council, 9 September. NAI S7440A.

Department of the President, 1927a. Letter from M. McDunphy to Private Secretary, Department of Finance, 21 April. NAI S7440A.

Department of the President, 1927b. Letter to Department of Fisheries, 22 August. NAI S7440B.

Department of the President, 1927c. Letter to Rev. M. J. Harkin, St Columba's, Carrick, Co. Donegal, 21 May. NAI S7439.

Department of the President, 1927d. Response to Gaeltacht Commission. 29 April. NAI S7440A.

Department of the President, 1932. Letter regarding enactment of bills in Irish, 30 December. NAI S6394A.

Department of the Taoiseach, 1958. 'Visit to Taoiseach by President of Gaelic League proposed for Friday, 3rd October'. NAI S11197B.

Department of Tourism, Arts, Heritage, Gaeltacht, Sport and Media, n.d. 'Amharcóir Pleanála Teanga'. Available at: <https://dahg.maps.arcgis.com/apps/webappviewer/index.html?id=7090794ee2ca4b53bb785b84c2bd9ad8>.

Department of Tourism, Arts, Heritage, Gaeltacht, Sport and Media, 2020. 'Language planning process'. Available at: <https://www.gov.ie/en/publicat ion/63ff2-language-planning-process/>.

Department of Tourism, Arts, Heritage, Gaeltacht, Sport and Media, 2021. 'Historic day as the Official Languages Bill is ready for enactment by the President of Ireland'. Press release, 15 December. Available at: <https://www.gov.ie/en/ press-release/b82ac-historic-day-as-the-official-languages-bill-is-ready-for-enactment-by-the-president-of-ireland/>.

Dublin North-East Community Communications Co-operation Society, 1989. Letter from P. T. Mac Ruairí to S. Mac Mathúna, 30 January. NUIG G60/36/6/2.

Duchêne, A. and Heller, M., 2007. *Discourses of Endangerment: Ideology and Interest in Defence of Languages*. London: Bloomsbury.

Dún Garbhán le Gaeilge, 2021. 'Bearta an Phlean Teanga le hAchoimre Bhéarla'. Consultation document published by Waterford County Council. Available at: <https://waterfordcouncilnews.com/wp-content/uploads/2021/08/ Bearta-an-Phlean-Teanga-le-hachoimre-Bearla-24-08.pdf>.

Dunbar, C., 2021. *Síolta: Pobail Ghaeilge Úra agus na Daoine a Thóg Iad*. Dublin: Coiscéim.

Elordui, A., 2018. 'Vernaculars in the stylization of new Basque youth media iden-tities: Is there a realignment of ideological relations?' *Discourse, Context and Media*, 26, 82–90.

Executive Council, 1924. Memorandum to government, 29 March. NAI S3717.

Executive Council, 1925a. Decision taken to set up Commission under chairman-ship of Gen. Mulcahy, 2 January. NAI S3717.

Executive Council, 1925b. Gaeltacht Commission appointments made, 27 January. NAI S3717.

Fáinne an Lae, 1926. 'Supplement to *Fáinne an Lae*, Mí na Nodlag, 1926: Save the Gaeltacht'. *Fáinne an Lae/An Claidheamh Soluis*, 7 (62), 7–19.

Fennell, D., 1969. 'Iosrael in Iar-Chonnachta'. *Inniu*, 28 February.

FIAT, n.d. 'Diagostic service. Keep your Fiat driving fit: go n-éirigh [sic] an bóthar leat'. Bilingual poster. NUIG G60/29/2/2.

Fishman, J., 1991. *Reversing Language Shift: Theoretical and Empirical Foundations of Assistance to Threatened Languages*. Clevedon: Multilingual Matters.

Flynn, C., 2020. *Adult Minority Language Learning: Motivation, Identity and Target Variety*. Bristol: Multilingual Matters.

Gaeilge Iorrais, 2018. *Plean Teanga Seacht mBliana (2018–2024) do Limistéar Pleanála Teanga Mhaigh Eo Thuaidh/Seven Year Language Plan (2018–2024) for the Language Planning Area of Mayo North*. An Fód Dubh: Gaeilge Iorrais. Available at: <http://gaeilgeiorrais.ie/images/plean.pdf>.

Gael-Linn, 1993. 'Preas Ráiteas'. Press release on launch of Raidió na Life, 29 September. NUIG G60/36/11/1.

Gaeltacht Commission, 1925. *Minutes of evidence taken before Coimisiún na Gaeltachta*. Dublin: The Stationery Office.

Gaeltacht Commission, 1926. *Coimisiún na Gaeltachta: Report*. Dublin: Stationery Office.

Gaeltarra Éireann & SFADCO, 1971. 'Gníomh don Ghaeltacht: An action plan for the Gaeltacht'. Report for Minister for Finance and the Gaeltacht.

García, O., 2013. 'Ethnic identity and language policy'. In: Spolsky, B. (ed.) *The Cambridge Handbook of Language Policy*. Cambridge: Cambridge University Press, 79–99.

García, O., Flores, N. and Spotti, M., 2017. 'Introduction. Language and society: A critical post-structuralist perspective'. In García, O., Flores, N. and Spotti, M. (eds) *The Oxford Handbook of Language and Society*. New York and Oxford: Oxford University Press, 1–16.

Garvin, T., 2009. *Judging Lemass*. Dublin: Royal Irish Academy.

Government of Ireland, 1928. *Government Policy on Recommendations of the Commission*. Dublin: Stationery Office.

Government of Ireland, 1965a. *Athbheochan na Gaeilge/The Restoration of the Irish Language*. Dublin: Stationery Office.

Government of Ireland, 1965b. Minute of cabinet meeting recording that the Minister for Finance recommended A.J. O'Reilly, chief officer, An Bord Bainne and M.J. Dargan, Assistant General Manager, Aer Lingus to Comhlacht Comhairleach na Gaeilge. 5 March, NAI TAOIS/2000/6/440.

Government of Ireland, 1966. *An Páipéar Bán um Athbheochan na Gaeilge: Tuarascáil don Tréimhse dar chríoch 31 Márta, 1966/White Paper on the Restoration of the Irish Language: Progress Report for the Period Ended 31 March, 1966*. Dublin: Stationery Office.

Government of Ireland, 1969. *An Páipéar Bán um Athbheochan na Gaeilge: Tuarascáil don Tréimhse dar chríoch 31 Márta, 1968/White Paper on the Restoration of the Irish Language: Progress Report for the Period ended 31 March, 1968*. Dublin: Stationery Office.

Government of Ireland, 1980. *White Paper on Educational Development*. Dublin: Stationery Office.

Government of Ireland, 2010. *20-Year Strategy for the Irish Language 2010-2030*. Dublin: Government Publications.

Hamilton, H., 2004. *The Speckled People*. New York: Fourth Estate.

Hanly, J., 1931. *The National Ideal: A Practical Exposition of True Nationality Appertaining to Ireland*. Dublin: Dollard.

Hanly, J., 1932. 'Chapter XII – Agriculture'. *Saorstát Éireann/Irish Free State Official Handbook*. Dublin: The Talbot Press, 115–127.

Harris, J., 2008. 'Irish in the education system'. In: Nic Pháidín, C. and Ó Cearnaigh, S. (eds) *A New View of the Irish Language*. Dublin: Cois Life, 178–190.

Harris, J., Forde P., Archer P., Nic Fhearaile, S. and O'Gorman, M., 2006. *Irish in Primary schools: Long-Term National Trends in Achievement*. Dublin: Department of Education and Science.

Hickey, T., 2001. 'Mixing beginners and native speakers in minority language immersion: Who is immersing whom?' *Canadian Modern Language Review*, 57 (3), 443–474.

Higgins, M. D., 1996. Speech by Michael D. Higgins, Minister for Arts, Culture and the Gaeltacht. Teilifís na Gaeilge, Baile na hAbhann, 31 October.

Hindley, R., 1990. *The Death of the Irish Language: A Qualified Obituary*. London: Routledge.

Hindley, R., 1991. 'Defining the Gaeltacht: Dilemmas in Irish language planning'. In: Williams, C. H. (ed.) *Linguistic Minorities, Society and Territory*. Clevedon: Multilingual Matters, 66–95.

Hjarvard, S., 2013. *The Mediatization of Culture and Society*. Abingdon: Routledge.

Hoare, Q. and Nowell Smith, G. (eds), 1991. *Selections from the Prison Notebooks of Antonio Gramsci*. London: Lawrence and Wishart.

Hogan, J., 1976. 'Michael Tierney 1894–1975'. *Studies: An Irish Quarterly Review*, 65 (259), 177–191.

Horgan, J., 2001. *Irish Media: A Critical History since 1922*. London: Routledge.

Hourigan, N., 2003. *Escaping the Global Village: Media, Language and Protest*. Lanham: Lexington Books.

Houses of the Oireachtas, 2021. 'Patrick J. Hogan'. *TDs and Senators*. Dublin: Houses of the Oireachtas. Available at: <https://www.oireachtas.ie/en/members/member/Patrick-J-Hogan.D.1921-08-16/>.

Independent Radio and Television Commission, 1989. Letter from P. Appelby to P. Mac Aonghusa, 7 September. NUIG G60/36/12.

Independent Radio and Television Commission, 1990. Letter from S. Ó Conaíle to S. Mac Mathúna, 9 April. NUIG G60/36/6/3.

Independent Radio Mayo, 1988. Letter to C. Ó Raghallaigh, 20 June. NUIG G60/36/6/2.

Inniu, 1977. 'Ainm Gaeilge: cúis le maslaí agus béicíl in Aerfort Ghlaschú'. *Inniu*, 21 October. NUIG G60/29/3.

Inniu, 1979a. 'Raidió an Phobail sa Ghaeltacht'. *Inniu*, 14 December.

Inniu, 1979b. 'Raidió an Phobail: "Saor-stáisiún" do Ghaeilgeoirí'. *Inniu*, 19 October.

Inniu, 1979c. 'Raidió an Phobail'. *Inniu*, 9 November.

Inniu, 1980. 'Radio an Phobail ar ais'. *Inniu*, 10 October.

Interprovincial Lottery Corporation [Canada], 1988. Bilingual (EN/FR) lottery ticket. NUIG G60/29/2/2.

Irish Farmers' Journal, 1960. 'F.J. Hanly: Obituary'. *Irish Farmers' Journal*, 13 August, 4.

Jernudd, B. and Nekvapil, J., 2012. 'History of the field: A sketch'. In: Spolsky, B. (ed.) *The Cambridge Handbook of Language Policy*. Cambridge: Cambridge University Press, 16–36.

Johnson, N., 1993. 'Building a nation: An examination of the Irish Gaeltacht Commission Report of 1926'. *Journal of Historical Geography*, 19 (2), 157–168.

Johnson, N., 1997. 'Making space. Gaeltacht policy and the politics of identity'. In: Graham, B. (ed.) *In Search of Ireland: A Cultural Geography*. London: Routledge, 174–191.

Jones, K., 2022. 'Placemaking: Towards rethinking land-use planning and language planning for a thriving Welsh language'. In: McLeod, W., Dunbar, R., Jones, K. and Walsh, J. (eds) *Language, Policy and Territory: A Festschrift for Colin Williams*. London: Routledge, 159–180.

Jones, R. and Lewis, H., 2019. *New Geographies of Language: Language, Culture and Politics in Wales*. London: Palgrave Macmillan.

Jones, V., 2006. *A Gaelic Experiment: The Preparatory System 1926–1961 and Coláiste Moibhí*. Dublin: The Woodfield Press.

Kelly, A. 2002. *Compulsory Irish: Language and Education in Ireland*. Dublin: Irish Academic Press.

Kelly-Holmes, H., 2011. 'Sex, lies and thematising Irish: New media, old discourses?' *Journal of Language and Politics*, 10 (4), 511–534.

Keogh, D. and McCarthy, A., 2007. *The Making of the Irish Constitution 1937*. Cork: Cork University Press.

Kirby, K., 2021. Personal communication with Karen Kirby, BBC Gaeilge, 30 November.

Kirby, P., 2010. *The Celtic Tiger in Collapse: Explaining the Weaknesses of the Irish Model*. London: Palgrave Macmillan.

Kissane, C., 2007. 'From pilot to policy: The development of a community radio movement, 1989–1997'. In: Day, R. (ed.) *Bicycle Highway: Celebrating Community Radio in Ireland*. Dublin: The Liffey Press, 29–36.

Kohn, L., 1932. *The Constitution of the Irish Free State*. London: George Allen and Unwin.

'Laurence C. Moriarty', 1911. Census return for Iona Drive, Glasnevin, Dublin: Public Record Office of Ireland. Available at: <http://www.census.nationalarchives. ie/reels/nai000038263/>.

'Laurence Moriarty', 1958. Certified copy of death certificate for Laurence Moriarty, 4 November 1958. Roman Catholic church records, Diocese of Dublin. Available

at: <https://civilrecords.irishgenealogy.ie/churchrecords/images/deaths_retu
rns/deaths_1958/04370/4134070.pdf>.

Land Commission, 1927. Response to Gaeltacht Commission, 30 April. NAI
S7440A.

Lee, J. J., 1989. *Ireland 1912–1985: Politics and Society*. Cambridge: Cambridge
University Press.

Loughlin, J. and Williams, C., 2007. 'Governance and language: The intellectual foundations'. In: Williams, C. (ed.) *Language and Governance*. Cardiff: University
of Wales Press, 57–103.

Mac Airt, C., 1929. 'Our weekly causerie'. *The Derry Journal*, 18 September, 8.

Mac Aodha, B., 1969. *An tSuirbhéireacht ar Ghaeltacht na Gaillimhe/The Galway
Gaeltacht Survey*. Galway: University College Galway.

Mac Aoidh, S., 2016. 'Gaelphobail úra ag teastáil'. *Mionlach*, 8 (Samhain), 4.

Mac Cárthaigh, D. (ed.), 1998. *I dTreo Deilbhcháipéise d'Acht Teanga Éireannach*.
Dublin: Coiscéim.

Mac Cárthaigh, D., 2020. *An Ghaeilge sa Dlí*. Indreabhán: Leabhar Breac.

Mac Conghail, M., 2009. *Aghaidheanna fidil agus Púicíní: Seoirse Mac Tomáis in
Éirinn, 1923–1934*. Dublin: Sairséal Ó Marcaigh.

Mac Congáil, N. and Ó Duibhín, C., 2009. *Glórtha ón tSeanaimsir*.
Belfast: Comhaltas Uladh.

Mac Donnacha, S., 2008. 'Seirbhís chraolacháin nó seirbhís phleanála teanga?'
In: O'Connell, E., Walsh, J. and Denvir, G. (eds) *TG4@10: Deich mBliana de
TG4*. Indreabhán: Cló Iar-Chonnacht, 103–116.

Mac Donnacha, S., 2021. Personal communication with Seosamh Mac Donnacha,
National University of Ireland, Galway, 30 August.

Mac Donnacha, S., Ní Chualáin, F., Ní Shéaghdha, A. and Ní Mhainín, T., 2004.
Staid Reatha na Scoileanna Gaeltachta. Dublin: COGG.

Mac Éinrí, E., 2019. 'An Ghaeilge sa chóras oideachais i dTuaisceart Éireann'.
In: Ó hIfearnáin, T. (ed.) *An tSochtheangeolaíocht: Taighde agus Gníomh*.
Dublin: Cois Life, 211–242.

Mac Fhearghusa, P., 1986. Letter to Electricity Supply Board, 19 January. NUIG
G60/29/2/1.

Mac Giolla Chríost, D., 2005. *The Irish Language in Ireland: From Goídel to
Globalisation*. London: Routledge.

Mac Giolla Chríost, D., 2012. *Jailtacht: The Irish Language, Symbolic Power and
Political Violence in Northern Ireland, 1972–2008*. Cardiff: University of
Wales Press.

Mac Giolla Chríost, D., 2016. *The Welsh Language Commissioner in Context: Roles,
Methods and Relationships*. Cardiff: University of Wales Press.

Mac Gréil, M. and Rhatigan, F., 2009. *The Irish Language and the Irish People: Report on the Attitudes towards, Competence in and Use of the Irish Language in the Republic of Ireland in 2007–08.* Maynooth: National University of Ireland, Maynooth.

Mac Ionnrachtaigh, F., 2013. *Language, Resistance and Revival: Republic Prisoners and the Irish Language in the North of Ireland.* London: Pluto Press.

Mac Mathúna, L., 2007. *Béarla sa Ghaeilge – Cabhair Choigríche: An Códmheascadh Gaeilge/Béarla i Litríocht na Gaeilge 1600–1900.* Dublin: An Clóchomhar.

Mac Mathúna, L., 2008. 'Linguistic change and standardization'. In: Nic Pháidín, C. and Ó Cearnaigh, S. (eds) *A New View of the Irish Language.* Dublin: Cois Life, 76–92.

Mac Mathúna, S., 1976. 'An Fochoiste Cearta – Téarmaí Tagartha – Moltaí', 18 June. NUIG G60/29/4/2.

Mac Murchú, I., 2008. 'Teilifís, tionscal agus teanga'. In: O'Connell, E., Walsh, J. and Denvir, G. (eds) *TG4@10: Deich mBliana de TG4.* Indreabhán: Cló Iar-Chonnacht, 157–161.

Mac Mathúna, S., 1986. 'Bille Cearta: Freagra ó Ard-Rúnaí Chonradh na Gaeilge'. *Anois*, 23 February.

Mac Néill, E., 1924. 'The Gaelicizing of Ireland'. Memorandum to government. NAI S3717.

Mac Néill, E., 1925. Proposal to add Prof. Tomás O'Rahilly and Fr Brian Crehan to Commission, 3 March. NAI S3717.

Mac Póilin, A., 2003a. 'Irish language television in NI'. In: Ó Riagáin, D. (ed.) *Language and Law in Northern Ireland.* Belfast: Cló Ollscoil na Ríona, 88–112.

Mac Póilin, A., 2003b. 'Irish language writing in Belfast after 1900'. In: Allen, N. and Kelly, A. (eds) *The Cities of Belfast.* Dublin: Four Courts Press, 127–151.

Mac Póilin, A., 2007. 'Nua-Ghaeltacht Phobal Feirste: ceachtanna le foghlaim?' In: McLeod, W. (ed.) *Gàidhealtachdan Ùra: Leasachadh na Gàidhlig agus na Gaeilge sa Bhaile Mhòr/Nua-Ghaeltachtaí: Cur chun cinn na Gàidhlig agus na Gaeilge sa Chathair.* Edinburgh: Celtic and Scottish Studies, Edinburgh University, 31–60.

Mac Póilin, A., 2018. 'The Pobal Feirste Neo-Gaeltacht: Lessons to learn?' In: Ní Bhaoill, R. (ed.) *Our Tangled Speech: Essays on Language and Culture.* Belfast: Ulster Historical Founadation and Ultach Trust, 240–265.

Mac Síomóin, T., 2006. *Ó Mhársa go Magla: Straitéis Nua don Ghaeilge.* Dublin: Coiscéim.

MacBride, S., 1980. *Communication and Society Today and Tomorrow, Many Voices One World, Towards a New More Just and More Efficient World Information and Communication Order.* Paris: UNESCO. Available at: <https://unesdoc. unesco.org/ark:/48223/pf0000040066>.

Macnamara, J., 1966. *Bilingualism and Primary Education: A Study of Irish Experience*. Edinburgh: Edinburgh University Press.

MacNelis, M., 1926. Letter to President Cosgrave. 13 December. NAI S7349.

Mag Eacháin, C., 2014. *Téarmaíocht Ghaeilge na hAthbheochana*. Dublin: Cois Life.

Mag Fhearraigh, P., 1987. Letter to First National Building Society, 14 January. NUIG G60 29/2/2.

Martin, F. X., 1980. 'Introduction'. In: Martin, F. X. (ed.) and Tierney, M. *Eoin MacNeill: Scholar and Man of Action, 1867–1945*. Oxford: Clarendon Press, vii–xiv.

Martin, F. X. (ed.) and Tierney, M., 1980. *Eoin MacNeill: Scholar and Man of Action, 1867–1945*. Oxford: Clarendon Press.

Mayo News, 1979. 'Pirate radio station for election special'. *Mayo News*, 15 December.

McCartney, D., 2009. 'Tierney, Michael'. Dictionary of Irish Biography. Dublin: Royal Irish Academy. Available at: <https://www.dib.ie/biography/tierney-michael-a8556>.

McCullagh, D., 1998. *A Makeshift Majority: The First Inter-Party Government, 1948–1951*. Dublin: IPA.

McCullagh, D., 2010. *The Reluctant Taoiseach: A Biography of John A. Costello*. Dublin: Gill and Macmillan.

McGilligan, P., 1924. 'Private business – Unemployment problem'. Dáil debates, 9 (6), 30 October. Available at: <https://www.oireachtas.ie/en/debates/debate/dail/1924-10-30/15/>.

McManus, R., 2021. *Dublin, 1910–1940: Shaping the City and Suburbs* (2nd edn). Dublin: Four Courts Press.

McMorrow, C., 2021. 'Why the housing crisis poses a threat to the Gaeltacht'. *Prime Time*, RTÉ television, 8 October. Available at: <https://www.rte.ie/news/primetime/2021/1007/1252390-housing-crisis-gaeltacht/>

Mhic Mhathúna, M. and Mac Con Iomaire, M., 2022. 'Early childhood education and care provision through the medium of the Irish language'. In: Hayes, N. & Walsh, T. (eds) *Early Childhood Education and Care in Ireland: Charting a Century of Developments (1921–2021)*. Oxford: Peter Lang, 75–100.

Mills, M., 1985. Speech by Ombudsman at 'Mórthionól' [Large assembly of CnaG], n.d. NUIG G60/29/2/1.

Moal, S., Ó Murchadha, N. and Walsh, J., 2018. 'New Speakers and language in the media: Audience design in Breton and Irish broadcast media'. In: Smith-Christmas, C., Ó Murchadha, N., Hornsby, M. and Moriarty, M. (eds) *New Speakers of Minority Languages: Linguistic Ideologies and Practices*. London: Palgrave Macmillan, 189–212.

Moriarty, M., 2015. *Globalizing Language Policy and Planning: An Irish Language Perspective*. London: Palgrave Macmillan.

Mulcahy, R., 2009. *My Father, the General: Richard Mulcahy and the Military History of the Revolution*. Dublin: Liberties Press.

Muller, J., 2010. *Language and Conflict in Northern Ireland and Canada: A Silent War*. Houndmills: Palgrave Macmillan.

Muller, J., 2022. 'Lessons learned, lessons ignored: The continuing road to an Irish Language Act in Northern Ireland'. In: McLeod, W., Dunbar, R., Jones, K. and Walsh, J. (eds) *Language, Policy and Territory: A Festschrift for Colin Williams*. London: Routledge, 325–344.

Murphy, J. A., 1976. 'Identity change in the Republic of Ireland'. *Études irlandaises*, 1, 143–158.

National University of Ireland, Galway, 2020. *Shared Vision, Shaped by Values: Strategy 2020–2025*. Galway: NUI Galway. Available at: <https://www.nuigalway.ie/media/strategicplanning/NUI-Galway-Strategy-2020-2025---Shared-Vision,-Shaped-by-Values.pdf>.

Nekvapil, J., 2006. 'From language planning to language management'. *Sociolinguistica*, 20, 92–104.

New Departures Media, 2021. *Uimhir 6*. Television programme, TG4, Baile na hAbhann, 14 April. Available at: <https://www.tg4.ie/ga/player/catagoir/faisneis/?series=Uimhir%206&genre=Faisneis>.

Newstalk, 2021. 'The Pat Kenny Show highlights: Irish language requirement for Gardaí'. Radio interview, Newstalk, 16 December. Available at: <https://www.newstalk.com/podcasts/highlights-from-the-pat-kenny-show/irish-language-requirement-for-gardai>.

Ní Bhaoill, R., 2010. *Ulster Gaelic Voices: Bailiúchán Doegen 1931*. Belfast: ULTACH Trust.

Ní Bhrádaigh, E., 2008a. 'Emergence and evolution of entrepreneurship in the Galway Gaeltacht'. Unpublished PhD thesis, Trinity College Dublin.

Ní Bhrádaigh, E., 2008b. 'Entrepreneurship capital emerging in a coastal community'. *International Journal of Entrepreneurship and Small Business*, 6 (3), 290–406.

Ní Bhrádaigh, E., 2008c. 'TG4@10: an léargas fiontraíochta'. In: O'Connell, E., Walsh, J. and Denvir, G. (eds) *TG4@10: Deich mBliana de TG4*. Indreabhán: Cló Iar-Chonnacht, 137–156.

Ní Bhrádaigh, E., McCarron, S. G., Walsh, J. and Duffy, P., 2007. 'Using GIS to map the Gaeltacht'. *Irish Geography*, 40 (1), 98–108.

Ní Chionnaith, Í., 2008. 'Fíorú aislinge: cuimhní cinn agus smaoine feachtasóra'. In: O'Connell, E., Walsh, J. and Denvir, G. (eds) *TG4@10: Deich mBliana de TG4*. Indreabhán: Cló Iar-Chonnacht, 27–41.

Ní Chuaig, N., Ó Brolcháin, C., Ní Chlochasaigh, K. and Ó Ceallaigh, T. J., 2021. *Staidéar ar Theaghlaigh atá ag Tógáil a gClann le Gaeilge laistigh de na Limistéir Oifigiúla Gaeltachta*. An Cheathrú Rua: Tuismitheoirí na Gaeltachta.

Ní Dhiorbháin, A., Mhic Mhathúna, M. and Ó Duibhir, P., 2021. 'Parents' experiences of a language-focused home visiting scheme in Ireland'. *Journal of Home Language Research*, 4 (1), 3, 1–14.

Ní Dhúda, L., 2017. 'Language management and language managers: Who are the Irish language managers in *Breacbhaile*?' *International Journal of the Sociology of Language*, 245, 217–243.

Ní Ghallachair, A., 2008. 'Súil(e) eile: srian nó féidearthachtaí?' In: O'Connell, E., Walsh, J. and Denvir, G. (eds) *TG4@10: Deich mBliana de TG4*. Indreabhán: Cló Iar-Chonnacht, 117–122.

Ní Ghallchobhair, F., 2014. *Ár dTéarmaí Féin*. Dublin: Cois Life.

Ní Ghréacháin, B., 2021. Personal communication with B. Ní Ghréacháin, Senior Executive, Gaeloideachas, 15 December.

Ní Mhunghaile, L., 2015. 'Pádraig Ó Siochfhradha: samhlú an náisiúin agus Coimisiún na Gaeltachta'. In: Ní Loingsigh, D., Ní Mhunghaile, L. and uí Ógáin, R. (eds) *'Rí na Gréine': Aistí i gCuimhne ar An Seabhac*. Dublin: An Cumann le Béaloideas Éireann, 23–46.

Ní Shéaghdha, A., 2010. *Taighde ar dhea-chleachtais bhunscoile i dtaca le saibhriú/ sealbhú agus sóisialú teanga do dhaltaí arb í an Ghaeilge a gcéad teanga*. Dublin: An Chomhairle um Oideachais Gaeltachta agus Gaelscolaíochta.

Ní Thuairisg, L. and Ó Duibhir, P., 2019. *Teacht in Inmhe: Tuarascáil taighde do Tuismitheoirí na Gaeltachta agus Teacht Aniar arna mhaoiniú ag an gComhairle um Oideachas Gaeltachta agus Gaelscolaíochta*. Dublin: SEALBHÚ, Dublin City University. Available at: <https://www.cogg.ie/wp-content/uploads/Tea cht-in-Inmhe.pdf>.

Ní Uallacháin, P., 2003. *A Hidden Ulster: People, Songs and Traditions of Oriel*. Dublin: Four Courts Press.

Nic Eoin, M., 1996. 'Pidgin, Gaelscoilis, Créól agus leaganacha cainte eile'. *Lá*, 1 February, 18.

Nic Eoin, M., 2005. *Trén bhFearann Breac: An Díláithriú Cultúir agus Nualitríocht na Gaeilge*. Dublin: Cois Life.

Nic Eoin, M., 2018. Interview with Máirín Nic Eoin on 'Dúiseacht na hAislinge'. Raidió na Life, 25 December. Available at: <https://soundcloud.com/rnl/rai dio-na-life-duiseacht-na-haislinge>.

Nic Eoin, M., 2021. Interview with Máirín Nic Eoin, Dublin, 25 September.

Nic Eoin, M. and Nic Dhonnchadha, A. (eds), 2008. *Ar an gCoigríoch: Díolaim Litríochta ar Scéal na hImirce*. Indreabhán: Cló Iar-Chonnacht.

Nic Fhionnachtaigh, M., 2019. Interview with Máire Nic Fhionnachtaigh, Finance and Administration Manager, Raidió Fáilte, Belfast, 6 July.

Nic Pháidín, C., 2008. 'Corpus planning for Irish: Dictionaries and terminology'. In: Nic Pháidín, C. and Ó Cearnaigh, S. (eds) *A New View of the Irish Language.* Dublin: Cois Life, 93–107.

Nic Shuibhne, N., 1998a. 'Stádas dlíthiúil na Gaeilge in Éirinn faoi láthair'. In: Mac Cárthaigh, D. (ed.) *I dTreo Deilbhcháipéise d'Acht Teanga Éireannach.* Dublin: Coiscéim, 1–7.

Nic Shuibhne, N., 1998b. *Cearta Teanga mar Fhíorchearta Daonna?/Language Rights as Human Rights!* Dublin: Dúid na Gaeilge.

North Dublin Community Radio, 1983. 'North Dublin Community Radio 890 kHz/Radio Pobal [sic] Thuaisceart BÁC'. Letter to newspaper editors, n.d. NUIG G60/36/6/2.

Northern Ireland Statistics and Research Agency, 2012. *Census 2011 Key Statistics for Northern Ireland.* Belfast: NISRA. Available at: <https://www.nisra.gov.uk/sites/nisra.gov.uk/files/publications/2011-census-results-key-statistics-north ern-ireland-report-11-december-2012.pdf>.

Northern Ireland Statistics and Research Agency, 2014. *Northern Ireland Census 2011 Key Statistics Summary Report.* Belfast: NISRA. Available at: <https://www.nisra.gov.uk/sites/nisra.gov.uk/files/publications/2011-census-results-key-statistics-summary-report.pdf>.

Nuacht RTÉ, 2021. 'Litreacha meabhrúcháin scríofa ag daltaí Gaelscoileanna'. Nuacht RTÉ, 15 December. Available at: <https://www.rte.ie/news/nua cht/2021/1215/1266850-litreacha-meabhruchain-scriofa-ag-daltai-gaelsco ileanna/>.

Ó Baoill, D. P., 1986. *Lárchanúint don Ghaeilge.* Dublin: Institiúid Teangeolaíochta Éireann.

Ó Baoill, D. P., 2000. '"Athchaighdeanú" na Nua-Ghaeilge'. In: Ó Cearúil, M. (ed.) *An Aimsir Óg (Cuid a Dó).* Dublin: Coiscéim, 128–140.

Ó Broin, L., 1986. *Just Like Yesterday: An Autobiography.* Dublin: Gill and Macmillan.

Ó Broin, E., 2019. *Home: Why Public Housing is the Answer.* Dublin: Merrion Press.

Ó Buachalla, S., 1994. 'Structural inequalities and the state's policy on the Irish language in the education system'. *Studies in Education*, 10 (1), 1–6.

Ó Cadhla, S., 2011. *An tSlat Féithleoige: Ealaíona an Dúchais 1800–2000.* Indreabhán: Cló Iar-Chonnacht.

Ó Caoimh, P., 2019. *Richard Mulcahy: From the Politics of War to the Politics of Peace, 1913–1924.* Dublin: Irish Academic Press.

Ó Caollaí, É., 2021. 'Call for Leaving Cert Irish proposal to be set aside'. *The Irish Times*, 3 November. Available at: <https://www.irishtimes.com/news/educat ion/call-for-leaving-cert-irish-proposals-to-be-set-aside-1.4718639>.

Ó Caollaí, M., 1979. 'Raidió an Phobail – Tuarascáil'. Report, 10 October. NUIG G60/36/10.

Ó Caollaí, M., 1980. Handwritten note, 6 March. NUIG G60/29/4/7.

Ó Caollaí, M., 1982. 'Craoladh Tráchtála'. Memorandum, n.d. NUIG G60/36/6/2.

Ó Caollaí, M., 1983. 'Local broadcasting: Non-stop pop or community development'. *Treoir: Iris Oifigiúil Chomhaltas Ceoltóirí Éireann*, 15 (2/3), 8–11. NUIG G60/6/6/2.

Ó Cearúil, M. 1999. *Bunreacht na hÉireann: A Study of the Irish Text*. Dublin: Stationery Office.

Ó Cearúil, M., 2002. *Bunreacht na hÉireann: Two Texts or Two Constitutions?* Dublin: Ireland Institute.

Ó Céidigh, P., 2018. *Socio-economic Profile of the Seven Gaeltacht Areas in Ireland: November 2018*. Maynooth: Maynooth University.

Ó Ceithearnaigh, P., 2006. 'An tAcht um Pleanáil agus Forbairt 2000 mar a feidhmíodh é ó thaobh na Gaeilge de i gceantar an Spidéil agus na bhForbacha'. Unpublished MA thesis, Dublin City University.

Ó Ciardha, P., 2008. 'Súil siar ar an "tSúil Eile"'. In O'Connell, E., Walsh, J. and Denvir, G. (eds) *TG4@10: Deich mBliana de TG4*. Indreabhán: Cló Iar-Chonnacht, 17–19.

Ó Ciardha, P., 2021. 'Athbhreithniú iomlán ag teastáil ar na hathruithe atá beartaithe ar scrúdú Gaeilge na hArdteiste – tuarascáil. *Tuairisc.ie*, 21 October'. Available at: <https://tuairisc.ie/athbhreithniu-iomlan-ag-teastail-ar-na-hathruithe-ata-beartaithe-ar-scrudu-gaeilge-na-hardteiste-tuarascail/>.

Ó Cinnéide, M., Keane, M. and Cawley, M., 1985. 'Industrialization and linguistic change among Gaelic-speaking communities in the west of Ireland'. *Language Planning and Language Problems*, 9 (1), 3–15.

Ó Cinnéide, M., Mac Donnacha, S. and Ní Chonghaile, S., 2001. *Polasaithe agus Cleachtais Eagaíochtaí Éagsúla le Feidhm sa Ghaeltacht*. Galway: NUI Galway.

Ó Cinnéide, M. and Ní Chonghaile, S., 1996. *An Ghaeilge san Earnáil Phoiblí i gCeantar na Gaillimhe: Tuarascáil do Bhord na Gaeilge agus d'Údarás na Gaeltachta*. Galway: University College Galway.

Ó Ciosáin, É., 1998. 'Scéalta i mbarr bata agus pictiúir as an spéir'. *Léachtaí Cholm Cille*, xxviii, 7–24.

Ó Ciosáin, É., 2018. Interview with Éamon Ó Ciosáin on 'Dúiseacht na hAislinge'. Raidió na Life, 25 December. Available at: <https://soundcloud.com/rnl/raidio-na-life-duiseacht-na-haislinge>.

Ó Ciosáin, S., 1988. 'Language planning and Irish'. *Language, Culture and Curriculum*, 1 (3), 263–280.

Ó Cuaig, S., 1969. *The Connacht Tribune*, 17 October, 10.

Ó Cuív, B., 1950. 'The Gaeltacht – Past and present'. In: Ó Cuív, B. (ed.) *Irish Dialects and Irish-Speaking Districts*. Dublin: Dublin Institute for Advanced Studies, 7–32.

Ó Cuív, É., 1998. 'Keynote address by Éamon Ó Cuív, TD, Minister of State, Department of Arts, Heritage, Gaeltacht and the Islands on the occasion of the opening of the International Conference on Language Legislation at Killiney, County Dublin, Ireland, 15 October 1998'. *Comhdháil Idirnáisiúnta ar Chearta Teanga/International Conference on Language Legislation/Conférence internationale sur la législation de la langue: Tuarascáil ar Imeachtaí na Comhdhála/Conférence Proceedings/Compte-rendu de conférence*, 7 12.

Ó Cuív, É., 2003. 'Official Languages Bill 2002: Second stage'. Dáil debates, 22 May. Available at: <https://www.oireachtas.ie/en/debates/debate/dail/2003-05-22/7/>.

Ó Cuív, É., 2021. Interviewed by Máirtín Mac Donncha. *Comhrá*. TG4, 2 September.

Ó Curraoin, S., 1976. Letter to S. Mac Mathúna, 4 November. NUIG G60/29/4/7.

Ó Drisceoil, F., 2007. 'Raidió na Life: raidió na réabhlóide'. In: Day, R. (ed.) *Bicycle Highway: Celebrating Community Radio in Ireland*. Dublin: The Liffey Press, 173–178.

Ó Drisleáin, M., 2012. 'Tuilleadh scéalta agus seanchais ó chnuasach an Dr. Piaras de Hindeberg, S.J.' *An Linn Bhuí: Iris Ghaeltacht na nDéise*, 16. Crosspatrick and Dublin, Leabhair na Linne, 120–142.

Ó Duibhir, P., 2018. *Immersion Education: Lessons from a Minority Language Context*. Bristol: Multilingual Matters.

Ó Dúlacháin, C., 1998. 'Acht Teanga nó Acht Cearta'. In: Mac Cárthaigh, D. (ed.) *I dTreo Deilbhcháipéise d'Acht Teanga Éireannach*. Dublin: Coiscéim, 55–61.

Ó Faoláin, C., Ó Drisleáin, M. and Breathnach, C., 2018. *Plean Teanga na nDéise 2018–2024*. An Rinn: Comhlacht Forbartha na nDéise.

Ó Fathartaigh, M. and Weeks, L., 2021. *Birth of a State: The Anglo-Irish Treaty*. Dublin: Irish Academic Press.

Ó Fiaich, T., 1964. Letter from Fr T. Ó Fiaich, chair, An Comhchoiste Sealadach Feidhmiúcháin to S. Lemass, Taoiseach, 24 November. NUIG G60/29/4/2.

Ó Fiannachta, M., 2017. Interview with Muiris Ó Fiannachta, manager, Raidió na Life, Dublin, 1 December.

Ó Flatharta, P., 2007. *Struchtúr Oideachais na Gaeltachta*. Dublin: Comhairle um Oideachas Gaeilge agus Gaeltachta.

Ó Flathartaigh, M., 2008. 'Cumann na nGaedheal, sea fishing and west Galway, 1923–32'. *Irish Historical Studies*, 36 (141), 72–90.

Ó Frighil, É., 1921. *Handbook of Irish Terms for the Use of Public Bodies*. Dublin: Irish County Councils General Office.

Ó Gadhra, N., 1989a. *An Chéad Dáil Éireann (1919–1921) (agus an Ghaeilge).* Dublin: Coiscéim.

Ó Gadhra, N., 1989b. *An Ghaeltacht (Oifigiúil) – agus 1992?* Dublin: Coiscéim.

Ó Gairbhí, S. T., 2018. *Súil Eile.* Dublin: Cois Life.

Ó Giollagáin, C., 2006. 'Gnéithe de stair theorainn na Gaeltachta: coimhlint idir dhá riachtanas'. In Doyle, A. and Ní Laoire, S. (eds) *Aistí ar an Nua-Ghaeilge in Ómós do Bhreandán Ó Buachalla.* Dublin: Cois Life, 95–116.

Ó Giollagáin, C., 2014. 'From revivalist to undertaker: New developments in official policies and attitudes towards Ireland's "first language"'. *Language Policy and Language Planning*, 38 (2), 101–127.

Ó Giollagáin, C. and Charlton, M., 2015. *Nuashonrú ar an Staidéar Cuimsitheach Teangeolaíoch ar Úsáid na Gaeilge sa Ghaeltacht: 2006–2011.* Na Forbacha: Údarás na Gaeltachta.

Ó Giollagáin, C., Mac Donnacha, S., Ní Chualáin, F., Ní Shéaghdha, A. and O'Brien, M., 2007a. *Comprehensive Linguistic Study of the Use of Irish in the Gaeltacht: Principal Findings and Recommendations.* Dublin: Department of Community, Rural and Gaeltacht Affairs.

Ó Giollagáin, C., Mac Donnacha, S., Ní Chualáin, F., Ní Shéaghdha, A. and O'Brien, M., 2007b. *Staidéar Cuimsitheach Teangeolaíoch ar Úsáid na Gaeilge sa Ghaeltacht: Tuarascáil Chríochnaitheach.* Dubin: Stationery Office.

Ó Glaisne, R., 1982. *Raidió na Gaeltachta.* Indreabhán: Cló Chois Fharraige.

Ó hAirt, D., 1988. *Díolaim Dhéiseach.* Dublin: Royal Irish Academy.

Ó hIfearnáin, T., 2006. *Beartas Teanga.* Dublin: Coiscéim.

Ó hIfearnáin, T., 2007. 'Raising children to be bilingual in the Gaeltacht: Language preference and practice'. *International Journal of Bilingual Education and Bilingualism*, 10 (4), 510–528.

Ó hIfearnáin, T., 2008. 'Endangering language vitality through institutional development: Ideology, authority and official standard Irish in the Gaeltacht'. In: King, K. A., Schilling-Estes, N., Fogle, L, Lou, J. J. & Soukup, B. (eds) *Sustaining Linguistic Diversity: Endangered and Minority Languages and Language Varieties.* Washington, DC: Georgetown University Press, 113–128.

Ó hIfearnáin, T., 2013. 'Family language policy, first language Irish speaker attitudes and community based response to language shift'. *Journal of Multilingual and Multicultural Development*, 34 (4), 348–365.

Ó Huallacháin, C., 1994. *The Irish and Irish: A Sociolinguistic Analysis of the Relationship between a People and their Language.* Dublin: Assisi Press.

Ó Laighin, P., 2003. *Acht na Gaeilge – Acht ar Strae: Léirmheas ar Acht na dTeangacha Oifigiúla 2003.* Dublin: Coiscéim.

Ó Laoire, L., 2004. 'Níl sí doiligh a iompar/No load to carry: A personal response to the current situation of Irish'. In: Mac Murchaidh (ed.) *Who Needs Irish? Reflections on the Importance of the Irish Language Today*. Dublin: Veritas, 46–63.

Ó Laoire, M., 2002. 'An Ghaeilge sa chóras oideachais: polasaí, pleanáil agus teagasc'. In: Ó hUiginn, R. (ed.) *Curaclam na Gaeilge: Léachtaí Cholm Cille XXXII*. Maynooth: An Sagart, 74–104.

Ó Laoire, M., 2004. *Siollabais Chumarsáide na Gaeilge*. Dublin: Coiscéim.

Ó Laoire, M., 2006. 'Múineadh na Gaeilge agus na nuatheangacha eile: polasaí agus pleanáil teanga'. In: Gallagher A. and Ó Laoire, M. (eds) *Language Education in Ireland: Current Practice and Future Needs/Teagasc na dTeangacha in Éirinn: Cleachtas an Lae Inniu agus Riachtanais an Lae Amáraigh*. Dublin: Irish Association for Applied Linguistics, 1–23.

Ó Laoire, M., 2019. 'An Ghaeilge sa chóras oideachais: pleanáil sealbhaithe agus curaclam'. In: Ó hIfearnáin, T. (ed.) *An tSochtheangeolaíocht: Taighde agus Gníomh*. Dublin: Cois Life, 243–264.

Ó Macháin, P., 2019. 'Ón mBéarla go Gaelainn na nDéise: an Cadhlach agus an Tóibíneach'. *An Linn Bhuí: Iris Ghaeltacht na nDéise*, 23. Crosspatrick and Dublin, Leabhair na Linne, 85–97.

Ó Madagáin, B., 1999. 'Irish: A difficult birth'. In: Foley, T. (ed.) *From Queen's College to National University: Essays on the Academic History of QCG/UCG/ NUI, Galway*. Dublin: Four Courts Press, 344–359.

Ó Máille, T., 1990. *Stádas na Gaeilge: Dearcadh Dlíthiúil/The Status of the Irish Language: A Legal Perspective*. Dublin: Bord na Gaeilge.

Ó Míleadha, P., 1926. 'Seanchas Shliabh gCua'. *Béaloideas*, 6, 2, 169–259.

Ó Murchadha, N., 2019. *An Ghaeilge sa Nua-Aoiseacht Dhéanach: An Meon i leith Éagsúlacht Teanga sa Ghaeilge*. Indreabhán: Cló Iar-Chonnacht.

Ó Murchadha, N. and Flynn, C., 2018. 'Language educators' regard for variation in late modernity: Perceptions of linguistic variation in minority contexts'. *Journal of Sociolinguistics*, 22 (3), 288–311.

Ó Murchú, H., 2007. 'Cur chun cinn na Gàidhlig agus na Gaeilge sa chathair'. In: McLeod, W. (ed.) *Gàidhealtachdan Ùra: Leasachadh na Gàidhlig agus na Gaeilge sa Bhaile Mhòr/Nua-Ghaeltachtaí: Cur chun cinn na Gàidhlig agus na Gaeilge sa Chathair*. Edinburgh: Celtic and Scottish Studies, Edinburgh University, 5–18.

Ó Murchú, H., 2008. *More Facts about Irish*. Dublin: European Bureau for Lesser Used Languages.

Ó Murchú, H., 2014. *More Facts about Irish: Volume 2*. Dublin: European Bureau for Lesser Used Languages.

Ó Murchú, M., 1985. *The Irish Language*. Dublin: Government of Ireland.

Ó Murchú, M., 2006 [2002]. *Ag Dul ó Chion? Cás na Gaeilge 1952–2002.* Dublin: Coiscéim.

Ó Murchú, S., 2018. Interview with Seosamh Ó Murchú on 'Dúiseacht na hAislinge'. Raidió na Life, 25 December. Available at: <https://soundcloud.com/rnl/raidio-na-life-duiseacht-na-haislinge>.

Ó Néill, E., 2005. 'Éirigh as do shuan!' *Lá*, 4 February, 1.

Ó Néill, E., 2019. Interview with Eoghan Ó Néill, journalist, Raidió Fáilte. Belfast, 6 July.

Ó Néill, E., 2021. Personal communication with Eoghan Ó Néill, journalist, Raidió Fáilte, 1 October.

Ó Riagáin, D., 2011. 'The concept of Gaeltacht: Time to revisit?' In: Kirk, J. M. & Ó Baoill, D. P. (eds) *Sustaining Minority Language Communities: Northern Ireland, the Republic of Ireland, and Scotland.* Belfast: Cló Ollscoil na Banríona, 89–95.

Ó Riagáin, P., 1971. *The Gaeltacht Studies: A Development Plan for the Gaeltacht.* Dublin: An Foras Forbartha.

Ó Riagáin, P., 1982. 'Athrú agus buanú teanga sa Ghaeltacht'. *Taighde Sochtheangeolaíochta agus Teangeolaíochta sa Ghaeltacht: Riachtanais an Lae Inniu.* Dublin: Institiúid Teangeolaíochta Éireann, 3–28.

Ó Riagáin, P., 1988. 'Bilingualism in Ireland 1973–1983: An overview of national sociolinguistic surveys'. *International Journal of the Sociology of Language*, 70, 29–52.

Ó Riagáin, P., 1992. *Language Maintenance and Language Shift as Strategies of Social Reproduction: Irish in the Corca Dhuibhne Gaeltacht 1926–1986.* Dublin: Instititiúid Teangeolaíochta Éireann.

Ó Riagáin, P., 1997. *Language Policy and Social Reproduction: Ireland 1893–1993.* Oxford: Clarendon Press.

Ó Riagáin, P., 2007. 'Relationships between attitude to Irish and social class, religion and national identity in the Republic of Ireland and Northern Ireland'. *International Journal of Bilingual Education and Bilingualism*, 10 (4), 369–393.

Ó Riagáin, P., 2012. 'Teanga, féiniúlacht agus an dearcadh náisiúnta'. In: Ó hIfearnáin, T. and Ní Neachtain, M. (eds) *An tSochtheangeolaíocht: Feidhm agus Tuairisc.* Dublin: Cois Life, 111–128.

Ó Riagáin, P., 2018. *Measures of Language Proficiency in Censuses and Surveys: A Comparative Analysis and Assessment.* Cham: Palgrave Macmillan.

Ó Riagáin, P. and Ó Gliasáin, M., 1994. *National Survey on Language Use: Preliminary Report.* Dublin: Institiúid Teangeolaíochta Éireann.

Ó Riain, S., 1994. *Pleanáil Teanga in Éirinn 1919–1985.* Dublin: Carbad/Bord na Gaeilge.

Ó Sé, M. M., 1998. 'An gá atá le hAcht Chearta Teanga in Éirinn'. In: Mac Cárthaigh, D. (ed.) *I dTreo Deilbhcháipéise d'Acht Teanga Éireannach*. Dublin: Coiscéim, 49–54.

Ó Torna, C., 2005. *Cruthú na Gaeltachta: 1893–1922*. Dublin: Cois Life.

Ó Tuathaigh, G., 1990. *The Development of the Gaeltacht as a Bilingual Entity* (Occasional Paper 8). Dublin: Institiúid Teangeolaíochta Éireann.

Ó Tuathaigh, G., 2008. 'The state and the Irish language: An historical perspective'. In: Nic Pháidín, C. and Ó Cearnaigh, S. (eds) *A New View of the Irish Language*. Dublin: Cois Life, 26–42.

Ó Tuathaigh, G., 2011. 'An stat, an fhéiniúlacht náisiúnta agus an teanga: cás na hÉireann'. In: Mac Cormaic, B. (ed.) *Féiniulacht, Cultúr agus Teanga i Ré an Domhandaithe*. Dublin: Coiscéim, 76–112.

Ó Tuathaigh, G., 2021. 'An Gúm: comhthéacs a bhunaithe'. In: Coilféir, M. (ed.) *An Scéim: An Gúm 1926–2016. Cnuasach Aistí*. Dublin: An Gúm, 1–18.

Ó Tuathail [O'Toole], P., 1986. Letter to Ned O'Keeffe TD, 8 April. NUIG G60/29/4/8.

Ó Tuathail, S., 2002. *Gaeilge agus Bunreacht*. Dublin: Coiscéim.

O'Connell, E., Walsh, J. and Denvir, G., 2008. 'Réamhrá'. In: O'Connell, E., Walsh, J. and Denvir, G. (eds) *TG4@10: Deich mBliana de TG4*. Indreabhán: Cló Iar-Chonnacht, 9–16.

O'Connor, T., Mortell, P. and de Róiste, Á., 2007. *Gaeltacht na nDéise: Anailís Riachtanas Socheacnamaíoch agus Cultúrtha/A Socio-economic and Cultural Needs Analysis*. Cork: CIT Press.

O'Hare, F., 2019. Interview with Fergus O'Hare, former manager, Raidió Fáilte, Belfast, 6th July.

O'Leary, P., 1994. *The Prose Literature of the Gaelic Revival, 1881–1921: Ideology and Innovation*. University Park: Pennsylvania State University Press.

O'Rourke, B. and Pujolar, J. (eds), 2019. *From New Speaker to Speaker: Outcomes, Reflections and Policy Recommendations from COST Action IS1306 on New Speakers in a Multilingual Europe: Opportunities and Challenges*. Newcastle Emlyn: IAITH, Welsh Centre for Language Planning.

O'Rourke, B., 2011. 'Whose language is it? Struggles for language ownership in an Irish language classroom'. *Journal of Language, Identity and Education*, 10 (5), 327–345.

O'Rourke, B., 2015. Language revitalisation models in minority language contexts: Tensions between ideologies of authenticity and anonymity'. *Anthropological Journal of European Cultures*, 24 (1), 63–82.

O'Rourke, B. and Walsh, J., 2015. 'New speakers of Irish: Shifting boundaries across time and space'. *International Journal of the Sociology of Language*, 231, 63–83.

O'Rourke, B. and Walsh, J., 2020. *New Speakers of Irish in the Global Context: New Revival?* Abingdon: Routledge.

O'Rourke, B., Pujolar, J. and Frekko, S., 2019a. 'New speakers: Umbrella term, analytical concept or lens?' In: O'Rourke, B. and Pujolar, J. (eds) *From New Speaker to Speaker: Outcomes, Reflections and Policy Recommendations from COST Action IS1306 on New Speakers in a Multilingual Europe: Opportunities and Challenges.* Newcastle Emlyn: IAITH, Welsh Centre for Language Planning, 25–27.

O'Rourke, B., Pujolar, J. and Frekko, S., 2019b. 'Researching new speakers and debating the concept'. In: O'Rourke, B. and Pujolar, J. (eds) *From New Speaker to Speaker: Outcomes, Reflections and Policy Recommendations from COST Action IS1306 on New Speakers in a Multilingual Europe: Opportunities and Challenges.* Newcastle Emlyn: IAITH, Welsh Centre for Language Planning, 14–19.

O'Rourke, B., Pujolar, J. and Ramallo, F., 2015. 'New speakers of minority languages: The challenging opportunity – Foreword'. *International Journal of the Sociology of Language*, 231, 1–20.

O'Rourke, B., Pujolar, J. and Walsh, J., 2017. 'Language education for new speakers'. In: McCarty, T. and May, S. (eds) *Language Policy and Political Issues in Education. Encyclopedia of Language and Education* (3rd edn). New York: Springer, 273–284.

O'Rourke, S., 1979. 'We're doing what RTÉ should do'. *Sunday Press*, 21 October.

Office of the Ombudsman, 1989. *Annual Report of the Ombudsman.* Dublin: Office of the Ombudsman.

Office of the Ombudsman, 1996. *Annual Report of the Ombudsman.* Dublin: Office of the Ombudsman.

Office of the Ombudsman, 1997. *Annual Report of the Ombudsman.* Dublin: Office of the Ombudsman.

Office of the Ombudsman, 1998. *Annual Report of the Ombudsman.* Dublin: Office of the Ombudsman.

Office of the Ombudsman, 1999. *Annual Report of the Ombudsman.* Dublin: Office of the Ombudsman.

Oifig an Choimisinéara Teanga, 2020. *Tuarascáil Bhliantúil/Annual Report 2019.* An Spidéal: Oifig an Choimisinéara Teanga.

Otheguy, R., García, O. and Reid, W., 2015. 'Clarifying translanguaging and deconstructing named languages: A perspective from linguistics'. *Applied Linguistics Review*, 6, 281–307.

Péterváry, T., Ó Curnáin, B., Ó Giollagáin, C. and Sheahan, J., 2014. *Iniúchadh ar an gcumas dátheangach: an sealbhú teanga i measc ghlúin óg na Gaeltachta.* Dublin: COGG.

Petit, K., 2016. 'Successful learners of Irish as an L2: Motivation, identity and linguistic *mudes*'. *Studia Celtica Posnaniensia*, 1, 39–57. Available at: <https://scie ndo.com/article/10.1515/scp-2016-0003>.

Petit, K., 2020. 'Creating places through language rules: A historical and ethnographic perspective on the "Rule of Irish"'. *Journal of Sociolinguistics*, 24, 228–244.

Pine, R., 2002. *2RN and the Origins of Irish Radio*. Dublin: Four Courts Press.

Plataforma per la Llengua, 2010. *Guia per a nous i futurs parlants de català*. Barcelona: Fundació Vincle. Available at: <http://www.plataforma-llengua. cat/media/assets/1880/guia_nousparlants_web_DEF.pdf>.

POBAL, 2004. *Acht na Gaeilge TÉ/The Irish Language Act NI*. Belfast: POBAL.

POBAL, 2005. *An Chairt Eorpach do Theangacha Réigiúnacha nó Mionlaigh: Feidhmiú na Cairte i leith na Gaeilge, Iúil 2002–2005/The European Charter for Regional of Minority Languages: The Implementation of the Charter with Regard to the Irish Language, July 2002–2005*. Belfast: POBAL.

POBAL, 2006. *Acht na Gaeilge do TÉ. Ag Fíorú na hAislinge: Ceachtanna ó Chéin is ó Chóngar/Vision to Enactment: Lessons from Far and Near*. Belfast: POBAL.

POBAL, 2012. *Acht na Gaeilge TÉ/The Irish Language Act NI, Eisiúint/Issue II*. Belfast: POBAL.

Premier County Communications, 1989. Letter from S. Ó Dúill, 11 February. NUIG G60/36/6/2.

Public Services Organisation Review Group, 1969. *Report of Public Services Organisation Review Group, 1966–1969 Presented to the Minister for Finance*. Dublin: Stationery Office.

Puigdevall, M., 2014. 'New speakers of minority languages: Belonging and legitimacy'. *Digithum*, 16, 44–46. Available at: <https://raco.cat/index.php/Digit hum/article/view/n16-puigdevall/394155>.

Puigdevall, M., Walsh, J., Amorrortu, E. and Ortega, A., 2018. '"I'll be one of them": Linguistic *mudes* and new speakers in three minority language contexts'. *Journal of Multilingual and Multicultural Development*, 39 (5), 445–457.

Quinnsworth, 1984. Bilingual receipt, 13 January. NUIG G60/29/4/6.

Raidió Fáilte, 2022. 'Athbhreithniú Straitéiseach & Plean Gnó/Strategic Review & Business Plan: January 2022–December 2024'. Belfast: Raidió Fáilte.

Raidió na Life, 1993. *Nuachtlitir*. Imleabhar 1, 1 December. NUIG G60/36/11/1.

Raidió na Life, 1994. *Nuachtlitir*. Imleabhar 2, 2 December. NUIG G60/36/11/1.

Raidió na Life, 2021. 'About us'. Available at: <http://www.raidionalife.ie/en/ about/>.

Raidió na Life, c. 1993. 'Raidió na Life 102 FM'. Advertising pack. NUIG G60/36/ 11/1.

Ricento, T., 2006. 'Language policy: Theory and practice – An introduction'. In: Ricento, T. (ed.) *An Introduction to Language Policy: Theory and Method*. Malden: Blackwell, 10–23.

Robert, E., 2009. 'Accommodating new speakers? An attitudinal investigation of L2 speakers of Welsh in south-east Wales'. *International Journal of the Sociology of Language*, 195, 93–116.

Romaine, S., 2006. 'Planning for the survival of linguistic diversity'. *Language Policy*, 5, 441–473.

Rowland, H., 2014. 'Conradh na Gaeilge agus an Language Freedom Movement: coimhlint idé-eolaíochta'. Unpublished PhD thesis, National University of Ireland, Galway.

Royal Irish Academy, 2009. 'The Doegen Records Web Project/Tionscadal Gréasáin Cheirníní Doegen'. Available at: <www.doegen.ie>.

Ryan, J., 1965. Letter from J. Ryan, Minister for Finance to S. Lemass, Taoiseach. 27 January. NAI TAOIS/2000/6/440.

S4C, 2021. *Adroddiad Blynyddol a Datganiad Ariannol ar gyfer y cyfnod 12 mis hyd at 31 Mawrth 2021/Annual Report and Statement of Accounts for the 12 Month Period to 31 March 2021*. Cardiff: S4C.

Sallabank, J., 2013. 'Diversity and language policy for endangered languages'. In: Spolsky, B. (ed.) *The Cambridge Handbook of Language Policy*. Cambridge: Cambridge University Press, 100–123.

Scottish National Party, 1977. 'Draft Articles of a Scottish Constitution'. NUIG G60/29/4/4.

Scottish National Party, 1981. Gaelic (Miscellaneous Provisions) Bill. NUIG G60/29/4/4.

SEALBHÚ, 2019. 'Treo an Pholasaí sa Todhchaí maidir le Díolúintí ó Staidéar ar an nGaeilge. Aighneacht arna haighniú ag SEALBHÚ: Lárionad Taighde DCU um Fhoghlaim agus Teagasc na Gaeilge'. Submission to consultation process by Department of Education. Dublin: SEALBHÚ, Dublin City University.

Seanad Éireann, 1938. 'Election of Leas-Chathaoirleach'. Seanad debates, 16 November, 22 (2). Available at: <https://www.oireachtas.ie/en/debates/debate/seanad/1938-11-16/2/>.

Seanad Éireann, 1959. 'Death of Leas-Chathaoirleach: Expression of sympathy'. Seanad debates, 29 April, 51 (1). Available at: <https://www.oireachtas.ie/en/debates/debate/seanad/1959-04-29/2/>.

Sebba, M. and Ayres-Bennett, W., 2021. 'Censoring multilingualism? Language questions in the 2021 census'. *Languages, Society and Policy*. Available at: <https://www.meits.org/opinion-articles/article/censoring-multilingualism-language-questions-in-the-2021-census>.

Seoighe, S., 2018. 'Is libhse an chathair' – Pop Up Gaeltacht agus nuachainteoirí na Gaeilge'. *COMHARTaighde* 4. <http://comhartaighde.ie/eagrain/4/seoighe/>. Accessed 20 October 2019.

Seven-Up International, 1987. 'Cuidíonn 7Up le beocht sa chóisir'. Bilingual card. NUIG G60/29/4/9.

Sheehan [Ó Síothcháin], M., 1906. *Sean-Chaint na nDéise: The Idiom of Living Irish*. Dublin: MH Gill & Son.

Shohamy, E., 2006. *Language Policy: Hidden Agendas and New Approaches*. Abingdon: Routledge.

Simpson, C., 2021a. 'Linda Ervine on how an Irish medium pre-school in east Belfast found a home after a campaign of intimidation'. *The Irish News*, 25 October. Available at: <https://www.irishnews.com/news/northernirelandnews/2021/10/25/news/linda-ervine-on-how-an-irish-medium-pre-school-in-east-belfast-found-a-home-after-a-campaign-of-intimidation-2488353/>.

Simpson, C., 2021b. 'United Nations should support immediate implementation of Irish language act'. *The Irish News*, 3 December. Available at: <https://www.irishnews.com/paywall/tsb/irishnews/irishnews/irishnews//news/northernirelandnews/2021/12/03/news/united-nations-should-support-immediate-implementation-of-irish-language-act-2525384/content.html>.

Singleton, D. and Flynn, C., 2021. 'Translanguaging: A pedagogical concept that went wandering'. *International Multilingual Research Journal*. Online first. DOI: <10.1080/19313152.2021.1985692>.

Smith-Christmas, C., 2020. 'Double-voicing and rubber ducks: The dominance of English in the imaginative play of two bilingual sisters'. *International Journal of Bilingual Education and Bilingualism*, 25 (4) 1–13.

Smith-Christmas, C., Ó Murchadha, N., Hornsby, M. and Moriarty, M. (eds), 2018. *New Speakers of Minority Languages: Linguistic Ideologies and Practices*. London: Palgrave Macmillan.

Smith-Christmas, C. and Ruiséal, O., 2019. *An nasc idir an teanga agus an pobal i gCorca Dhuibhne/The Intersection of Language and Community in Corca Dhuibhne*. Report for the 'Sustaining Minoritized Languages in Europe (SMiLE)' project. Washington, DC: Smithsonian Centre for Folklife and Cultural Heritage.

Spolsky, B., 2004. *Language Policy*. Cambridge: Cambridge University Press.

Spolsky, B., 2009. *Language Management*. Cambridge: Cambridge University Press.

Spolsky, B., 2012. 'What is language policy?' In *The Cambridge Handbook of Language Policy*. Cambridge: Cambridge University Press, 3–15.

Spolsky, B. (ed.), 2012. *The Cambridge Handbook of Language Policy*. Cambridge: Cambridge University Press.

Spolsky, B., 2021. *Rethinking Language Policy*. Edinburgh: Edinburgh University Press.

Telecom Éireann, 1985. 'Telephone Service Account'. Telephone bill, 14 November. NUIG G60/29/2/1.

TG4, 2020. *TG4 Annual Report 2020*. Baile na hAbhann: TG4. Available at: <https://d1ogos8nlbdohm.cloudfront.net/tg4-redesign-2015/wp-content/uploads/2021/10/TG4-Tuarascail-20-B.pdf>.

TG4, 2021. 'An additional €4.2m for TG4 in Budget 2022'. Press release, 12 October. Available at: <https://www.tg4.ie/en/information/press/press-releases/2021-2/an-additional-e4-2m-for-tg4-in-budget-2022/>.

The Connacht Tribune, 1927. '"Blot on the country": Minister's declaration about the Gaeltacht'. *The Connacht Tribune*, 29 January, 5.

The Cork Examiner, 1958. 'Death of parish priest who edited Irish catechism'. *The Cork Examiner*, 20 February, 4.

The Derry Journal, 1953. 'Donegal priest's golden jubilee'. *The Derry Journal*, 11 September, 1.

The Irish Independent, 1978. '"Piracy" through the medium'. *The Irish Independent*, 31 January, 6.

The Irish Press, 1969. 'Comhairle na Gaeilge'. *The Irish Press*, 30 June, 8.

The Irish Times, 1978. 'Irish language pirate station proposed'. *The Irish Times*, 21 January, 8.

The Irish Times, 2001. 'Local feels plan threatens future of Ring'. *The Irish Times*, 27 June, 2.

The North/South Language Body, 2002. *The North/South Language Body: Annual Report and Accounts for the Year Ended 31 December 2002/An Foras Teanga: Tuarascáil Bhliantúil agus Cuntais don Bhliain dár chríoch 31 Nollaig 2002/Tha Boord o Leid: An Accont o tha Darg for the Year himnaist 31 Decemmer 2002*. Dublin & Belfast: North/South Language Body.

Tierney, M., 1927. 'The revival of the Irish language'. *Studies: An Irish Quarterly Review*, 16 (61), 1–22.

Toblerone, n.d. Trilingual (FR/NL/DE) packaging on chocolate bar, presumably from Belgium. NUIG G60/29/4/9.

Tuairisc.ie, 2019. 'Cad atá sa Bhille Teanga nua agus cén difear a dhéanfaidh sé do phobal na Gaeilge?' *Tuairisc.ie,* 13 December. Available at: <https://tuairisc.ie/cad-ata-sa-bhille-teanga-nua-agus-cen-difear-a-dheanfaidh-se-do-phobal-na-gaeilge/>.

Tuairisc.ie, 2021a. '"Lá stairiúil" – Bille Teanga rite i dTithe an Oireachtais. *Tuairisc.ie*, 15 December. Available at: <https://tuairisc.ie/la-stairiuil-bille-teanga-nua-rite-i-dtithe-an-oireachtais/>.

Tuairisc.ie, 2021b. 'An Bille Teanga rite sa Dáil agus a cheann scribe nach mór sroichte aige'. *Tuairisc.ie*, 6 October. Available at: <https://tuairisc.ie/an-bille-teanga-rite-sa-dail-agus-a-cheann-scribe-nach-mor-sroichte-aige/>.

Tuairisc.ie, 2021c. 'An rialtas chun toghchán Údarás na Gaeltachta a thabhairt ar ais'. *Tuairisc.ie*, 16 April. Available at: <https://tuairisc.ie/an-rialtas-chun-toghc han-udaras-na-gaeltachta-a-thabhairt-ar-ais/>.

Tuairisc.ie, 2021d. 'Bille Teanga "níos láidre" ann agus deireadh lena phlé sa Seanad'. *Tuairisc.ie*, 8 December. Available at: <https://tuairisc.ie/bille-teanga-nios-lai dre-ann-agus-deireadh-lena-phle-sa-seanad/>.

Tuairisc.ie, 2021e. 'Cead pleanála d'óstán agus scéim 30 teach sa Ghaeltacht curtha ar ceal san Ard-Chúirt'. *Tuairisc.ie*, 10 Samhain. Available at: <https://tuair isc.ie/cead-pleanala-dostan-agus-sceim-30-teach-sa-ghaeltacht-curtha-ar-ceal-san-ard-chuirt/>.

Tuairisc.ie, 2021f. 'Cinneadh déanta ag an rialtas nach mbeidh ag teastáil feasta chun a bheith i do Gharda ach teanga amháin'. *Tuairisc.ie*, 16 December. Available at: <https://tuairisc.ie/cinneadh-deanta-ag-an-rialtas-nach-mbeidh-ag-teastail -feasta-chun-a-bheith-i-do-gharda-ach-teanga-amhain/>.

Tuairisc.ie, 2021g. 'Dul chun cinn déanta maidir le hAcht na dTeangacha Oifigiúla a neartú tar éis plé 25 uair an chloig. *Tuairisc.ie*, 16 April. Available at: <https:// tuairisc.ie/dul-chun-cinn-deanta-maidir-le-hacht-na-dteangacha-oifigiula-a-neartu-tar-eis-ple-25-uair-an-chloig/>.

Tuairisc.ie, 2021h. 'Fáilte curtha ag seanadóir roimh chinneadh gan cead pleanála a thabhairt d'fhorbairt chonspóideach sa Ghaeltacht'. *Tuairisc.ie*, 30 August. Available at: <https://tuairisc.ie/failte-curtha-ag-seanadoir-roimh-chinne adh-gan-cead-pleanala-a-thabhairt-dfhorbairt-chonspoideach-sa-ghaelta cht/>.

Turraoin, D., 2019. 'Maidhc Dháith, mo sheanathair'. *An Linn Bhuí: Iris Ghaeltacht na nDéise*, 23. Crosspatrick and Dublin: Leabhair na Linne. 6–9.

Uí Chollatáin, R., 2004. *An Claidheamh Soluis agus Fáinne an Lae 1899–1932*. Dublin: Cois Life.

Uí Fhoghlú, Á., 2000. 'An Rinn: Déise Mumhan'. In: Ó Tuathaigh, G., Ó Laoire, L. and Ua Súilleabháin, S. (eds) *Pobal na Gaeltachta: A Scéal agus a Dhán*. Indreabhán: Cló Iar-Chonnacht/Raidió na Gaeltachta, 624–636.

Uí Fhoghlú, Á., 2004. 'An briathar mí-rialta i nGaeluinn na nDéise'. Unpublished MPhil thesis, University College Cork.

uí Ógáin, R., 2009. *Going to the Well for Water: The Séamus Ennis Field Diary 1942–1946*. Cork: Cork University Press.

University College Galway, 1925. Letter from J. Hynes to Executive Council, 8 April. NAI S3717.

Verling, M., 2007. Leabhar Mhaidhc Dháith: Scéalta agus Seanchas ón Rinn. An Daingean: An Sagart.

Walsh, J., 2002. *Díchoimisiúnú Teanga: Coimisiún na Gaeltachta 1926*. Dublin: Cois Life.

Walsh, J., 2011. 'Athchuairt ar an mBreac-Ghaeltacht: fianaise stairiúil ar an athrú teanga i gCúige Mumhan'. *Béascna*, 7, 115–156.

Walsh, J., 2012. *Contests and Contexts: The Irish Language and Ireland's Socio-Economic Development* (2nd edn). Oxford: Peter Lang.

Walsh, J., 2015. 'The Irish language regime and language ideology in Ireland'. In: Cardinal, L. and Sonntag, S. (eds) *State Traditions and Language Regimes: Conceptualizing Language Policy Choices*. Montréal: McGill-Queen's University Press, 62–78.

Walsh, J., 2016. '"Chuireag na smóilíní a' sclimpireacht istig in mo chroí": athrú teanga agus idé-eolaíocht teanga i mBreac-Ghaeltacht na nDéise'. In: Walsh, J. and Ó Muircheartaigh, P. (eds) *Ag Siúl an Bhealaigh Mhóir: Aistí in Ómós don Ollamh Nollaig Mac Congáil*. Dublin: Leabhair Comhar, 414–449.

Walsh, J., 2017. 'Enactments concerning the Irish language, 1922–2016'. *Dublin University Law Journal*, 39 (2), 449–466.

Walsh, J., 2018. 'An Gael agus an raidió'. *Comhar*, 78 (9). Available at: <https://comhar.ie/iris/78/9/an-gael-agus-an-raidio/>.

Walsh, J., 2019a. 'National identity and belonging among gay "new speakers" of Irish'. *Journal of Language and Sexuality*, 8 (1), 53–81.

Walsh, J., 2019b. 'Sainiú na Gaeltachta: pobail, ceantair agus líonraí'. In: Ó hIfearnáin, T. (ed.) *An tSochtheangeolaíocht: Taighde agus Gníomh*. Dublin: Cois Life, 185–210.

Walsh, J., 2019c. 'The role of emotions and positionality in the trajectories of "new speakers" of Irish'. *International Journal of Bilingualism*, 23 (1), 221–235.

Walsh, J., 2021a. '"Real" language policy in a time of crisis: Covid-19, the state and the Irish language'. In: Maher, E. and O'Brien, E. (eds) *Reimagining Irish Studies for the 21st Century*. Oxford: Peter Lang, 229–246.

Walsh, J., 2021b. 'The governance of Irish in the neoliberal age: The retreat of the state under the guise of partnership'. In: Lewis, H. and McLeod, W. (eds) *Language Revitalisation and Social Transformation*. Basingstoke: Palgrave Macmillan, 311–342.

Walsh, J., 2021c. *Research on Use of the Irish Language on Radio – Phase 3*. Galway: National University of Ireland, Galway. Available at: <https://aran.library.nuigalway.ie/handle/10379/16584>.

Walsh, J. and Day, R., 2021. '"New speakers" on Irish language community radio: New understandings of linguistic variation on Raidió na Life'. *Journal of Multilingual and Multicultural Development*, online first. DOI: 10.1080/01434632.2021.1955893.

Walsh, J. and Greene, B., 2020. 'Irish pirate radio 1978–1988: How political stasis allowed unlicensed radio to flourish and innovate'. *Journal of Radio and Audio Media*, 27 (2), 274–297.

Walsh, J. and Ní Dhúda, L., 2015. '"New speakers" of Irish in the United States: Practices and motivations'. *Applied Linguistics Review*, 6, 173–193.

Walsh, J., Day, R. and Fogarty, P., 2018. *Research on Use of the Irish Language on Radio (Phase 2)*. Galway and Limerick: NUI Galway and University of Limerick. Available at: <https://audioresearchcentre.wordpress.com/research/>.

Walsh, J., Ní Uigín, D., Rowland, H., Fogarty, P. and Callinan, L., 2021. *Plean Teanga Chathair na Gaillimhe, 2020–2026*. Galway: Gaillimh le Gaeilge. Available at: <https://gleg.ie/wp-content/uploads/2021/06/Plean_Teanga_Chathair_na_Gaillimhe_2020-2026_210621-1.pdf>.

Walsh, J., O'Rourke, B. and Rowland, H., 2015. *Research Report on New Speakers of Irish for Foras na Gaeilge*. Dublin: Foras na Gaeilge. Available at: <https://www.forasnagaeilge.ie/wp-content/uploads/2015/10/New-speakers-of-Irish-report.pdf>.

Waterford City and County Council, 2021. *Draft Waterford City and County Development Plan 2022–2028*. Dungarvan: Waterford City and County Council. Available at: <https://consult.waterfordcouncil.ie/en/consultation/draft-waterford-city-and-county-development-plan-2022-2028>.

Waterford County Council, 1999. *1999 Waterford County Development Plan*. Dungarvan: Waterford County Council.

Waterford County Council, 2004. *Waterford County Development Plan Review 2005: Draft*. Dungarvan: Waterford County Council.

Waterford County Council, 2011. *Waterford County Development Plan 2011–2017*. Dungarvan: Waterford County Council.

Watson, I., 2003. *Broadcasting in Irish: Minority Language, Radio, Television and Identity*. Dublin: Four Courts Press.

Whelan, N., 2009. *Fianna Fáil: A Biography of the Party*. Dublin: Gill & Macmillan.

Williams, C. (ed.), 2007. *Language and Governance*. Cardiff: University of Wales Press.

Williams, C., 2013. 'Language policy, territorialism and regional autonomy'. In: Spolsky, B. (ed.) *The Cambridge Handbook of Language Policy*. Cambridge: Cambridge University Press, 174–202.

Williams, C., 2018. 'Creative ambiguity in the service of language policy and new speakers'. *Language Policy*, 18, 593–608.

Williams, C., 2019. 'The policy community and recommendations on new speakers'. In: O'Rourke, B. and Pujolar, J. (eds) *From New Speaker to Speaker: Outcomes,*

Reflections and Policy Recommendations from COST Action IS1306 on New Speakers in a Multilingual Europe: Opportunities and Challenges. Newcastle Emlyn: IAITH, Welsh Centre for Language Planning, 29–54.

Williams, C., 2022. *Language Policy and the New Speaker Challenge.* Cambridge: Cambridge University Press.

Williams, G., 1992. *Sociolinguistics: A Sociological Critique.* London: Routledge.

Williams, N. J. A., 1985a. Letter to Rights Bureau, 1 August. NUIG G60/29/2/1.

Williams, N. J. A., 1985b. Letter to Rights Bureau, 9 April. NUIG G60/29/2/1.

Wills, C., 2015. *The Best Are Leaving: Emigration and Post-War Irish Culture.* Cambridge: Cambridge University Press.

Woolard, K., 2016. *Singular and Plural: Ideologies of Linguistic Authority in 21st Century Catalonia.* Oxford: Oxford University Press.

Wright, S., 2013. 'Language policy, the nation and nationalism'. In: Spolsky, B. (ed.) *The Cambridge Handbook of Language Policy.* Cambridge: Cambridge University Press, 59–78.

Zenker, O., 2013. *Irish/ness is All Around Us: Language Revivalism and the Culture of Ethnic Identity in Northern Ireland.* New York: Berghahn Books.

Index

1916 Rising 93, 213, 262, 310
2RN 116, 249, 250, 251, 252
  see also Radio Éireann
20-Year Strategy for the Irish Language 2010–2030 3, 25, 38, 145, 148, 150, 192, 193, 320

'A' schools 146, 147, 176, 181, 182

Acadamh na hOllscolaíochta Gaeilge 151, 192–193
Académie française see French Academy
Acaill (Mayo) 101–102, 106
acquisition language planning 10, 141
Action Plan for Irish 1983–1986 221
activism 5, 9, 27, 56, 91, 94, 172, 194, 213, 248, 292, 300, 312, 313, 314, 317
  in media 260, 303
  professionalisation of 312
activists 10, 90, 93, 95, 99, 256, 261, 278, 279, 284, 304, 322
Administration of Justice (Ireland) Act (1737) 212
Aer Lingus 217
AMARC (World Association of Community Radio Broadcasters) 269
Anglo-Irish Treaty 1
Attorney General vs. Coyne and Wallace (1984) 199

Baile an Fheirtéaraigh (Kerry) 99
Baile Bhuirne (Cork) 97
Bailiúchán na Scol 50

Basque Country 3, 5, 19, 21, 22, 223, 230, 237, 307, 313, 316
BBC (British Broadcasting Corporation) 250, 259, 260–261, 264, 304
  BBC Irish Language Unit 259
  BBC Radio Ulster 259, 295
  BBC Scotland 259
  BBC Wales 259
Belfast 24, 26, 33, 40, 249, 254, 260, 276, 293, 296–298, 302, 304, 313, 314
Belfast Agreement (1998) 152, 153, 191, 211, 212, 233, 247, 259, 304, 312
Belgium 218, 312
bilingualism 5, 46, 120, 157, 158, 164, 166, 170, 185, 189, 208, 227
Bolzano/Bozen 237
Bord na Gaeilge 173, 176, 177, 178, 179, 181, 183, 186, 190–191, 193, 221–223, 225–229, 230–231, 234, 237, 238–239, 244, 275–276
Bord na Leabhar Gaeilge 184
Breatnach, Nioclás 44, 48, 50, 51–58, 67, 74, 75
Broadcasting Authority of Ireland 258
  see also Independent Radio and Television Commission
broadcasting legislation 254, 260, 266, 303, 307, 314
broadcasting policy 269, 303, 313, 314
Breac-Ghaeltacht 44–46, 49, 51, 52, 53–54, 55, 57, 58, 74, 100–101, 107, 108, 109, 111, 118, 132, 135, 136, 138, 151, 308
  see also Fíor-Ghaeltacht; Gaeltacht

Brexit 321
Britain 30, 83, 102, 137, 260, 268, 296

Caighdeán Oifigiúil na Gaeilge 154
Canada 185, 218, 231, 237, 240, 242,
        245, 312
Canadian Commissioner of Official
        Languages 219
Carraig, An Charraig (Donegal) 128
Catalan 20, 288, 289
Catalonia 5, 9, 19, 22, 223, 229, 237, 309
Catholic Church 113, 125, 135, 153
Cavan 80, 93, 108, 117
Ceantar na nOileán (Galway) 33
Celtic Tiger 68, 85, 245
census
        Irish Free State (1926) 135, 250
        Republic of Ireland
                (2002) 31, 70, 87
                (2006) 59
                (2016) 31–32, 37, 62
                (2022) 31
        Northern Ireland
                (2001) 295
                (2011) 33
                (2021) 33
Century Radio 271–272
civil service 79, 99, 113, 117, 123, 125, 126,
        129, 131, 132, 138, 155, 169, 180,
        184, 214, 226, 231, 312
Civil War, Irish 52, 133, 138, 309
Clann na Talmhan 93
classic language planning 8–9
climate change 15, 68, 321
coalition government 144, 155, 190,
        226, 230
Coiste Comhairleach Pleanála, An 223
Coláiste na Rinne 57, 68, 94
colonialism 15, 139, 268
Comhairle na Gaeilge 26, 84, 142, 155–
        156, 160, 161, 163, 168, 169–174,

        178, 180, 182, 184–185, 189–190,
        191, 192, 193, 194, 222, 311
Comhairle na Gaelscolaíochta 153
Comhairle um Oideachas Gaeltachta
        agus Gaelscolaíochta,
        An Chomhairle um
        Oideachas Gaeltachta agus
        Gaelscolaíochta 148, 149,
        150, 191
Comhaltas Ceoltóirí Éireann 211, 271
Comhar Naíonraí na Gaeltachta 37
Comharchumann Raidió Átha
        Cliath 271
Comhchoiste Réamhscolaíochta, An 191
Comhdháil Náisiúnta na Gaeilge 26,
        229, 233, 237, 242, 246, 247, 255,
        269, 272, 275
Comhlacht Comhairleach na
        Gaeilge 165
Comhlacht Forbartha na
        nDéise 60, 63, 67
Commission on Higher Education 162,
        163, 173, 176
Commission on the Restoration of the
        Irish Language 156, 255
Committee on Irish Language Attitudes
        Research 36, 171, 184–189, 190,
        193, 194, 215, 311
Commonwealth 196
community development 26, 40, 270,
        274, 278–279, 286, 292, 296, 299,
        302, 304
*Comprehensive Linguistic Study of the Use
        of Irish in the Gaeltacht* 36, 60,
        69, 58, 81, 87–88, 89, 150
'compulsory' Irish 160, 161, 167
Congested Districts Board 80, 114,
        115, 130
Conradh na Gaeilge 1, 26, 77, 78, 91, 92,
        94, 95, 96, 98, 118, 133, 143, 191,
        197, 198, 199, 212–213, 215, 216,

217, 218, 219, 220–221, 222, 230,
246, 247, 250, 256, 264, 265,
266, 267, 269, 272–273, 303, 312,
313, 316
archive of 23, 270
Ard-Fheis (assembly) of 199, 218, 272
branches of 115, 117, 265, 272
business committee of 99
campaign by 197, 212, 214, 255, 312
co-founder of 116
Craobh an Chéitinnigh branch of 96
executive committee of 94, 264
influence of 142
intervention from 216
legal notice from 213
president of 78, 116
reforms in 264
Rights Bureau of 214, 312
seminar organised by 223
sub-committee of 215, 267
submission by 268
conservatism 118, 130, 135, 139, 309, 310
Constitutional Review
Group 224–225, 229
constitutional status of Irish 2, 10, 26, 79,
139, 181, 195, 196, 197, 198, 202,
220, 224, 225, 232, 237, 246
Cork city 89, 233, 256
Cork Gaeltacht 65, 93
corpus language planning 10, 154,
155, 209
Cosgrave, WT 79, 90, 115, 117,
128–130, 134
see also Fine Gael
County
Clare 84, 94, 95, 98, 109, 117, 172
Cork 43, 83, 87, 97, 98, 108, 109, 135,
262, 270
Donegal 83, 88, 94, 98, 105, 107, 108,
109, 111, 114, 115, 116, 117, 215

Galway 68, 84, 88, 89, 98, 104, 107,
117, 127, 227
Kerry 87, 89, 97, 98, 104, 117
Mayo 87, 97, 266, 111, 117, 270, 272
Meath 74, 80, 87, 164, 272, 275
Tipperary 42, 44, 47, 49, 50, 51, 54,
94, 108, 109, 270
Waterford 25, 29, 33, 42, 43, 44, 46,
47, 48, 49, 51, 53, 60, 67, 68, 74,
75, 87, 94, 97, 98, 103, 107, 108,
109, 308
see also Gaeltacht na nDéise
Covid-19 31, 205, 208, 302, 318
cross-border governance 24, 191, 238, 312,
214, 322
see also Foras na Gaeilge
Cultúrlann, An Chultúrlann 295,
296, 300
Cymdeithas Yr Iaith Gymraeg (Welsh
Language Society) 218
Czech 8
Czechoslovakia 7, 8

daily Irish speakers 32–33, 43, 59,
61, 87–88
Daingean, An (Kerry) 89, 96, 204
Declaration of Rights for the Irish
Language see *Forógra Cearta don
Ghaeilge* 215
De Hindeberg, Fr Piaras 48, 50
demographic change 5, 17, 69
Democratic Unionist Party 212
De Valera, Éamon 50, 96, 116, 146, 154,
156, 157, 198, 213–214, 229,
250, 252
see also Fianna Fáil
dialectology 45, 46
diaspora 137, 252
diglossia 9, 170–172, 178, 181, 189, 194
Doegen, Wilhelm 47
Donegal Gaeltacht 32, 37, 221, 298

Dromaid, An (Kerry) 107
Dublin Institute of Advanced
	Studies 46, 185
Dublin radio co-operative see
	Comharchumann Raidió
	Átha Cliath
Dublin Vocational Education
	Committee 210

Economic and Social Research
	Institute 34, 35
economic development policy 26,
	118, 172
economic protectionism 83, 156, 310
Education Act (1998) 148, 150
Estonia 20
European Bureau for Lesser Used
	Languages 229
European Charter for Regional or
	Minority Languages 26, 221,
	235, 259
European Co-operation in Science and
	Technology (COST) 19, 22
European Court of Justice 210–211
European Economic Community see
	European Union
European Union 16, 17, 19, 26, 167, 179,
	195, 209–210, 231, 322

Fáinne, An 97
Fáinne an Lae 116
Fál Carrach, An (Donegal) 217
Falls Road 292, 293, 295, 300
	see also Belfast
Farmers' Party 93
Faroe Islands 256
Feachtas Náisiúnta Teilifíse 256
	see also TG4
Fianna Fáil 2, 116, 134, 139, 146, 155, 156,
	170, 180, 189–190, 220, 226, 229,
	230, 267, 268, 310

Fine Gael 2, 93, 96, 155, 180, 190, 198, 220
Finland 7, 307
Fíor-Ghaeltacht 44, 45, 46, 49, 107,
	108–109, 111, 120, 121, 135, 136, 138
	see also Breac-Ghaeltacht; Gaeltacht
Fishman, Joshua 8, 10, 18, 39, 167–168,
	170, 185
Forógra Cearta don Ghaeilge 215
Foras na Gaeilge 34, 40, 89, 155, 191,
	212, 238–239, 292, 302, 312, 314,
	315, 318
Foras Teanga, An 238
foreign direct investment 83, 156
France 11
French 7, 94, 108, 144, 152, 166,
	241–242, 245
French Academy 7

Gaelic Athletic Association 64, 221, 222,
	271, 296
Gaelic League see Conradh na Gaeilge
gaelicisation 5, 79, 92, 118, 134, 139, 155,
	157, 158–159, 194
Gael-Linn 169, 275
gaelscoileanna 1, 2, 3, 147, 152, 154, 190,
	191, 275, 279, 280
Gaeltacht
	boundaries of 137
	contraction of 137
	economy of 81, 102, 112, 123, 175, 320
	education board for 150
	governance of 82, 84, 126, 130, 172
	housing in 55, 80, 86, 112
	policy towards 24, 80, 139, 310
	schools in 25, 68, 110, 117, 124, 128,
		141, 142, 147, 148–150, 176, 191
	status of 61, 62, 64, 80, 88, 89
	see also Breac-Ghaeltacht; Cork;
		Donegal; Fíor- Ghaeltacht;
		Galway; Kerry; Mayo; Meath;
		Waterford

Gaeltacht Act (2012) 25, 62, 88, 148
Gaeltacht Area Orders (1956) 82
Gaeltacht Bhóthar Seoighe 39, 40, 292
Gaeltacht Civil Rights Movement *see*
    Gluaiseacht Cearta Sibhialta na
    Gaeltachta
Gaeltacht Commission
    (1925–1926) 25, 42, 44, 49, 57, 58, 67,
    74, 77, 79, 80, 90–137, 151, 309,
    310, 315, 318
    (2000–2002) 60, 86, 87, 149
Gaeltacht Education Policy 148, 150, 191
Gaeltacht na nDéise 29, 38, 42–75
Gaeltacht Service Town 62, 67, 88,
    89, 309
Gaeltacht Services 80
Gaeltarra Éireann 25, 83–84, 85, 172, 173
Galicia 21, 22, 237
Galway city 33, 88, 89, 151, 183, 298
Galway City Language Plan 89
Galway Gaeltacht 33, 36, 37, 87, 108,
    109, 221
Garda Síochána 2, 3, 4, 263
Garda Síochána Act (1924) 121
German 144, 152, 166
Glasgow 215
globalisation 17, 18, 320
Glór na nGael 68
Gluaiseacht Cearta Sibhialta na
    Gaeltachta 83, 84, 261, 263, 303
Graded Intergenerational Disruption
    Scale 10
    see also Fishman, Joshua
Green Party 2, 318
Groener, Anita 210, 226
Gúm, An 184

Haughey, Charles 167, 169, 220, 256, 268
    see also Fianna Fáil
Higgins, Michael D. 230, 256, 273,
    276, 312

    see also Labour Party
housing 43, 59, 68, 70, 71, 72, 85, 236
Housing (Gaeltacht) Act (1929) 98, 121
Hyde, Douglas 78, 116, 250, 252

identity 11, 24, 41, 309
ideology 57, 288
immigrant languages 258, 283
Implementing a Language Policy 173
independent broadcasting 221, 233
Independent Radio and Television
    Commission 271, 272, 274
Industrial Development Agency 84,
    172, 191
Institiúid Teangeolaíochta Éireann *see*
    Linguistics Institute of Ireland
intergenerational transmission 10–11, 18,
    38, 75, 319
Iontaobhas na Gaelscolaíochta 153
Irish Folklore Commission 49, 50, 51, 56,
    74, 97, 308
Irish in Education 174, 178
Irish language
    as academic subject 151, 153
    broadcasting 259–260, 314
    governance of 60, 114, 309, 314, 315
    language planning officers for 75, 76,
        90, 308
    language schemes for 203–204, 208,
        238, 242–243, 247
    marginalisation of 251, 259, 268,
        303, 322
    networks 40, 88, 89, 309, 319
    revitalisation of 304
    signage in 12, 67, 203, 204, 209, 216,
        227, 228, 238, 244
    as standalone subject 142, 152, 174
    voluntary sector of 267, 275, 320
Irish Language Broadcast Fund
    (Northern Ireland) 258

Irish Language in a Changing Society,
  The 223
Irish language ombudsman 236
  see also Oifig an
    Choimisinéara Teanga
Irish Language Services Advisory
  Committee 206–207
Irish language television 221, 230, 246,
  255, 257, 273
  see also TG4
Irish-medium pre-schools (*naíonraí*) 147
Irish-medium schools *see* 'A' schools,
  gaelscoileanna
Irish National Teachers'
  Organisation 146
Isle of Man 50
Isle of Skye 294
Italian 152

Lá 276, 291, 292, 293, 295
Labour Party 95, 155, 220, 226
Land Commission 80, 91, 112, 115, 126,
  127, 132
Language and Community 170
language acquisition 42, 64, 150, 160, 317
language beliefs 13, 56, 58
language commissioner
  see Oifig an Choimisinéara Teanga
Language Freedom Movement 144, 157,
  170, 180, 214, 311
language governance 6, 16, 238, 315
language maintenance 61, 65, 78, 320
language management 6, 13–15, 44, 56,
  58, 74, 75, 247, 313, 314, 321, 322
language normalisation 7, 304
language policy
  development of 58
  framework of 1, 4, 247
  governance of 190, 311
  implementation of 15
  implications for 18, 19, 20

models of 12, 23
professionalisation of 163, 193
shifts in 135
study of 16, 31
theory of 13
language practice 12, 45, 46, 49, 50, 52,
  56, 57, 58, 74, 308, 322
language revitalisation 7, 10, 18, 22, 278,
  279, 283, 304, 314, 319
Language Revitalisation and Social
  Transformation 17
language revival 6, 7, 97, 124, 133, 145
language shift 14, 15, 23, 36, 37, 45–47, 49,
  50, 51, 54, 55, 58, 59, 60, 74, 87, 95,
  161, 191, 186, 290, 307, 310, 317, 318
Lemass, Seán 83, 156, 157–158, 318
  see also Fianna Fáil
liberalisation, economic 83, 84, 156,
  194, 310
Limerick 80, 108, 183
Linguistic Atlas and Survey of Irish
  Dialects 47
linguistic balance 43, 85
linguistic boundaries 19
linguistic diversity 153, 289
linguistic endangerment 55
linguistic impact 68, 69, 71, 320
Linguistics Institute of Ireland 166–169,
  185, 186, 189, 193, 194, 311
Lios Póil (Kerry) 104
Local Government and Development
  Institutions for the Gaeltacht 172
Local Offices and Executives Order
  (Gaeltacht) (1928) 79
Local Radio Bill (1983) 267–268
Louth 80, 98

Mac Cuinnigeáin, Fr Seaghan 94,
  114–115, 139
MacNeill, Eoin 78, 90–92, 96, 98, 118,
  124, 133, 138, 318

Maltese 210
Manx Gaelic 50
Mayo Gaeltacht 83, 108, 109, 266
middle class 78, 93, 98, 118, 138
migrants 20, 22, 319
minority language education 183
minority language media 255, 278, 283, 286, 290, 291
minority language policy 17, 19
minority language promotion 10
Misneach 39
muda 20

Naíscoileanna Gaelacha, na (Naíonraí Gaelacha, na) 191
National Association of Community Broadcasting 270
National College of Physical Education 183
National Council for Curriculum and Assessment 144, 148
National Folklore Collection 23
National Institute for Higher Education 183
national language policy 16, 17, 193
National University of Ireland, Galway 23, 93, 94, 98, 111, 151, 162, 164, 174, 176, 177, 182, 192, 225, 227
nationalism 9, 20, 57, 58, 157, 158, 307, 309, 310, 320
nationalists 31, 34, 40, 268, 292, 313
neoliberalism 6, 15, 17, 18, 68, 268, 303, 313, 314
New Decade, New Approach (NDNA) 212
New International Information Order 268, 303
new speakers 19–20, 21–22, 29, 41, 42, 43, 304
Nic Shuibhne, Niamh 228–229, 231–232

Northern Ireland Act (1998) 212
Northern Ireland Executive 212, 213
Norway 7, 20, 237, 307

Ó Beoláin vs. Fahy (2001) 200–201
Ó Buachalla, Breandán 141, 169
Ó Cairealláin, Gearóid 292–293, 296
Ó Cuaig, Seosamh 261–262
Ó Cuív, Éamon 87, 229–230, 233, 237–238, 239–240, 244, 246, 318
Ó Foghludha vs. McClean (1931) 197, 231
Ó Huallacháin, Fr Colmán 143, 163–168, 185, 189, 193, 194
Ó Laighin, Pádraig 240–246
Ó Monacháin vs. Ireland (1986) 220
Ó Murchú vs. Taoiseach (2010) 201
Ó Murchú, Máirtín 146, 170, 185, 239, 310

OFCOM 291, 295, 296
Official Languages Act (Canada) (1985) 240
Official Languages Act (2003) 4, 24, 26, 195, 201, 202–204, 208, 209, 213, 214, 225, 230, 246, 312, 313
Official Languages (Amendment) Act (2021) 205–208, 247, 313
Official Languages (Equality) Bill (2002) 239, 240, 318
Official Standard of Irish *see* Caighdeán Oifigiúil na Gaeilge
Oifig an Choimisinéara Teanga 73, 202, 204, 207, 236, 238, 247, 312
Oireachtas Éireann 158, 196, 197, 199, 202, 204, 209, 210, 219, 220, 230, 231, 236, 241, 243, 245, 268
Oireachtas na Gaeilge 163, 275
Ombudsman, Office of 223–224, 225
overt language policy 247, 300, 313

pandemic *see* Covid-19

pirate broadcasting
  radio 251, 253, 260–266, 267, 268,
    269–270, 272, 274, 292–296, 303
  television 256
  see also Raidió an Phobail; Raidió
    Fáilte; Saor-Raidió Chonamara
placenames 24, 202, 204, 209, 216
Placenames Committee 207
Planning and Development Act
  (2000) 69, 72, 85
POBAL 211–212, 318
Polish 288
Pop-Up Gaeltacht 283
Portuguese 288
poverty 102, 107, 110, 116, 119, 124,
  125, 128
Prague School 8
Protestants 35, 40, 153–154, 299
public administration, use of Irish in 79,
  105, 154, 163, 167, 171, 180, 189,
  195, 213–214, 216, 311, 218
Public Appointments Service 206
public broadcasting 173

qualitative research 31, 40, 87

Radio and Television Bill (1987) 269
Radio Caroline 260–261
Radio Éireann 162, 249, 250, 251, 252,
  253–254, 255, 261
Radio Free Belfast 293
Radio Free Derry 261
Raidió an Phobail 264–266
Raidió Fáilte
  history 292–296
  unionist involvement with 299
Raidió na Gaeltachta
  campaign for 26, 263
  establishment of 83, 251, 252, 254, 303
Raidió na Life
  establishment of 273–277, 303

linguistic standards of 287, 304
Raidió Rí-Rá 254
Raidió Teilifís Éireann *see* Radio Éireann,
  Raidió na Gaeltachta, Telefís
  Éireann, TG4
Ráth Chairn 38, 65, 74
'real' language policy 3, 12–13, 157, 159,
  193, 304, 309
resettlement 111–112, 114, 127, 129, 131,
  136, 137, 310
Reversing Language Shift 10
Revival policy 1, 24, 52, 74, 77, 78, 82,
  90, 92, 93, 94, 96–97, 99, 116, 118,
  120, 134, 136, 137, 138–139, 146,
  157, 166, 189, 215, 255, 288, 292,
  298, 308, 310, 321, 322
rights
  framework 202, 212, 234, 247, 312
  for Irish speakers 26, 212, 214, 235,
    238, 241
Rinn, An (Waterford) 43, 55, 59, 60, 70,
  71, 73, 94, 103
romanticism 7, 20, 21, 138
Ros Muc (Galway) 262
Russian 7

S4C 257, 259
  see also Wales
St Andrews Agreement (2006) 211, 212
Saor-Raidió Chonamara 253, 262, 263,
  293, 303
Scéim Labhairt na Gaeilge 37, 59, 81, 87
School Meals (Gaeltacht) Act (1930) 121
Schools Collection *see* Bailiúchán na Scol
Scottish Gaelic 294
Seanphobal, An (Waterford) 43,
  54, 59, 60
Shaw's Road Gaeltacht *see* Gaeltacht
  Bhóthar Seoighe
Sinn Féin 93, 95, 98, 212
Sliabh gCua (Tipperary) 50, 94

Sligo 80, 108, 109
Slovakia 7
social class 187–188
  intersection of 187, 189
  structures 31
social media 205, 296
socio-economic factors
  areas of disadvantage 302
  deprivation 36, 297
  development of the Gaeltacht 84, 85
  socioeconomic transformation 5, 317
 South Kerry 95, 96
Soviet Union 7, 9
Spain 19, 21
Spanish 21, 114, 152, 276, 288
Spolsky, Bernard 7, 12–16, 44, 51, 56,
  247, 321
standardisation 8, 79, 100, 154–155
  see also Caighdeán Oifigiúil na
  Gaeilge
*An Stát (Mac Fhearraigh) vs. Mac
  Gamhnia* (1983) 231
An Stát (Mac Fhearraigh) vs. Neilan
  (1984) 199
state intervention 77, 124, 309
Stormont 154, 211–212, 295
*Submissions to the Higher Education
  Authority* 174, 176
supranational language policy 210
syllabus for Gaeltacht pupils 148

teacher training 149, 160, 175, 182
Teastas Eorpach na Gaeilge 72
Teileann (Donegal) 108
Teilifís na Gaeilge *see* TG4
Telefís Éireann 249, 252, 253, 255
TG4 26, 43, 230, 247, 257–258, 259
Toraigh (Donegal) 33
Towards a Language Policy 1971 171
translanguaging 286, 291
Tuismitheoirí na Gaeltachta 37

Údarás na Gaeltachta 25, 63, 84–85, 86,
  89, 173, 191, 227, 230, 234, 236,
  256, 266, 320
  elections to 71
Ulster Scots 33, 212
unionists 40, 123, 153, 154, 296, 299,
  313, 317
United Ireland 321
United Nations 212
University College Cork 23, 169
University College Galway *see* National
  University of Ireland, Galway
University College Galway Act
  (1929) 151
University College (Amendment)
  Galway Act (2006) 192
University of Galway *see* National
  University of Ireland, Galway
University of Wales 185
upper class 35

Wagner, Heinrich 47–48
Wales 2, 5, 10, 19, 22, 137, 152, 183, 204,
  208, 218, 223, 229, 231, 237, 257,
  259, 307, 312, 313, 316, 320
Waterford Gaeltacht *see* Gaeltacht
  na nDéise
Welsh language 152, 166, 183, 218, 238,
  247, 259, 321
Welsh Language Act 1993 243, 244
West Belfast 33, 34, 39–40, 41, 291, 294,
  296, 302, 304
West Clare 100, 101, 103, 108
West Kerry Gaeltacht 36, 89, 101, 108, 109
Westminster 211, 212
Whitaker, T.K. 83, 156–158, 169, 170,
  185, 318
  see also Lemass, Seán
White Paper on Gaeltacht Commission
  (1928) 80, 90, 130–133, 136

White Paper on Restoration of Irish
    (1965) 155, 157, 158–163, 165, 169,
    174, 179, 181, 184, 185, 194, 213
working class 73, 118, 187, 190

World Association of Community Radio
    Broadcasters *see* AMARC

Reimagining Ireland

Series Editor: Dr Eamon Maher, Technological
University Dublin

The concepts of Ireland and 'Irishness' are in constant flux in the wake of an ever-increasing reappraisal of the notion of cultural and national specificity in a world assailed from all angles by the forces of globalisation and uniformity. Reimagining Ireland interrogates Ireland's past and present and suggests possibilities for the future by looking at Ireland's literature, culture and history and subjecting them to the most up-to-date critical appraisals associated with sociology, literary theory, historiography, political science and theology.

Some of the pertinent issues include, but are not confined to, Irish writing in English and Irish, Nationalism, Unionism, the Northern 'Troubles', the Peace Process, economic development in Ireland, the impact and decline of the Celtic Tiger, Irish spirituality, the rise and fall of organised religion, the visual arts, popular cultures, sport, Irish music and dance, emigration and the Irish diaspora, immigration and multiculturalism, marginalisation, globalisation, modernity/postmodernity and postcolonialism. The series publishes monographs, comparative studies, interdisciplinary projects, conference proceedings and edited books. Proposals should be sent either to Dr Eamon Maher at eamon.maher@ittdublin.ie or to ireland@peterlang.com.

Vol. 1   Eugene O'Brien: 'Kicking Bishop Brennan up the Arse': Negotiating Texts and Contexts in Contemporary Irish Studies
ISBN 978-3-03911-539-6. 219 pages. 2009.

Vol. 2   James P.Byrne, Padraig Kirwan and Michael O'Sullivan (eds): Affecting Irishness: Negotiating Cultural Identity Within and Beyond the Nation
ISBN 978-3-03911-830-4. 334 pages. 2009.

Vol. 3   Irene Lucchitti: The Islandman: The Hidden Life of Tomás O'Crohan
ISBN 978-3-03911-837-3. 232 pages. 2009.

Vol. 4   Paddy Lyons and Alison O'Malley-Younger (eds): No Country for Old Men: Fresh Perspectives on Irish Literature
ISBN 978-3-03911-841-0. 289 pages. 2009.

Vol. 5   Eamon Maher (ed.): Cultural Perspectives on Globalisation and
Ireland
ISBN 978-3-03911-851-9. 256 pages. 2009.

Vol. 6   Lynn Brunet: 'A Course of Severe and Arduous Trials': Bacon, Beckett
and Spurious Freemasonry in Early Twentieth-Century Ireland
ISBN 978-3-03911-854-0. 218 pages. 2009.

Vol. 7   Claire Lynch: Irish Autobiography: Stories of Self in the Narrative of
a Nation
ISBN 978-3-03911-856-4. 234 pages. 2009.

Vol. 8   Victoria O'Brien: A History of Irish Ballet from 1927 to 1963
ISBN 978-3-03911-873-1. 208 pages. 2011.

Vol. 9   Irene Gilsenan Nordin and Elin Holmsten (eds): Liminal Borderlands
in Irish Literature and Culture
ISBN 978-3-03911-859-5. 208 pages. 2009.

Vol. 10   Claire Nally: Envisioning Ireland: W. B. Yeats's Occult Nationalism
ISBN 978-3-03911-882-3. 320 pages. 2010.

Vol. 11   Raita Merivirta: The Gun and Irish Politics: Examining National
History in Neil Jordan's *Michael Collins*
ISBN 978-3-03911-888-5. 202 pages. 2009.

Vol. 12   John Strachan and Alison O'Malley-Younger
(eds): Ireland: Revolution and Evolution
ISBN 978-3-03911-881-6. 248 pages. 2010.

Vol. 13   Barbara Hughes: Between Literature and History: The Diaries and
Memoirs of Mary Leadbeater and Dorothea Herbert
ISBN 978-3-03911-889-2. 255 pages. 2010.

Vol. 14   Edwina Keown and Carol Taaffe (eds): Irish Modernism: Origins,
Contexts, Publics
ISBN 978-3-03911-894-6. 256 pages. 2010.

Vol. 15   John Walsh: Contests and Contexts: The Irish Language and
Ireland's Socio-Economic Development
ISBN 978-3-03911-914-1. 492 pages. 2011.

Vol. 16   Zélie Asava: The Black Irish Onscreen: Representing Black and
           Mixed-Race Identities on Irish Film and Television
           ISBN 978-3-0343-0839-7. 213 pages. 2013.

Vol. 17   Susan Cahill and Eóin Flannery (eds): This Side of Brightness: Essays
           on the Fiction of Colum McCann
           ISBN 978-3-03911-935-6. 189 pages. 2012.

Vol. 18   Brian Arkins: The Thought of W. B. Yeats
           ISBN 978-3-03911-939-4. 204 pages. 2010.

Vol. 19   Maureen O'Connor: The Female and the Species: The Animal in Irish
           Women's Writing
           ISBN 978-3-03911-959-2. 203 pages. 2010.

Vol. 20   Rhona Trench: Bloody Living: The Loss of Selfhood in the Plays of
           Marina Carr
           ISBN 978-3-03911-964-6. 327 pages. 2010.

Vol. 21   Jeannine Woods: Visions of Empire and Other Imaginings: Cinema,
           Ireland and India, 1910–1962
           ISBN 978-3-03911-974-5. 230 pages. 2011.

Vol. 22   Neil O'Boyle: New Vocabularies, Old Ideas: Culture, Irishness and the
           Advertising Industry
           ISBN 978-3-03911-978-3. 233 pages. 2011.

Vol. 23   Dermot McCarthy: John McGahern and the Art of Memory
           ISBN 978-3-0343-0100-8. 344 pages. 2010.

Vol. 24   Francesca Benatti, Sean Ryder and Justin Tonra (eds): Thomas
           Moore: Texts, Contexts, Hypertexts
           ISBN 978-3-0343-0900-4. 220 pages. 2013.

Vol. 25   Sarah O'Connor: No Man's Land: Irish Women and the Cultural
           Present
           ISBN 978-3-0343-0111-4. 230 pages. 2011.

Vol. 26   Caroline Magennis: Sons of Ulster: Masculinities in the Contem-
           porary Northern Irish Novel
           ISBN 978-3-0343-0110-7. 192 pages. 2010.

Vol. 27 Dawn Duncan: Irish Myth, Lore and Legend on Film
ISBN 978-3-0343-0140-4. 181 pages. 2013.

Vol. 28 Eamon Maher and Catherine Maignant (eds): Franco-Irish
Connections in Space and Time: Peregrinations and Ruminations
ISBN 978-3-0343-0870-0. 295 pages. 2012.

Vol. 29 Holly Maples: Culture War: Conflict, Commemoration and the
Contemporary Abbey Theatre
ISBN 978-3-0343-0137-4. 294 pages. 2011.

Vol. 30 Maureen O'Connor (ed.): Back to the Future of Irish
Studies: Festschrift for Tadhg Foley
ISBN 978-3-0343-0141-1. 359 pages. 2010.

Vol. 31 Eva Urban: Community Politics and the Peace Process in
Contemporary Northern Irish Drama
ISBN 978-3-0343-0143-5. 303 pages. 2011.

Vol. 32 Mairéad Conneely: Between Two Shores/*Idir Dhá Chladach*: Writing
the Aran Islands, 1890–1980
ISBN 978-3-0343-0144-2. 299 pages. 2011.

Vol. 33 Gerald Morgan and Gavin Hughes (eds): Southern Ireland and the
Liberation of France: New Perspectives
ISBN 978-3-0343-0190-9. 250 pages. 2011.

Vol. 34 Anne MacCarthy: Definitions of Irishness in the 'Library of
Ireland' Literary Anthologies
ISBN 978-3-0343-0194-7. 271 pages. 2012.

Vol. 35 Irene Lucchitti: Peig Sayers: In Her Own Write
ISBN 978-3-0343-0253-1. Forthcoming.

Vol. 36 Eamon Maher and Eugene O'Brien (eds): Breaking the
Mould: Literary Representations of Irish Catholicism
ISBN 978-3-0343-0232-6. 249 pages. 2011.

Vol. 37 Mícheál Ó hAodha and John O'Callaghan (eds): Narratives of the
Occluded Irish Diaspora: Subversive Voices
ISBN 978-3-0343-0248-7. 227 pages. 2012.

Vol. 38   Willy Maley and Alison O'Malley-Younger (eds): Celtic
           Connections: Irish–Scottish Relations and the Politics of Culture
           ISBN 978-3-0343-0214-2. 247 pages. 2013.

Vol. 39   Sabine Egger and John McDonagh (eds): Polish–Irish Encounters in
           the Old and New Europe
           ISBN 978-3-0343-0253-1. 322 pages. 2011.

Vol. 40   Elke D'hoker, Raphaël Ingelbien and Hedwig Schwall (eds): Irish
           Women Writers: New Critical Perspectives
           ISBN 978-3-0343-0249-4. 318 pages. 2011.

Vol. 41   Peter James Harris: From Stage to Page: Critical Reception of Irish
           Plays in the London Theatre, 1925–1996
           ISBN 978-3-0343-0266-1. 311 pages. 2011.

Vol. 42   Hedda Friberg-Harnesk, Gerald Porter and Joakim Wrethed
           (eds): Beyond Ireland: Encounters Across Cultures
           ISBN 978-3-0343-0270-8. 342 pages. 2011.

Vol. 43   Irene Gilsenan Nordin and Carmen Zamorano Llena (eds): Urban
           and Rural Landscapes in Modern Ireland: Language, Literature and
           Culture
           ISBN 978-3-0343-0279-1. 238 pages. 2012.

Vol. 44   Kathleen Costello-Sullivan: Mother/Country: Politics of the Personal
           in the Fiction of Colm Tóibín
           ISBN 978-3-0343-0753-6. 247 pages. 2012.

Vol. 45   Lesley Lelourec and Gráinne O'Keeffe-Vigneron (eds): Ireland and
           Victims: Confronting the Past, Forging the Future
           ISBN 978-3-0343-0792-5. 331 pages. 2012.

Vol. 46   Gerald Dawe, Darryl Jones and Nora Pelizzari (eds): Beautiful
           Strangers: Ireland and the World of the 1950s
           ISBN 978-3-0343-0801-4. 207 pages. 2013.

Vol. 47   Yvonne O'Keeffe and Claudia Reese (eds): New Voices, Inherited
           Lines: Literary and Cultural Representations of the Irish Family
           ISBN 978-3-0343-0799-4. 238 pages. 2013.

Vol. 48   Justin Carville (ed.): Visualizing Dublin: Visual Culture, Modernity and the Representation of Urban Space
ISBN 978-3-0343-0802-1. 326 pages. 2014.

Vol. 49   Gerald Power and Ondřej Pilný (eds): Ireland and the Czech Lands: Contacts and Comparisons in History and Culture
ISBN 978-3-0343-1701-6. 243 pages. 2014.

Vol. 50   Eoghan Smith: John Banville: Art and Authenticity
ISBN 978-3-0343-0852-6. 199 pages. 2014.

Vol. 51   María Elena Jaime de Pablos and Mary Pierse (eds): George Moore and the Quirks of Human Nature
ISBN 978-3-0343-1752-8. 283 pages. 2014.

Vol. 52   Aidan O'Malley and Eve Patten (eds): Ireland, West to East: Irish Cultural Connections with Central and Eastern Europe
ISBN 978-3-0343-0913-4. 307 pages. 2014.

Vol. 53   Ruben Moi, Brynhildur Boyce and Charles I. Armstrong (eds): The Crossings of Art in Ireland
ISBN 978-3-0343-0983-7. 319 pages. 2014.

Vol. 54   Sylvie Mikowski (ed.): Ireland and Popular Culture
ISBN 978-3-0343-1717-7. 257 pages. 2014.

Vol. 55   Benjamin Keatinge and Mary Pierse (eds): France and Ireland in the Public Imagination
ISBN 978-3-0343-1747-4. 279 pages. 2014.

Vol. 56   Raymond Mullen, Adam Bargroff and Jennifer Mullen (eds): John McGahern: Critical Essays
ISBN 978-3-0343-1755-9. 253 pages. 2014.

Vol. 57   Máirtín Mac Con Iomaire and Eamon Maher (eds): 'Tickling the Palate': Gastronomy in Irish Literature and Culture
ISBN 978-3-0343-1769-6. 253 pages. 2014.

Vol. 58   Heidi Hansson and James H. Murphy (eds): Fictions of the Irish Land War
ISBN 978-3-0343-0999-8. 237 pages. 2014.

Vol. 59   Fiona McCann: A Poetics of Dissensus: Confronting Violence in Contemporary Prose Writing from the North of Ireland ISBN 978-3-0343-0979-0. 238 pages. 2014.

Vol. 60   Marguérite Corporaal, Christopher Cusack, Lindsay Janssen and Ruud van den Beuken (eds): Global Legacies of the Great Irish Famine: Transnational and Interdisciplinary Perspectives ISBN 978-3-0343-0903-5. 357 pages. 2014.

Vol. 61   Katarzyna Ojrzyn'ska: 'Dancing As If Language No Longer Existed': Dance in Contemporary Irish Drama ISBN 978-3-0343-1813-6. 318 pages. 2015.

Vol. 62   Whitney Standlee: 'Power to Observe': Irish Women Novelists in Britain, 1890–1916 ISBN 978-3-0343-1837-2. 288 pages. 2015.

Vol. 63   Elke D'hoker and Stephanie Eggermont (eds): The Irish Short Story: Traditions and Trends ISBN 978-3-0343-1753-5. 330 pages. 2015.

Vol. 64   Radvan Markus: Echoes of the Rebellion: The Year 1798 in Twentieth-Century Irish Fiction and Drama ISBN 978-3-0343-1832-7. 248 pages. 2015.

Vol. 65   B. Mairéad Pratschke: Visions of Ireland: Gael Linn's *Amharc Éireann* Film Series, 1956–1964 ISBN 978-3-0343-1872-3. 301 pages. 2015.

Vol. 66   Una Hunt and Mary Pierse (eds): France and Ireland: Notes and Narratives ISBN 978-3-0343-1914-0. 272 pages. 2015.

Vol. 67   John Lynch and Katherina Dodou (eds): The Leaving of Ireland: Migration and Belonging in Irish Literature and Film ISBN 978-3-0343-1896-9. 313 pages. 2015.

Vol. 68   Anne Goarzin (ed.): New Critical Perspectives on Franco-Irish Relations ISBN 978-3-0343-1781-8. 271 pages. 2015.

Vol. 69   Michel Brunet, Fabienne Gaspari and Mary Pierse (eds): George
           Moore's Paris and His Ongoing French Connections
           ISBN 978-3-0343-1973-7. 279 pages. 2015.

Vol. 70   Carine Berbéri and Martine Pelletier (eds): Ireland: Authority
           and Crisis
           ISBN 978-3-0343-1939-3. 296 pages. 2015.

Vol. 71   David Doolin: Transnational Revolutionaries: The Fenian Invasion of
           Canada, 1866
           ISBN 978-3-0343-1922-5. 348 pages. 2016.

Vol. 72   Terry Phillips: Irish Literature and the First World War: Culture,
           Identity and Memory
           ISBN 978-3-0343-1969-0. 297 pages. 2015.

Vol. 73   Carmen Zamorano Llena and Billy Gray (eds): Authority and
           Wisdom in the New Ireland: Studies in Literature and Culture
           ISBN 978-3-0343-1833-4. 263 pages. 2016.

Vol. 74   Flore Coulouma (ed.): New Perspectives on Irish TV Series: Identity
           and Nostalgia on the Small Screen
           ISBN 978-3-0343-1977-5. 222 pages. 2016.

Vol. 75   Fergal Lenehan: Stereotypes, Ideology and Foreign
           Correspondents: German Media Representations of Ireland,
           1946–2010
           ISBN 978-3-0343-2222-5. 306 pages. 2016.

Vol. 76   Jarlath Killeen and Valeria Cavalli (eds): 'Inspiring a Mysterious
           Terror': 200 Years of Joseph Sheridan Le Fanu
           ISBN 978-3-0343-2223-2. 260 pages. 2016.

Vol. 77   Anne Karhio: 'Slight Return': Paul Muldoon's Poetics of Place
           ISBN 978-3-0343-1986-7. 272 pages. 2017.

Vol. 78   Margaret Eaton: Frank Confessions: Performance in the Life-Writings
           of Frank McCourt
           ISBN 978-1-906165-61-1. 294 pages. 2017.

Vol. 79   Marguérite Corporaal, Christopher Cusack and Ruud van den
           Beuken (eds): Irish Studies and the Dynamics of Memory: Transitions
           and Transformations
           ISBN 978-3-0343-2236-2. 360 pages. 2017.

Vol. 80   Conor Caldwell and Eamon Byers (eds): New Crops, Old
           Fields: Reimagining Irish Folklore
           ISBN 978-3-0343-1912-6. 200 pages. 2017.

Vol. 81   Sinéad Wall: Irish Diasporic Narratives in Argentina: A
           Reconsideration of Home, Identity and Belonging
           ISBN 978-1-906165-66-6. 282 pages. 2017.

Vol. 82   Ute Anna Mittermaier: Images of Spain in Irish Literature, 1922–1975
           ISBN 978-3-0343-1993-5. 386 pages. 2017.

Vol. 83   Lauren Clark: Consuming Irish Children: Advertising and the Art of
           Independence, 1860–1921
           ISBN 978-3-0343-1989-8. 288 pages. 2017.

Vol. 84   Lisa FitzGerald: Re-Place: Irish Theatre Environments
           ISBN 978-1-78707-359-3. 222 pages. 2017.

Vol. 85   Joseph Greenwood: 'Hear My Song': Irish Theatre and Popular Song
           in the 1950s and 1960s
           ISBN 978-3-0343-1915-7. 320 pages. 2017.

Vol. 86   Nils Beese: Writing Slums: Dublin, Dirt and Literature
           ISBN 978-1-78707-959-5. 250 pages. 2018.

Vol. 87   Barry Houlihan (ed.): Navigating Ireland's Theatre Archive: Theory,
           Practice, Performance
           ISBN 978-1-78707-372-2. 306 pages. 2019.

Vol. 88   María Elena Jaime de Pablos (ed.): Giving Shape to the Moment: The
           Art of Mary O'Donnell: Poet, Novelist and Short Story Writer
           ISBN 978-1-78874-403-4. 228 pages. 2018.

Vol. 89   Marguérite Corporaal and Peter Gray (eds): The Great Irish Famine
           and Social Class: Conflicts, Responsibilities, Representations
           ISBN 978-1-78874-166-8. 330 pages. 2019.

Vol. 90   Patrick Speight: Irish-Argentine Identity in an Age of Political
           Challenge and Change, 1875–1983
           ISBN 978-1-78874-417-1. 360 pages. 2020.

Vol. 91   Fionna Barber, Heidi Hansson, and Sara Dybris McQuaid
           (eds): Ireland and the North
           ISBN 978-1-78874-289-4. 338 pages. 2019.

Vol. 92   Ruth Sheehy: The Life and Work of Richard King: Religion,
           Nationalism and Modernism
           ISBN 978-1-78707-246-6. 482 pages. 2019.

Vol. 93   Brian Lucey, Eamon Maher and Eugene O'Brien (eds): Recalling the
           Celtic Tiger
           ISBN 978-1-78997-286-3. 386 pages. 2019.

Vol. 94   Melania Terrazas Gallego (ed.): Trauma and Identity in Contemporary
           Irish Culture
           ISBN 978-1-78997-557-4. 302 pages. 2020.

Vol. 95   Patricia Medcalf: Advertising the Black Stuff in Ireland 1959–1999:
           Increments of Change
           ISBN 978-1-78997-345-7. 218 pages. 2020.

Vol. 96   Anne Goarzin and Maria Parsons (eds): New Cartographies, Nomadic
           Methologies: Contemporary Arts, Culture and Politics in Ireland
           ISBN 978-1-78874-651-9. 204 pages. 2020.

Vol. 97   Hiroko Ikeda and Kazuo Yokouchi (eds): Irish Literature in the British
           Context and Beyond: New Perspectives from Kyoto
           ISBN 978-1-78997-566-6. 250 pages. 2020.

Vol. 98   Catherine Nealy Judd: Travel Narratives of the Irish Famine: Politics,
           Tourism, and Scandal, 1845–1853
           ISBN 978-1-80079-084-1. 468 pages. 2020.

Vol. 99   Lesley Lelourec and Gráinne O'Keeffe-Vigneron (eds): Northern Ireland after the Good Friday Agreement: Building a Shared Future from a Troubled Past?
ISBN 978-1-78997-746-2. 262 pages. 2021.

Vol. 100   Eamon Maher and Eugene O'Brien (eds): Reimagining Irish Studies for the Twenty-First Century
ISBN 978-1-80079-191-6. 384 pages. 2021.

Vol. 101   Nathalie Sebbane: Memorialising the Magdalene Laundries: From Story to History
ISBN 978-1-78707-589-4. 334 pages. 2021.

Vol 102   Roz Goldie: A Dangerous Pursuit: The Anti-Sectarian Work of Counteract
ISBN 978-1-80079-187-9. 268 pages. 2021.

Vol. 103   Ann Wilson: The Picture Postcard: A New Window into Edwardian Ireland
ISBN 978-1-78874-079-1. 282 pages. 2021.

Vol. 104   Anna Charczun: Irish Lesbian Writing Across Time: A New Framework for Rethinking Love Between Women
ISBN 978-1-78997-864-3. 320 pages. 2022.

Vol. 105   Olivier Coquelin, Brigitte Bastiat and Frank Healy (eds): Northern Ireland: Challenges of Peace and Reconciliation Since the Good Friday Agreement
ISBN 978-1-78997-817-9. 298 pages. 2022.

Vol. 106   Jo Murphy-Lawless and Laury Oaks (eds): The Salley Gardens: Women, Sex, and Motherhood in Ireland
ISBN 978-1-80079-417-7. 338 pages. 2022.

Vol. 107   Mercedes del Campo: Voices from the Margins: Gender and the Everyday in Women's Pre- and Post-Agreement Troubles Short Fiction
ISBN 978-1-78874-330-3. 324 pages. 2022.

Vol. 108   Sean McGraw and Jonathan Tiernan: The Politics of Irish Primary Education: Reform in an Era of Secularisation
ISBN 978-1-80079-709-3. 532 pages. 2022.

Vol. 109   Gerald Dawe: Northern Windows/Southern Stars: Selected Early
            Essays 1983–1994
            ISBN 978-1-80079-652-2. 180 pages. 2022.

Vol. 110   John Fanning: The Mandarin, the Musician and the Mage:
            Seán Ó Riada, Thomas Kinsella and the Lessons of Ireland's
            Mid-Twentieth-Century Revival
            ISBN 978-1-80079-599-0. *Forthcoming*. 2022.

Vol. 111   Gerald Dawe: Dreaming of Home: Seven Irish Writers
            ISBN 978-1-80079-655-3. 108 pages. 2022.

Vol. 112   John Walsh: One Hundred Years of Irish Language Policy, 1922–2022
            ISBN 978-1-78997-892-6. 394 pages. 2022.

Printed by
CPI books GmbH, Leck